ENGLISH
HEBREW

THEME-BASED
DICTIONARY

Contains over 9000 commonly
used words

T&P BOOKS PUBLISHING

Theme-based dictionary British English-Hebrew - 9000 words
British English collection

By Andrey Taranov

T&P Books vocabularies are intended for helping you learn, memorize and review foreign words. The dictionary is divided into themes, covering all major spheres of everyday activities, business, science, culture, etc.

The process of learning words using T&P Books' theme-based dictionaries gives you the following advantages:

- Correctly grouped source information predetermines success at subsequent stages of word memorization
- Availability of words derived from the same root allowing memorization of word units (rather than separate words)
- Small units of words facilitate the process of establishing associative links needed for consolidation of vocabulary
- Level of language knowledge can be estimated by the number of learned words

T&P Books Publishing
www.tpbooks.com

ISBN: 978-1-78716-432-1

This book is also available in E-book formats.
Please visit www.tpbooks.com or the major online bookstores.

HEBREW THEME-BASED DICTIONARY
British English collection

T&P Books vocabularies are intended to help you learn, memorize, and review foreign words. The vocabulary contains over 9000 commonly used words arranged thematically.

- Vocabulary contains the most commonly used words
- Recommended as an addition to any language course
- Meets the needs of beginners and advanced learners of foreign languages
- Convenient for daily use, revision sessions, and self-testing activities
- Allows you to assess your vocabulary

Special features of the vocabulary

- Words are organized according to their meaning, not alphabetically
- Words are presented in three columns to facilitate the reviewing and self-testing processes
- Words in groups are divided into small blocks to facilitate the learning process
- The vocabulary offers a convenient and simple transcription of each foreign word

The vocabulary has 256 topics including:

Basic Concepts, Numbers, Colors, Months, Seasons, Units of Measurement, Clothing & Accessories, Food & Nutrition, Restaurant, Family Members, Relatives, Character, Feelings, Emotions, Diseases, City, Town, Sightseeing, Shopping, Money, House, Home, Office, Working in the Office, Import & Export, Marketing, Job Search, Sports, Education, Computer, Internet, Tools, Nature, Countries, Nationalities and more ...

TABLE OF CONTENTS

PRONUNCIATION GUIDE

Letter's name	Letter	Hebrew example	T&P phonetic alphabet	English example
Alef	א	אריה	[a], [ɑ:]	bath, to pass
	א	אחד	[ɛ], [ɛ:]	habit, bad
	א	מָאָה	[']	glottal stop
Bet	ב	בית	[b]	baby, book
Gimel	ג	גמל	[g]	game, gold
Gimel+geresh	ג'	ג'ונגל	[dʒ]	joke, general
Dalet	ד	דג	[d]	day, doctor
Hei	ה	הר	[h]	home, have
Vav	ו	וסת	[v]	very, river
Zayin	ז	זאב	[z]	zebra, please
Zayin+geresh	ז'	ז'ורנל	[ʒ]	forge, pleasure
Chet	ח	חוט	[x]	as in Scots 'loch'
Tet	ט	טוב	[t]	tourist, trip
Yud	י	יום	[j]	yes, New York
Kaph	ך כ	כריש	[k]	clock, kiss
Lamed	ל	לחם	[l]	lace, people
Mem	ם מ	מלך	[m]	magic, milk
Nun	ן נ	נר	[n]	name, normal
Samech	ס	סוס	[s]	city, boss
Ayin	ע	עין	[a], [ɑ:]	bath, to pass
	ע	תָשָׁעִים	[']	voiced pharyngeal fricative
Pei	ף פ	פיל	[p]	pencil, private
Tsadi	ץ צ	צעצוע	[ts]	cats, tsetse fly
Tsadi+geresh	צ'י'צ'	צ'ק	[tʃ]	church, French
Qoph	ק	קוף	[k]	clock, kiss
Resh	ר	רכבת	[r]	French (guttural) R
Shin	ש	שלחן, עָשֹרֵים	[s], [ʃ]	city, machine
Tav	ת	תפוז	[t]	tourist, trip

ABBREVIATIONS
used in the dictionary

English abbreviations

ab.	-	about
adj	-	adjective
adv	-	adverb
anim.	-	animate
as adj	-	attributive noun used as adjective
e.g.	-	for example
etc.	-	et cetera
fam.	-	familiar
fem.	-	feminine
form.	-	formal
inanim.	-	inanimate
masc.	-	masculine
math	-	mathematics
mil.	-	military
n	-	noun
pl	-	plural
pron.	-	pronoun
sb	-	somebody
sing.	-	singular
sth	-	something
v aux	-	auxiliary verb
vi	-	intransitive verb
vi, vt	-	intransitive, transitive verb
vt	-	transitive verb

Hebrew abbreviations

ז	-	masculine
ז"ר	-	masculine plural
ז, נ	-	masculine, feminine
נ	-	feminine
נ"ר	-	feminine plural

BASIC CONCEPTS

Basic concepts. Part 1

1. Pronouns

I, me	ani	אֲנִי (ז, נ)
you (masc.)	ata	אַתָּה (ז)
you (fem.)	at	אַתְּ (נ)
he	hu	הוּא (ז)
she	hi	הִיא (נ)
we	a'naxnu	אֲנַחְנוּ (ז, נ)
you (masc.)	atem	אַתֶּם (ז"ר)
you (fem.)	aten	אַתֶּן (נ"ר)
you (polite, sing.)	ata, at	אַתָּה (ז), אַתְּ (נ)
you (polite, pl)	atem, aten	אַתֶּם (ז"ר), אַתֶּן (נ"ר)
they (masc.)	hem	הֵם (ז"ר)
they (fem.)	hen	הֵן (נ"ר)

2. Greetings. Salutations. Farewells

Hello! (fam.)	ʃalom!	שָׁלוֹם!
Hello! (form.)	ʃalom!	שָׁלוֹם!
Good morning!	'boker tov!	בּוֹקֶר טוֹב!
Good afternoon!	tsaha'rayim tovim!	צָהֳרַיִים טוֹבִים!
Good evening!	'erev tov!	עֶרֶב טוֹב!
to say hello	lomar ʃalom	לוֹמַר שָׁלוֹם
Hi! (hello)	hai!	הַיי!
greeting (n)	ahlan	אַהְלַן
to greet (vt)	lomar ʃalom	לוֹמַר שָׁלוֹם
How are you? (form.)	ma ʃlomeχ?, ma ʃlomχa?	מַה שְׁלוֹמֵךְ? (נ), מַה שְׁלוֹמְךָ? (ז)
How are you? (fam.)	ma niʃma?	מַה נִשְׁמָע?
What's new?	ma χadaʃ?	מַה חָדָשׁ?
Bye-Bye! Goodbye!	lehitra'ot!	לְהִתְרָאוֹת!
Bye!	bai!	בַּיי!
See you soon!	lehitra'ot bekarov!	לְהִתְרָאוֹת בְּקָרוֹב!
Farewell!	heye ʃalom!	הֱיֵה שָׁלוֹם!
Farewell! (form.)	lehitra'ot!	לְהִתְרָאוֹת!
to say goodbye	lomar lehitra'ot	לוֹמַר לְהִתְרָאוֹת
Cheers!	bai!	בַּיי!
Thank you! Cheers!	toda!	תּוֹדָה!
Thank you very much!	toda raba!	תּוֹדָה רַבָּה!

My pleasure!	bevakaʃa	בְּבַקָּשָׁה
Don't mention it!	al lo davar	עַל לֹא דָּבָר
It was nothing	ein be'ad ma	אֵין בְּעַד מָה

| Excuse me! | sliχa! | סְלִיחָה! |
| to excuse (forgive) | lis'loaχ | לִסְלוֹחַ |

to apologize (vi)	lehitnatsel	לְהִתְנַצֵּל
My apologies	ani mitnatsel, ani mitna'tselet	אֲנִי מִתְנַצֵּל (ז), אֲנִי מִתְנַצֶּלֶת (נ)
I'm sorry!	ani mitsta'er, ani mitsta''eret	אֲנִי מִצְטַעֵר (ז), אֲנִי מִצְטַעֶרֶת (נ)
to forgive (vt)	lis'loaχ	לִסְלוֹחַ
It's okay! (that's all right)	lo nora	לֹא נוֹרָא
please (adv)	bevakaʃa	בְּבַקָּשָׁה

Don't forget!	al tiʃkaχ!	אַל תִּשְׁכַּח! (ז)
Certainly!	'betaχ!	בֶּטַח!
Of course not!	'betaχ ʃelo!	בֶּטַח שֶׁלֹּא!
Okay! (I agree)	okei!	אוֹקֵיי!
That's enough!	maspik!	מַסְפִּיק!

3. How to address

Excuse me, ...	sliχa!	סְלִיחָה!
mister, sir	adon	אָדוֹן
madam	gvirti	גְּבִרְתִּי
miss	'gveret	גְּבֶרֶת
young man	baχur tsa'ir	בָּחוּר צָעִיר
young man (little boy)	'yeled	יֶלֶד
miss (little girl)	yalda	יַלְדָּה

4. Cardinal numbers. Part 1

0 zero	'efes	אֶפֶס (ז)
1 one	eχad	אֶחָד (ז)
1 one (fem.)	aχat	אַחַת (נ)
2 two	'ʃtayim	שְׁתַּיִים (נ)
3 three	ʃaloʃ	שָׁלוֹש (נ)
4 four	arba	אַרְבַּע (נ)

5 five	χameʃ	חָמֵש (נ)
6 six	ʃeʃ	שֵׁש (נ)
7 seven	'ʃeva	שֶׁבַע (נ)
8 eight	'ʃmone	שְׁמוֹנֶה (נ)
9 nine	'teʃa	תֵּשַׁע (נ)

10 ten	'eser	עֶשֶׂר (נ)
11 eleven	aχat esre	אַחַת-עֶשְׂרֵה (נ)
12 twelve	ʃteim esre	שְׁתֵּים-עֶשְׂרֵה (נ)
13 thirteen	ʃloʃ esre	שְׁלוֹש-עֶשְׂרֵה (נ)
14 fourteen	arba esre	אַרְבַּע-עֶשְׂרֵה (נ)
15 fifteen	χameʃ esre	חָמֵש-עֶשְׂרֵה (נ)
16 sixteen	ʃeʃ esre	שֵׁש-עֶשְׂרֵה (נ)

17 seventeen	ʃva esre	שְׁבַע־עֶשְׂרֵה (נ)
18 eighteen	ʃmone esre	שְׁמוֹנֶה־עֶשְׂרֵה (נ)
19 nineteen	tʃa esre	תְּשַׁע־עֶשְׂרֵה (נ)

20 twenty	esrim	עֶשְׂרִים
21 twenty-one	esrim ve'eχad	עֶשְׂרִים וְאֶחָד
22 twenty-two	esrim u'ʃnayim	עֶשְׂרִים וּשְׁנַיִים
23 twenty-three	esrim uʃloʃa	עֶשְׂרִים וּשְׁלוֹשָׁה

30 thirty	ʃloʃim	שְׁלוֹשִׁים
31 thirty-one	ʃloʃim ve'eχad	שְׁלוֹשִׁים וְאֶחָד
32 thirty-two	ʃloʃim u'ʃnayim	שְׁלוֹשִׁים וּשְׁנַיִים
33 thirty-three	ʃloʃim uʃloʃa	שְׁלוֹשִׁים וּשְׁלוֹשָׁה

40 forty	arba'im	אַרְבָּעִים
41 forty-one	arba'im ve'eχad	אַרְבָּעִים וְאֶחָד
42 forty-two	arba'im u'ʃnayim	אַרְבָּעִים וּשְׁנַיִים
43 forty-three	arba'im uʃloʃa	אַרְבָּעִים וּשְׁלוֹשָׁה

50 fifty	χamiʃim	חֲמִישִׁים
51 fifty-one	χamiʃim ve'eχad	חֲמִישִׁים וְאֶחָד
52 fifty-two	χamiʃim u'ʃnayim	חֲמִישִׁים וּשְׁנַיִים
53 fifty-three	χamiʃim uʃloʃa	חֲמִישִׁים וּשְׁלוֹשָׁה

60 sixty	ʃiʃim	שִׁישִׁים
61 sixty-one	ʃiʃim ve'eχad	שִׁישִׁים וְאֶחָד
62 sixty-two	ʃiʃim u'ʃnayim	שִׁישִׁים וּשְׁנַיִים
63 sixty-three	ʃiʃim uʃloʃa	שִׁישִׁים וּשְׁלוֹשָׁה

70 seventy	ʃiv'im	שִׁבְעִים
71 seventy-one	ʃiv'im ve'eχad	שִׁבְעִים וְאֶחָד
72 seventy-two	ʃiv'im u'ʃnayim	שִׁבְעִים וּשְׁנַיִים
73 seventy-three	ʃiv'im uʃloʃa	שִׁבְעִים וּשְׁלוֹשָׁה

80 eighty	ʃmonim	שְׁמוֹנִים
81 eighty-one	ʃmonim ve'eχad	שְׁמוֹנִים וְאֶחָד
82 eighty-two	ʃmonim u'ʃnayim	שְׁמוֹנִים וּשְׁנַיִים
83 eighty-three	ʃmonim uʃloʃa	שְׁמוֹנִים וּשְׁלוֹשָׁה

90 ninety	tiʃim	תִּשְׁעִים
91 ninety-one	tiʃim ve'eχad	תִּשְׁעִים וְאֶחָד
92 ninety-two	tiʃim u'ʃayim	תִּשְׁעִים וּשְׁנַיִים
93 ninety-three	tiʃim uʃloʃa	תִּשְׁעִים וּשְׁלוֹשָׁה

5. Cardinal numbers. Part 2

100 one hundred	'me'a	מֵאָה (נ)
200 two hundred	ma'tayim	מָאתַיִים
300 three hundred	ʃloʃ me'ot	שְׁלוֹשׁ מֵאוֹת (נ)
400 four hundred	arba me'ot	אַרְבַּע מֵאוֹת (נ)
500 five hundred	χameʃ me'ot	חָמֵשׁ מֵאוֹת (נ)

| 600 six hundred | ʃeʃ me'ot | שֵׁשׁ מֵאוֹת (נ) |
| 700 seven hundred | ʃva me'ot | שְׁבַע מֵאוֹת (נ) |

800 eight hundred	ʃmone me'ot	שְׁמוֹנֶה מֵאוֹת (נ)
900 nine hundred	tʃa me'ot	תֵּשַׁע מֵאוֹת (נ)
1000 one thousand	'elef	אֶלֶף (ז)
2000 two thousand	al'payim	אַלְפַּיִים (ז)
3000 three thousand	ʃloʃet alafim	שְׁלוֹשֶׁת אֲלָפִים (ז)
10000 ten thousand	a'seret alafim	עֲשֶׂרֶת אֲלָפִים (ז)
one hundred thousand	'me'a 'elef	מֵאָה אֶלֶף (ז)
million	milyon	מִילְיוֹן (ז)
billion	milyard	מִילְיַארְד (ז)

6. Ordinal numbers

first (adj)	riʃon	רִאשׁוֹן
second (adj)	ʃeni	שֵׁנִי
third (adj)	ʃliʃi	שְׁלִישִׁי
fourth (adj)	revi'i	רְבִיעִי
fifth (adj)	χamiʃi	חֲמִישִׁי
sixth (adj)	ʃiʃi	שִׁישִׁי
seventh (adj)	ʃvi'i	שְׁבִיעִי
eighth (adj)	ʃmini	שְׁמִינִי
ninth (adj)	tʃi'i	תְּשִׁיעִי
tenth (adj)	asiri	עֲשִׂירִי

7. Numbers. Fractions

fraction	'ʃever	שֶׁבֶר (ז)
one half	'χetsi	חֲצִי (ז)
one third	ʃliʃ	שְׁלִישׁ (ז)
one quarter	'reva	רֶבַע (ז)
one eighth	ʃminit	שְׁמִינִית (נ)
one tenth	asirit	עֲשִׂירִית (נ)
two thirds	ʃnei ʃliʃim	שְׁנֵי שְׁלִישִׁים (ז)
three quarters	'ʃloʃet riv'ei	שְׁלוֹשֶׁת רְבָעֵי

8. Numbers. Basic operations

subtraction	χisur	חִיסּוּר (ז)
to subtract (vi, vt)	leχaser	לְחַסֵּר
division	χiluk	חִילּוּק (ז)
to divide (vt)	leχalek	לְחַלֵּק
addition	χibur	חִיבּוּר (ז)
to add up (vt)	leχaber	לְחַבֵּר
to add (vi)	leχaber	לְחַבֵּר
multiplication	'kefel	כֶּפֶל (ז)
to multiply (vt)	lehaχpil	לְהַכְפִּיל

9. Numbers. Miscellaneous

digit, figure	sifra	סִפְרָה (נ)
number	mispar	מִסְפָּר (ז)
numeral	ʃem mispar	שֵׁם מִסְפָּר (ז)
minus sign	'minus	מִינוּס (ז)
plus sign	plus	פְּלוּס (ז)
formula	nusxa	נוֹסְחָה (נ)

calculation	xiʃuv	חִישׁוּב (ז)
to count (vi, vt)	lispor	לִסְפּוֹר
to count up	lexaʃev	לְחַשֵׁב
to compare (vt)	lehaʃvot	לְהַשׁווֹת

How much?	'kama?	כַּמָה?
How many?	'kama?	כַּמָה?
sum, total	sxum	סְכוּם (ז)
result	totsa'a	תוֹצָאָה (נ)
remainder	ʃe'erit	שְׁאֵרִית (נ)

a few (e.g., ~ years ago)	'kama	כַּמָה
little (I had ~ time)	ktsat	קְצָת
few (I have ~ friends)	me'at	מְעַט
a little (~ tired)	me'at	מְעַט
the rest	ʃe'ar	שְׁאָר (ז)
one and a half	exad va'xetsi	אֶחָד וָחֵצִי (ז)
dozen	tresar	תְּרֵיסָר (ז)

in half (adv)	'xetsi 'xetsi	חֵצִי חֵצִי
equally (evenly)	ʃave beʃave	שָׁווֶה בְּשָׁווֶה
half	'xetsi	חֵצִי (ז)
time (three ~s)	'pa'am	פַּעַם (נ)

10. The most important verbs. Part 1

to advise (vt)	leya'ets	לְייַעֵץ
to agree (say yes)	lehaskim	לְהַסְכִּים
to answer (vi, vt)	la'anot	לַעֲנוֹת
to apologize (vi)	lehitnatsel	לְהִתְנַצֵל
to arrive (vi)	leha'gi'a	לְהַגִיעַ

to ask (~ oneself)	liʃ'ol	לִשְׁאוֹל
to ask (~ sb to do sth)	levakeʃ	לְבַקֵשׁ
to be (vi)	lihyot	לִהְיוֹת

to be afraid	lefaxed	לְפַחֵד
to be hungry	lihyot ra'ev	לִהְיוֹת רָעֵב
to be interested in …	lehit'anyen be…	לְהִתְעַנְיֵין בְּ…
to be needed	lehidareʃ	לְהִידָרֵשׁ
to be surprised	lehitpale	לְהִתְפַּלֵא

to be thirsty	lihyot tsame	לִהְיוֹת צָמֵא
to begin (vt)	lehatxil	לְהַתְחִיל

to belong to ...	lehiʃtayex	לְהִשְׁתַּייֵךְ
to boast (vi)	lehitravrev	לְהִתְרַבְרֵב
to break (split into pieces)	liʃbor	לִשְׁבּוֹר
to call (~ for help)	likro	לִקְרוֹא

can (v aux)	yaxol	יָכוֹל
to catch (vt)	litfos	לִתְפּוֹס
to change (vt)	leʃanot	לְשַׁנּוֹת
to choose (select)	livxor	לִבְחוֹר
to come down (the stairs)	la'redet	לָרֶדֶת

to compare (vt)	lehaʃvot	לְהַשְׁווֹת
to complain (vi, vt)	lehitlonen	לְהִתְלוֹנֵן
to confuse (mix up)	lehitbalbel	לְהִתְבַּלְבֵּל
to continue (vt)	lehamʃix	לְהַמְשִׁיךְ
to control (vt)	liʃlot	לִשְׁלוֹט
to cook (dinner)	levaʃel	לְבַשֵּׁל

to cost (vt)	la'alot	לַעֲלוֹת
to count (add up)	lispor	לִסְפּוֹר
to count on ...	lismox al	לִסְמוֹךְ עַל
to create (vt)	litsor	לִיצוֹר
to cry (weep)	livkot	לִבְכּוֹת

11. The most important verbs. Part 2

to deceive (vi, vt)	leramot	לְרַמּוֹת
to decorate (tree, street)	lekaʃet	לְקַשֵּׁט
to defend (a country, etc.)	lehagen	לְהָגֵן
to demand (request firmly)	lidroʃ	לִדְרוֹשׁ
to dig (vt)	laxpor	לַחְפּוֹר

to discuss (vt)	ladun	לָדוּן
to do (vt)	la'asot	לַעֲשׂוֹת
to doubt (have doubts)	lefakpek	לְפַקְפֵּק
to drop (let fall)	lehapil	לְהַפִּיל
to enter (room, house, etc.)	lehikanes	לְהִיכָּנֵס

to excuse (forgive)	lis'loax	לִסְלוֹחַ
to exist (vi)	lehitkayem	לְהִתְקַייֵם
to expect (foresee)	laxazot	לַחֲזוֹת
to explain (vt)	lehasbir	לְהַסְבִּיר
to fall (vi)	lipol	לִיפּוֹל

to fancy (vt)	limtso xen be'ei'nayim	לִמְצוֹא חֵן בְּעֵינַיים
to find (vt)	limtso	לִמְצוֹא
to finish (vt)	lesayem	לְסַייֵם
to fly (vi)	la'uf	לָעוּף
to follow ... (come after)	la'akov axarei	לַעֲקוֹב אַחֲרֵי

to forget (vi, vt)	liʃ'koax	לִשְׁכּוֹחַ
to forgive (vt)	lis'loax	לִסְלוֹחַ
to give (vt)	latet	לָתֵת
to give a hint	lirmoz	לִרְמוֹז

to go (on foot)	la'leχet	לָלֶכֶת
to go for a swim	lehitraχets	לְהִתְרַחֵץ
to go out (for dinner, etc.)	latset	לָצֵאת
to guess (the answer)	lenaχeʃ	לְנַחֵשׁ

to have (vt)	lehaχzik	לְהַחְזִיק
to have breakfast	le'eχol aruχat 'boker	לֶאֱכֹל אֲרוּחַת בּוֹקֶר
to have dinner	le'eχol aruχat 'erev	לֶאֱכֹל אֲרוּחַת עֶרֶב
to have lunch	le'eχol aruχat tsaha'rayim	לֶאֱכֹל אֲרוּחַת צָהֳרַיִם
to hear (vt)	liʃ'mo‘a	לִשְׁמוֹעַ

to help (vt)	la‘azor	לַעֲזוֹר
to hide (vt)	lehastir	לְהַסְתִּיר
to hope (vi, vt)	lekavot	לְקַוּוֹת
to hunt (vi, vt)	latsud	לָצוּד
to hurry (vi)	lemaher	לְמַהֵר

12. The most important verbs. Part 3

to inform (vt)	leho'dia	לְהוֹדִיעַ
to insist (vi, vt)	lehit‘akeʃ	לְהִתְעַקֵּשׁ
to insult (vt)	leha‘aliv	לְהַעֲלִיב
to invite (vt)	lehazmin	לְהַזְמִין
to joke (vi)	lehitba'deaχ	לְהִתְבַּדֵּחַ

to keep (vt)	liʃmor	לִשְׁמוֹר
to keep silent	liʃtok	לִשְׁתּוֹק
to kill (vt)	laharog	לַהֲרוֹג
to know (sb)	lehakir et	לְהַכִּיר אֶת
to know (sth)	la'da‘at	לָדַעַת
to laugh (vi)	litsχok	לִצְחוֹק

to liberate (city, etc.)	leʃaχrer	לְשַׁחְרֵר
to look for ... (search)	leχapes	לְחַפֵּשׂ
to love (sb)	le'ehov	לֶאֱהֹב
to make a mistake	lit'ot	לִטְעוֹת
to manage, to run	lenahel	לְנַהֵל

to mean (signify)	lomar	לוֹמַר
to mention (talk about)	lehazkir	לְהַזְכִּיר
to miss (school, etc.)	lehaχsir	לְהַחְסִיר
to notice (see)	lasim lev	לָשִׂים לֵב
to object (vi, vt)	lehitnaged	לְהִתְנַגֵּד

to observe (see)	litspot, lehaʃkif	לִצְפּוֹת, לְהַשְׁקִיף
to open (vt)	lif'toaχ	לִפְתּוֹחַ
to order (meal, etc.)	lehazmin	לְהַזְמִין
to order (mil.)	lifkod	לִפְקוֹד
to own (possess)	lihyot 'ba‘al ʃel	לִהְיוֹת בַּעַל שֶׁל

to participate (vi)	lehiʃtatef	לְהִשְׁתַּתֵּף
to pay (vi, vt)	leʃalem	לְשַׁלֵּם
to permit (vt)	leharʃot	לְהַרְשׁוֹת
to plan (vt)	letaχnen	לְתַכְנֵן

to play (children)	lesaχek	לְשַׂחֵק
to pray (vi, vt)	lehitpalel	לְהִתְפַּלֵּל
to prefer (vt)	leha'adif	לְהַעֲדִיף
to promise (vt)	lehav'tiaχ	לְהַבְטִיחַ
to pronounce (vt)	levate	לְבַטֵּא
to propose (vt)	leha'tsi'a	לְהַצִּיעַ
to punish (vt)	leha'aniʃ	לְהַעֲנִישׁ

13. The most important verbs. Part 4

to read (vi, vt)	likro	לִקְרוֹא
to recommend (vt)	lehamlits	לְהַמְלִיץ
to refuse (vi, vt)	lesarev	לְסָרֵב
to regret (be sorry)	lehitsta'er	לְהִצְטַעֵר
to rent (sth from sb)	liskor	לִשְׂכּוֹר
to repeat (say again)	laχazor al	לַחֲזוֹר עַל
to reserve, to book	lehazmin meroʃ	לְהַזְמִין מֵרֹאשׁ
to run (vi)	laruts	לָרוּץ
to save (rescue)	lehatsil	לְהַצִּיל
to say (~ thank you)	lomar	לוֹמַר
to scold (vt)	linzof	לִנְזוֹף
to see (vt)	lir'ot	לִרְאוֹת
to sell (vt)	limkor	לִמְכּוֹר
to send (vt)	liʃ'loaχ	לִשְׁלוֹחַ
to shoot (vi)	lirot	לִירוֹת
to shout (vi)	lits'ok	לִצְעוֹק
to show (vt)	lehar'ot	לְהַרְאוֹת
to sign (document)	laχtom	לַחְתּוֹם
to sit down (vi)	lehityaʃev	לְהִתְיַישֵׁב
to smile (vi)	leχayeχ	לְחַיֵּיךְ
to speak (vi, vt)	ledaber	לְדַבֵּר
to steal (money, etc.)	lignov	לִגְנוֹב
to stop (for pause, etc.)	la'atsor	לַעֲצוֹר
to stop (please ~ calling me)	lehafsik	לְהַפְסִיק
to study (vt)	lilmod	לִלְמוֹד
to swim (vi)	lisχot	לִשְׂחוֹת
to take (vt)	la'kaχat	לָקַחַת
to think (vi, vt)	laχʃov	לַחְשׁוֹב
to threaten (vt)	le'ayem	לְאַיֵּים
to touch (with hands)	la'ga'at	לָגַעַת
to translate (vt)	letargem	לְתַרְגֵּם
to trust (vt)	liv'toaχ	לִבְטוֹחַ
to try (attempt)	lenasot	לְנַסּוֹת
to turn (e.g., ~ left)	lifnot	לִפְנוֹת
to underestimate (vt)	leham'it be''ereχ	לְהַמְעִיט בְּעֵרֶךְ
to understand (vt)	lehavin	לְהָבִין
to unite (vt)	le'aχed	לְאַחֵד

to wait (vt)	lehamtin	לְהַמְתִּין
to want (wish, desire)	lirtsot	לִרְצוֹת
to warn (vt)	lehazhir	לְהַזְהִיר
to work (vi)	la'avod	לַעֲבוֹד
to write (vt)	lixtov	לִכְתּוֹב
to write down	lirʃom	לִרְשׁוֹם

14. Colours

colour	'tseva	צֶבַע (ז)
shade (tint)	gavan	גָּוֶן (ז)
hue	gavan	גָּוֶן (ז)
rainbow	'keʃet	קֶשֶׁת (נ)
white (adj)	lavan	לָבָן
black (adj)	ʃaxor	שָׁחוֹר
grey (adj)	afor	אָפוֹר
green (adj)	yarok	יָרוֹק
yellow (adj)	tsahov	צָהוֹב
red (adj)	adom	אָדוֹם
blue (adj)	kaxol	כָּחוֹל
light blue (adj)	taxol	תְּכוֹל
pink (adj)	varod	וָרוֹד
orange (adj)	katom	כָּתוֹם
violet (adj)	segol	סָגוֹל
brown (adj)	xum	חוּם
golden (adj)	zahov	זָהוֹב
silvery (adj)	kasuf	כָּסוּף
beige (adj)	beʒ	בֶּז'
cream (adj)	be'tseva krem	בְּצֶבַע קְרֶם
turquoise (adj)	turkiz	טוּרְקִיז
cherry red (adj)	bordo	בּוֹרְדוֹ
lilac (adj)	segol	סָגוֹל
crimson (adj)	patol	פָּטוֹל
light (adj)	bahir	בָּהִיר
dark (adj)	kehe	כֵּהֶה
bright, vivid (adj)	bohek	בּוֹהֵק
coloured (pencils)	tsiv'oni	צִבְעוֹנִי
colour (e.g. ~ film)	tsiv'oni	צִבְעוֹנִי
black-and-white (adj)	ʃaxor lavan	שָׁחוֹר-לָבָן
plain (one-coloured)	xad tsiv'i	חַד-צִבְעִי
multicoloured (adj)	sasgoni	סַסְגּוֹנִי

15. Questions

| Who? | mi? | מִי? |
| What? | ma? | מָה? |

Where? (at, in)	'eifo?	אֵיפֹה?
Where (to)?	le'an?	לְאָן?
From where?	me''eifo?	מֵאֵיפֹה?
When?	matai?	מָתַי?
Why? (What for?)	'lama?	לָמָה?
Why? (~ are you crying?)	ma'du'a?	מַדוּעַ?

What for?	biʃvil ma?	בִּשְׁבִיל מָה?
How? (in what way)	eix, keitsad?	כֵּיצַד? אֵיךְ?
What? (What kind of ...?)	'eize?	אֵיזֶה?
Which?	'eize?	אֵיזֶה?

To whom?	lemi?	לְמִי?
About whom?	al mi?	עַל מִי?
About what?	al ma?	עַל מָה?
With whom?	im mi?	עִם מִי?

| How many? How much? | 'kama? | כַּמָה? |
| Whose? | ʃel mi? | שֶׁל מִי? |

16. Prepositions

with (accompanied by)	im	עִם
without	bli, lelo	בְּלִי, לְלֹא
to (indicating direction)	le...	לְ...
about (talking ~ ...)	al	עַל
before (in time)	lifnei	לִפְנֵי
in front of ...	lifnei	לִפְנֵי

under (beneath, below)	mi'taxat le...	מִתַּחַת לְ...
above (over)	me'al	מֵעַל
on (atop)	al	עַל
from (off, out of)	mi, me	מִ, מֵ
of (made from)	mi, me	מִ, מֵ

| in (e.g. ~ ten minutes) | tox | תּוֹךְ |
| over (across the top of) | 'derex | דֶּרֶךְ |

17. Function words. Adverbs. Part 1

Where? (at, in)	'eifo?	אֵיפֹה?
here (adv)	po, kan	פֹּה, כָּאן
there (adv)	ʃam	שָׁם

| somewhere (to be) | 'eifo ʃehu | אֵיפֹה שֶׁהוּא |
| nowhere (not anywhere) | beʃum makom | בְּשׁוּם מָקוֹם |

| by (near, beside) | leyad ... | לְיַד ... |
| by the window | leyad haxalon | לְיַד הַחַלוֹן |

| Where (to)? | le'an? | לְאָן? |
| here (e.g. come ~!) | 'hena, lekan | הֵנָּה; לְכָאן |

there (e.g. to go ~)	leʃam	לְשָׁם
from here (adv)	mikan	מִכָּאן
from there (adv)	miʃam	מִשָּׁם
close (adv)	karov	קָרוֹב
far (adv)	raχok	רָחוֹק
near (e.g. ~ Paris)	leyad	לְיַד
nearby (adv)	karov	קָרוֹב
not far (adv)	lo raχok	לֹא רָחוֹק
left (adj)	smali	שְׂמָאלִי
on the left	mismol	מִשְׂמֹאל
to the left	'smola	שְׂמֹאלָה
right (adj)	yemani	יְמָנִי
on the right	miyamin	מִיָּמִין
to the right	ya'mina	יָמִינָה
in front (adv)	mika'dima	מִקָּדִימָה
front (as adj)	kidmi	קִדְמִי
ahead (the kids ran ~)	ka'dima	קָדִימָה
behind (adv)	me'aχor	מֵאָחוֹר
from behind	me'aχor	מֵאָחוֹר
back (towards the rear)	a'χora	אָחוֹרָה
middle	'emtsa	אֶמְצַע (ז)
in the middle	ba''emtsa	בָּאֶמְצַע
at the side	mehatsad	מֵהַצַּד
everywhere (adv)	beχol makom	בְּכָל מָקוֹם
around (in all directions)	misaviv	מִסָּבִיב
from inside	mibifnim	מִבִּפְנִים
somewhere (to go)	le'an ʃehu	לְאָן שֶׁהוּא
straight (directly)	yaʃar	יָשָׁר
back (e.g. come ~)	baχazara	בַּחֲזָרָה
from anywhere	me'ei ʃam	מֵאֵי שָׁם
from somewhere	me'ei ʃam	מֵאֵי שָׁם
firstly (adv)	reʃit	רֵאשִׁית
secondly (adv)	ʃenit	שֵׁנִית
thirdly (adv)	ʃliʃit	שְׁלִישִׁית
suddenly (adv)	pit'om	פִּתְאוֹם
at first (in the beginning)	behatslaχa	בַּהַתְחָלָה
for the first time	lariʃona	לָרִאשׁוֹנָה
long before ...	zman rav lifnei ...	זְמַן רַב לִפְנֵי ...
anew (over again)	meχadaʃ	מֵחָדָשׁ
for good (adv)	letamid	לְתָמִיד
never (adv)	af 'pa'am, me'olam	מֵעוֹלָם, אַף פַּעַם
again (adv)	ʃuv	שׁוּב
now (adv)	aχʃav, ka'et	עַכְשָׁיו, כָּעֵת

often (adv)	le'itim krovot	לְעִיתִים קְרוֹבוֹת
then (adv)	az	אָז
urgently (quickly)	bidχifut	בִּדְחִיפוּת
usually (adv)	be'dereχ klal	בְּדֶרֶךְ כְּלָל

by the way, ...	'dereχ 'agav	דֶּרֶךְ אַגַב
possible (that is ~)	efʃari	אֶפְשָׁרִי
probably (adv)	kanir'e	כַּנִרְאָה
maybe (adv)	ulai	אוּלַי
besides ...	χuts mize ...	חוּץ מִזֶה ...
that's why ...	laχen	לָכֵן
in spite of ...	lamrot ...	לַמְרוֹת ...
thanks to ...	hodot le...	הוֹדוֹת לְ...

what (pron.)	ma	מָה
that (conj.)	ʃe	שֶׁ
something	'maʃehu	מַשֶׁהוּ
anything (something)	'maʃehu	מַשֶׁהוּ
nothing	klum	כְּלוּם

who (pron.)	mi	מִי
someone	'miʃehu, 'miʃehi	מִישֶׁהוּ (ז), מִישֶׁהִי (נ)
somebody	'miʃehu, 'miʃehi	מִישֶׁהוּ (ז), מִישֶׁהִי (נ)

nobody	af eχad, af aχat	אַף אֶחָד (ז), אַף אַחַת (נ)
nowhere (a voyage to ~)	leʃum makom	לְשׁוּם מָקוֹם
nobody's	lo ʃayaχ le'af eχad	לֹא שַׁיָךְ לְאַף אֶחָד
somebody's	ʃel 'miʃehu	שֶׁל מִישֶׁהוּ

so (I'm ~ glad)	kol kaχ	כָּל-כָּךְ
also (as well)	gam	גַם
too (as well)	gam	גַם

18. Function words. Adverbs. Part 2

Why?	ma'du'a?	מַדוּעַ?
for some reason	miʃum ma	מִשׁוּם-מָה
because ...	miʃum ʃe	מִשׁוּם שֶׁ
for some purpose	lematara 'kolʃehi	לְמַטָרָה כָּלְשֶׁהִי

and	ve ...	ו ...
or	o	אוֹ
but	aval, ulam	אֲבָל, אוּלָם
for (e.g. ~ me)	biʃvil	בִּשְׁבִיל

too (excessively)	yoter midai	יוֹתֵר מִדַי
only (exclusively)	rak	רַק
exactly (adv)	bediyuk	בְּדִיוּק
about (more or less)	be''ereχ	בְּעֵרֶךְ

approximately (adv)	be''ereχ	בְּעֵרֶךְ
approximate (adj)	meʃo'ar	מְשׁוֹעָר
almost (adv)	kim'at	כִּמְעַט
the rest	ʃe'ar	שְׁאָר (ז)

the other (second)	aχer	אַחֵר
other (different)	aχer	אַחֵר
each (adj)	kol	כֹּל
any (no matter which)	kolʃehu	כָּלְשֶׁהוּ
many, much (a lot of)	harbe	הַרְבֵּה
many people	harbe	הַרְבֵּה
all (everyone)	kulam	כּוּלָם

in return for ...	tmurat ...	תְּמוּרַת ...
in exchange (adv)	bitmura	בִּתְמוּרָה
by hand (made)	bayad	בְּיָד
hardly (negative opinion)	safek im	סָפֵק אִם

probably (adv)	karov levadai	קָרוֹב לְוַודַאי
on purpose (intentionally)	'davka	דַּווקָא
by accident (adv)	bemikre	בְּמִקְרֶה

very (adv)	me'od	מְאוֹד
for example (adv)	lemaʃal	לְמָשָׁל
between	bein	בֵּין
among	be'kerev	בְּקֶרֶב
so much (such a lot)	kol kaχ harbe	כָּל־כָּך הַרְבֵּה
especially (adv)	bimyuχad	בְּמִיוּחָד

Basic concepts. Part 2

19. Weekdays

Monday	yom ʃeni	יוֹם שֵׁנִי (ז)
Tuesday	yom ʃliʃi	יוֹם שְׁלִישִׁי (ז)
Wednesday	yom revi'i	יוֹם רְבִיעִי (ז)
Thursday	yom χamiʃi	יוֹם חֲמִישִׁי (ז)
Friday	yom ʃiʃi	יוֹם שִׁישִׁי (ז)
Saturday	ʃabat	שַׁבָּת (נ)
Sunday	yom riʃon	יוֹם רִאשׁוֹן (ז)

today (adv)	hayom	הַיּוֹם
tomorrow (adv)	maχar	מָחָר
the day after tomorrow	maχara'tayim	מָחֳרָתַיִם
yesterday (adv)	etmol	אֶתְמוֹל
the day before yesterday	ʃilʃom	שִׁלְשׁוֹם

day	yom	יוֹם (ז)
working day	yom avoda	יוֹם עֲבוֹדָה (ז)
public holiday	yom χag	יוֹם חַג (ז)
day off	yom menuχa	יוֹם מְנוּחָה (ז)
weekend	sof ʃa'vu'a	סוֹף שָׁבוּעַ

all day long	kol hayom	כָּל הַיּוֹם
the next day (adv)	lamaχarat	לַמָּחֳרָת
two days ago	lifnei yo'mayim	לִפְנֵי יוֹמַיִם
the day before	'erev	עֶרֶב
daily (adj)	yomyomi	יוֹמְיוֹמִי
every day (adv)	midei yom	מְדֵי יוֹם

week	ʃa'vua	שָׁבוּעַ (ז)
last week (adv)	baʃa'vu'a ʃe'avar	בַּשָּׁבוּעַ שֶׁעָבַר
next week (adv)	baʃa'vu'a haba	בַּשָּׁבוּעַ הַבָּא
weekly (adj)	ʃvu'i	שָׁבוּעִי
every week (adv)	kol ʃa'vu'a	כָּל שָׁבוּעַ
twice a week	pa'a'mayim beʃa'vu'a	פַּעֲמַיִם בְּשָׁבוּעַ
every Tuesday	kol yom ʃliʃi	כָּל יוֹם שְׁלִישִׁי

20. Hours. Day and night

morning	'boker	בּוֹקֶר (ז)
in the morning	ba'boker	בַּבּוֹקֶר
noon, midday	tsaha'rayim	צָהֳרַיִם (ז"ר)
in the afternoon	aχar hatsaha'rayim	אַחַר הַצָּהֳרַיִם

| evening | 'erev | עֶרֶב (ז) |
| in the evening | ba''erev | בָּעֶרֶב |

night	'laila	לַיְלָה (ז)
at night	ba'laila	בַּלַּיְלָה
midnight	χatsot	חֲצוֹת (נ)

second	ʃniya	שְׁנִיָּה (נ)
minute	daka	דַּקָּה (נ)
hour	ʃa'a	שָׁעָה (נ)
half an hour	χatsi ʃa'a	חֲצִי שָׁעָה (נ)
a quarter-hour	'reva ʃa'a	רֶבַע שָׁעָה (ז)
fifteen minutes	χameʃ esre dakot	חֲמֵשׁ עָשְׂרֵה דַּקּוֹת
24 hours	yemama	יְמָמָה (נ)

sunrise	zriχa	זְרִיחָה (נ)
dawn	'ʃaχar	שַׁחַר (ז)
early morning	'ʃaχar	שַׁחַר (ז)
sunset	ʃki'a	שְׁקִיעָה (נ)

early in the morning	mukdam ba'boker	מוּקְדָּם בַּבּוֹקֶר
this morning	ha'boker	הַבּוֹקֶר
tomorrow morning	maχar ba'boker	מָחָר בַּבּוֹקֶר
this afternoon	hayom aχarei hatzaha'rayim	הַיּוֹם אַחֲרֵי הַצָּהֳרַיִם
in the afternoon	aχar hatsaha'rayim	אַחַר הַצָּהֳרַיִם
tomorrow afternoon	maχar aχarei hatsaha'rayim	מָחָר אַחֲרֵי הַצָּהֳרַיִם
tonight (this evening)	ha''erev	הָעֶרֶב
tomorrow night	maχar ba''erev	מָחָר בַּעֶרֶב

at 3 o'clock sharp	baʃa'a ʃaloʃ bediyuk	בְּשָׁעָה שָׁלוֹשׁ בְּדִיּוּק
about 4 o'clock	bisvivot arba	בִּסְבִיבוֹת אַרְבַּע
by 12 o'clock	ad ʃteim esre	עַד שְׁתֵּים־עָשְׂרֵה

in 20 minutes	be'od esrim dakot	בְּעוֹד עֶשְׂרִים דַּקּוֹת
in an hour	be'od ʃa'a	בְּעוֹד שָׁעָה
on time (adv)	bazman	בַּזְמַן

a quarter to ...	'reva le...	רֶבַע לְ...
within an hour	toχ ʃa'a	תּוֹךְ שָׁעָה
every 15 minutes	kol 'reva ʃa'a	כָּל רֶבַע שָׁעָה
round the clock	misaviv laʃa'on	מִסָּבִיב לַשָּׁעוֹן

21. Months. Seasons

January	'yanu'ar	יָנוּאָר (ז)
February	'febru'ar	פֶבְּרוּאָר (ז)
March	merts	מֶרְץ (ז)
April	april	אַפְּרִיל (ז)
May	mai	מַאי (ז)
June	'yuni	יוּנִי (ז)

July	'yuli	יוּלִי (ז)
August	'ogust	אוֹגוּסְט (ז)
September	sep'tember	סֶפְּטֶמְבָּר (ז)
October	ok'tober	אוֹקְטוֹבָּר (ז)
November	no'vember	נוֹבֶמְבָּר (ז)
December	de'tsember	דֶּצֶמְבָּר (ז)

27

spring	aviv	אָבִיב (ז)
in spring	ba'aviv	בָּאָבִיב
spring (as adj)	avivi	אָבִיבִי
summer	'kayits	קַיִץ (ז)
in summer	ba'kayits	בַּקַיִץ
summer (as adj)	ketsi	קֵיצִי
autumn	stav	סְתָיו (ז)
in autumn	bestav	בִּסְתָיו
autumn (as adj)	stavi	סְתָווִי
winter	'xoref	חוֹרֶף (ז)
in winter	ba'xoref	בַּחוֹרֶף
winter (as adj)	xorpi	חוֹרְפִי
month	'xodeʃ	חוֹדֶשׁ (ז)
this month	ha'xodeʃ	הַחוֹדֶשׁ
next month	ba'xodeʃ haba	בַּחוֹדֶשׁ הַבָּא
last month	ba'xodeʃ ʃe'avar	בַּחוֹדֶשׁ שֶׁעָבַר
a month ago	lifnei 'xodeʃ	לִפְנֵי חוֹדֶשׁ
in a month (a month later)	be'od 'xodeʃ	בְּעוֹד חוֹדֶשׁ
in 2 months (2 months later)	be'od xod'ʃayim	בְּעוֹד חוֹדְשַׁיִים
the whole month	kol ha'xodeʃ	כָּל הַחוֹדֶשׁ
all month long	kol ha'xodeʃ	כָּל הַחוֹדֶשׁ
monthly (~ magazine)	xodʃi	חוֹדְשִׁי
monthly (adv)	xodʃit	חוֹדְשִׁית
every month	kol 'xodeʃ	כָּל חוֹדֶשׁ
twice a month	pa'a'mayim be'xodeʃ	פַּעֲמַיִים בְּחוֹדֶשׁ
year	ʃana	שָׁנָה (נ)
this year	haʃana	הַשָׁנָה
next year	baʃana haba'a	בַּשָׁנָה הַבָּאָה
last year	baʃana ʃe'avra	בַּשָׁנָה שֶׁעָבְרָה
a year ago	lifnei ʃana	לִפְנֵי שָׁנָה
in a year	be'od ʃana	בְּעוֹד שָׁנָה
in two years	be'od ʃna'tayim	בְּעוֹד שְׁנָתַיִים
the whole year	kol haʃana	כָּל הַשָׁנָה
all year long	kol haʃana	כָּל הַשָׁנָה
every year	kol ʃana	כָּל שָׁנָה
annual (adj)	ʃnati	שְׁנָתִי
annually (adv)	midei ʃana	מִדֵי שָׁנָה
4 times a year	arba pa'amim be'xodeʃ	אַרְבַּע פְּעָמִים בְּחוֹדֶשׁ
date (e.g. today's ~)	ta'arix	תַאֲרִיךְ (ז)
date (e.g. ~ of birth)	ta'arix	תַאֲרִיךְ (ז)
calendar	'luax ʃana	לוּחַ שָׁנָה (ז)
half a year	xatsi ʃana	חֲצִי שָׁנָה (נ)
six months	ʃiʃa xodaʃim, xatsi ʃana	חֲצִי שָׁנָה, שִׁישָׁה חוֹדָשִׁים (נ)
season (summer, etc.)	ona	עוֹנָה (נ)
century	'me'a	מֵאָה (נ)

22. Time. Miscellaneous

time	zman	זְמַן (ז)
moment	'rega	רֶגַע (ז)
instant (n)	'rega	רֶגַע (ז)
instant (adj)	miyadi	מִיָּדִי
lapse (of time)	tkufa	תְּקוּפָה (נ)
life	χayim	חַיִּים (ז"ר)
eternity	'netsaχ	נֶצַח (ז)
epoch	idan	עִידָן (ז)
era	idan	עִידָן (ז)
cycle	maχzor	מַחֲזוֹר (ז)
period	tkufa	תְּקוּפָה (נ)
term (short-~)	tkufa	תְּקוּפָה (נ)
the future	atid	עָתִיד (ז)
future (as adj)	haba	הַבָּא
next time	ba'pa'am haba'a	בְּפַעַם הַבָּאָה
the past	avar	עָבָר (ז)
past (recent)	ʃe'avar	שֶׁעָבַר
last time	ba'pa'am hako'demet	בְּפַעַם הַקּוֹדֶמֶת
later (adv)	me'uχar yoter	מְאוּחָר יוֹתֵר
after (prep.)	aχarei	אַחֲרֵי
nowadays (adv)	kayom	כַּיּוֹם
now (adv)	aχʃav, ka'et	עַכְשָׁיו, כָּעֵת
immediately (adv)	miyad	מִיָּד
soon (adv)	bekarov	בְּקָרוֹב
in advance (beforehand)	meroʃ	מֵרֹאשׁ
a long time ago	mizman	מִזְּמַן
recently (adv)	lo mizman	לֹא מִזְּמַן
destiny	goral	גּוֹרָל (ז)
memories (childhood ~)	ziχronot	זִיכְרוֹנוֹת (ז"ר)
archives	arχiyon	אַרְכִיּוֹן (ז)
during ...	bezman ʃel ...	בְּזְמַן שֶׁל ...
long, a long time (adv)	zman rav	זְמַן רַב
not long (adv)	lo zman rav	לֹא זְמַן רַב
early (in the morning)	mukdam	מוּקְדָּם
late (not early)	me'uχar	מְאוּחָר
forever (for good)	la'netsaχ	לָנֶצַח
to start (begin)	lehatχil	לְהַתְחִיל
to postpone (vt)	lidχot	לִדְחוֹת
at the same time	bo zmanit	בּוֹ זְמַנִית
permanently (adv)	bikvi'ut	בִּקְבִיעוּת
constant (noise, pain)	ka'vu'a	קָבוּעַ
temporary (adj)	zmani	זְמַנִי
sometimes (adv)	lif'amim	לִפְעָמִים
rarely (adv)	le'itim reχokot	לְעִיתִים רְחוֹקוֹת
often (adv)	le'itim krovot	לְעִיתִים קְרוֹבוֹת

23. Opposites

rich (adj)	aʃir	עָשִׁיר
poor (adj)	ani	עָנִי
ill, sick (adj)	χole	חוֹלֶה
well (not sick)	bari	בָּרִיא
big (adj)	gadol	גָּדוֹל
small (adj)	katan	קָטָן
quickly (adv)	maher	מַהֵר
slowly (adv)	le'at	לְאַט
fast (adj)	mahir	מָהִיר
slow (adj)	iti	אִיטִי
glad (adj)	sa'meaχ	שָׂמֵחַ
sad (adj)	atsuv	עָצוּב
together (adv)	be'yaχad	בְּיַחַד
separately (adv)	levad	לְבַד
aloud (to read)	bekol ram	בְּקוֹל רָם
silently (to oneself)	belev, be'ʃeket	בְּלֵב, בְּשֶׁקֶט
tall (adj)	ga'voha	גָּבוֹהַ
low (adj)	namuχ	נָמוּךְ
deep (adj)	amok	עָמוֹק
shallow (adj)	radud	רָדוּד
yes	ken	כֵּן
no	lo	לֹא
distant (in space)	raχok	רָחוֹק
nearby (adj)	karov	קָרוֹב
far (adv)	raχok	רָחוֹק
nearby (adv)	samuχ	סָמוּךְ
long (adj)	aroχ	אָרוֹךְ
short (adj)	katsar	קָצָר
good (kindhearted)	tov lev	טוֹב לֵב
evil (adj)	raʃa	רָשָׁע
married (adj)	nasui	נָשׂוּי
single (adj)	ravak	רַוָּק
to forbid (vt)	le'esor al	לֶאֱסוֹר עַל
to permit (vt)	leharʃot	לְהַרְשׁוֹת
end	sof	סוֹף (ז)
beginning	hatχala	הַתְחָלָה (נ)

left (adj)	smali	שְׂמָאלִי
right (adj)	yemani	יְמָנִי
first (adj)	riʃon	רִאשׁוֹן
last (adj)	aχaron	אַחֲרוֹן
crime	'peʃa	פֶּשַׁע (ז)
punishment	'oneʃ	עוֹנֶשׁ (ז)
to order (vt)	letsavot	לְצַוּוֹת
to obey (vi, vt)	letsayet	לְצַיֵּת
straight (adj)	yaʃar	יָשָׁר
curved (adj)	me'ukal	מְעוּקָל
paradise	gan 'eden	גַּן עֵדֶן (ז)
hell	gehinom	גֵּיהִינוֹם (ז)
to be born	lehivaled	לְהִיוָּלֵד
to die (vi)	lamut	לָמוּת
strong (adj)	χazak	חָזָק
weak (adj)	χalaʃ	חַלָּשׁ
old (adj)	zaken	זָקֵן
young (adj)	tsa'ir	צָעִיר
old (adj)	yaʃan	יָשָׁן
new (adj)	χadaʃ	חָדָשׁ
hard (adj)	kaʃe	קָשֶׁה
soft (adj)	raχ	רַךְ
warm (tepid)	χamim	חָמִים
cold (adj)	kar	קַר
fat (adj)	ʃamen	שָׁמֵן
thin (adj)	raze	רָזֶה
narrow (adj)	tsar	צַר
wide (adj)	raχav	רָחָב
good (adj)	tov	טוֹב
bad (adj)	ra	רַע
brave (adj)	amits	אַמִּיץ
cowardly (adj)	paχdani	פַּחְדָנִי

24. Lines and shapes

square	ri'bu'a	רִיבּוּעַ (ז)
square (as adj)	meruba	מְרוּבָּע
circle	ma'agal, igul	מַעְגָּל, עִיגוּל (ז)
round (adj)	agol	עָגוֹל

| triangle | meʃulaʃ | מְשׁוּלָשׁ (ז) |
| triangular (adj) | meʃulaʃ | מְשׁוּלָשׁ |

oval	e'lipsa	אֶלִיפְּסָה (נ)
oval (as adj)	e'lipti	אֶלִיפְּטִי
rectangle	malben	מַלְבֵּן (ז)
rectangular (adj)	malbeni	מַלְבֵּנִי

pyramid	pira'mida	פִּירָמִידָה (נ)
rhombus	me'uyan	מְעוּיָּן (ז)
trapezium	trapez	טְרַפֵּז (ז)
cube	kubiya	קוּבִּיָּה (נ)
prism	minsara	מִנְסָרָה (נ)

circumference	ma'agal	מַעֲגָל (ז)
sphere	sfira	סְפִירָה (נ)
ball (solid sphere)	kadur	כַּדּוּר (ז)

diameter	'koter	קֹטֶר (ז)
radius	'radyus	רַדְיוּס (ז)
perimeter (circle's ~)	hekef	הֶיקֵף (ז)
centre	merkaz	מֶרְכָּז (ז)

horizontal (adj)	ofki	אוֹפְקִי
vertical (adj)	anaχi	אֲנָכִי
parallel (n)	kav makbil	קַו מַקְבִּיל (ז)
parallel (as adj)	makbil	מַקְבִּיל

line	kav	קַו (ז)
stroke	kav	קַו (ז)
straight line	kav yaʃar	קַו יָשָׁר (ז)
curve (curved line)	akuma	עֲקוּמָה (נ)
thin (line, etc.)	dak	דַּק
contour (outline)	mit'ar	מִתְאָר (ז)

intersection	χituχ	חִיתּוּךְ (ז)
right angle	zavit yaʃara	זָוִית יָשָׁרָה (נ)
segment	mikta	מִקְטָע (ז)
sector	gizra	גִּזְרָה (נ)
side (of triangle)	'tsela	צֶלַע (ז)
angle	zavit	זָוִית (נ)

25. Units of measurement

weight	miʃkal	מִשְׁקָל (ז)
length	'oreχ	אוֹרֶךְ (ז)
width	'roχav	רוֹחַב (ז)
height	'gova	גּוֹבַהּ (ז)
depth	'omek	עוֹמֶק (ז)
volume	'nefaχ	נֶפַח (ז)
area	'ʃetaχ	שֶׁטַח (ז)

| gram | gram | גְּרָם (ז) |
| milligram | miligram | מִילִיגְרָם (ז) |

kilogram	kilogram	קִילוֹגְרָם (ז)
ton	ton	טוֹן (ז)
pound	'pa'und	פָּאוּנד (ז)
ounce	'unkiya	אוּנקִיָה (נ)

metre	'meter	מֶטֶר (ז)
millimetre	mili'meter	מִילִימֶטֶר (ז)
centimetre	senti'meter	סָנטִימֶטֶר (ז)
kilometre	kilo'meter	קִילוֹמֶטֶר (ז)
mile	mail	מַייל (ז)

inch	intʃ	אִינצ' (ז)
foot	'regel	רֶגֶל (נ)
yard	yard	יַרד (ז)

| square metre | 'meter ra'vu'a | מֶטֶר רָבוּעַ (ז) |
| hectare | hektar | הֶקטָר (ז) |

litre	litr	לִיטֶר (ז)
degree	ma'ala	מַעֲלָה (נ)
volt	volt	ווֹלט (ז)
ampere	amper	אַמפֶּר (ז)
horsepower	'koaχ sus	כּוֹחַ סוּס (ז)

quantity	kamut	כַּמוּת (נ)
a little bit of ...	ktsat ...	קצָת ...
half	'χetsi	חֲצִי (ז)
dozen	tresar	תרֵיסָר (ז)
piece (item)	yeχida	יְחִידָה (נ)

| size | 'godel | גוֹדֶל (ז) |
| scale (map ~) | kne mida | קנֵה מִידָה (ז) |

minimal (adj)	mini'mali	מִינִימָאלִי
the smallest (adj)	hakatan beyoter	הַקָטָן בְּיוֹתֵר
medium (adj)	memutsa	מְמוּצָע
maximal (adj)	maksi'mali	מַקסִימָלִי
the largest (adj)	hagadol beyoter	הַגָדוֹל בְּיוֹתֵר

26. Containers

canning jar (glass ~)	tsin'tsenet	צנצֶנֶת (נ)
tin, can	paχit	פַּחִית (נ)
bucket	dli	דלִי (ז)
barrel	χavit	חָבִית (נ)

wash basin (e.g., plastic ~)	gigit	גִיגִית (נ)
tank (100L water ~)	meiχal	מֵיכָל (ז)
hip flask	meimiya	מֵימִיָה (נ)
jerrycan	'dʒerikan	גֶ'רִיקָן (ז)
tank (e.g., tank car)	meχalit	מֵיכָלִית (נ)

| mug | 'sefel | סֵפֶל (ז) |
| cup (of coffee, etc.) | 'sefel | סֵפֶל (ז) |

saucer	taχtit	תַּחְתִּית (נ)
glass (tumbler)	kos	כּוֹס (נ)
wine glass	ga'vi'a	גָּבִיעַ (ז)
stock pot (soup pot)	sir	סִיר (ז)

bottle (~ of wine)	bakbuk	בַּקְבּוּק (ז)
neck (of the bottle, etc.)	tsavar habakbuk	צַוַּאר הַבַּקְבּוּק (ז)

carafe (decanter)	kad	כַּד (ז)
pitcher	kankan	קַנְקַן (ז)
vessel (container)	kli	כְּלִי (ז)
pot (crock, stoneware ~)	sir 'χeres	סִיר חֶרֶס (ז)
vase	agartal	אֲגַרְטָל (ז)

bottle (perfume ~)	tsloχit	צְלוֹחִית (נ)
vial, small bottle	bakbukon	בַּקְבּוּקוֹן (ז)
tube (of toothpaste)	ffo'feret	שְׁפוֹפֶרֶת (נ)

sack (bag)	sak	שַׂק (ז)
bag (paper ~, plastic ~)	sakit	שַׂקִּית (נ)
packet (of cigarettes, etc.)	χafisa	חֲפִיסָה (נ)

box (e.g. shoebox)	kufsa	קוּפְסָה (נ)
crate	argaz	אַרְגָּז (ז)
basket	sal	סַל (ז)

27. Materials

material	'χomer	חוֹמֶר (ז)
wood (n)	ets	עֵץ (ז)
wood-, wooden (adj)	me'ets	מֵעֵץ

glass (n)	zχuχit	זְכוּכִית (נ)
glass (as adj)	mizχuχit	מִזְּכוּכִית

stone (n)	'even	אֶבֶן (נ)
stone (as adj)	me''even	מֵאֶבֶן

plastic (n)	'plastik	פְּלַסְטִיק (ז)
plastic (as adj)	mi'plastik	מִפְּלַסְטִיק

rubber (n)	'gumi	גּוּמִי (ז)
rubber (as adj)	mi'gumi	מִגּוּמִי

cloth, fabric (n)	bad	בַּד (ז)
fabric (as adj)	mibad	מִבַּד

paper (n)	neyar	נְיָיר (ז)
paper (as adj)	mineyar	מִנְּיָיר

cardboard (n)	karton	קַרְטוֹן (ז)
cardboard (as adj)	mikarton	מִקַּרְטוֹן
polyethylene	'nailon	נַיְילוֹן (ז)
cellophane	tselofan	צֶלוֹפָן (ז)

| linoleum | li'nole'um | לִינוֹלְיאוּם (ז) |
| plywood | dikt | דִּיקְט (ז) |

porcelain (n)	χar'sina	חַרְסִינָה (נ)
porcelain (as adj)	meχar'sina	מְחַרְסִינָה
clay (n)	χarsit	חַרְסִית (נ)
clay (as adj)	me'χeres	מֵחֶרֶס
ceramic (n)	ke'ramika	קֵרָמִיקָה (נ)
ceramic (as adj)	ke'rami	קֵרָמִי

28. Metals

metal (n)	ma'teχet	מַתֶּכֶת (נ)
metal (as adj)	mataχti	מַתַּכְתִּי
alloy (n)	sag'soget	סַגְסוֹגֶת (נ)

gold (n)	zahav	זָהָב (ז)
gold, golden (adj)	mizahav, zahov	מִזָּהָב, זָהוֹב
silver (n)	'kesef	כֶּסֶף (ז)
silver (as adj)	kaspi	כַּסְפִּי

iron (n)	barzel	בַּרְזֶל (ז)
iron-, made of iron (adj)	mibarzel	מִבַּרְזֶל
steel (n)	plada	פְּלָדָה (נ)
steel (as adj)	miplada	מִפְּלָדָה
copper (n)	ne'χoʃet	נְחוֹשֶׁת (נ)
copper (as adj)	mine'χoʃet	מִנְחוֹשֶׁת

aluminium (n)	alu'minyum	אָלוּמִינְיוּם (ז)
aluminium (as adj)	me'alu'minyum	מֵאָלוּמִינְיוּם
bronze (n)	arad	אָרָד (ז)
bronze (as adj)	me'arad	מֵאָרָד

brass	pliz	פְּלִיז (ז)
nickel	'nikel	נִיקֶל (ז)
platinum	'platina	פְּלָטִינָה (נ)
mercury	kaspit	כַּסְפִּית (נ)
tin	bdil	בְּדִיל (ז)
lead	o'feret	עוֹפֶרֶת (נ)
zinc	avats	אָבָץ (ז)

HUMAN BEING

Human being. The body

29. Humans. Basic concepts

human being	ben adam	בֶּן אָדָם (ז)
man (adult male)	'gever	גֶּבֶר (ז)
woman	iʃa	אִשָׁה (נ)
child	'yeled	יֶלֶד (ז)
girl	yalda	יַלְדָה (נ)
boy	'yeled	יֶלֶד (ז)
teenager	'naʿar	נַעַר (ז)
old man	zaken	זָקֵן (ז)
old woman	zkena	זְקֵנָה (נ)

30. Human anatomy

organism (body)	guf ha'adam	גוּף הָאָדָם (ז)
heart	lev	לֵב (ז)
blood	dam	דָם (ז)
artery	'orek	עוֹרֶק (ז)
vein	vrid	וְרִיד (ז)
brain	'moaχ	מוֹחַ (ז)
nerve	aʦav	עָצָב (ז)
nerves	aʦabim	עֲצַבִּים (ז"ר)
vertebra	χulya	חוּלְיָה (נ)
spine (backbone)	amud haʃidra	עַמוּד הַשִׁדְרָה (ז)
stomach (organ)	keiva	קֵיבָה (נ)
intestines, bowels	me"ayim	מְעַיִים (ז"ר)
intestine (e.g. large ~)	me'i	מְעִי (ז)
liver	kaved	כָּבֵד (ז)
kidney	kilya	כְּלְיָה (נ)
bone	'eʦem	עֶצֶם (נ)
skeleton	'ʃeled	שֶׁלֶד (ז)
rib	'ʦela	צֵלַע (ז)
skull	gul'golet	גוּלְגוֹלֶת (נ)
muscle	ʃrir	שְׁרִיר (ז)
biceps	ʃrir du raʃi	שְׁרִיר דוּ-רָאשִׁי (ז)
triceps	ʃrir tlat raʃi	שְׁרִיר תְּלָת-רָאשִׁי (ז)
tendon	gid	גִּיד (ז)
joint	'perek	פֶּרֶק (ז)

lungs	re'ot	רֵיאוֹת (נ״ר)
genitals	evrei min	אֶבְרֵי מִין (ז״ר)
skin	or	עוֹר (ז)

31. Head

head	roʃ	רֹאשׁ (ז)
face	panim	פָּנִים (ז״ר)
nose	af	אַף (ז)
mouth	pe	פֶּה (ז)

eye	'ayin	עַיִן (נ)
eyes	ei'nayim	עֵינַיִם (נ״ר)
pupil	iʃon	אִישׁוֹן (ז)
eyebrow	gaba	גַּבָּה (נ)
eyelash	ris	רִיס (ז)
eyelid	af'af	עַפְעַף (ז)

tongue	laʃon	לָשׁוֹן (נ)
tooth	ʃen	שֵׁן (נ)
lips	sfa'tayim	שְׂפָתַיִם (נ״ר)
cheekbones	atsamot leχa'yayim	עַצְמוֹת לְחָיַיִם (נ״ר)
gum	χani'χayim	חֲנִיכַיִים (ז״ר)
palate	χeχ	חֵךְ (ז)

nostrils	neχi'rayim	נְחִירַיִים (ז״ר)
chin	santer	סַנְטֵר (ז)
jaw	'leset	לֶסֶת (נ)
cheek	'leχi	לָחִי (נ)

forehead	'metsaχ	מֵצַח (ז)
temple	raka	רַקָּה (נ)
ear	'ozen	אוֹזֶן (נ)
back of the head	'oref	עוֹרֶף (ז)
neck	tsavar	צַוָּאר (ז)
throat	garon	גָּרוֹן (ז)

hair	se'ar	שֵׂיעָר (ז)
hairstyle	tis'roket	תִּסְרוֹקֶת (נ)
haircut	tis'poret	תִּסְפּוֹרֶת (נ)
wig	pe'a	פֵּאָה (נ)

moustache	safam	שָׂפָם (ז)
beard	zakan	זָקָן (ז)
to have (a beard, etc.)	legadel	לְגַדֵּל
plait	tsama	צַמָּה (נ)
sideboards	pe'ot leχa'yayim	פֵּאוֹת לְחָיַיִם (נ״ר)

red-haired (adj)	'dʒindʒi	ג׳ינג׳י
grey (hair)	kasuf	כָּסוּף
bald (adj)	ke'reaχ	קֵירֵחַ
bald patch	ka'raχat	קָרַחַת (נ)
ponytail	'kuku	קוּקוּ (ז)
fringe	'poni	פּוֹנִי (ז)

32. Human body

| hand | kaf yad | כַּף יָד (נ) |
| arm | yad | יָד (נ) |

finger	'etsba	אֶצְבַּע (נ)
toe	'bohen	בּוֹהֶן (נ)
thumb	agudal	אֲגוּדָל (ז)
little finger	'zeret	זֶרֶת (נ)
nail	tsi'poren	צִיפּוֹרֶן (נ)

fist	egrof	אֶגְרוֹף (ז)
palm	kaf yad	כַּף יָד (נ)
wrist	ʃoreʃ kaf hayad	שׁוֹרֶשׁ כַּף הַיָּד (ז)
forearm	ama	אַמָּה (נ)
elbow	marpek	מַרְפֵּק (ז)
shoulder	katef	כָּתֵף (נ)

leg	'regel	רֶגֶל (נ)
foot	kaf 'regel	כַּף רֶגֶל (נ)
knee	'berex	בֶּרֶךְ (נ)
calf (part of leg)	ʃok	שׁוֹק (נ)
hip	yarex	יָרֵךְ (נ)
heel	akev	עָקֵב (ז)

body	guf	גּוּף (ז)
stomach	'beten	בֶּטֶן (נ)
chest	xaze	חָזֶה (ז)
breast	ʃad	שַׁד (ז)
flank	tsad	צַד (ז)
back	gav	גַּב (ז)
lower back	mot'nayim	מוֹתְנַיִים (ז"ר)
waist	'talya	טַלְיָה (נ)

navel (belly button)	tabur	טַבּוּר (ז)
buttocks	axo'rayim	אֲחוֹרַיִים (ז"ר)
bottom	yaʃvan	יַשְׁבָן (ז)

beauty spot	nekudat xen	נְקוּדַת חֵן (נ)
birthmark (café au lait spot)	'ketem leida	כֶּתֶם לֵידָה (ז)
tattoo	ka'a'ku'a	קַעֲקוּעַ (ז)
scar	tsa'leket	צַלֶּקֶת (נ)

Clothing & Accessories

33. Outerwear. Coats

clothes	bgadim	בְּגָדִים (ז״ר)
outerwear	levuʃ elyon	לְבוּש עֶלְיוֹן (ז)
winter clothing	bigdei 'χoref	בִּגְדֵי חוֹרֶף (ז״ר)

coat (overcoat)	me'il	מְעִיל (ז)
fur coat	me'il parva	מְעִיל פַּרְוָה (ז)
fur jacket	me'il parva katsar	מְעִיל פַּרְוָה קָצָר (ז)
down coat	me'il puχ	מְעִיל פּוּך (ז)

jacket (e.g. leather ~)	me'il katsar	מְעִיל קָצָר (ז)
raincoat (trenchcoat, etc.)	me'il 'geʃem	מְעִיל גֶּשֶׁם (ז)
waterproof (adj)	amid be'mayim	עָמִיד בְּמַיִם

34. Men's & women's clothing

shirt (button shirt)	χultsa	חוּלְצָה (נ)
trousers	miχna'sayim	מִכְנָסַיִם (ז״ר)
jeans	miχnesei 'dʒins	מִכְנְסֵי ג'ִינְס (ז״ר)
suit jacket	ʒaket	ז'ָקֵט (ז)
suit	χalifa	חֲלִיפָה (נ)

dress (frock)	simla	שִׂמְלָה (נ)
skirt	χatsa'it	חֲצָאִית (נ)
blouse	χultsa	חוּלְצָה (נ)
knitted jacket (cardigan, etc.)	ʒaket 'tsemer	ז'ָקֵט צֶמֶר (ז)
jacket (of woman's suit)	ʒaket	ז'ָקֵט (ז)

T-shirt	ti ʃert	טִי שֶׁרְט (ז)
shorts (short trousers)	miχna'sayim ktsarim	מִכְנָסַיִם קְצָרִים (ז״ר)
tracksuit	'trening	טְרֶנִינְג (ז)
bathrobe	χaluk raχatsa	חָלוּק רַחְצָה (ז)
pyjamas	pi'dʒama	פִּיג'ָמָה (נ)

jumper (sweater)	'sveder	סְוֶודֶר (ז)
pullover	afuda	אֲפוּדָה (נ)

waistcoat	vest	וֶסְט (ז)
tailcoat	frak	פְרַאק (ז)
dinner suit	tuk'sido	טוּקְסִידוֹ (ז)

uniform	madim	מַדִּים (ז״ר)
workwear	bigdei avoda	בִּגְדֵי עֲבוֹדָה (ז״ר)
boiler suit	sarbal	סַרְבָּל (ז)
coat (e.g. doctor's smock)	χaluk	חָלוּק (ז)

35. Clothing. Underwear

underwear	levanim	לְבָנִים (ז״ר)
pants	taxtonim	תַחְתּוֹנִים (ז״ר)
panties	taxtonim	תַחְתּוֹנִים (ז״ר)
vest (singlet)	gufiya	גוּפִייָה (נ)
socks	gar'bayim	גַרְבַּיִם (ז״ר)

nightgown	'ktonet 'laila	כְּתוֹנֶת לַיְלָה (נ)
bra	xaziya	חֲזִייָה (נ)
knee highs (knee-high socks)	birkon	בִּרְכּוֹן (ז)
tights	garbonim	גַרְבּוֹנִים (ז״ר)
stockings (hold ups)	garbei 'nailon	גַרְבֵּי נַיְלוֹן (ז״ר)
swimsuit, bikini	'beged yam	בֶּגֶד יָם (ז)

36. Headwear

hat	'kova	כּוֹבַע (ז)
trilby hat	'kova 'leved	כּוֹבַע לֶבֶד (ז)
baseball cap	'kova 'beisbol	כּוֹבַע בֵּייסְבּוֹל (ז)
flatcap	'kova mitsxiya	כּוֹבַע מִצְחִייָה (ז)

beret	baret	בֶּרֶט (ז)
hood	bardas	בַּרְדָס (ז)
panama hat	'kova 'tembel	כּוֹבַע טֶמְבֶּל (ז)
knit cap (knitted hat)	'kova 'gerev	כּוֹבַע גֶרֶב (ז)

| headscarf | mit'paxat | מִטְפַּחַת (נ) |
| women's hat | 'kova | כּוֹבַע (ז) |

hard hat	kasda	קַסְדָה (נ)
forage cap	kumta	כּוּמְתָה (נ)
helmet	kasda	קַסְדָה (נ)

| bowler | mig'ba'at me'u'gelet | מִגְבַּעַת מְעוּגֶלֶת (נ) |
| top hat | tsi'linder | צִילִינְדֶר (ז) |

37. Footwear

footwear	han'ala	הַנְעָלָה (נ)
shoes (men's shoes)	na'a'layim	נַעֲלַיִם (נ״ר)
shoes (women's shoes)	na'a'layim	נַעֲלַיִם (נ״ר)
boots (e.g., cowboy ~)	maga'fayim	מַגָפַיִם (ז״ר)
carpet slippers	na'alei 'bayit	נַעֲלֵי בַּיִת (נ״ר)

trainers	na'alei sport	נַעֲלֵי סְפּוֹרְט (נ״ר)
trainers	na'alei sport	נַעֲלֵי סְפּוֹרְט (נ״ר)
sandals	sandalim	סַנְדָלִים (ז״ר)

| cobbler (shoe repairer) | sandlar | סַנְדְלָר (ז) |
| heel | akev | עָקֵב (ז) |

pair (of shoes)	zug	זוּג (ז)
lace (shoelace)	sroχ	שְׂרוֹךְ (ז)
to lace up (vt)	lisroχ	לִשְׂרוֹךְ
shoehorn	kaf na'a'layim	כַּף נַעֲלַיִים (נ)
shoe polish	miʃχat na'a'layim	מִשְׁחַת נַעֲלַיִים (נ)

38. Textile. Fabrics

cotton (n)	kutna	כּוּתְנָה (נ)
cotton (as adj)	mikutna	מְכּוּתְנָה
flax (n)	piʃtan	פִּשְׁתָּן (ז)
flax (as adj)	mipiʃtan	מִפִּשְׁתָּן

silk (n)	'meʃi	מֶשִׁי (ז)
silk (as adj)	miʃyi	מֶשְׁיִי
wool (n)	'tsemer	צֶמֶר (ז)
wool (as adj)	tsamri	צַמְרִי

velvet	ktifa	קְטִיפָה (נ)
suede	zamʃ	זָמְשׁ (ז)
corduroy	'korderoi	קוֹרְדָּרוֹי (ז)

nylon (n)	'nailon	נַיְילוֹן (ז)
nylon (as adj)	mi'nailon	מְנַיְילוֹן
polyester (n)	poli''ester	פּוֹלִיאָסְטֶר (ז)
polyester (as adj)	mipoli''ester	מְפּוֹלִיאָסְטֶר

leather (n)	or	עוֹר (ז)
leather (as adj)	me'or	מֵעוֹר
fur (n)	parva	פַּרְוָוה (נ)
fur (e.g. ~ coat)	miparva	מִפַּרְוָוה

39. Personal accessories

gloves	kfafot	כְּפָפוֹת (נ"ר)
mittens	kfafot	כְּפָפוֹת (נ"ר)
scarf (muffler)	tsa'if	צָעִיף (ז)

glasses	miʃka'fayim	מִשְׁקָפַיִים (ז"ר)
frame (eyeglass ~)	mis'geret	מִסְגֶרֶת (נ)
umbrella	mitriya	מִטְרִייָה (נ)
walking stick	makel haliχa	מַקֵל הֲלִיכָה (ז)
hairbrush	miv'reʃet se'ar	מִבְרֶשֶׁת שֵׂיעָר (נ)
fan	menifa	מְנִיפָה (נ)

tie (necktie)	aniva	עֲנִיבָה (נ)
bow tie	anivat parpar	עֲנִיבַת פַּרְפַּר (נ)
braces	ktefiyot	כְּתֵפִיוֹת (נ"ר)
handkerchief	mimχata	מִמְחָטָה (נ)

| comb | masrek | מַסְרֵק (ז) |
| hair slide | sikat roʃ | סִיכַּת רֹאשׁ (נ) |

| hairpin | sikat se'ar | סִיכַּת שֵׂעָר (נ) |
| buckle | avzam | אַבְזָם (ז) |

| belt | χagora | חֲגוֹרָה (נ) |
| shoulder strap | retsu'at katef | רְצוּעַת כָּתֵף (נ) |

bag (handbag)	tik	תִּיק (ז)
handbag	tik	תִּיק (ז)
rucksack	tarmil	תַּרְמִיל (ז)

40. Clothing. Miscellaneous

fashion	ofna	אוֹפְנָה (נ)
in vogue (adj)	ofnati	אוֹפְנָתִי
fashion designer	me'atsev ofna	מְעַצֵּב אוֹפְנָה (ז)

collar	tsavaron	צַוָּארוֹן (ז)
pocket	kis	כִּיס (ז)
pocket (as adj)	ʃel kis	שֶׁל כִּיס
sleeve	ʃarvul	שַׁרְווּל (ז)
hanging loop	mitle	מִתְלָה (נ)
flies (on trousers)	χanut	חֲנוּת (נ)

zip (fastener)	roχsan	רוֹכְסָן (ז)
fastener	'keres	קֶרֶס (ז)
button	kaftor	כַּפְתּוֹר (ז)
buttonhole	lula'a	לוּלָאָה (נ)
to come off (ab. button)	lehitaleʃ	לְהִיתָּלֵשׁ

to sew (vi, vt)	litpor	לִתְפּוֹר
to embroider (vi, vt)	lirkom	לִרְקוֹם
embroidery	rikma	רִקְמָה (נ)
sewing needle	'maχat tfira	מַחַט תְּפִירָה (נ)
thread	χut	חוּט (ז)
seam	'tefer	תֶּפֶר (ז)

to get dirty (vi)	lehitlaχleχ	לְהִתְלַכְלֵךְ
stain (mark, spot)	'ketem	כֶּתֶם (ז)
to crease, crumple (vi)	lehitkamet	לְהִתְקַמֵּט
to tear, to rip (vt)	lik'ro'a	לִקְרוֹעַ
clothes moth	aʃ	עָשׁ (ז)

41. Personal care. Cosmetics

toothpaste	miʃχat ʃi'nayim	מִשְׁחַת שִׁינַּיִים (נ)
toothbrush	miv'reʃet ʃi'nayim	מִבְרֶשֶׁת שִׁינַּיִים (נ)
to clean one's teeth	letsaχ'tseaχ ʃi'nayim	לְצַחְצֵחַ שִׁינַּיִים

razor	'ta'ar	תַּעַר (ז)
shaving cream	'ketsef gi'luaχ	קֶצֶף גִּילּוּחַ (ז)
to shave (vi)	lehitga'leaχ	לְהִתְגַּלֵּחַ
soap	sabon	סַבּוֹן (ז)

shampoo	ʃampu	שַׁמְפּוּ (ז)
scissors	mispa'rayim	מִסְפָּרַיִים (ז״ר)
nail file	ptsira	פְּצִירָה (נ)
nail clippers	gozez tsipor'nayim	גּוֹזֵז צִיפּוֹרְנַיִים (ז)
tweezers	pin'tseta	פִּינְצֶטָה (נ)

cosmetics	tamrukim	תַּמְרוּקִים (ז״ר)
face mask	maseχa	מַסֵכָה (נ)
manicure	manikur	מָנִיקוּר (ז)
to have a manicure	la'asot manikur	לַעֲשׂוֹת מָנִיקוּר
pedicure	pedikur	פֶּדִיקוּר (ז)

make-up bag	tik ipur	תִּיק אִיפּוּר (ז)
face powder	'pudra	פּוּדְרָה (נ)
powder compact	pudriya	פּוּדְרִיָיה (נ)
blusher	'somek	סוֹמֶק (ז)

perfume (bottled)	'bosem	בּוֹשֶׂם (ז)
toilet water (lotion)	mei 'bosem	מֵי בּוֹשֶׂם (ז״ר)
lotion	mei panim	מֵי פָּנִים (ז״ר)
cologne	mei 'bosem	מֵי בּוֹשֶׂם (ז״ר)

eyeshadow	tslalit	צְלָלִית (נ)
eyeliner	ai 'lainer	אַיי לַיינֶר (ז)
mascara	'maskara	מַסְקָרָה (נ)

lipstick	sfaton	שְׂפָתוֹן (ז)
nail polish	'laka letsipor'nayim	לַכָּה לְצִיפּוֹרְנַיִים (נ)
hair spray	tarsis lese'ar	תַּרְסִיס לְשֵׂיעָר (ז)
deodorant	de'odo'rant	דָאוֹדוֹרַנְט (ז)

cream	krem	קְרֶם (ז)
face cream	krem panim	קְרֶם פָּנִים (ז)
hand cream	krem ya'dayim	קְרֶם יָדַיִים (ז)
anti-wrinkle cream	krem 'neged kmatim	קְרֶם נֶגֶד קְמָטִים (ז)
day cream	krem yom	קְרֶם יוֹם (ז)
night cream	krem 'laila	קְרֶם לַילָה (ז)
day (as adj)	yomi	יוֹמִי
night (as adj)	leili	לֵילִי

tampon	tampon	טַמְפּוֹן (ז)
toilet paper (toilet roll)	neyar tu'alet	נְיַיר טוּאָלֶט (ז)
hair dryer	meyabeʃ se'ar	מְיַיבֵּשׁ שֵׂיעָר (ז)

42. Jewellery

jewellery	taχʃitim	תַכְשִׁיטִים (ז״ר)
precious (e.g. ~ stone)	yekar 'ereχ	יְקַר עֵרֶךְ
hallmark stamp	tav tsorfim, bχina	תָו צוֹרְפִים (ז), בְּחִינָה (נ)

ring	ta'ba'at	טַבַּעַת (נ)
wedding ring	ta'ba'at nisu'in	טַבַּעַת נִישׂוּאִין (נ)
bracelet	tsamid	צָמִיד (ז)
earrings	agilim	עֲגִילִים (ז״ר)

necklace (~ of pearls)	maχ'rozet	מַחרוֹזֶת (נ)
crown	'keter	כֶּתֶר (ז)
bead necklace	maχ'rozet	מַחרוֹזֶת (נ)

diamond	yahalom	יַהֲלוֹם (ז)
emerald	ba'reket	בָּרֶקֶת (נ)
ruby	'odem	אוֹדֶם (ז)
sapphire	sapir	סַפִּיר (ז)
pearl	pnina	פְּנִינָה (נ)
amber	inbar	עִנבָּר (ז)

43. Watches. Clocks

watch (wristwatch)	ʃe'on yad	שָׁעוֹן יָד (ז)
dial	'luaχ ʃa'on	לוּחַ שָׁעוֹן (ז)
hand (of clock, watch)	maχog	מָחוֹג (ז)
metal bracelet	tsamid	צָמִיד (ז)
watch strap	retsu'a leʃa'on	רְצוּעָה לְשָׁעוֹן (נ)

battery	solela	סוֹלְלָה (נ)
to be flat (battery)	lehitroken	לְהִתרוֹקֵן
to change a battery	lehaχlif	לְהַחלִיף
to run fast	lemaher	לְמַהֵר
to run slow	lefager	לְפַגֵר

wall clock	ʃe'on kir	שָׁעוֹן קִיר (ז)
hourglass	ʃe'on χol	שָׁעוֹן חוֹל (ז)
sundial	ʃe'on 'ʃemeʃ	שָׁעוֹן שֶׁמֶשׁ (ז)
alarm clock	ʃa'on me'orer	שָׁעוֹן מְעוֹרֵר (ז)
watchmaker	ʃa'an	שַׁעָן (ז)
to repair (vt)	letaken	לְתַקֵן

Food. Nutricion

44. Food

meat	basar	בָּשָׂר (ז)
chicken	of	עוֹף (ז)
poussin	pargit	פַּרְגִּית (נ)
duck	barvaz	בַּרְוָז (ז)
goose	avaz	אַוָּז (ז)
game	'tsayid	צַיִד (ז)
turkey	'hodu	הוֹדוּ (ז)

pork	basar χazir	בְּשַׂר חֲזִיר (ז)
veal	basar 'egel	בְּשַׂר עֵגֶל (ז)
lamb	basar 'keves	בְּשַׂר כֶּבֶשׂ (ז)
beef	bakar	בָּקָר (ז)
rabbit	arnav	אַרְנָב (ז)

sausage (bologna, pepperoni, etc.)	naknik	נַקְנִיק (ז)
vienna sausage (frankfurter)	naknikiya	נַקְנִיקִיָּה (נ)
bacon	'kotel χazir	קוֹתֶל חֲזִיר (ז)
ham	basar χazir me'uʃan	בְּשַׂר חֲזִיר מְעוּשָּׁן (ז)
gammon	'kotel χazir me'uʃan	קוֹתֶל חֲזִיר מְעוּשָּׁן (ז)

pâté	pate	פָּטֶה (ז)
liver	kaved	כָּבֵד (ז)
mince (minced meat)	basar taχun	בָּשָׂר טָחוּן (ז)
tongue	laʃon	לָשׁוֹן (נ)

egg	beitsa	בֵּיצָה (נ)
eggs	beitsim	בֵּיצִים (נ"ר)
egg white	χelbon	חֶלְבּוֹן (ז)
egg yolk	χelmon	חֶלְמוֹן (ז)

fish	dag	דָּג (ז)
seafood	perot yam	פֵּירוֹת יָם (ז"ר)
crustaceans	sartana'im	סַרְטָנָאִים (ז"ר)
caviar	kavyar	קַוְיָאר (ז)

crab	sartan yam	סַרְטָן יָם (ז)
prawn	ʃrimps	שְׁרִימְפְּס (ז"ר)
oyster	tsidpat ma'aχal	צִדְפַּת מַאֲכָל (נ)
spiny lobster	'lobster kotsani	לוֹבְּסְטֶר קוֹצָנִי (ז)
octopus	tamnun	תַּמְנוּן (ז)
squid	kala'mari	קָלָמָארִי (ז)

sturgeon	basar haχidkan	בְּשַׂר הַחִדְקָן (ז)
salmon	'salmon	סַלְמוֹן (ז)
halibut	putit	פּוּטִית (נ)

cod	ſibut	שִׁיבּוּט (ז)
mackerel	kolyas	קוֹלְיָס (ז)
tuna	'tuna	טוּנָה (נ)
eel	tslofaχ	צְלוֹפָח (ז)
trout	forel	פּוֹרֶל (ז)
sardine	sardin	סַרְדִּין (ז)
pike	ze'ev 'mayim	זְאֵב מַיִם (ז)
herring	ma'liaχ	מָלִים (ז)
bread	'leχem	לֶחֶם (ז)
cheese	gvina	גְּבִינָה (נ)
sugar	sukar	סוּכָּר (ז)
salt	'melaχ	מֶלַח (ז)
rice	'orez	אוֹרֶז (ז)
pasta (macaroni)	'pasta	פַּסְטָה (נ)
noodles	irtiyot	אִטְרִיּוֹת (נ״ר)
butter	χem'a	חֶמְאָה (נ)
vegetable oil	'ſemen tsimχi	שֶׁמֶן צִמְחִי (ז)
sunflower oil	'ſemen χamaniyot	שֶׁמֶן חַמָּנִיוֹת (ז)
margarine	marga'rina	מַרְגָּרִינָה (נ)
olives	zeitim	זֵיתִים (ז״ר)
olive oil	'ſemen 'zayit	שֶׁמֶן זַיִת (ז)
milk	χalav	חָלָב (ז)
condensed milk	χalav merukaz	חָלָב מְרוּכָּז (ז)
yogurt	'yogurt	יוֹגוּרְט (ז)
soured cream	ſa'menet	שַׁמֶּנֶת (נ)
cream (of milk)	ſa'menet	שַׁמֶּנֶת (נ)
mayonnaise	mayonez	מָיוֹנֶז (ז)
buttercream	ka'tsefet χem'a	קַצֶּפֶת חֶמְאָה (נ)
cereal grains (wheat, etc.)	grisim	גְּרִיסִים (ז״ר)
flour	'kemaχ	קֶמַח (ז)
tinned food	ſimurim	שִׁימוּרִים (ז״ר)
cornflakes	ptitei 'tiras	פְּתִיתֵי תִּירָס (ז״ר)
honey	dvaſ	דְּבַשׁ (ז)
jam	riba	רִיבָּה (נ)
chewing gum	'mastik	מַסְטִיק (ז)

45. Drinks

water	'mayim	מַיִם (ז״ר)
drinking water	mei ſtiya	מֵי שְׁתִיָּה (ז״ר)
mineral water	'mayim mine'raliyim	מַיִם מִינֵרָלְיִים (ז״ר)
still (adj)	lo mugaz	לֹא מוּגָז
carbonated (adj)	mugaz	מוּגָז
sparkling (adj)	mugaz	מוּגָז

ice	'keraχ	קֶרַח (ז)
with ice	im 'keraχ	עִם קֶרַח

non-alcoholic (adj)	natul alkohol	נְטוּל אַלכּוֹהוֹל
soft drink	maʃke kal	מַשׁקֶה קַל (ז)
refreshing drink	maʃke mera'anen	מַשׁקֶה מְרַעֲנֵן (ז)
lemonade	limo'nada	לִימוֹנָדָה (נ)

spirits	maʃka'ot χarifim	מַשׁקָאוֹת חָרִיפִים (ז"ר)
wine	'yayin	יַיִן (ז)
white wine	'yayin lavan	יַיִן לָבָן (ז)
red wine	'yayin adom	יַיִן אָדוֹם (ז)

liqueur	liker	לִיקֶר (ז)
champagne	ʃam'panya	שַׁמפַּניָה (נ)
vermouth	'vermut	וֶרמוּט (ז)

whisky	'viski	וִיסקִי (ז)
vodka	'vodka	וֹדקָה (נ)
gin	dʒin	ג'ִין (ז)
cognac	'konyak	קוֹניָאק (ז)
rum	rom	רוֹם (ז)

coffee	kafe	קָפֶּה (ז)
black coffee	kafe ʃaχor	קָפֶּה שָׁחוֹר (ז)
white coffee	kafe hafuχ	קָפֶּה הָפוּך (ז)
cappuccino	kapu'tʃino	קָפּוּצ'ִינוֹ (ז)
instant coffee	kafe names	קָפֶּה נָמֵס (ז)

milk	χalav	חָלָב (ז)
cocktail	kokteil	קוֹקטֵיל (ז)
milkshake	'milkʃeik	מִילקשֵׁייק (ז)

juice	mits	מִיץ (ז)
tomato juice	mits agvaniyot	מִיץ עַגבָנִיוֹת (ז)
orange juice	mits tapuzim	מִיץ תַפּוּזִים (ז)
freshly squeezed juice	mits saχut	מִיץ סָחוּט (ז)

beer	'bira	בִּירָה (נ)
lager	'bira bahira	בִּירָה בָּהִירָה (נ)
bitter	'bira keha	בִּירָה כֵּהָה (נ)

tea	te	תֵה (ז)
black tea	te ʃaχor	תֵה שָׁחוֹר (ז)
green tea	te yarok	תֵה יָרוֹק (ז)

46. Vegetables

vegetables	yerakot	יְרָקוֹת (ז"ר)
greens	'yerek	יֶרֶק (ז)

tomato	agvaniya	עַגבָנִייָה (נ)
cucumber	melafefon	מְלָפְפוֹן (ז)
carrot	'gezer	גֶזֶר (ז)

potato	ta'puaχ adama	תַּפּוּחַ אֲדָמָה (ז)
onion	batsal	בָּצָל (ז)
garlic	ʃum	שׁוּם (ז)

cabbage	kruv	כְּרוּב (ז)
cauliflower	kruvit	כְּרוּבִית (נ)
Brussels sprouts	kruv nitsanim	כְּרוּב נִצָּנִים (ז)
broccoli	'brokoli	בְּרוֹקוֹלִי (ז)

beetroot	'selek	סֶלֶק (ז)
aubergine	χatsil	חָצִיל (ז)
courgette	kiʃu	קִישׁוּא (ז)
pumpkin	'dla'at	דְּלַעַת (נ)
turnip	'lefet	לֶפֶת (נ)

parsley	petro'zilya	פֶּטְרוֹזִילְיָה (נ)
dill	ʃamir	שָׁמִיר (ז)
lettuce	'χasa	חַסָּה (נ)
celery	'seleri	סֶלֶרִי (ז)
asparagus	aspa'ragos	אַסְפָּרָגוֹס (ז)
spinach	'tered	תֶּרֶד (ז)

pea	afuna	אֲפוּנָה (נ)
beans	pol	פּוֹל (ז)
maize	'tiras	תִּירָס (ז)
kidney bean	ʃu'it	שְׁעוּעִית (נ)

sweet paper	'pilpel	פִּלְפֵּל (ז)
radish	tsnonit	צְנוֹנִית (נ)
artichoke	artiʃok	אַרְטִישׁוֹק (ז)

47. Fruits. Nuts

fruit	pri	פְּרִי (ז)
apple	ta'puaχ	תַּפּוּחַ (ז)
pear	agas	אַגָּס (ז)
lemon	limon	לִימוֹן (ז)
orange	tapuz	תַּפּוּז (ז)
strawberry (garden ~)	tut sade	תּוּת שָׂדֶה (ז)

tangerine	klemen'tina	קְלֶמָנְטִינָה (נ)
plum	ʃezif	שְׁזִיף (ז)
peach	afarsek	אֲפַרְסֵק (ז)
apricot	'miʃmeʃ	מִשְׁמֵשׁ (ז)
raspberry	'petel	פֶּטֶל (ז)
pineapple	'ananas	אֲנָנָס (ז)

banana	ba'nana	בָּנָנָה (נ)
watermelon	ava'tiaχ	אֲבַטִּיחַ (ז)
grape	anavim	עֲנָבִים (ז"ר)
sour cherry	duvdevan	דּוּבְדְּבָן (ז)
sweet cherry	gudgedan	גּוּדְגְּדָן (ז)
melon	melon	מֶלוֹן (ז)
grapefruit	eʃkolit	אֶשְׁכּוֹלִית (נ)

avocado	avo'kado	אֲבוֹקָדוֹ (ז)
papaya	pa'paya	פַּפָּאיָה (נ)
mango	'mango	מַנְגּוֹ (ז)
pomegranate	rimon	רִימוֹן (ז)

redcurrant	dumdemanit aduma	דּוּמְדְּמָנִית אֲדוֹמָה (נ)
blackcurrant	dumdemanit ʃχora	דּוּמְדְּמָנִית שְׁחוֹרָה (נ)
gooseberry	χazarzar	חֲזַרְזָר (ז)
bilberry	uχmanit	אוּכְמָנִית (נ)
blackberry	'petel ʃaχor	פֶּטֶל שָׁחוֹר (ז)

raisin	tsimukim	צִימוּקִים (ז״ר)
fig	te'ena	תְּאֵנָה (נ)
date	tamar	תָּמָר (ז)

peanut	botnim	בּוֹטְנִים (ז״ר)
almond	ʃaked	שָׁקֵד (ז)
walnut	egoz 'meleχ	אֱגוֹז מֶלֶךְ (ז)
hazelnut	egoz ilsar	אֱגוֹז אִלְסָר (ז)
coconut	'kokus	קוֹקוּס (ז)
pistachios	'fistuk	פִּיסְטוּק (ז)

48. Bread. Sweets

bakers' confectionery (pastry)	mutsrei kondi'torya	מוּצְרֵי קוֹנְדִיטוֹרִיָה (ז״ר)
bread	'leχem	לֶחֶם (ז)
biscuits	ugiya	עוּגִיָּה (נ)

chocolate (n)	'ʃokolad	שׁוֹקוֹלָד (ז)
chocolate (as adj)	mi'ʃokolad	מְשׁוֹקוֹלָד
candy (wrapped)	sukariya	סוּכָּרִיָה (נ)
cake (e.g. cupcake)	uga	עוּגָּה (נ)
cake (e.g. birthday ~)	uga	עוּגָּה (נ)

pie (e.g. apple ~)	pai	פַּאי (ז)
filling (for cake, pie)	milui	מִילוּי (ז)

jam (whole fruit jam)	riba	רִיבָּה (נ)
marmalade	marme'lada	מַרְמֶלָדָה (נ)
waffles	'vaflim	וָפְלִים (ז״ר)
ice-cream	'glida	גְלִידָה (נ)
pudding (Christmas ~)	'puding	פּוּדִינְג (ז)

49. Cooked dishes

course, dish	mana	מָנָה (נ)
cuisine	mitbaχ	מִטְבָּח (ז)
recipe	matkon	מַתְכּוֹן (ז)
portion	mana	מָנָה (נ)

salad	salat	סָלָט (ז)
soup	marak	מָרָק (ז)

clear soup (broth)	marak ʦaχ, ʦir	מָרָק צַח, צִיר (ז)
sandwich (bread)	kariχ	כָּרִיך (ז)
fried eggs	beiʦat ain	בֵּיצַת עַיִן (נ)

| hamburger (beefburger) | 'hamburger | הַמבּוּרגֶר (ז) |
| beefsteak | umʦa, steik | אוּמצָה (נ), סטֵייק (ז) |

side dish	to'sefet	תּוֹסֶפֶת (נ)
spaghetti	spa'geti	ספָּגֶטִי (ז)
mash	meχit tapuχei adama	מְחִית תַּפּוּחֵי אֲדָמָה (נ)
pizza	'piʦa	פִּיצָה (נ)
porridge (oatmeal, etc.)	daysa	דַייסָה (נ)
omelette	χavita	חֲבִיתָה (נ)

boiled (e.g. ~ beef)	mevuʃal	מְבוּשָל
smoked (adj)	me'uʃan	מְעוּשָן
fried (adj)	metugan	מְטוּגָן
dried (adj)	meyubaʃ	מְיוּבָּש
frozen (adj)	kafu	קָפוּא
pickled (adj)	kavuʃ	כָּבוּש

sweet (sugary)	matok	מָתוֹק
salty (adj)	ma'luaχ	מָלוּחַ
cold (adj)	kar	קָר
hot (adj)	χam	חַם
bitter (adj)	marir	מָרִיר
tasty (adj)	ta'im	טָעִים

to cook in boiling water	levaʃel be'mayim rotχim	לְבַשֵל בְּמַיִם רוֹתחִים
to cook (dinner)	levaʃel	לְבַשֵל
to fry (vt)	letagen	לְטַגֵן
to heat up (food)	leχamem	לְחַמֵם

to salt (vt)	leham'liaχ	לְהַמלִיחַ
to pepper (vt)	lefalpel	לְפַלפֵּל
to grate (vt)	lerasek	לְרַסֵק
peel (n)	klipa	קלִיפָּה (נ)
to peel (vt)	lekalef	לְקַלֵף

50. Spices

salt	'melaχ	מֶלַח (ז)
salty (adj)	ma'luaχ	מָלוּחַ
to salt (vt)	leham'liaχ	לְהַמלִיחַ

black pepper	'pilpel ʃaχor	פִּלפֵּל שָחוֹר (ז)
red pepper (milled ~)	'pilpel adom	פִּלפֵּל אָדוֹם (ז)
mustard	χardal	חַרדָל (ז)
horseradish	χa'zeret	חֲזֶרֶת (נ)

condiment	'rotev	רוֹטֶב (ז)
spice	tavlin	תַּבלִין (ז)
sauce	'rotev	רוֹטֶב (ז)
vinegar	'χomeʦ	חוֹמֶץ (ז)

anise	kamnon	כַּמְנוֹן (ז)
basil	reχan	רֵיחָן (ז)
cloves	tsi'poren	צִיפּוֹרֶן (ז)
ginger	'dʒindʒer	גִ'ינגִ'ר (ז)
coriander	'kusbara	כּוּסְבָּרָה (נ)
cinnamon	kinamon	קִינָמוֹן (ז)

sesame	'ʃumʃum	שׁוּמְשׁוֹם (ז)
bay leaf	ale dafna	עֲלֵה דַּפְנָה (ז)
paprika	'paprika	פַּפְרִיקָה (נ)
caraway	'kimel	קִימָל (ז)
saffron	ze'afran	זְעַפְרָן (ז)

51. Meals

| food | 'oχel | אוֹכֶל (ז) |
| to eat (vi, vt) | le'eχol | לֶאֱכוֹל |

breakfast	aruχat 'boker	אֲרוּחַת בּוֹקֶר (נ)
to have breakfast	le'eχol aruχat 'boker	לֶאֱכוֹל אֲרוּחַת בּוֹקֶר
lunch	aruχat tsaha'rayim	אֲרוּחַת צָהֳרַיִם (נ)
to have lunch	le'eχol aruχat tsaha'rayim	לֶאֱכוֹל אֲרוּחַת צָהֳרַיִם
dinner	aruχat 'erev	אֲרוּחַת עֶרֶב (נ)
to have dinner	le'eχol aruχat 'erev	לֶאֱכוֹל אֲרוּחַת עֶרֶב

| appetite | te'avon | תֵּיאָבוֹן (ז) |
| Enjoy your meal! | betei'avon! | בְּתֵיאָבוֹן! |

to open (~ a bottle)	lif'toaχ	לִפְתּוֹחַ
to spill (liquid)	liʃpoχ	לִשְׁפּוֹךְ
to spill out (vi)	lehiʃapeχ	לְהִישָּׁפֵךְ

to boil (vi)	lir'toaχ	לִרְתּוֹחַ
to boil (vt)	lehar'tiaχ	לְהַרְתִּיחַ
boiled (~ water)	ra'tuaχ	רָתוּחַ
to chill, cool down (vt)	lekarer	לְקָרֵר
to chill (vi)	lehitkarer	לְהִתְקָרֵר

| taste, flavour | 'ta'am | טַעַם (ז) |
| aftertaste | 'ta'am levai | טַעַם לְווַאי (ז) |

to slim down (lose weight)	lirzot	לִרְזוֹת
diet	di''eta	דִּיאֵטָה (נ)
vitamin	vitamin	וִיטָמִין (ז)
calorie	ka'lorya	קָלוֹרְיָה (נ)
vegetarian (n)	tsimχoni	צִמְחוֹנִי (ז)
vegetarian (adj)	tsimχoni	צִמְחוֹנִי

fats (nutrient)	ʃumanim	שׁוּמָנִים (ז"ר)
proteins	χelbonim	חֶלְבּוֹנִים (ז"ר)
carbohydrates	paχmema	פַּחְמֵימָה (נ)
slice (of lemon, ham)	prusa	פְּרוּסָה (נ)
piece (of cake, pie)	χatiχa	חֲתִיכָה (נ)
crumb (of bread, cake, etc.)	perur	פֵּירוּר (ז)

52. Table setting

spoon	kaf	כַּף (ז)
knife	sakin	סַכִּין (ז), (נ)
fork	mazleg	מַזְלֵג (ז)

cup (e.g., coffee ~)	'sefel	סֵפֶל (ז)
plate (dinner ~)	tsa'laxat	צַלַחַת (נ)
saucer	taxtit	תַחְתִּית (נ)
serviette	mapit	מַפִּית (נ)
toothpick	keisam ʃi'nayim	קֵיסָם שִׁינַיִים (ז)

53. Restaurant

restaurant	mis'ada	מִסְעָדָה (נ)
coffee bar	beit kafe	בֵּית קָפֶה (ז)
pub, bar	bar, pab	בָּר, פָּאבּ (ז)
tearoom	beit te	בֵּית תָה (ז)

waiter	meltsar	מֶלְצָר (ז)
waitress	meltsarit	מֶלְצָרִית (נ)
barman	'barmen	בַּרְמֶן (ז)

menu	tafrit	תַפְרִיט (ז)
wine list	reʃimat yeynot	רְשִׁימַת יֵינוֹת (נ)
to book a table	lehazmin ʃulxan	לְהַזְמִין שׁוּלְחָן

course, dish	mana	מָנָה (נ)
to order (meal)	lehazmin	לְהַזְמִין
to make an order	lehazmin	לְהַזְמִין

aperitif	maʃke meta'aven	מַשְׁקֶה מְתַאֲבֵן (ז)
starter	meta'aven	מְתַאֲבֵן (ז)
dessert, pudding	ki'nuax	קִינוּחַ (ז)

bill	xeʃbon	חֶשְׁבּוֹן (ז)
to pay the bill	leʃalem	לְשַׁלֵם
to give change	latet 'odef	לָתֵת עוֹדֶף
tip	tip	טִיפּ (ז)

Family, relatives and friends

54. Personal information. Forms

name (first name)	ʃem	שֵׁם (ז)
surname (last name)	ʃem miʃpaχa	שֵׁם מִשְׁפָּחָה (ז)
date of birth	ta'ariχ leda	תַּאֲרִיךְ לֵידָה (ז)
place of birth	mekom leda	מְקוֹם לֵידָה (ז)
nationality	le'om	לְאוֹם (ז)
place of residence	mekom megurim	מְקוֹם מְגוּרִים (ז)
country	medina	מְדִינָה (נ)
profession (occupation)	mik'tso'a	מִקְצוֹעַ (ז)
gender, sex	min	מִין (ז)
height	'gova	גּוֹבַה (ז)
weight	miʃkal	מִשְׁקָל (ז)

55. Family members. Relatives

mother	em	אֵם (נ)
father	av	אָב (ז)
son	ben	בֵּן (ז)
daughter	bat	בַּת (נ)
younger daughter	habat haktana	הַבַּת הַקְטַנָּה (נ)
younger son	haben hakatan	הַבֵּן הַקָטָן (ז)
eldest daughter	habat habχora	הַבַּת הַבְּכוֹרָה (נ)
eldest son	haben habχor	הַבֵּן הַבְּכוֹר (ז)
brother	aχ	אָח (ז)
elder brother	aχ gadol	אָח גָּדוֹל (ז)
younger brother	aχ katan	אָח קָטָן (ז)
sister	aχot	אָחוֹת (נ)
elder sister	aχot gdola	אָחוֹת גְדוֹלָה (נ)
younger sister	aχot ktana	אָחוֹת קְטַנָּה (נ)
cousin (masc.)	ben dod	בֶּן דּוֹד (ז)
cousin (fem.)	bat 'doda	בַּת דּוֹדָה (נ)
mummy	'ima	אִמָּא (נ)
dad, daddy	'aba	אַבָּא (ז)
parents	horim	הוֹרִים (ז"ר)
child	'yeled	יֶלֶד (ז)
children	yeladim	יְלָדִים (ז"ר)
grandmother	'savta	סַבְתָּא (נ)
grandfather	'saba	סַבָּא (ז)
grandson	'neχed	נֶכֶד (ז)

| granddaughter | neχda | נֶכְדָּה (נ) |
| grandchildren | neχadim | נְכָדִים (ז"ר) |

uncle	dod	דּוֹד (ז)
aunt	'doda	דּוֹדָה (נ)
nephew	aχyan	אַחְיָן (ז)
niece	aχyanit	אַחְיָנִית (נ)

mother-in-law (wife's mother)	χamot	חָמוֹת (נ)
father-in-law (husband's father)	χam	חָם (ז)
son-in-law (daughter's husband)	χatan	חָתָן (ז)
stepmother	em χoreget	אֵם חוֹרֶגֶת (נ)
stepfather	av χoreg	אָב חוֹרֵג (ז)

infant	tinok	תִּינוֹק (ז)
baby (infant)	tinok	תִּינוֹק (ז)
little boy, kid	pa'ot	פָּעוֹט (ז)

wife	iʃa	אִשָּׁה (נ)
husband	'ba'al	בַּעַל (ז)
spouse (husband)	ben zug	בֶּן זוּג (ז)
spouse (wife)	bat zug	בַּת זוּג (נ)

married (masc.)	nasui	נָשׂוּי
married (fem.)	nesu'a	נְשׂוּאָה
single (unmarried)	ravak	רַוָּק
bachelor	ravak	רַוָּק (ז)
divorced (masc.)	garuʃ	גָּרוּשׁ
widow	almana	אַלְמָנָה (נ)
widower	alman	אַלְמָן (ז)

relative	karov miʃpaχa	קָרוֹב מִשְׁפָּחָה (ז)
close relative	karov miʃpaχa	קָרוֹב מִשְׁפָּחָה (ז)
distant relative	karov raχok	קָרוֹב רָחוֹק (ז)
relatives	krovei miʃpaχa	קְרוֹבֵי מִשְׁפָּחָה (ז"ר)

orphan (boy)	yatom	יָתוֹם (ז)
orphan (girl)	yetoma	יְתוֹמָה (נ)
guardian (of a minor)	apo'tropos	אַפּוֹטְרוֹפּוֹס (ז)
to adopt (a boy)	le'amets	לְאַמֵּץ
to adopt (a girl)	le'amets	לְאַמֵּץ

56. Friends. Colleagues

friend (masc.)	χaver	חָבֵר (ז)
friend (fem.)	χavera	חֲבֵרָה (נ)
friendship	yedidut	יְדִידוּת (נ)
to be friends	lihyot yadidim	לִהְיוֹת יְדִידִים

| pal (masc.) | χaver | חָבֵר (ז) |
| pal (fem.) | χavera | חֲבֵרָה (נ) |

partner	ʃutaf	שׁוּתָף (ז)
chief (boss)	menahel, roʃ	מְנַהֵל (ז), רֹאשׁ (ז)
superior (n)	memune	מְמוּנֶה (ז)
owner, proprietor	be'alim	בְּעָלִים (ז)
subordinate (n)	kafuf le	כָּפוּף לְ (ז)
colleague	amit	עָמִית (ז)

acquaintance (person)	makar	מַכָּר (ז)
fellow traveller	ben levaya	בֶּן לְוָיָה (ז)
classmate	xaver lekita	חָבֵר לְכִיתָה (ז)

neighbour (masc.)	ʃaxen	שָׁכֵן (ז)
neighbour (fem.)	ʃxena	שְׁכֵנָה (נ)
neighbours	ʃxenim	שְׁכֵנִים (ז״ר)

57. Man. Woman

woman	iʃa	אִשָּׁה (נ)
girl (young woman)	baxura	בַּחוּרָה (נ)
bride	kala	כַּלָּה (נ)

beautiful (adj)	yafa	יָפָּה
tall (adj)	gvoha	גְבוֹהָה
slender (adj)	tmira	תְמִירָה
short (adj)	namux	נָמוּך

blonde (n)	blon'dinit	בְּלוֹנְדִינִית (נ)
brunette (n)	bru'netit	בְּרוּנֶטִית (נ)
ladies' (adj)	ʃel naʃim	שֶׁל נָשִׁים
virgin (girl)	betula	בְּתוּלָה (נ)
pregnant (adj)	hara	הָרָה

man (adult male)	'gever	גֶּבֶר (ז)
blonde haired man	blon'dini	בְּלוֹנְדִינִי (ז)
dark haired man	ʃxarxar	שְׁחַרְחַר
tall (adj)	ga'voha	גָבוֹהַ
short (adj)	namux	נָמוּך
rude (rough)	gas	גַס
stocky (adj)	guʦ	גּוּץ
robust (adj)	xason	חָסֹן
strong (adj)	xazak	חָזָק
strength	'koax	כֹּחַ (ז)

stout, fat (adj)	ʃamen	שָׁמֵן
swarthy (adj)	ʃaxum	שָׁחוּם
slender (well-built)	tamir	תָמִיר
elegant (adj)	ele'ganti	אֶלֶגַנְטִי

58. Age

| age | gil | גִיל (ז) |
| youth (young age) | ne'urim | נְעוּרִים (ז״ר) |

55

young (adj)	tsa'ir	צָעִיר
younger (adj)	tsa'ir yoter	צָעִיר יוֹתֵר
older (adj)	mevugar yoter	מְבוּגָר יוֹתֵר

young man	baxur	בָּחוּר (ז)
teenager	'na'ar	נַעַר (ז)
guy, fellow	baxur	בָּחוּר (ז)

| old man | zaken | זָקֵן (ז) |
| old woman | zkena | זְקֵנָה (נ) |

adult (adj)	mevugar	מְבוּגָר (ז)
middle-aged (adj)	bagil ha'amida	בַּגִּיל הָעֲמִידָה
elderly (adj)	zaken	זָקֵן
old (adj)	zaken	זָקֵן

retirement	'pensya	פֶּנְסִיָה (נ)
to retire (from job)	latset legimla'ot	לָצֵאת לְגִימְלָאוֹת
pensioner	pensyoner	פֶּנְסִיוֹנֶר (ז)

59. Children

child	'yeled	יֶלֶד (ז)
children	yeladim	יְלָדִים (ז״ר)
twins	te'omim	תְּאוֹמִים (ז״ר)

cradle	arisa	עֲרִיסָה (נ)
rattle	ra'ashan	רַעֲשָׁן (ז)
nappy	xitul	חִיתוּל (ז)

dummy, comforter	motsets	מוֹצֵץ (ז)
pram	agala	עֲגָלָה (נ)
nursery	gan yeladim	גַּן יְלָדִים (ז)
babysitter	beibi'siter	בֵּיבִּיסִיטֶר (ז, נ)

childhood	yaldut	יַלְדוּת (נ)
doll	buba	בּוּבָּה (נ)
toy	tsa'a'tsu'a	צַעֲצוּעַ (ז)
construction set (toy)	misxak harkava	מִשְׂחַק הַרְכָּבָה (ז)
well-bred (adj)	mexunax	מְחוּנָךְ
ill-bred (adj)	lo mexunax	לֹא מְחוּנָךְ
spoilt (adj)	mefunak	מְפוּנָק

to be naughty	lehishtovev	לְהִשְׁתּוֹבֵב
mischievous (adj)	shovav	שׁוֹבָב
mischievousness	ma'ase 'kundes	מַעֲשֵׂה קוּנְדֵס (ז)
mischievous child	'yeled shovav	יֶלֶד שׁוֹבָב (ז)

| obedient (adj) | tsaytan | צַיְיתָן |
| disobedient (adj) | lo memushma | לֹא מְמוּשְׁמָע |

docile (adj)	ka'nu'a	כָּנוּעַ
clever (intelligent)	xaxam	חָכָם
child prodigy	'yeled 'pele	יֶלֶד פֶּלֶא (ז)

60. Married couples. Family life

to kiss (vt)	lenaʃek	לְנַשֵׁק
to kiss (vi)	lehitnaʃek	לְהִתְנַשֵׁק
family (n)	miʃpaχa	מִשְׁפָּחָה (נ)
family (as adj)	miʃpaχti	מִשְׁפַּחְתִּי
couple	zug	זוּג (ז)
marriage (state)	nisu'im	נִישׂוּאִים (ז״ר)
hearth (home)	aχ, ken	אָח (ז), קֵן (ז)
dynasty	ʃo'ʃelet	שׁוֹשֶׁלֶת (נ)

date	deit	דֵּייט (ז)
kiss	neʃika	נְשִׁיקָה (נ)

love (for sb)	ahava	אַהֲבָה (נ)
to love (sb)	le'ehov	לֶאֱהוֹב
beloved	ahuv	אָהוּב

tenderness	roχ	רוֹךְ (ז)
tender (affectionate)	adin, raχ	עָדִין, רַךְ
faithfulness	ne'emanut	נֶאֱמָנוּת (נ)
faithful (adj)	masur	מָסוּר
care (attention)	de'aga	דְּאָגָה (נ)
caring (~ father)	do'eg	דּוֹאֵג

newlyweds	zug tsa'ir	זוּג צָעִיר (ז)
honeymoon	ya'reaχ dvaʃ	יָרֵחַ דְּבַשׁ (ז)
to get married (ab. woman)	lehitχaten	לְהִתְחַתֵּן
to get married (ab. man)	lehitχaten	לְהִתְחַתֵּן

wedding	χatuna	חֲתוּנָה (נ)
golden wedding	χatunat hazahav	חֲתוּנַת הַזָּהָב (נ)
anniversary	yom nisu'in	יוֹם נִישׂוּאִין (ז)

lover (masc.)	me'ahev	מְאַהֵב (ז)
mistress (lover)	mea'hevet	מְאַהֶבֶת (נ)

adultery	bgida	בְּגִידָה (נ)
to cheat on ... (commit adultery)	livgod be...	לִבְגּוֹד בְּ...
jealous (adj)	kanai	קַנַּאי
to be jealous	lekane	לְקַנֵּא
divorce	geruʃin	גֵּרוּשִׁין (ז״ר)
to divorce (vi)	lehitgareʃ mi...	לְהִתְגָּרֵשׁ מְ...

to quarrel (vi)	lariv	לָרִיב
to be reconciled (after an argument)	lehitpayes	לְהִתְפַּייֵס
together (adv)	be'yaχad	בְּיַחַד
sex	min	מִין (ז)

happiness	'oʃer	אוֹשֶׁר (ז)
happy (adj)	me'uʃar	מְאוּשָׁר
misfortune (accident)	ason	אָסוֹן (ז)
unhappy (adj)	umlal	אוּמְלָל

Character. Feelings. Emotions

61. Feelings. Emotions

feeling (emotion)	'regef	רֶגֶשׁ (ז)
feelings	regafot	רְגָשׁוֹת (ז"ר)
to feel (vt)	lehargif	לְהַרְגִּישׁ
hunger	'ra'av	רָעָב (ז)
to be hungry	lihyot ra'ev	לִהְיוֹת רָעֵב
thirst	tsima'on	צִמָּאוֹן (ז)
to be thirsty	lihyot tsame	לִהְיוֹת צָמֵא
sleepiness	yafnuniyut	יַשְׁנוּנִיּוּת (נ)
to feel sleepy	lirtsot lifon	לִרְצוֹת לִישׁוֹן
tiredness	ayefut	עֲיֵפוּת (נ)
tired (adj)	ayef	עָיֵף
to get tired	lehit'ayef	לְהִתְעַיֵּף
mood (humour)	matsav 'ruax	מַצַּב רוּחַ (ז)
boredom	fi'amum	שִׁעֲמוּם (ז)
to be bored	lehifta'amem	לְהִשְׁתַּעֲמֵם
seclusion	hitbodedut	הִתְבּוֹדְדוּת (נ)
to seclude oneself	lehitboded	לְהִתְבּוֹדֵד
to worry (make anxious)	lehad'ig	לְהַדְאִיג
to be worried	lid'og	לִדְאוֹג
worrying (n)	de'aga	דְּאָגָה (נ)
anxiety	xarada	חֲרָדָה (נ)
preoccupied (adj)	mutrad	מוּטְרָד
to be nervous	lihyot atsbani	לִהְיוֹת עַצְבָּנִי
to panic (vi)	lehibahel	לְהִיבָּהֵל
hope	tikva	תִּקְוָה (נ)
to hope (vi, vt)	lekavot	לְקַוּוֹת
certainty	vada'ut	וַדָּאוּת (נ)
certain, sure (adj)	vada'i	וַדָּאִי
uncertainty	i vada'ut	אִי וַדָּאוּת (נ)
uncertain (adj)	lo ba'tuax	לֹא בָּטוּחַ
drunk (adj)	fikor	שִׁיכּוֹר
sober (adj)	pi'keax	פִּיכֵּחַ
weak (adj)	xalaf	חַלָּשׁ
happy (adj)	me'ufar	מְאוּשָׁר
to scare (vt)	lehafxid	לְהַפְחִיד
fury (madness)	teruf	טֵירוּף
rage (fury)	'za'am	זַעַם (ז)
depression	dika'on	דִּיכָּאוֹן (ז)
discomfort (unease)	i noxut	אִי נוֹחוּת (נ)

comfort	noχut	נוֹחוּת (נ)
to regret (be sorry)	lehitsta'er	לְהִצְטַעֵר
regret	χarata	חֲרָטָה (נ)
bad luck	'χoser mazal	חוֹסֶר מַזָל (ז)
sadness	'etsev	עֶצֶב (ז)

shame (remorse)	buʃa	בּוּשָׁה (נ)
gladness	simχa	שִׂמְחָה (נ)
enthusiasm, zeal	hitlahavut	הִתְלַהֲבוּת (נ)
enthusiast	mitlahev	מִתְלַהֵב
to show enthusiasm	lehitlahev	לְהִתְלַהֵב

62. Character. Personality

character	'ofi	אוֹפִי (ז)
character flaw	pgam be''ofi	פְּגָם בָּאוֹפִי (ז)
mind	'seχel	שֵׂכֶל (ז)
reason	bina	בִּינָה (נ)

conscience	matspun	מַצְפּוּן (ז)
habit (custom)	hergel	הֶרְגֵל (ז)
ability (talent)	ye'χolet	יְכוֹלֶת (נ)
can (e.g. ~ swim)	la'da'at	לָדַעַת

patient (adj)	savlan	סַבְלָן
impatient (adj)	χasar savlanut	חֲסַר סַבְלָנוּת
curious (inquisitive)	sakran	סַקְרָן
curiosity	sakranut	סַקְרָנוּת (נ)

modesty	tsni'ut	צְנִיעוּת (נ)
modest (adj)	tsa'nu'a	צָנוּעַ
immodest (adj)	lo tsa'nu'a	לֹא צָנוּעַ

laziness	atslut	עַצְלוּת (נ)
lazy (adj)	atsel	עָצֵל
lazy person (masc.)	atslan	עַצְלָן (ז)

cunning (n)	armumiyut	עַרְמוּמִיוּת (נ)
cunning (as adj)	armumi	עַרְמוּמִי
distrust	'χoser emun	חוֹסֶר אֵמוּן (ז)
distrustful (adj)	χadʃani	חַדְשָׁנִי

generosity	nedivut	נְדִיבוּת (נ)
generous (adj)	nadiv	נָדִיב
talented (adj)	muχʃar	מוּכְשָׁר
talent	kiʃaron	כִּישָׁרוֹן (ז)

courageous (adj)	amits	אַמִיץ
courage	'omets	אוֹמֶץ (ז)
honest (adj)	yaʃar	יָשָׁר
honesty	'yoʃer	יוֹשֶׁר (ז)

careful (cautious)	zahir	זָהִיר
brave (courageous)	amits	אַמִיץ

serious (adj)	retsini	רְצִינִי
strict (severe, stern)	χamur	חָמוּר
decisive (adj)	neχrats	נֶחֱרָץ
indecisive (adj)	hasesan	הַסְּסָן
shy, timid (adj)	baiʃan	בַּיישָׁן
shyness, timidity	baiʃanut	בַּיישָׁנוּת (נ)
confidence (trust)	emun	אֵמוּן (ז)
to believe (trust)	leha'amin	לְהַאֲמִין
trusting (credulous)	tam	תָּם
sincerely (adv)	beχenut	בְּכֵנוּת
sincere (adj)	ken	כֵּן
sincerity	kenut	כֵּנוּת (נ)
open (person)	pa'tuaχ	פָּתוּחַ
calm (adj)	ʃalev	שָׁלֵו
frank (sincere)	glui lev	גְלוּי לֵב
naïve (adj)	na''ivi	נָאִיבִי
absent-minded (adj)	mefuzar	מְפֻזָר
funny (odd)	matsχik	מַצְחִיק
greed	ta'avat 'betsa	תַּאֲוַות בֶּצַע (נ)
greedy (adj)	rodef 'betsa	רוֹדֵף בֶּצַע
stingy (adj)	kamtsan	קַמְצָן
evil (adj)	raʃa	רָשָׁע
stubborn (adj)	akʃan	עַקְשָׁן
unpleasant (adj)	lo na'im	לֹא נָעִים
selfish person (masc.)	ego'ist	אֶגוֹאִיסְט (ז)
selfish (adj)	anoχi	אֲנוֹכִי
coward	paχdan	פַּחְדָן (ז)
cowardly (adj)	paχdani	פַּחְדָנִי

63. Sleep. Dreams

to sleep (vi)	liʃon	לִישׁוֹן
sleep, sleeping	ʃena	שֵׁינָה (נ)
dream	χalom	חֲלוֹם (ז)
to dream (in sleep)	laχalom	לַחֲלוֹם
sleepy (adj)	radum	רָדוּם
bed	mita	מִיטָה (נ)
mattress	mizran	מִזְרָן (ז)
blanket (eiderdown)	smiχa	שְׂמִיכָה (נ)
pillow	karit	כָּרִית (נ)
sheet	sadin	סָדִין (ז)
insomnia	nedudei ʃena	נְדוּדֵי שֵׁינָה (ז"ר)
sleepless (adj)	χasar ʃena	חֲסַר שֵׁינָה
sleeping pill	kadur ʃena	כַּדוּר שֵׁינָה (ז)
to take a sleeping pill	la'kaχat kadur ʃena	לָקַחַת כַּדוּר שֵׁינָה
to feel sleepy	lirtsot liʃon	לִרְצוֹת לִישׁוֹן

to yawn (vi)	lefahek	לְפַהֵק
to go to bed	la'leχet liʃon	לָלֶכֶת לִישׁוֹן
to make up the bed	leha'ʦi'a mita	לְהַצִּיעַ מִיטָה
to fall asleep	leheradem	לְהֵירָדֵם

nightmare	siyut	סִיּוּט (ז)
snore, snoring	neχira	נְחִירָה (נ)
to snore (vi)	linχor	לִנְחוֹר

alarm clock	ʃa'on me'orer	שָׁעוֹן מְעוֹרֵר (ז)
to wake (vt)	leha'ir	לְהָעִיר
to wake up	lehit'orer	לְהִתְעוֹרֵר
to get up (vi)	lakum	לָקוּם
to have a wash	lehitraχeʦ	לְהִתְרַחֵץ

64. Humour. Laughter. Gladness

humour (wit, fun)	humor	הוּמוֹר (ז)
sense of humour	χuʃ humor	חוּשׁ הוּמוֹר (ז)
to enjoy oneself	lehanot	לֵיהָנוֹת
cheerful (merry)	sa'meaχ	שָׂמֵחַ
merriment (gaiety)	aliʦut	עֲלִיצוּת (נ)

smile	χiyuχ	חִיּוּךְ (ז)
to smile (vi)	leχayeχ	לְחַיֵּיךְ
to start laughing	lifroʦ biʦχok	לִפְרוֹץ בְּצְחוֹק
to laugh (vi)	liʦχok	לִצְחוֹק
laugh, laughter	ʦχok	צְחוֹק (ז)

anecdote	anek'dota	אֲנֶקְדּוֹטָה (נ)
funny (anecdote, etc.)	maʦχik	מַצְחִיק
funny (odd)	meʃa'a'ʃe'a	מְשַׁעֲשֵׁעַ

to joke (vi)	lehitba'deaχ	לְהִתְבַּדֵּחַ
joke (verbal)	bdiχa	בְּדִיחָה (נ)
joy (emotion)	simχa	שִׂמְחָה (נ)
to rejoice (vi)	lis'moaχ	לִשְׂמוֹחַ
joyful (adj)	sa'meaχ	שָׂמֵחַ

65. Discussion, conversation. Part 1

| communication | 'keʃer | קֶשֶׁר (ז) |
| to communicate | letakʃer | לְתַקְשֵׁר |

conversation	siχa	שִׂיחָה (נ)
dialogue	du 'siaχ	דּוּ-שִׂיחַ (ז)
discussion (discourse)	diyun	דִּיּוּן (ז)
dispute (debate)	vi'kuaχ	וִיכּוּחַ (ז)
to dispute	lehitva'keaχ	לְהִתְוַוכֵּחַ

| interlocutor | ben 'siaχ | בֶּן שִׂיחַ (ז) |
| topic (theme) | nose | נוֹשֵׂא (ז) |

point of view	nekudat mabat	נְקוּדַת מַבָּט (נ)
opinion (point of view)	de'a	דֵּעָה (נ)
speech (talk)	ne'um	נְאוּם (ז)

discussion (of report, etc.)	diyun	דִּיּוּן (ז)
to discuss (vt)	ladun	לָדוּן
talk (conversation)	siχa	שִׂיחָה (נ)
to talk (to chat)	leso'χeaχ	לְשׂוֹחֵחַ
meeting	pgiʃa	פְּגִישָׁה (נ)
to meet (vi, vt)	lehipageʃ	לְהִיפָּגֵשׁ

proverb	pitgam	פִּתְגָּם (ז)
saying	pitgam	פִּתְגָּם (ז)
riddle (poser)	χida	חִידָה (נ)
to pose a riddle	laχud χida	לָחוּד חִידָה
password	sisma	סִיסְמָה (נ)
secret	sod	סוֹד (ז)

oath (vow)	ʃvu'a	שְׁבוּעָה (נ)
to swear (an oath)	lehiʃava	לְהִישָׁבַע
promise	havtaχa	הַבְטָחָה (נ)
to promise (vt)	lehav'tiaχ	לְהַבְטִיחַ

advice (counsel)	etsa	עֵצָה (נ)
to advise (vt)	leya'ets	לְיַיעֵץ
to follow one's advice	lif'ol lefi ha'etsa	לִפְעוֹל לְפִי הָעֵצָה
to listen to … (obey)	lehiʃama	לְהִישָׁמַע

news	χadaʃot	חֲדָשׁוֹת (נ"ר)
sensation (news)	sen'satsya	סֶנְסַצְיָה (נ)
information (data)	meida	מֵידָע (ז)
conclusion (decision)	maskana	מַסְקָנָה (נ)
voice	kol	קוֹל (ז)
compliment	maχma'a	מַחְמָאָה (נ)
kind (nice)	adiv	אָדִיב

word	mila	מִילָה (נ)
phrase	miʃpat	מִשְׁפָּט (ז)
answer	tʃuva	תְּשׁוּבָה (נ)

truth	emet	אֱמֶת (נ)
lie	'ʃeker	שֶׁקֶר (ז)

thought	maχʃava	מַחְשָׁבָה (נ)
idea (inspiration)	ra'ayon	רַעֲיוֹן (ז)
fantasy	fan'tazya	פַנְטַזְיָה (נ)

66. Discussion, conversation. Part 2

respected (adj)	meχubad	מְכוּבָּד
to respect (vt)	leχabed	לְכַבֵּד
respect	kavod	כָּבוֹד (ז)
Dear … (letter)	hayakar …	הַיָּקָר …
to introduce (sb to sb)	la'asot hekerut	לַעֲשׂוֹת הֶיכֵּרוּת

to make acquaintance	lehakir	לְהַכִּיר
intention	kavana	כַּוָונָה (נ)
to intend (have in mind)	lehitkaven	לְהִתְכַּוֵון
wish	iχul	אִיחוּל (ז)
to wish (~ good luck)	le'aχel	לְאַחֵל
surprise (astonishment)	hafta'a	הַפתָעָה (נ)
to surprise (amaze)	lehaf'ti'a	לְהַפתִיעַ
to be surprised	lehitpale	לְהִתפַּלֵא
to give (vt)	latet	לָתֵת
to take (get hold of)	la'kaχat	לָקַחַת
to give back	lehaχzir	לְהַחזִיר
to return (give back)	lehaʃiv	לְהָשִיב
to apologize (vi)	lehitnatsel	לְהִתנַצֵל
apology	hitnatslut	הִתנַצלוּת (נ)
to forgive (vt)	lis'loaχ	לִסלוֹחַ
to talk (speak)	ledaber	לְדַבֵּר
to listen (vi)	lehakʃiv	לְהַקשִיב
to hear out	liʃ'mo'a	לִשמוֹעַ
to understand (vt)	lehavin	לְהָבִין
to show (to display)	lehar'ot	לְהַראוֹת
to look at …	lehistakel	לְהִסתַכֵּל
to call (yell for sb)	likro le…	…לִקרוֹא לְ
to distract (disturb)	lehaf'ri'a	לְהַפרִיעַ
to disturb (vt)	lehaf'ri'a	לְהַפרִיעַ
to pass (to hand sth)	limsor	לִמסוֹר
demand (request)	bakaʃa	בַּקָשָה (נ)
to request (ask)	levakeʃ	לְבַקֵש
demand (firm request)	driʃa	דרִישָה (נ)
to demand (request firmly)	lidroʃ	לִדרוֹש
to tease (call names)	lehitgarot	לְהִתגָרוֹת
to mock (make fun of)	lil'og	לִלעוֹג
mockery, derision	'la'ag	לַעַג (ז)
nickname	kinui	כִּינוּי (ז)
insinuation	'remez	רֶמֶז (ז)
to insinuate (imply)	lirmoz	לִרמוֹז
to mean (vt)	lehitkaven le…	…לְהִתכַּוֵון לְ
description	te'ur	תֵיאוּר (ז)
to describe (vt)	leta'er	לְתָאֵר
praise (compliments)	'ʃevaχ	שֶבַח (ז)
to praise (vt)	leʃa'beaχ	לְשַבֵּחַ
disappointment	aχzava	אַכזָבָה (נ)
to disappoint (vt)	le'aχzev	לְאַכזֵב
to be disappointed	lehit'aχzev	לְהִתאַכזֵב
supposition	hanaχa	הַנָחָה (נ)
to suppose (assume)	leʃa'er	לְשַעֵר

| warning (caution) | azhara | אַזהָרָה (נ) |
| to warn (vt) | lehazhir | לְהַזהִיר |

67. Discussion, conversation. Part 3

| to talk into (convince) | leʃaχ'ne'a | לְשַׁכנֵעַ |
| to calm down (vt) | lehar'gi'a | לְהַרגִּיעַ |

silence (~ is golden)	ʃtika	שתִיקָה (נ)
to be silent (not speaking)	liʃtok	לִשׁתּוֹק
to whisper (vi, vt)	lilχoʃ	לִלחוֹשׁ
whisper	leχiʃa	לְחִישָׁה (נ)

| frankly, sincerely (adv) | beχenut | בְּכֵנוּת |
| in my opinion ... | leda'ati ... | לְדַעתִּי ... |

detail (of the story)	prat	פּרָט (ז)
detailed (adj)	meforat	מְפוֹרָט
in detail (adv)	bimfurat	בְּמפוֹרָט

| hint, clue | 'remez | רֶמֶז (ז) |
| to give a hint | lirmoz | לִרמוֹז |

look (glance)	mabat	מַבָּט (ז)
to have a look	lehabit	לְהַבִּיט
fixed (look)	kafu	קָפוּא
to blink (vi)	lematsmets	לְמַצמֵץ
to wink (vi)	likrots	לִקרוֹץ
to nod (in assent)	lehanhen	לְהַנהֵן

sigh	anaχa	אֲנָחָה (נ)
to sigh (vi)	lehe'anaχ	לְהֵיאָנַח
to shudder (vi)	lir'od	לִרעוֹד
gesture	meχva	מֶחווָה (נ)
to touch (one's arm, etc.)	la'ga'at be...	לָגַעַת בְּ...
to seize (e.g., ~ by the arm)	litfos	לִתפוֹס
to tap (on the shoulder)	lit'poaχ	לִטפּוֹחַ

Look out!	zehirut!	זְהִירוּת!
Really?	be'emet?	בֶּאֱמֶת?
Are you sure?	ata ba'tuaχ?	אַתָּה בָּטוּחַ?
Good luck!	behatslaχa!	בְּהַצלָחָה!
I see!	muvan!	מוּבָן!
What a pity!	χaval!	חֲבָל!

68. Agreement. Refusal

consent	haskama	הַסכָּמָה (נ)
to consent (vi)	lehaskim	לְהַסכִּים
approval	iʃur	אִישׁוּר (ז)
to approve (vt)	le'aʃer	לְאַשֵׁר
refusal	siruv	סֵירוּב (ז)

to refuse (vi, vt)	lesarev	לְסָרֵב
Great!	metsuyan!	מְצוּיָן!
All right!	tov!	טוֹב!
Okay! (I agree)	be'seder!	בְּסֵדֶר!

forbidden (adj)	asur	אָסוּר
it's forbidden	asur	אָסוּר
it's impossible	'bilti efʃari	בִּלְתִי אֶפְשָׁרִי
incorrect (adj)	ʃagui	שָׁגוּי

to reject (~ a demand)	lidχot	לִדְחוֹת
to support (cause, idea)	litmoχ be...	לִתְמוֹךְ בְּ...
to accept (~ an apology)	lekabel	לְקַבֵּל

to confirm (vt)	le'aʃer	לְאַשֵׁר
confirmation	iʃur	אִישׁוּר (ז)
permission	reʃut	רְשׁוּת (נ)
to permit (vt)	leharʃot	לְהַרְשׁוֹת
decision	haχlata	הַחְלָטָה (נ)
to say nothing (hold one's tongue)	liʃtok	לִשְׁתוֹק

condition (term)	tnai	תְנַאי (ז)
excuse (pretext)	teruts	תֵירוּץ (ז)
praise (compliments)	'ʃevaχ	שֶׁבַח (ז)
to praise (vt)	leʃa'beaχ	לְשַׁבֵּחַ

69. Success. Good luck. Failure

success	hatsala	הַצְלָחָה (נ)
successfully (adv)	behatslaχa	בְּהַצְלָחָה
successful (adj)	mutslaχ	מוּצְלָח

luck (good luck)	mazal	מַזָל (ז)
Good luck!	behatslaχa!	בְּהַצְלָחָה!
lucky (e.g. ~ day)	mutslaχ	מוּצְלָח
lucky (fortunate)	bar mazal	בַּר מַזָל

failure	kiʃalon	כִּישָׁלוֹן (ז)
misfortune	'χoser mazal	חוֹסֶר מַזָל (ז)
bad luck	'χoser mazal	חוֹסֶר מַזָל (ז)
unsuccessful (adj)	lo mutslaχ	לֹא מוּצְלָח
catastrophe	ason	אָסוֹן (ז)

pride	ga'ava	גַאֲוָה (נ)
proud (adj)	ge'e	גֵאֶה
to be proud	lehitga'ot	לְהִתְגָאוֹת

winner	zoχe	זוֹכֶה (ז)
to win (vi)	lena'tseaχ	לְנַצֵחַ
to lose (not win)	lehafsid	לְהַפְסִיד
try	nisayon	נִיסָיוֹן (ז)
to try (vi)	lenasot	לְנַסוֹת
chance (opportunity)	hizdamnut	הִזְדַמְנוּת (נ)

70. Quarrels. Negative emotions

shout (scream)	tseʿaka	צְעָקָה (נ)
to shout (vi)	litsʿok	לִצְעוֹק
to start to cry out	lehatχil litsʿok	לְהַתְחִיל לִצְעוֹק
quarrel	riv	רִיב (ז)
to quarrel (vi)	lariv	לָרִיב
fight (squabble)	riv	רִיב (ז)
to make a scene	lariv	לָרִיב
conflict	siχsuχ	סִכְסוּךְ (ז)
misunderstanding	i havana	אִי הֲבָנָה (נ)
insult	elbon	עֶלְבּוֹן (ז)
to insult (vt)	lehaʿaliv	לְהַעֲלִיב
insulted (adj)	neʿelav	נֶעֱלָב
resentment	tina	טִינָה (נ)
to offend (vt)	lifʾgoʿa	לִפְגוֹעַ
to take offence	lehipaga	לְהִיפָּגַע
indignation	hitmarmerut	הִתְמַרְמְרוּת (נ)
to be indignant	lehitraʿem	לְהִתְרַעֵם
complaint	tluna	תְּלוּנָה (נ)
to complain (vi, vt)	lehitlonen	לְהִתְלוֹנֵן
apology	hitnatslut	הִתְנַצְּלוּת (נ)
to apologize (vi)	lehitnatsel	לְהִתְנַצֵּל
to beg pardon	levakeʃ sliχa	לְבַקֵּשׁ סְלִיחָה
criticism	bi'koret	בִּיקּוֹרֶת (נ)
to criticize (vt)	levaker	לְבַקֵּר
accusation	haʾaʃama	הַאֲשָׁמָה (נ)
to accuse (vt)	lehaʾaʃim	לְהַאֲשִׁים
revenge	nekama	נְקָמָה (נ)
to avenge (get revenge)	linkom	לִנְקוֹם
to pay back	lehaχzir	לְהַחְזִיר
disdain	zilzul	זִלְזוּל (ז)
to despise (vt)	lezalzel be...	לְזַלְזֵל בְּ...
hatred, hate	sinʾa	שִׂנְאָה (נ)
to hate (vt)	lisno	לִשְׂנוֹא
nervous (adj)	atsbani	עַצְבָּנִי
to be nervous	lihyot atsbani	לִהְיוֹת עַצְבָּנִי
angry (mad)	kaʿus	כָּעוּס
to make angry	lehargiz	לְהַרְגִיז
humiliation	haʃpala	הַשְׁפָּלָה (נ)
to humiliate (vt)	lehaʃpil	לְהַשְׁפִּיל
to humiliate oneself	lehaʃpil et atsmo	לְהַשְׁפִּיל אֶת עַצְמוֹ
shock	'helem	הֶלֶם (ז)
to shock (vt)	lezaʿa'zeʿa	לְזַעֲזֵעַ
trouble (e.g. serious ~)	tsara	צָרָה (נ)

unpleasant (adj)	lo naʿim	לֹא נָעִים
fear (dread)	'paχad	פַּחַד (ז)
terrible (storm, heat)	nora	נוֹרָא
scary (e.g. ~ story)	mafχid	מַפְחִיד
horror	zvaʿa	זְוָעָה (נ)
awful (crime, news)	ayom	אָיֹם

to begin to tremble	leheraʿed	לְהֵירָעֵד
to cry (weep)	livkot	לִבְכּוֹת
to start crying	lehatχil livkot	לְהַתְחִיל לִבְכּוֹת
tear	dimʿa	דְּמָעָה (נ)

fault	aʃma	אַשְׁמָה (נ)
guilt (feeling)	rigʃei aʃam	רִגְשֵׁי אָשָׁם (ז״ר)
dishonor (disgrace)	χerpa	חֶרְפָּה (נ)
protest	meχa'a	מֶחָאָה (נ)
stress	'laχats	לַחַץ (ז)

to disturb (vt)	lehaf'riʿa	לְהַפְרִיעַ
to be furious	liχ'os	לִכְעוֹס
angry (adj)	zoʿem	זוֹעֵם
to end (~ a relationship)	lesayem	לְסַיֵּים
to swear (at sb)	lekalel	לְקַלֵּל

to scare (become afraid)	lehibahel	לְהִיבָּהֵל
to hit (strike with hand)	lehakot	לְהַכּוֹת
to fight (street fight, etc.)	lehitkotet	לְהִתְקוֹטֵט

to settle (a conflict)	lehasdir	לְהַסְדִּיר
discontented (adj)	lo merutse	לֹא מְרוּצֶה
furious (adj)	metoraf	מְטוֹרָף

| It's not good! | ze lo tov! | זֶה לֹא טוֹב! |
| It's bad! | ze ra! | זֶה רַע! |

Medicine

71. Diseases

illness	maxala	מַחֲלָה (נ)
to be ill	lihyot xole	לִהְיוֹת חוֹלֶה
health	bri'ut	בְּרִיאוּת (נ)
runny nose (coryza)	na'zelet	נַזֶּלֶת (נ)
tonsillitis	da'leket ʃkedim	דַּלֶּקֶת שְׁקֵדִים (נ)
cold (illness)	hitstanenut	הִצְטַנְּנוּת (נ)
to catch a cold	lehitstanen	לְהִצְטַנֵּן
bronchitis	bron'xitis	בְּרוֹנְכִיטִיס (ז)
pneumonia	da'leket re'ot	דַּלֶּקֶת רֵיאוֹת (נ)
flu, influenza	ʃa'pa'at	שַׁפַּעַת (נ)
shortsighted (adj)	ktsar re'iya	קְצַר רְאִיָּה
longsighted (adj)	rexok re'iya	רְחוֹק־רְאִיָּה
strabismus (crossed eyes)	pzila	פְּזִילָה (נ)
squint-eyed (adj)	pozel	פּוֹזֵל
cataract	katarakt	קָטָרַקְט (ז)
glaucoma	gla'u'koma	גְּלָאוּקוֹמָה (נ)
stroke	ʃavats moxi	שָׁבָץ מוֹחִי (ז)
heart attack	hetkef lev	הֶתְקֵף לֵב (ז)
myocardial infarction	'otem ʃrir halev	אוֹטֶם שְׁרִיר הַלֵּב (ז)
paralysis	ʃituk	שִׁיתוּק (ז)
to paralyse (vt)	leʃatek	לְשַׁתֵּק
allergy	a'lergya	אָלֶרְגְיָה (נ)
asthma	'astma, ka'tseret	אַסְתְמָה, קַצֶּרֶת (נ)
diabetes	su'keret	סוּכֶּרֶת (נ)
toothache	ke'ev ʃi'nayim	כְּאֵב שִׁנַּיִים (ז)
caries	a'ʃeʃet	עַשֶּׁשֶׁת (נ)
diarrhoea	ʃilʃul	שִׁלְשׁוּל (ז)
constipation	atsirut	עֲצִירוּת (נ)
stomach upset	kilkul keiva	קִלְקוּל קֵיבָה (ז)
food poisoning	har'alat mazon	הַרְעָלַת מָזוֹן (נ)
to get food poisoning	laxatof har'alat mazon	לַחֲטוֹף הַרְעָלַת מָזוֹן
arthritis	da'leket mifrakim	דַּלֶּקֶת מִפְרָקִים (נ)
rickets	ra'kexet	רַכֶּבֶת (נ)
rheumatism	ʃigaron	שִׁיגָרוֹן (ז)
atherosclerosis	ar'teryo skle'rosis	אַרְטֶרְיוֹ־סְקלֶרוֹסִיס (ז)
gastritis	da'leket keiva	דַּלֶּקֶת קֵיבָה (נ)
appendicitis	da'leket toseftan	דַּלֶּקֶת תּוֹסֶפְתָּן (נ)

| cholecystitis | da'leket kis hamara | דַּלֶּקֶת כִּיס הַמָּרָה (נ) |
| ulcer | 'ulkus, kiv | אוּלְקוּס, כִּיב (ז) |

measles	xa'tsevet	חַצֶּבֶת (נ)
rubella (German measles)	a'demet	אַדֶּמֶת (נ)
jaundice	tsa'hevet	צַהֶבֶת (נ)
hepatitis	da'leket kaved	דַּלֶּקֶת כָּבֵד (נ)

schizophrenia	sxizo'frenya	סְכִיזוֹפְרֶנְיָה (נ)
rabies (hydrophobia)	ka'levet	כַּלֶּבֶת (נ)
neurosis	noi'roza	נוֹירוֹזָה (נ)
concussion	za'a'zu'a 'moax	זַעֲזוּעַ מוֹחַ (ז)

cancer	sartan	סַרְטָן (ז)
sclerosis	ta'refet	טָרֶשֶׁת (נ)
multiple sclerosis	ta'refet nefotsa	טָרֶשֶׁת נְפוֹצָה (נ)

alcoholism	alkoholizm	אַלְכּוֹהוֹלִיזְם (ז)
alcoholic (n)	alkoholist	אַלְכּוֹהוֹלִיסְט (ז)
syphilis	a'gevet	עַגֶּבֶת (נ)
AIDS	eids	אֵיידְס (ז)

tumour	gidul	גִּידוּל (ז)
malignant (adj)	mam'ir	מַמְאִיר
benign (adj)	ʃapir	שָׁפִיר

fever	ka'daxat	קַדַּחַת (נ)
malaria	ma'larya	מָלַרְיָה (נ)
gangrene	gan'grena	גַּנְגְרֶנָה (נ)
seasickness	maxalat yam	מַחֲלַת יָם (נ)
epilepsy	maxalat hanefila	מַחֲלַת הַנְּפִילָה (נ)

epidemic	magefa	מַגֵּיפָה (נ)
typhus	'tifus	טִיפוּס (ז)
tuberculosis	ʃa'xefet	שַׁחֶפֶת (נ)
cholera	ko'lera	כּוֹלֵרָה (נ)
plague (bubonic ~)	davar	דֶּבֶר (ז)

72. Symptoms. Treatments. Part 1

symptom	simptom	סִימְפְּטוֹם (ז)
temperature	xom	חוֹם (ז)
high temperature (fever)	xom ga'voha	חוֹם גָּבוֹהַּ (ז)
pulse	'dofek	דוֹפֶק (ז)

dizziness (vertigo)	sxar'xoret	סְחַרְחוֹרֶת (נ)
hot (adj)	xam	חַם
shivering	tsmar'moret	צְמַרְמוֹרֶת (נ)
pale (e.g. ~ face)	xiver	חִיוֵּר

cough	ʃi'ul	שִׁיעוּל (ז)
to cough (vi)	lehiʃta'el	לְהִשְׁתַּעֵל
to sneeze (vi)	lehit'ateʃ	לְהִתְעַטֵּשׁ
faint	ilafon	עִילָפוֹן (ז)

to faint (vi)	lehit'alef	לְהִתְעַלֵף
bruise (hématome)	χabura	חַבּוּרָה (נ)
bump (lump)	blita	בְּלִיטָה (נ)
to bang (bump)	lekabel maka	לְקַבֵּל מַכָּה
contusion (bruise)	maka	מַכָּה (נ)
to get a bruise	lekabel maka	לְקַבֵּל מַכָּה

to limp (vi)	lits'lo'a	לִצְלוֹעַ
dislocation	'neka	נֶקַע (ז)
to dislocate (vt)	lin'ko'a	לִנקוֹעַ
fracture	'fever	שֶׁבֶר (ז)
to have a fracture	lifbor	לִשׁבּוֹר

cut (e.g. paper ~)	χataχ	חָתָך (ז)
to cut oneself	lehiχateχ	לְהֵיחָתֵך
bleeding	dimum	דִימוּם (ז)

burn (injury)	kviya	כְּווִיָה (נ)
to get burned	laχatof kviya	לַחֲטוֹף כְּווִיָה

to prick (vt)	lidkor	לִדקוֹר
to prick oneself	lehidaker	לְהִידָקֵר
to injure (vt)	lif'tso'a	לִפצוֹעַ
injury	ptsi'a	פְּצִיעָה (נ)
wound	'petsa	פֶּצַע (ז)
trauma	'tra'uma	טרָאוּמָה (נ)

to be delirious	lahazot	לַהֲזוֹת
to stutter (vi)	legamgem	לְגַמגֵם
sunstroke	makat 'femef	מַכַּת שֶׁמֶשׁ (נ)

73. Symptoms. Treatments. Part 2

pain, ache	ke'ev	כְּאֵב (ז)
splinter (in foot, etc.)	kots	קוֹץ (ז)

sweat (perspiration)	ze'a	זֵיעָה (נ)
to sweat (perspire)	leha'zi'a	לְהַזִיעַ
vomiting	haka'a	הָקָאָה (נ)
convulsions	pirkusim	פִּירכּוּסִים (ז"ר)

pregnant (adj)	hara	הָרָה
to be born	lehivaled	לְהִיווָלֵד
delivery, labour	leda	לֵידָה (נ)
to deliver (~ a baby)	la'ledet	לָלֶדֶת
abortion	hapala	הַפָּלָה (נ)

breathing, respiration	nefima	נְשִׁימָה (נ)
in-breath (inhalation)	fe'ifa	שְׁאִיפָה (נ)
out-breath (exhalation)	nefifa	נְשִׁיפָה (נ)
to exhale (breathe out)	linfof	לִנשׁוֹף
to inhale (vi)	lifof	לִשׁאוֹף
disabled person	naχe	נָכֶה (ז)
cripple	naχe	נָכֶה (ז)

drug addict	narkoman	נַרקוֹמָן (ז)
deaf (adj)	xeref	חֵירֵשׁ
mute (adj)	ilem	אִילֵם
deaf mute (adj)	xeref-ilem	חֵירֵשׁ־אִילֵם

mad, insane (adj)	mefuga	מְשׁוּגָע
madman (demented person)	mefuga	מְשׁוּגָע (ז)
madwoman	mefu'ga'at	מְשׁוּגַעַת (נ)
to go insane	lehifta'ge'a	לְהִשׁתַגֵע

gene	gen	גֵן (ז)
immunity	xasinut	חֲסִינוּת (נ)
hereditary (adj)	torafti	תוֹרַשׁתִי
congenital (adj)	mulad	מוּלָד

virus	'virus	וִירוּס (ז)
microbe	xaidak	חַיידָק (ז)
bacterium	bak'terya	בַּקטֶריָה (נ)
infection	zihum	זִיהוּם (ז)

74. Symptoms. Treatments. Part 3

| hospital | beit xolim | בֵּית חוֹלִים (ז) |
| patient | metupal | מְטוּפָּל (ז) |

diagnosis	avxana	אַבחָנָה (נ)
cure	ripui	רִיפּוּי (ז)
medical treatment	tipul refu'i	טִיפּוּל רְפוּאִי (ז)
to get treatment	lekabel tipul	לְקַבֵּל טִיפּוּל
to treat (~ a patient)	letapel be...	לְטַפֵּל בְּ...
to nurse (look after)	letapel be...	לְטַפֵּל בְּ...
care (nursing ~)	tipul	טִיפּוּל (ז)

operation, surgery	ni'tuax	נִיתוּחַ (ז)
to bandage (head, limb)	laxbof	לַחבּוֹשׁ
bandaging	xavifa	חֲבִישָׁה (נ)

vaccination	xisun	חִיסוּן (ז)
to vaccinate (vt)	lexasen	לְחַסֵן
injection	zrika	זרִיקָה (נ)
to give an injection	lehazrik	לְהַזרִיק

attack	hetkef	הַתקֵף (ז)
amputation	kti'a	קְטִיעָה (נ)
to amputate (vt)	lik'to'a	לִקטוֹעַ
coma	tar'demet	תַרדֶמֶת (נ)
to be in a coma	lihyot betar'demet	לִהיוֹת בְּתַרדֶמֶת
intensive care	tipul nimrats	טִיפּוּל נִמרָץ (ז)

to recover (~ from flu)	lehaxlim	לְהַחלִים
condition (patient's ~)	matsav	מַצָב (ז)
consciousness	hakara	הַכָּרָה (נ)
memory (faculty)	zikaron	זִיכָּרוֹן (ז)

to pull out (tooth)	la'akor	לַעֲקוֹר
filling	stima	סתִימָה (נ)
to fill (a tooth)	la'asot stima	לַעֲשׂוֹת סתִימָה

| hypnosis | hip'noza | הִיפּנוֹזָה (נ) |
| to hypnotize (vt) | lehapnet | לְהַפּנֵט |

75. Doctors

doctor	rofe	רוֹפֵא (ז)
nurse	aχot	אָחוֹת (נ)
personal doctor	rofe iʃi	רוֹפֵא אִישִׁי (ז)

dentist	rofe ʃi'nayim	רוֹפֵא שִׁינַיִים (ז)
optician	rofe ei'nayim	רוֹפֵא עֵינַיִים (ז)
general practitioner	rofe pnimi	רוֹפֵא פּנִימִי (ז)
surgeon	kirurg	כִּירוּרג (ז)

psychiatrist	psiχi''ater	פּסִיכִיאָטֶר (ז)
paediatrician	rofe yeladim	רוֹפֵא יְלָדִים (ז)
psychologist	psiχolog	פּסִיכוֹלוֹג (ז)
gynaecologist	rofe naʃim	רוֹפֵא נָשִׁים (ז)
cardiologist	kardyolog	קַרדִיוֹלוֹג (ז)

76. Medicine. Drugs. Accessories

medicine, drug	trufa	תרוּפָה (נ)
remedy	trufa	תרוּפָה (נ)
to prescribe (vt)	lirʃom	לִרשׁוֹם
prescription	mirʃam	מִרשָׁם (ז)

tablet, pill	kadur	כַּדוּר (ז)
ointment	miʃχa	מִשׁחָה (נ)
ampoule	'ampula	אַמפּוּלָה (נ)
mixture	ta'a'rovet	תַעֲרוֹבֶת (נ)
syrup	sirop	סִירוֹפּ (ז)
pill	gluya	גלוּיָה (נ)
powder	avka	אַבקָה (נ)

gauze bandage	taχ'boʃet 'gaza	תַחבּוֹשֶׁת גָאזָה (ז)
cotton wool	'tsemer 'gefen	צֶמֶר גֶפֶן (ז)
iodine	yod	יוֹד (ז)

plaster	'plaster	פּלַסטֶר (ז)
eyedropper	taf'tefet	טַפטֶפֶת (נ)
thermometer	madχom	מַדחוֹם (ז)
syringe	mazrek	מַזרֵק (ז)

wheelchair	kise galgalim	כִּיסֵא גַלגַלִים (ז)
crutches	ka'bayim	קַבַּיִים (ז"ר)
painkiller	meʃakeχ ke'evim	מְשַׁכֵּך כְּאֵבִים (ז)
laxative	trufa meʃal'ʃelet	תרוּפָה מְשַׁלשֶׁלֶת (נ)

spirits (ethanol)	'kohal	בֹּהֵל (ז)
medicinal herbs	isvei marpe	עִשְׂבֵי מַרְפֵּא (ז"ר)
herbal (~ tea)	ʃel asavim	שֶׁל עֲשָׂבִים

77. Smoking. Tobacco products

tobacco	'tabak	טַבָּק (ז)
cigarette	si'garya	סִיגַרְיָה (נ)
cigar	sigar	סִיגָר (ז)
pipe	mik'teret	מִקְטֶרֶת (נ)
packet (of cigarettes)	χafisa	חֲפִיסָה (נ)
matches	gafrurim	גַּפְרוּרִים (ז"ר)
matchbox	kufsat gafrurim	קוּפְסַת גַּפְרוּרִים (נ)
lighter	matsit	מַצִּית (ז)
ashtray	ma'afera	מַאֲפֵרָה (נ)
cigarette case	nartik lesi'garyot	נַרְתִּיק לְסִיגַרְיוֹת (ז)
cigarette holder	piya	פִּיָּה (נ)
filter (cigarette tip)	'filter	פִילְטֶר (ז)
to smoke (vi, vt)	le'aʃen	לְעַשֵּׁן
to light a cigarette	lehadlik si'garya	לְהַדְלִיק סִיגַרְיָה
smoking	iʃun	עִישׁוּן (ז)
smoker	me'aʃen	מְעַשֵּׁן (ז)
cigarette end	bdal si'garya	בְּדַל סִיגַרְיָה (ז)
smoke, fumes	aʃan	עָשָׁן (ז)
ash	'efer	אֵפֶר (ז)

HUMAN HABITAT

City

78. City. Life in the city

city, town	ir	עִיר (נ)
capital city	ir bira	עִיר בִּירָה (נ)
village	kfar	כְּפָר (ז)
city map	mapat ha'ir	מַפַּת הָעִיר (נ)
city centre	merkaz ha'ir	מֶרְכַּז הָעִיר (ז)
suburb	parvar	פַּרְוָר (ז)
suburban (adj)	parvari	פַּרְוָרִי
outskirts	parvar	פַּרְוָר (ז)
environs (suburbs)	svivot	סְבִיבוֹת (נ"ר)
city block	ʃxuna	שְׁכוּנָה (נ)
residential block (area)	ʃxunat megurim	שְׁכוּנַת מְגוּרִים (נ)
traffic	tnu'a	תְּנוּעָה (נ)
traffic lights	ramzor	רַמְזוֹר (ז)
public transport	taxbura tsiburit	תַּחְבּוּרָה צִיבּוּרִית (נ)
crossroads	'tsomet	צוֹמֶת (ז)
zebra crossing	ma'avar xatsaya	מַעֲבָר חֲצָיָה (ז)
pedestrian subway	ma'avar tat karka'i	מַעֲבָר תַּת־קַרְקָעִי (ז)
to cross (~ the street)	laxatsot	לַחֲצוֹת
pedestrian	holex 'regel	הוֹלֵךְ רֶגֶל (ז)
pavement	midraxa	מִדְרָכָה (נ)
bridge	'geʃer	גֶּשֶׁר (ז)
embankment (river walk)	ta'yelet	טַיֶּלֶת (נ)
fountain	mizraka	מִזְרָקָה (נ)
allée (garden walkway)	sdera	שְׂדֵרָה (נ)
park	park	פָּארְק (ז)
boulevard	sdera	שְׂדֵרָה (נ)
square	kikar	כִּיכָּר (נ)
avenue (wide street)	rexov raʃi	רְחוֹב רָאשִׁי (ז)
street	rexov	רְחוֹב (ז)
side street	simta	סִמְטָה (נ)
dead end	mavoi satum	מָבוֹי סָתוּם (ז)
house	'bayit	בַּיִת (ז)
building	binyan	בִּנְיָן (ז)
skyscraper	gored ʃxakim	גּוֹרֵד שְׁחָקִים (ז)
facade	xazit	חָזִית (נ)
roof	gag	גַּג (ז)

window	χalon	חַלוֹן (ז)
arch	'keʃet	קֶשֶׁת (נ)
column	amud	עַמוּד (ז)
corner	pina	פִּינָה (נ)

shop window	χalon ra'ava	חַלוֹן רַאֲוָה (ז)
signboard (store sign, etc.)	'ʃelet	שֶׁלֶט (ז)
poster	kraza	כְּרָזָה (נ)
advertising poster	'poster	פּוֹסְטֶר (ז)
hoarding	'luaχ pirsum	לוּחַ פִּרְסוּם (ז)

rubbish	'zevel	זֶבֶל (ז)
rubbish bin	paχ aʃpa	פַּח אַשְׁפָּה (ז)
to litter (vi)	lelaχleχ	לְלַכְלֵךְ
rubbish dump	mizbala	מִזְבָּלָה (נ)

telephone box	ta 'telefon	תָּא טֶלֶפוֹן (ז)
lamppost	amud panas	עַמוּד פַּנָס (ז)
bench (park ~)	safsal	סַפְסָל (ז)

police officer	ʃoter	שׁוֹטֵר (ז)
police	miʃtara	מִשְׁטָרָה (נ)
beggar	kabtsan	קַבְּצָן (ז)
homeless (n)	χasar 'bayit	חֲסַר בַּיִת (ז)

79. Urban institutions

shop	χanut	חֲנוּת (נ)
chemist, pharmacy	beit mir'kaχat	בֵּית מִרְקַחַת (ז)
optician (spectacles shop)	χanut miʃka'fayim	חֲנוּת מִשְׁקָפַיִים (נ)
shopping centre	kanyon	קַנְיוֹן (ז)
supermarket	super'market	סוּפֶּרמַרְקֶט (ז)

bakery	ma'afiya	מַאֲפִיָּה (נ)
baker	ofe	אוֹפֶה (ז)
cake shop	χanut mamtakim	חֲנוּת מַמְתָּקִים (נ)
grocery shop	ma'kolet	מַכּוֹלֶת (נ)
butcher shop	itliz	אִטְלִיז (ז)

greengrocer	χanut perot viyerakot	חֲנוּת פֵּירוֹת וִירָקוֹת (נ)
market	ʃuk	שׁוּק (ז)

coffee bar	beit kafe	בֵּית קָפֶה (ז)
restaurant	mis'ada	מִסְעָדָה (נ)
pub, bar	pab	פָּאבּ (ז)
pizzeria	pi'tseriya	פִּיצֶרְיָה (נ)

hairdresser	mispara	מִסְפָּרָה (נ)
post office	'do'ar	דּוֹאַר (ז)
dry cleaners	nikui yaveʃ	נִיקּוּי יָבֵשׁ (ז)
photo studio	'studyo letsilum	סְטוּדִיוֹ לְצִילוּם (ז)

shoe shop	χanut na'a'layim	חֲנוּת נַעֲלַיִים (נ)
bookshop	χanut sfarim	חֲנוּת סְפָרִים (נ)

sports shop	χanut sport	חֲנוּת סְפּוֹרְט (נ)
clothes repair shop	χanut tikun bgadim	חֲנוּת תִּיקּוּן בְּגָדִים (נ)
formal wear hire	χanut haskarat bgadim	חֲנוּת הַשְׂכָּרַת בְּגָדִים (נ)
video rental shop	χanut haʃalat sratim	חֲנוּת הַשְׁאָלַת סְרָטִים (נ)

circus	kirkas	קִרְקָס (ז)
zoo	gan hayot	גַן חַיּוֹת (ז)
cinema	kol'no'a	קוֹלְנוֹעַ (ז)
museum	muze'on	מוּזֵיאוֹן (ז)
library	sifriya	סִפְרִייָה (נ)

theatre	te'atron	תֵּיאַטְרוֹן (ז)
opera (opera house)	beit 'opera	בֵּית אוֹפֵּרָה (ז)
nightclub	mo'adon 'laila	מוֹעֲדוֹן לַיְלָה (ז)
casino	ka'zino	קָזִינוֹ (ז)

mosque	misgad	מִסְגָּד (ז)
synagogue	beit 'kneset	בֵּית כְּנֶסֶת (ז)
cathedral	kated'rala	קָתֶדְרָלָה (נ)
temple	mikdaʃ	מִקְדָּשׁ (ז)
church	knesiya	כְּנֵסִייָה (נ)

college	miχlala	מִכְלָלָה (נ)
university	uni'versita	אוּנִיבֶרְסִיטָה (נ)
school	beit 'sefer	בֵּית סֵפֶר (ז)

prefecture	maχoz	מָחוֹז (ז)
town hall	iriya	עִירִייָה (נ)
hotel	beit malon	בֵּית מָלוֹן (ז)
bank	bank	בַּנק (ז)

embassy	ʃagrirut	שַׁגְרִירוּת (נ)
travel agency	soχnut nesi'ot	סוֹכְנוּת נְסִיעוֹת (נ)
information office	modi'in	מוֹדִיעִין (ז)
currency exchange	misrad hamarat mat'be'a	מִשְׂרַד הֲמָרַת מַטְבֵּעַ (ז)

underground, tube	ra'kevet taχtit	רַכֶּבֶת תַּחְתִּית (נ)
hospital	beit χolim	בֵּית חוֹלִים (ז)

petrol station	taχanat 'delek	תַּחֲנַת דֶּלֶק (נ)
car park	migraʃ χanaya	מִגְרַשׁ חֲנָיָה (ז)

80. Signs

signboard (store sign, etc.)	'ʃelet	שֶׁלֶט (ז)
notice (door sign, etc.)	moda'a	מוֹדָעָה (נ)
poster	'poster	פּוֹסְטֶר (ז)
direction sign	tamrur	תַּמְרוּר (ז)
arrow (sign)	χeʦ	חֵץ (ז)

caution	azhara	אַזְהָרָה (נ)
warning sign	'ʃelet azhara	שֶׁלֶט אַזְהָרָה (ז)
to warn (vt)	lehazhir	לְהַזְהִיר
rest day (weekly ~)	yom 'χofeʃ	יוֹם חוֹפֶשׁ (ז)

timetable (schedule)	'luaχ zmanim	לוּחַ זְמַנִּים (ז)
opening hours	ʃa'ot avoda	שְׁעוֹת עֲבוֹדָה (נ"ר)
WELCOME!	bruχim haba'im!	בְּרוּכִים הַבָּאִים!
ENTRANCE	knisa	כְּנִיסָה
WAY OUT	yetsi'a	יְצִיאָה
PUSH	dχof	דְּחוֹף
PULL	mʃoχ	מְשׁוֹך
OPEN	pa'tuaχ	פָּתוּחַ
CLOSED	sagur	סָגוּר
WOMEN	lenaʃim	לְנָשִׁים
MEN	legvarim	לִגְבָרִים
DISCOUNTS	hanaχot	הַנָּחוֹת
SALE	mivtsa	מִבְצָע
NEW!	χadaʃ!	חָדָשׁ!
FREE	χinam	חִינָּם
ATTENTION!	sim lev!	שִׂים לֵב!
NO VACANCIES	ein makom panui	אֵין מָקוֹם פָּנוּי
RESERVED	ʃamur	שָׁמוּר
ADMINISTRATION	hanhala	הַנְהָלָה
STAFF ONLY	le'ovdim bilvad	לְעוֹבְדִים בְּלְבָד
BEWARE OF THE DOG!	zehirut 'kelev noʃeχ!	זְהִירוּת, כֶּלֶב נוֹשֵׁךְ!
NO SMOKING	asur le'aʃen!	אָסוּר לְעַשֵּׁן!
DO NOT TOUCH!	lo lagaat!	לֹא לָגַעַת!
DANGEROUS	mesukan	מְסוּכָּן
DANGER	sakana	סַכָּנָה
HIGH VOLTAGE	'metaχ ga'voha	מֶתַח גָּבוֹהַ
NO SWIMMING!	haraχatsa asura!	הָרַחָצָה אֲסוּרָה!
OUT OF ORDER	lo oved	לֹא עוֹבֵד
FLAMMABLE	dalik	דָּלִיק
FORBIDDEN	asur	אָסוּר
NO TRESPASSING!	asur la'avor	אָסוּר לַעֲבוֹר
WET PAINT	'tseva laχ	צֶבַע לַח

81. Urban transport

bus, coach	'otobus	אוֹטוֹבּוּס (ז)
tram	ra'kevet kala	רַכֶּבֶת קַלָּה (נ)
trolleybus	tro'leibus	טְרוֹלֵייבּוּס (ז)
route (of bus, etc.)	maslul	מַסְלוּל (ז)
number (e.g. bus ~)	mispar	מִסְפָּר (ז)
to go by ...	lin'so'a be...	לִנְסוֹעַ בְּ...
to get on (~ the bus)	la'alot	לַעֲלוֹת
to get off ...	la'redet mi...	לָרֶדֶת מֵ...
stop (e.g. bus ~)	taχana	תַּחֲנָה (נ)

next stop	hataxana haba'a	הַתַחֲנָה הַבָּאָה (נ)
terminus	hataxana ha'axrona	הַתַחֲנָה הָאַחֲרוֹנָה (נ)
timetable	'luax zmanim	לוּחַ זְמַנִים (ז)
to wait (vt)	lehamtin	לְהַמְתִין

| ticket | kartis | כַּרְטִיס (ז) |
| fare | mexir hanesiya | מְחִיר הַנְסִיעָה (ז) |

cashier (ticket seller)	kupai	קוּפַאי (ז)
ticket inspection	bi'koret kartisim	בִּיקוֹרֶת כַּרְטִיסִים (נ)
ticket inspector	mevaker	מְבַקֵר (ז)

to be late (for ...)	le'axer	לְאַחֵר
to miss (~ the train, etc.)	lefasfes	לְפַסְפֵס
to be in a hurry	lemaher	לְמַהֵר

taxi, cab	monit	מוֹנִית (נ)
taxi driver	nahag monit	נֶהָג מוֹנִית (ז)
by taxi	bemonit	בְּמוֹנִית
taxi rank	taxanat moniyot	תַחֲנַת מוֹנִיוֹת (נ)
to call a taxi	lehazmin monit	לְהַזְמִין מוֹנִית
to take a taxi	la'kaxat monit	לָקַחַת מוֹנִית

traffic	tnu'a	תְנוּעָה (נ)
traffic jam	pkak	פְקָק (ז)
rush hour	ʃa'ot 'omes	שְעוֹת עוֹמֶס (נ"ר)
to park (vi)	laxanot	לַחֲנוֹת
to park (vt)	lehaxnot	לְהַחְנוֹת
car park	xanaya	חֲנָיָה (נ)

underground, tube	ra'kevet taxtit	רַכֶּבֶת תַחְתִית (נ)
station	taxana	תַחֲנָה (נ)
to take the tube	lin'so'a betaxtit	לִנְסוֹעַ בְּתַחְתִית
train	ra'kevet	רַכֶּבֶת (נ)
train station	taxanat ra'kevet	תַחֲנַת רַכֶּבֶת (נ)

82. Sightseeing

monument	an'darta	אַנְדַרְטָה (נ)
fortress	mivtsar	מִבְצָר (ז)
palace	armon	אַרְמוֹן (ז)
castle	tira	טִירָה (נ)
tower	migdal	מִגְדָל (ז)
mausoleum	ma'uzo'le'um	מָאוּזוֹלֵיאוּם (ז)

architecture	adrixalut	אַדְרִיכָלוּת (נ)
medieval (adj)	benaimi	בֵּינַיימִי
ancient (adj)	atik	עַתִיק
national (adj)	le'umi	לְאוּמִי
famous (monument, etc.)	mefursam	מְפוּרְסָם

tourist	tayar	תַיָיר (ז)
guide (person)	madrix tiyulim	מַדְרִיך טִיוּלִים (ז)
excursion, sightseeing tour	tiyul	טִיוּל (ז)

to show (vt)	lehar'ot	לְהַרְאוֹת
to tell (vt)	lesaper	לְסַפֵּר
to find (vt)	limtso	לִמְצוֹא
to get lost (lose one's way)	la'lexet le'ibud	לָלֶכֶת לְאִיבּוּד
map (e.g. underground ~)	mapa	מַפָּה (נ)
map (e.g. city ~)	tarʃim	תַּרְשִׁים (ז)
souvenir, gift	maz'keret	מַזְכֶּרֶת (נ)
gift shop	xanut matanot	חֲנוּת מַתָּנוֹת (נ)
to take pictures	letsalem	לְצַלֵם
to have one's picture taken	lehitstalem	לְהִצְטַלֵם

83. Shopping

to buy (purchase)	liknot	לִקְנוֹת
shopping	kniya	קְנִיָה (נ)
to go shopping	la'lexet lekniyot	לָלֶכֶת לִקְנִיוֹת
shopping	arixat kniyot	עֲרִיכַת קְנִיוֹת (נ)
to be open (ab. shop)	pa'tuax	פָּתוּחַ
to be closed	sagur	סָגוּר
footwear, shoes	na'a'layim	נַעֲלַיִים (נ"ר)
clothes, clothing	bgadim	בְּגָדִים (ז"ר)
cosmetics	tamrukim	תַּמְרוּקִים (ז"ר)
food products	mutsrei mazon	מוּצְרֵי מָזוֹן (ז"ר)
gift, present	matana	מַתָּנָה (נ)
shop assistant (masc.)	moxer	מוֹכֵר (ז)
shop assistant (fem.)	mo'xeret	מוֹכֶרֶת (נ)
cash desk	kupa	קוּפָּה (נ)
mirror	mar'a	מַרְאָה (נ)
counter (shop ~)	duxan	דוּכָן (ז)
fitting room	'xeder halbaʃa	חֲדַר הַלְבָּשָׁה (ז)
to try on	limdod	לִמְדוֹד
to fit (ab. dress, etc.)	lehat'im	לְהַתְאִים
to fancy (vt)	limtso xen be'ei'nayim	לִמְצוֹא חֵן בְּעֵינַיִים
price	mexir	מְחִיר (ז)
price tag	tag mexir	תָּג מְחִיר (ז)
to cost (vt)	la'alot	לַעֲלוֹת
How much?	'kama?	כַּמָה?
discount	hanaxa	הֲנָחָה (נ)
inexpensive (adj)	lo yakar	לֹא יָקָר
cheap (adj)	zol	זוֹל
expensive (adj)	yakar	יָקָר
It's expensive	ze yakar	זֶה יָקָר
hire (n)	haskara	הַשְׂכָּרָה (נ)
to hire (~ a dinner jacket)	liskor	לִשְׂכּוֹר

| credit (trade credit) | aʃrai | אַשְׁרַאי (ז) |
| on credit (adv) | be'aʃrai | בְּאַשְׁרַאי |

84. Money

money	'kesef	כֶּסֶף (ז)
currency exchange	hamara	הֲמָרָה (נ)
exchange rate	'ʃa'ar χalifin	שַׁעַר חֲלִיפִין (ז)
cashpoint	kaspomat	כַּסְפּוֹמָט (ז)
coin	mat'be'a	מַטְבֵּעַ (ז)

| dollar | 'dolar | דּוֹלָר (ז) |
| euro | 'eiro | אֵירוֹ (ז) |

lira	'lira	לִירָה (נ)
Deutschmark	mark germani	מַרְק גֶּרְמָנִי (ז)
franc	frank	פְרַנְק (ז)
pound sterling	'lira 'sterling	לִירָה שְׁטֶרְלִינְג (נ)
yen	yen	יֶן (ז)

debt	χov	חוֹב (ז)
debtor	'ba'al χov	בַּעַל חוֹב (ז)
to lend (money)	lehalvot	לְהַלְווֹת
to borrow (vi, vt)	lilvot	לִלְווֹת

bank	bank	בַּנְק (ז)
account	χeʃbon	חֶשְׁבּוֹן (ז)
to deposit (vt)	lehafkid	לְהַפְקִיד
to deposit into the account	lehafkid leχeʃbon	לְהַפְקִיד לְחֶשְׁבּוֹן
to withdraw (vt)	limʃoχ meχeʃbon	לִמְשׁוֹךְ מֵחֶשְׁבּוֹן

credit card	kartis aʃrai	כַּרְטִיס אַשְׁרַאי (ז)
cash	mezuman	מְזוּמָן
cheque	tʃek	צֵ'ק (ז)
to write a cheque	liχtov tʃek	לִכְתּוֹב צֵ'ק
chequebook	pinkas 'tʃekim	פִּנְקָס צֵ'קִים (ז)

wallet	arnak	אַרְנָק (ז)
purse	arnak lematbe''ot	אַרְנָק לְמַטְבְּעוֹת (ז)
safe	ka'sefet	כַּסֶּפֶת (נ)

heir	yoreʃ	יוֹרֵשׁ (ז)
inheritance	yeruʃa	יְרוּשָׁה (נ)
fortune (wealth)	'oʃer	עוֹשֶׁר (ז)

lease	χoze sχirut	חוֹזֶה שְׂכִירוּת (ז)
rent (money)	sχar dira	שְׂכַר דִּירָה (ז)
to rent (sth from sb)	liskor	לִשְׂכּוֹר

price	meχir	מְחִיר (ז)
cost	alut	עֲלוּת (נ)
sum	sχum	סְכוּם (ז)
to spend (vt)	lehotsi	לְהוֹצִיא
expenses	hotsa'ot	הוֹצָאוֹת (נ"ר)

| to economize (vi, vt) | laχasoχ | לַחֲסוֹךְ |
| economical | χesχoni | חֶסְכוֹנִי |

to pay (vi, vt)	leʃalem	לְשַׁלֵם
payment	taʃlum	תַשְׁלוּם (ז)
change (give the ~)	'odef	עוֹדֶף (ז)

tax	mas	מַס (ז)
fine	knas	קְנָס (ז)
to fine (vt)	liknos	לִקְנוֹס

85. Post. Postal service

post office	'do'ar	דוֹאַר (ז)
post (letters, etc.)	'do'ar	דוֹאַר (ז)
postman	davar	דַוָּר (ז)
opening hours	ʃa'ot avoda	שְׁעוֹת עֲבוֹדָה (נ״ר)

letter	miχtav	מִכְתָּב (ז)
registered letter	miχtav raʃum	מִכְתָּב רָשׁוּם (ז)
postcard	gluya	גְלוּיָה (נ)
telegram	mivrak	מִבְרָק (ז)
parcel	χavila	חֲבִילָה (נ)
money transfer	ha'avarat ksafim	הַעֲבָרַת כְּסָפִים (נ)

to receive (vt)	lekabel	לְקַבֵּל
to send (vt)	liʃloaχ	לִשְׁלוֹחַ
sending	ʃliχa	שְׁלִיחָה (נ)

address	'ktovet	כְּתוֹבֶת (נ)
postcode	mikud	מִיקוּד (ז)
sender	ʃo'leaχ	שׁוֹלֵחַ (ז)
receiver	nim'an	נִמְעָן (ז)

| name (first name) | ʃem prati | שֵׁם פְּרָטִי (ז) |
| surname (last name) | ʃem miʃpaχa | שֵׁם מִשְׁפָּחָה (ז) |

postage rate	ta'arif	תַעֲרִיף (ז)
standard (adj)	ragil	רָגִיל
economical (adj)	χesχoni	חֶסְכוֹנִי

weight	miʃkal	מִשְׁקָל (ז)
to weigh (~ letters)	liʃkol	לִשְׁקוֹל
envelope	ma'atafa	מַעֲטָפָה (נ)
postage stamp	bul 'do'ar	בּוּל דוֹאַר (ז)
to stamp an envelope	lehadbik bul	לְהַדְבִּיק בּוּל

Dwelling. House. Home

86. House. Dwelling

house	'bayit	בַּיִת (ז)
at home (adv)	ba'bayit	בַּבַּיִת
yard	χatser	חָצֵר (נ)
fence (iron ~)	gader	גָּדֵר (נ)
brick (n)	levena	לְבֵנָה (נ)
brick (as adj)	milevenim	מִלְבֵנִים
stone (n)	'even	אֶבֶן (נ)
stone (as adj)	me''even	מֵאֶבֶן
concrete (n)	beton	בֶּטוֹן (ז)
concrete (as adj)	mibeton	מִבֶּטוֹן
new (new-built)	χadaʃ	חָדָשׁ
old (adj)	yaʃan	יָשָׁן
decrepit (house)	balui	בָּלוּי
modern (adj)	mo'derni	מוֹדֶרנִי
multistorey (adj)	rav komot	רַב־קוֹמוֹת
tall (~ building)	ga'voha	גָּבוֹהַ
floor, storey	'koma	קוֹמָה (נ)
single-storey (adj)	χad komati	חַד־קוֹמָתִי
ground floor	komat 'karka	קוֹמַת קַרקַע (נ)
top floor	hakoma ha'elyona	הַקוֹמָה הָעֶלִיוֹנָה (נ)
roof	gag	גַּג (ז)
chimney	aruba	אֲרוּבָּה (נ)
roof tiles	'ra'af	רַעַף (ז)
tiled (adj)	mere'afim	מְרֻעָפִּים
loft (attic)	aliyat gag	עֲלִייַת גַּג (נ)
window	χalon	חַלוֹן (ז)
glass	zχuχit	זכוּכִית (נ)
window ledge	'eden χalon	אֶדֶן חַלוֹן (ז)
shutters	trisim	תרִיסִים (ז"ר)
wall	kir	קִיר (ז)
balcony	mir'peset	מִרפֶּסֶת (נ)
downpipe	marzev	מַרזֵב (ז)
upstairs (to be ~)	le'mala	לְמַעלָה
to go upstairs	la'alot bemadregot	לַעֲלוֹת בְּמַדרֵגוֹת
to come down (the stairs)	la'redet bemadregot	לָרֶדֶת בְּמַדרֵגוֹת
to move (to new premises)	la'avor	לַעֲבוֹר

87. House. Entrance. Lift

entrance	knisa	כְּנִיסָה (נ)
stairs (stairway)	madregot	מַדְרֵגוֹת (נ"ר)
steps	madregot	מַדְרֵגוֹת (נ"ר)
banisters	ma'ake	מַעֲקֶה (ז)
lobby (hotel ~)	'lobi	לוֹבִּי (ז)

postbox	teivat 'do'ar	תֵּיבַת דּוֹאַר (נ)
waste bin	pax 'zevel	פַּח זֶבֶל (ז)
refuse chute	merik aʃpa	מֵרִיק אַשְׁפָּה (ז)

lift	ma'alit	מַעֲלִית (נ)
goods lift	ma'alit masa	מַעֲלִית מַשָּׂא (נ)
lift cage	ta ma'alit	תָּא מַעֲלִית (ז)
to take the lift	lin'so'a bema'alit	לִנְסוֹעַ בְּמַעֲלִית

flat	dira	דִּירָה (נ)
residents (~ of a building)	dayarim	דַּיָּירִים (ז"ר)
neighbour (masc.)	ʃaxen	שָׁכֵן (ז)
neighbour (fem.)	ʃxena	שְׁכֵנָה (נ)
neighbours	ʃxenim	שְׁכֵנִים (ז"ר)

88. House. Electricity

electricity	xaʃmal	חַשְׁמַל (ז)
light bulb	nura	נוּרָה (נ)
switch	'meteg	מֶתֶג (ז)
fuse (plug fuse)	natix	נָתִיךְ (ז)

cable, wire (electric ~)	xut	חוּט (ז)
wiring	xivut	חִיווּט (ז)
electricity meter	mone xaʃmal	מוֹנֶה חַשְׁמַל (ז)
readings	kri'a	קְרִיאָה (נ)

89. House. Doors. Locks

door	'delet	דֶּלֶת (נ)
gate (vehicle ~)	'ʃa'ar	שַׁעַר (ז)
handle, doorknob	yadit	יָדִית (נ)
to unlock (unbolt)	lif'toax	לִפְתּוֹחַ
to open (vt)	lif'toax	לִפְתּוֹחַ
to close (vt)	lisgor	לִסְגּוֹר

key	maf'teax	מַפְתֵּחַ (ז)
bunch (of keys)	tsror maftexot	צְרוֹר מַפְתְּחוֹת (ז)
to creak (door, etc.)	laxarok	לַחֲרוֹק
creak	xarika	חֲרִיקָה (נ)
hinge (door ~)	tsir	צִיר (ז)
doormat	ʃtixon	שְׁטִיחוֹן (ז)
door lock	man'ul	מַנְעוּל (ז)

keyhole	χor haman'ul	חוֹר הַמַּנְעוּל (ז)
crossbar (sliding bar)	'briaχ	בְּרִיחַ (ז)
door latch	'briaχ	בְּרִיחַ (ז)
padlock	man'ul	מַנְעוּל (ז)

to ring (~ the door bell)	letsaltsel	לְצַלְצֵל
ringing (sound)	tsiltsul	צִלְצוּל (ז)
doorbell	pa'amon	פַּעֲמוֹן (ז)
doorbell button	kaftor	כַּפְתוֹר (ז)
knock (at the door)	hakaʃa	הַקָּשָׁה (נ)
to knock (vi)	lehakiʃ	לְהַקִּישׁ

code	kod	קוֹד (ז)
combination lock	man'ul kod	מַנְעוּל קוֹד (ז)
intercom	'interkom	אִינְטֶרְקוֹם (ז)
number (on the door)	mispar	מִסְפָּר (ז)
doorplate	luχit	לוּחִית (נ)
peephole	einit	עֵינִית (נ)

90. Country house

village	kfar	כְּפָר (ז)
vegetable garden	gan yarak	גַּן יָרָק (ז)
fence	gader	גָּדֵר (נ)
picket fence	gader yetedot	גֶּדֶר יְתֵדוֹת (נ)
wicket gate	piʃpaʃ	פִּשְׁפָּשׁ (ז)

granary	asam	אָסָם (ז)
cellar	martef	מַרְתֵּף (ז)
shed (garden ~)	maχsan	מַחְסָן (ז)
well (water)	be'er	בְּאֵר (נ)

stove (wood-fired ~)	aχ	אָח (נ)
to stoke the stove	lehasik et ha'aχ	לְהַסִּיק אֶת הָאָח
firewood	atsei hasaka	עֲצֵי הַסָּקָה (נ"ר)
log (firewood)	bul ets	בּוּל עֵץ (ז)

veranda	mir'peset mekora	מִרְפֶּסֶת מְקוֹרָה (נ)
deck (terrace)	mir'peset	מִרְפֶּסֶת (נ)
stoop (front steps)	madregot ba'petaχ 'bayit	מַדְרֵגוֹת בְּפֶתַח בַּיִת (נ"ר)
swing (hanging seat)	nadneda	נַדְנֵדָה (נ)

91. Villa. Mansion

country house	'bayit bakfar	בַּיִת בַּכְּפָר (ז)
country-villa	'vila	וִילָה (נ)
wing (~ of a building)	agaf	אָגָף (ז)

garden	gan	גַּן (ז)
park	park	פָּארְק (ז)
tropical glasshouse	χamama	חֲמָמָה (נ)
to look after (garden, etc.)	legadel	לְגַדֵּל

swimming pool	breχat sχiya	בְּרֵיכַת שְׂחִיָּה (נ)
gym (home gym)	'χeder 'koʃer	חֲדַר כּוֹשֶׁר (ז)
tennis court	migraʃ 'tenis	מִגְרַשׁ טֶנִיס (ז)
home theater (room)	'χeder hakrana beiti	חֲדַר הַקְרָנָה בֵּיתִי (ז)
garage	musaχ	מוּסָךְ (ז)

| private property | reχuʃ prati | רְכוּשׁ פְּרָטִי (ז) |
| private land | 'ʃetaχ prati | שֶׁטַח פְּרָטִי (ז) |

| warning (caution) | azhara | אַזְהָרָה (נ) |
| warning sign | 'ʃelet azhara | שֶׁלֶט אַזְהָרָה (ז) |

security	avtaχa	אַבְטָחָה (נ)
security guard	ʃomer	שׁוֹמֵר (ז)
burglar alarm	ma'a'reχet az'aka	מַעֲרֶכֶת אַזְעָקָה (נ)

92. Castle. Palace

castle	tira	טִירָה (נ)
palace	armon	אַרְמוֹן (ז)
fortress	mivtsar	מִבְצָר (ז)

wall (round castle)	χoma	חוֹמָה (נ)
tower	migdal	מִגְדָּל (ז)
keep, donjon	migdal merkazi	מִגְדָּל מֶרְכָּזִי (ז)

portcullis	'ʃa'ar anaχi	שַׁעַר אָנָכִי (ז)
subterranean passage	ma'avar tat karka'i	מַעֲבָר תַּת־קַרְקָעִי (ז)
moat	χafir	חָפִיר (ז)
chain	ʃal'ʃelet	שַׁלְשֶׁלֶת (נ)
arrow loop	eʃnav 'yeri	אֶשְׁנָב יָרִי (ז)

magnificent (adj)	mefo'ar	מְפוֹאָר
majestic (adj)	malχuti	מַלְכוּתִי
impregnable (adj)	'bilti χadir	בִּלְתִּי חָדִיר
medieval (adj)	benaimi	בֵּינַיִּמִי

93. Flat

flat	dira	דִּירָה (נ)
room	'χeder	חֶדֶר (ז)
bedroom	χadar ʃena	חֲדַר שֵׁינָה (ז)
dining room	pinat 'oχel	פִּינַת אוֹכֶל (נ)
living room	salon	סָלוֹן (ז)
study (home office)	χadar avoda	חֲדַר עֲבוֹדָה (ז)
entry room	prozdor	פְּרוֹזְדוֹר (ז)
bathroom	χadar am'batya	חֲדַר אַמְבַּטְיָה (ז)
water closet	ʃerutim	שֵׁירוּתִים (ז"ר)

ceiling	tikra	תִּקְרָה (נ)
floor	ritspa	רִצְפָּה (נ)
corner	pina	פִּינָה (נ)

94. Flat. Cleaning

to clean (vi, vt)	lenakot	לְנַקּוֹת
to put away (to stow)	lefanot	לְפַנּוֹת
dust	avak	אָבָק (ז)
dusty (adj)	me'ubak	מְאוּבָּק
to dust (vt)	lenakot avak	לְנַקּוֹת אָבָק
vacuum cleaner	ʃo'ev avak	שׁוֹאֵב אָבָק (ז)
to vacuum (vt)	liʃov avak	לִשְׁאוֹב אָבָק
to sweep (vi, vt)	letate	לְטַאטֵא
sweepings	'psolet ti'tu	פְּסוֹלֶת טָאטוּא (נ)
order	'seder	סֵדֶר (ז)
disorder, mess	i 'seder	אִי סֵדֶר (ז)
mop	magev im smartut	מַגָּב עִם סְמַרְטוּט (ז)
duster	smartut avak	סְמַרְטוּט אָבָק (ז)
short broom	mat'ate katan	מַטְאֲטֵא קָטָן (ז)
dustpan	ya'e	יָעֶה (ז)

95. Furniture. Interior

furniture	rehitim	רָהִיטִים (ז"ר)
table	ʃulχan	שׁוֹלְחָן (ז)
chair	kise	כִּסֵּא (ז)
bed	mita	מִיטָה (נ)
sofa, settee	sapa	סַפָּה (נ)
armchair	kursa	כּוּרְסָה (נ)
bookcase	aron sfarim	אֲרוֹן סְפָרִים (ז)
shelf	madaf	מַדָּף (ז)
wardrobe	aron bgadim	אֲרוֹן בְּגָדִים (ז)
coat rack (wall-mounted ~)	mitle	מִתְלֶה (ז)
coat stand	mitle	מִתְלֶה (ז)
chest of drawers	ʃida	שִׁידָה (נ)
coffee table	ʃulχan itonim	שׁוֹלְחָן עִיתּוֹנִים (ז)
mirror	mar'a	מַרְאָה (נ)
carpet	ʃa'tiaχ	שָׁטִיחַ (ז)
small carpet	ʃa'tiaχ	שָׁטִיחַ (ז)
fireplace	aχ	אָח (נ)
candle	ner	נֵר (ז)
candlestick	pamot	פָּמוֹט (ז)
drapes	vilonot	וִילוֹנוֹת (ז"ר)
wallpaper	tapet	טַפֶּט (ז)
blinds (jalousie)	trisim	תְּרִיסִים (ז"ר)
table lamp	menorat ʃulχan	מְנוֹרַת שׁוֹלְחָן (נ)
wall lamp (sconce)	menorat kir	מְנוֹרַת קִיר (נ)

standard lamp	menora o'medet	מְנוֹרָה עוֹמֶדֶת (נ)
chandelier	niv'reʃet	נִבְרֶשֶׁת (נ)

leg (of chair, table)	'regel	רֶגֶל (נ)
armrest	miʃ'enet yad	מִשְׁעֶנֶת יָד (נ)
back (backrest)	miʃ'enet	מִשְׁעֶנֶת (נ)
drawer	megera	מְגֵירָה (נ)

96. Bedding

bedclothes	matsa'im	מַצָּעִים (ז"ר)
pillow	karit	כָּרִית (נ)
pillowslip	tsipit	צִיפִית (נ)
duvet	smiχa	שְׂמִיכָה (נ)
sheet	sadin	סָדִין (ז)
bedspread	kisui mita	כִּיסוּי מִיטָה (ז)

97. Kitchen

kitchen	mitbaχ	מִטְבָּח (ז)
gas	gaz	גָּז (ז)
gas cooker	tanur gaz	תַּנּוּר גָּז (ז)
electric cooker	tanur χaʃmali	תַּנּוּר חַשְׁמַלִּי (ז)
oven	tanur afiya	תַּנּוּר אֲפִיָּיה (ז)
microwave oven	mikrogal	מִיקְרוֹגַל (ז)

refrigerator	mekarer	מְקָרֵר (ז)
freezer	makpi	מַקְפִּיא (ז)
dishwasher	me'diaχ kelim	מֵדִיחַ כֵּלִים (ז)

mincer	matχenat basar	מַטְחֲנַת בָּשָׂר (נ)
juicer	masχeta	מַסְחֵטָה (נ)
toaster	'toster	טוֹסְטֶר (ז)
mixer	'mikser	מִיקְסֶר (ז)

coffee machine	meχonat kafe	מְכוֹנַת קָפֶה (נ)
coffee pot	findʒan	פִינְגָ׳אן (ז)
coffee grinder	matχenat kafe	מַטְחֲנַת קָפֶה (נ)

kettle	kumkum	קוּמְקוּם (ז)
teapot	kumkum	קוּמְקוּם (ז)
lid	miχse	מִכְסֶה (ז)
tea strainer	mis'nenet te	מְסַנֶּנֶת תֵּה (נ)

spoon	kaf	כַּף (נ)
teaspoon	kapit	כַּפִּית (נ)
soup spoon	kaf	כַּף (נ)
fork	mazleg	מַזְלֵג (ז)
knife	sakin	סַכִּין (ז, נ)

tableware (dishes)	kelim	כֵּלִים (ז"ר)
plate (dinner ~)	tsa'laχat	צַלַּחַת (נ)

saucer	taχtit	תַּחְתִּית (נ)
shot glass	kosit	כּוֹסִית (נ)
glass (tumbler)	kos	כּוֹס (נ)
cup	'sefel	סֵפֶל (ז)

sugar bowl	mis'keret	מִסְכֶּרֶת (נ)
salt cellar	milχiya	מִלְחִיָּה (נ)
pepper pot	pilpeliya	פִּלְפְּלִיָּה (נ)
butter dish	maχame'a	מַחְמָאָה (נ)

stock pot (soup pot)	sir	סִיר (ז)
frying pan (skillet)	maχvat	מַחֲבַת (נ)
ladle	tarvad	תַּרְוָד (ז)
colander	mis'nenet	מְסַנֶּנֶת (נ)
tray (serving ~)	magaʃ	מַגָּשׁ (ז)

bottle	bakbuk	בַּקְבּוּק (ז)
jar (glass)	tsin'tsenet	צִנְצֶנֶת (נ)
tin (can)	paχit	פַּחִית (נ)

bottle opener	potχan bakbukim	פּוֹתְחָן בַּקְבּוּקִים (ז)
tin opener	potχan kufsa'ot	פּוֹתְחָן קוּפְסָאוֹת (ז)
corkscrew	maχlets	מַחְלֵץ (ז)
filter	'filter	פִילְטֶר (ז)
to filter (vt)	lesanen	לְסַנֵּן

| waste (food ~, etc.) | 'zevel | זֶבֶל (ז) |
| waste bin (kitchen ~) | paχ 'zevel | פַּח זֶבֶל (ז) |

98. Bathroom

bathroom	χadar am'batya	חֲדַר אַמְבַּטְיָה (ז)
water	'mayim	מַיִם (ז״ר)
tap	'berez	בֶּרֶז (ז)
hot water	'mayim χamim	מַיִם חַמִּים (ז״ר)
cold water	'mayim karim	מַיִם קָרִים (ז״ר)

toothpaste	miʃχat ʃi'nayim	מִשְׁחַת שִׁנַּיִים (נ)
to clean one's teeth	letsaχ'tseaχ ʃi'nayim	לְצַחְצֵחַ שִׁנַּיִים
toothbrush	miv'reʃet ʃi'nayim	מִבְרֶשֶׁת שִׁנַּיִים (נ)

to shave (vi)	lehitga'leaχ	לְהִתְגַּלֵּחַ
shaving foam	'ketsef gi'luaχ	קֶצֶף גִּילּוּחַ (ז)
razor	'ta‘ar	תַּעַר (ז)

to wash (one's hands, etc.)	liʃtof	לִשְׁטוֹף
to have a bath	lehitraχets	לְהִתְרַחֵץ
shower	mik'laχat	מִקְלַחַת (נ)
to have a shower	lehitka'leaχ	לְהִתְקַלֵּחַ

bath	am'batya	אַמְבַּטְיָה (נ)
toilet (toilet bowl)	asla	אַסְלָה (נ)
sink (washbasin)	kiyor	כִּיּוֹר (ז)
soap	sabon	סַבּוֹן (ז)

soap dish	saboniya	סַבּוֹנִיָּה (נ)
sponge	sfog 'lifa	סְפוֹג לִיפָה (ז)
shampoo	ʃampu	שַׁמְפּוּ (ז)
towel	ma'gevet	מַגֶּבֶת (נ)
bathrobe	χaluk raχatsa	חֲלוּק רַחְצָה (ז)

laundry (process)	kvisa	כְּבִיסָה (נ)
washing machine	meχonat kvisa	מְכוֹנַת כְּבִיסָה (נ)
to do the laundry	leχabes	לְכַבֵּס
washing powder	avkat kvisa	אַבְקַת כְּבִיסָה (נ)

99. Household appliances

TV, telly	tele'vizya	טֶלֶוִיזְיָה (נ)
tape recorder	teip	טֵייפּ (ז)
video	maχʃir 'vide'o	מַכְשִׁיר וִידָאוֹ (ז)
radio	'radyo	רַדְיוֹ (ז)
player (CD, MP3, etc.)	nagan	נַגָּן (ז)

video projector	makren	מַקְרֵן (ז)
home cinema	kol'no'a beiti	קוֹלְנוֹעַ בֵּיתִי (ז)
DVD player	nagan dividi	נַגָּן DVD (ז)
amplifier	magber	מַגְבֵּר (ז)
video game console	maχʃir plei'steiʃen	מַכְשִׁיר פְּלֵייסְטֵיישֶׁן (ט)

video camera	matslemat 'vide'o	מַצְלֵמַת וִידָאוֹ (נ)
camera (photo)	matslema	מַצְלֵמָה (נ)
digital camera	matslema digi'talit	מַצְלֵמָה דִיגִיטָלִית (נ)

vacuum cleaner	ʃo'ev avak	שׁוֹאֵב אָבָק (ז)
iron (e.g. steam ~)	maghets	מַגְהֵץ (ז)
ironing board	'kereʃ gihuts	קֶרֶשׁ גִיהוּץ (ז)

telephone	'telefon	טֶלֶפוֹן (ז)
mobile phone	'telefon nayad	טֶלֶפוֹן נַיָּיד (ז)
typewriter	meχonat ktiva	מְכוֹנַת כְּתִיבָה (נ)
sewing machine	meχonat tfira	מְכוֹנַת תְּפִירָה (נ)

microphone	mikrofon	מִיקְרוֹפוֹן (ז)
headphones	ozniyot	אוֹזְנִיּוֹת (נ״ר)
remote control (TV)	'ʃelet	שֶׁלֶט (ז)

CD, compact disc	taklitor	תַּקְלִיטוֹר (ז)
cassette, tape	ka'letet	קַלֶּטֶת (נ)
vinyl record	taklit	תַּקְלִיט (ז)

100. Repairs. Renovation

renovations	ʃiputs	שִׁיפּוּץ (ז)
to renovate (vt)	leʃapets	לְשַׁפֵּץ
to repair, to fix (vt)	letaken	לְתַקֵּן
to put in order	lesader	לְסַדֵּר

89

to redo (do again)	la'asot meχadaʃ	לַעֲשׂוֹת מֵחָדָשׁ
paint	'tseva	צֶבַע (ז)
to paint (~ a wall)	lits'bo'a	לִצְבּוֹעַ
house painter	tsaba'i	צַבָּעִי (ז)
paintbrush	mikχol	מִכְחוֹל (ז)

| whitewash | sid | סִיד (ז) |
| to whitewash (vt) | lesayed | לְסַיֵּד |

wallpaper	tapet	טַפֶּט (ז)
to wallpaper (vt)	lehadbik ta'petim	לְהַדְבִּיק טַפֶּטִים
varnish	'laka	לַכָּה (נ)
to varnish (vt)	lim'roaχ 'laka	לִמְרוֹחַ לַכָּה

101. Plumbing

water	'mayim	מַיִם (ז״ר)
hot water	'mayim χamim	מַיִם חַמִּים (ז״ר)
cold water	'mayim karim	מַיִם קָרִים (ז״ר)
tap	'berez	בֶּרֶז (ז)

drop (of water)	tipa	טִיפָּה (נ)
to drip (vi)	letaftef	לְטַפְטֵף
to leak (ab. pipe)	lidlof	לִדְלוֹף
leak (pipe ~)	dlifa	דְּלִיפָה (נ)
puddle	ʃlulit	שְׁלוּלִית (נ)

pipe	tsinor	צִינוֹר (ז)
valve (e.g., ball ~)	'berez	בֶּרֶז (ז)
to be clogged up	lehisatem	לְהִיסָּתֵם

tools	klei avoda	כְּלֵי עֲבוֹדָה (ז״ר)
adjustable spanner	maf'teaχ mitkavnen	מַפְתֵּחַ מִתְכַּוֵּון (ז)
to unscrew (lid, filter, etc.)	lif'toaχ	לִפְתּוֹחַ
to screw (tighten)	lehavrig	לְהַבְרִיג

to unclog (vt)	lif'toaχ et hastima	לִפְתּוֹחַ אֶת הַסְּתִימָה
plumber	ʃravrav	שְׁרַבְרַב (ז)
basement	martef	מַרְתֵּף (ז)
sewerage (system)	biyuv	בִּיּוּב (ז)

102. Fire. Conflagration

fire (accident)	srefa	שְׂרֵיפָה (נ)
flame	lehava	לֶהָבָה (נ)
spark	nitsots	נִיצוֹץ (ז)
smoke (from fire)	aʃan	עָשָׁן (ז)
torch (flaming stick)	lapid	לַפִּיד (ז)
campfire	medura	מְדוּרָה (נ)

| petrol | 'delek | דֶּלֶק (ז) |
| paraffin | kerosin | קֵרוֹסִין (ז) |

flammable (adj)	dalik	דָּלִיק
explosive (adj)	nafits	נָפִיץ
NO SMOKING	asur le'aʃen!	אָסוּר לְעַשֵן!

safety	betiχut	בְּטִיחוּת (נ)
danger	sakana	סַכָּנָה (נ)
dangerous (adj)	mesukan	מְסוּכָּן

to catch fire	lehidalek	לְהִידָלֵק
explosion	pitsuts	פִּיצוּץ (ז)
to set fire	lehatsit	לְהַצִּית
arsonist	matsit	מַצִּית (ז)
arson	hatsata	הַצָּתָה (נ)

to blaze (vi)	liv'or	לִבְעוֹר
to burn (be on fire)	la'alot be'eʃ	לַעֲלוֹת בָּאֵש
to burn down	lehisaref	לְהִישָׂרֵף

to call the fire brigade	lehazmin meχabei eʃ	לְהַזְמִין מְכַבֵּי אֵש
firefighter, fireman	kabai	כַּבַּאי (ז)
fire engine	'reχev kibui	רֶכֶב כִּיבּוּי (ז)
fire brigade	meχabei eʃ	מְכַבֵּי אֵש (ז"ר)
fire engine ladder	sulam kaba'im	סוּלָם כַּבָּאִים (ז)

fire hose	zarnuk	זַרְנוּק (ז)
fire extinguisher	mataf	מַטָף (ז)
helmet	kasda	קַסְדָה (נ)
siren	tsofar	צוֹפָר (ז)

to cry (for help)	lits'ok	לִצְעוֹק
to call for help	likro le'ezra	לִקְרוֹא לְעֶזְרָה
rescuer	matsil	מַצִּיל (ז)
to rescue (vt)	lehatsil	לְהַצִּיל

to arrive (vi)	leha'gi'a	לְהַגִּיעַ
to extinguish (vt)	leχabot	לְכַבּוֹת
water	'mayim	מַיִם (ז"ר)
sand	χol	חוֹל (ז)

ruins (destruction)	χoravot	חוֹרְבוֹת (נ"ר)
to collapse (building, etc.)	likros	לִקְרוֹס
to fall down (vi)	likros	לִקְרוֹס
to cave in (ceiling, floor)	lehitmotet	לְהִתְמוֹטֵט

| piece of debris | pisat χoravot | פִּיסַת חוֹרְבוֹת (נ) |
| ash | 'efer | אֵפֶר (ז) |

| to suffocate (die) | lehiχanek | לְהֵיחָנֵק |
| to be killed (perish) | lehihareg | לְהֵיהָרֵג |

HUMAN ACTIVITIES

Job. Business. Part 1

103. Office. Working in the office

office (company ~)	misrad	מִשְׂרָד (ז)
office (of director, etc.)	misrad	מִשְׂרָד (ז)
reception desk	kabala	קַבָּלָה (נ)
secretary	mazkir	מַזְכִּיר (ז)
secretary (fem.)	mazkira	מַזְכִּירָה (נ)
director	menahel	מְנַהֵל (ז)
manager	menahel	מְנַהֵל (ז)
accountant	menahel xeʃbonot	מְנַהֵל חֶשְׁבּוֹנוֹת (ז)
employee	oved	עוֹבֵד (ז)
furniture	rehitim	רָהִיטִים (ז"ר)
desk	ʃulxan	שׁוּלְחָן (ז)
desk chair	kursa	כּוּרְסָה (נ)
drawer unit	ʃidat megerot	שִׁידַת מְגֵירוֹת (נ)
coat stand	mitle	מִתְלֶה (ז)
computer	maxʃev	מַחְשֵׁב (ז)
printer	mad'peset	מַדְפֶּסֶת (נ)
fax machine	faks	פַקְס (ז)
photocopier	mexonat tsilum	מְכוֹנַת צִילוּם (נ)
paper	neyar	נְיָיר (ז)
office supplies	tsiyud misradi	צִיוּד מִשְׂרָדִי (ז)
mouse mat	ʃa'tiax le'axbar	שְׁטִיחַ לְעַכְבָּר (ז)
sheet of paper	daf	דַף (ז)
binder	klaser	קְלַסֵר (ז)
catalogue	katalog	קָטָלוֹג (ז)
phone directory	madrix 'telefon	מַדְרִיך טֶלֶפוֹן (ז)
documentation	ti'ud	תִיעוּד (ז)
brochure (e.g. 12 pages ~)	xo'veret	חוֹבֶרֶת (נ)
leaflet (promotional ~)	alon	עָלוֹן (ז)
sample	dugma	דוּגְמָה (נ)
training meeting	yeʃivat hadraxa	יְשִׁיבַת הַדְרָכָה (נ)
meeting (of managers)	yeʃiva	יְשִׁיבָה (נ)
lunch time	hafsakat tsaha'rayim	הַפְסָקַת צָהֳרַיִים (נ)
to make a copy	letsalem mismax	לְצַלֵם מִסְמָך
to make multiple copies	lehaxin mispar otakim	לְהָכִין מִסְפָּר עוֹתָקִים
to receive a fax	lekabel faks	לְקַבֵּל פַקְס
to send a fax	liʃloax faks	לִשְׁלוֹחַ פַקְס

to call (by phone)	lehitkaʃer	לְהִתְקַשֵּׁר
to answer (vt)	la'anot	לַעֲנוֹת
to put through	lekaʃer	לְקַשֵּׁר

to arrange, to set up	lik'bo'a pgiʃa	לִקְבּוֹעַ פְּגִישָׁה
to demonstrate (vt)	lehadgim	לְהַדְגִּים
to be absent	lehe'ader	לְהֵיעָדֵר
absence	he'adrut	הֵיעָדְרוּת (נ)

104. Business processes. Part 1

business	'esek	עֵסֶק (ז)
occupation	isuk	עִיסוּק (ז)
firm	xevra	חֶבְרָה (נ)
company	xevra	חֶבְרָה (נ)
corporation	ta'agid	תַּאֲגִיד (ז)
enterprise	'esek	עֵסֶק (ז)
agency	soxnut	סוֹכְנוּת (נ)

agreement (contract)	heskem	הֶסְכֵּם (ז)
contract	xoze	חוֹזֶה (ז)
deal	iska	עִסְקָה (נ)
order (to place an ~)	hazmana	הַזְמָנָה (נ)
terms (of the contract)	tnai	תְּנַאי (ז)

wholesale (adv)	besitonut	בְּסִיטוֹנוּת
wholesale (adj)	sitona'i	סִיטוֹנָאִי
wholesale (n)	sitonut	סִיטוֹנוּת (נ)
retail (adj)	kim'oni	קִמְעוֹנִי
retail (n)	kim'onut	קִמְעוֹנוּת (נ)

competitor	mitxare	מִתְחָרֶה (ז)
competition	taxarut	תַּחֲרוּת (נ)
to compete (vi)	lehitxarot	לְהִתְחָרוֹת

| partner (associate) | ʃutaf | שׁוּתָף (ז) |
| partnership | ʃutafa | שׁוּתָפוּת (נ) |

crisis	maʃber	מַשְׁבֵּר (ז)
bankruptcy	pʃitat 'regel	פְּשִׁיטַת רֶגֶל (נ)
to go bankrupt	lifʃot 'regel	לִפְשׁוֹט רֶגֶל
difficulty	'koʃi	קוֹשִׁי (ז)
problem	be'aya	בְּעָיָה (נ)
catastrophe	ason	אָסוֹן (ז)

economy	kalkala	כַּלְכָּלָה (נ)
economic (~ growth)	kalkali	כַּלְכָּלִי
economic recession	mitun kalkali	מִיתוּן כַּלְכָּלִי (ז)

| goal (aim) | matara | מַטָּרָה (נ) |
| task | mesima | מְשִׂימָה (נ) |

| to trade (vi) | lisxor | לִסְחוֹר |
| network (distribution ~) | 'reʃet | רֶשֶׁת (נ) |

inventory (stock)	maxsan	מַחסָן (ז)
range (assortment)	mivxar	מִבחָר (ז)

leader (leading company)	manhig	מַנהִיג (ז)
large (~ company)	gadol	גָדוֹל
monopoly	'monopol	מוֹנוֹפּוֹל (ז)

theory	te''orya	תִיאוֹריָה (נ)
practice	'praktika	פּרַקטִיקָה (נ)
experience (in my ~)	nisayon	נִיסיוֹן (ז)
trend (tendency)	megama	מְגַמָה (נ)
development	pi'tuax	פִּיתוּחַ (ז)

105. Business processes. Part 2

profit (foregone ~)	'revax	רֶווַח (ז)
profitable (~ deal)	rivxi	רִווחִי

delegation (group)	miʃ'laxat	מִשלַחַת (נ)
salary	mas'koret	מַשכּוֹרֶת (נ)
to correct (an error)	letaken	לְתַקֵן
business trip	nesi'a batafkid	נְסִיעָה בַּתַפקִיד (נ)
commission	amla	עַמלָה (נ)

to control (vt)	liʃlot	לִשלוֹט
conference	kinus	כִּינוּס (ז)
licence	riʃayon	רִישָיוֹן (ז)
reliable (~ partner)	amin	אָמִין

initiative (undertaking)	yozma	יוֹזמָה (נ)
norm (standard)	'norma	נוֹרמָה (נ)
circumstance	nesibot	נְסִיבּוֹת (נ״ר)
duty (of employee)	xova	חוֹבָה (נ)

organization (company)	irgun	אִרגוּן (ז)
organization (process)	hit'argenut	הִתאַרגְנוּת (נ)
organized (adj)	me'urgan	מְאוּרגָן
cancellation	bitul	בִּיטוּל (ז)
to cancel (call off)	levatel	לְבַטֵל
report (official ~)	dox	דוֹחַ (ז)

patent	patent	פָּטֶנט (ז)
to patent (obtain patent)	lirʃom patent	לִרשוֹם פָּטֶנט
to plan (vt)	letaxnen	לְתַכנֵן

bonus (money)	'bonus	בּוֹנוּס (ז)
professional (adj)	miktso'i	מִקצוֹעִי
procedure	'nohal	נוֹהַל (ז)

to examine (contract, etc.)	livxon	לִבחוֹן
calculation	xiʃuv	חִישוּב (ז)
reputation	monitin	מוֹנִיטִין (ז״ר)
risk	sikun	סִיכּוּן (ז)
to manage, to run	lenahel	לְנַהֵל

information	meida	מֵידָע (ז)
property	ba'alut	בַּעֲלוּת (נ)
union	igud	אִיגוּד (ז)

life insurance	bi'tuax xayim	בִּיטוּחַ חַיִּים (ז)
to insure (vt)	leva'teax	לְבַטֵּחַ
insurance	bi'tuax	בִּיטוּחַ (ז)

auction (~ sale)	mexira 'pombit	מְכִירָה פּוּמְבִּית (נ)
to notify (inform)	leho'dia	לְהוֹדִיעַ
management (process)	nihul	נִיהוּל (ז)
service (~ industry)	ʃirut	שֵׁירוּת (ז)

forum	'forum	פוֹרוּם (ז)
to function (vi)	letafked	לְתַפְקֵד
stage (phase)	ʃalav	שָׁלָב (ז)
legal (~ services)	miʃpati	מִשְׁפָּטִי
lawyer (legal advisor)	orex din	עוֹרֵךְ דִּין (ז)

106. Production. Works

plant	mif'al	מִפְעָל (ז)
factory	beit xa'roʃet	בֵּית חֲרוֹשֶׁת (ז)
workshop	agaf	אֲגָף (ז)
works, production site	mif'al	מִפְעָל (ז)

industry (manufacturing)	ta'asiya	תַּעֲשִׂיָּיה (נ)
industrial (adj)	ta'asiyati	תַּעֲשִׂיָּיתִי
heavy industry	ta'asiya kveda	תַּעֲשִׂיָּיה כְּבֵדָה (נ)
light industry	ta'asiya kala	תַּעֲשִׂיָּיה קַלָּה (נ)

products	to'tseret	תּוֹצֶרֶת (נ)
to produce (vt)	leyatser	לְיַיצֵּר
raw materials	'xomer 'gelem	חוֹמֶר גֶּלֶם (ז)

foreman (construction ~)	menahel avoda	מְנַהֵל עֲבוֹדָה (ז)
workers team (crew)	'tsevet ovdim	צֶוֶות עוֹבְדִים (ז)
worker	po'el	פּוֹעֵל (ז)

working day	yom avoda	יוֹם עֲבוֹדָה (ז)
pause (rest break)	hafsaka	הַפְסָקָה (נ)
meeting	yeʃiva	יְשִׁיבָה (נ)
to discuss (vt)	ladun	לָדוּן

plan	toxnit	תּוֹכְנִית (נ)
to fulfil the plan	leva'tse'a et hatoxnit	לְבַצֵּעַ אֶת הַתּוֹכְנִית
rate of output	'ketsev tfuka	קֶצֶב תְּפוּקָה (ז)
quality	eixut	אֵיכוּת (נ)
control (checking)	bakara	בַּקָּרָה (נ)
quality control	bakarat eixut	בַּקָּרַת אֵיכוּת (נ)

workplace safety	betixut beavoda	בְּטִיחוּת בָּעֲבוֹדָה (נ)
discipline	miʃma'at	מִשְׁמַעַת (נ)
violation (of safety rules, etc.)	hafara	הָפָרָה (נ)

to violate (rules)	lehafer	לְהָפֵר
strike	ʃvita	שְׁבִיתָה (נ)
striker	ʃovet	שׁוֹבֵת (ז)
to be on strike	liʃbot	לִשְׁבּוֹת
trade union	igud ovdim	אִיגוּד עוֹבְדִים (ז)

to invent (machine, etc.)	lehamtsi	לְהַמְצִיא
invention	hamtsa'a	הַמְצָאָה (נ)
research	meχkar	מֶחְקָר (ז)
to improve (make better)	leʃaper	לְשַׁפֵּר
technology	teχno'logya	טֶכְנוֹלוֹגְיָה (נ)
technical drawing	sirtut	שִׂרְטוּט (ז)

load, cargo	mit'an	מִטְעָן (ז)
loader (person)	sabal	סַבָּל (ז)
to load (vehicle, etc.)	leha'amis	לְהַעֲמִיס
loading (process)	ha'amasa	הַעֲמָסָה (נ)
to unload (vi, vt)	lifrok mit'an	לִפְרוֹק מִטְעָן
unloading	prika	פְּרִיקָה (נ)

transport	hovala	הוֹבָלָה (נ)
transport company	χevrat hovala	חֶבְרַת הוֹבָלָה (נ)
to transport (vt)	lehovil	לְהוֹבִיל

wagon	karon	קָרוֹן (ז)
tank (e.g., oil ~)	meχalit	מֵיכָלִית (נ)
lorry	masa'it	מַשָּׂאִית (נ)

| machine tool | meχonat ibud | מְכוֹנַת עִיבּוּד (נ) |
| mechanism | manganon | מַנְגָּנוֹן (ז) |

industrial waste	'psolet ta'asiyatit	פְּסוֹלֶת תַּעֲשִׂייָתִית (נ)
packing (process)	ariza	אֲרִיזָה (נ)
to pack (vt)	le'eroz	לֶאֱרוֹז

107. Contract. Agreement

contract	χoze	חוֹזֶה (ז)
agreement	heskem	הֶסְכֵּם (ז)
addendum	'sefaχ	סֶפַח (ז)

to sign a contract	la'aroχ heskem	לַעֲרוֹךְ הֶסְכֵּם
signature	χatima	חֲתִימָה (נ)
to sign (vt)	laχtom	לַחְתּוֹם
seal (stamp)	χo'temet	חוֹתֶמֶת (נ)

subject of contract	nose haχoze	נוֹשֵׂא הַחוֹזֶה (ז)
clause	se'if	סָעִיף (ז)
parties (in contract)	tsdadim	צְדָדִים (ז"ר)
legal address	'ktovet miʃpatit	כְּתוֹבֶת מִשְׁפָּטִית (נ)

to violate the contract	lehafer χoze	לְהָפֵר חוֹזֶה
commitment (obligation)	hitχaivut	הִתְחַייְבוּת (נ)
responsibility	aχrayut	אַחְרָיוּת (נ)

force majeure	'koaχ elyon	כֹּוֹחַ עֶלְיוֹן (ז)
dispute	vi'kuaχ	וִיכּוּחַ (ז)
penalties	itsumim	עִיצוּמִים (ז"ר)

108. Import & Export

import	ye'vu'a	יְבוּא (ז)
importer	yevu'an	יְבוּאָן (ז)
to import (vt)	leyabe	לְיַבֵּא
import (as adj.)	meyuba	מְיוּבָּא
export (exportation)	yitsu	יִיצוּא (ז)
exporter	yetsu'an	יְצוּאָן (ז)
to export (vi, vt)	leyatse	לְיַצֵּא
export (as adj.)	ʃel yitsu	שֶׁל יִיצוּא
goods (merchandise)	sχora	סְחוֹרָה (נ)
consignment, lot	miʃ'loaχ	מִשְׁלוֹחַ (ז)
weight	miʃkal	מֵשְׁקָל (ז)
volume	'nefaχ	נֶפַח (ז)
cubic metre	'meter me'ukav	מֶטֶר מְעוּקָב (ז)
manufacturer	yatsran	יַצְרָן (ז)
transport company	χevrat hovala	חֶבְרַת הוֹבָלָה (נ)
container	meχula	מְכוּלָה (נ)
border	gvul	גְבוּל (ז)
customs	'meχes	מֶכֶס (ז)
customs duty	mas 'meχes	מַס מֶכֶס (ז)
customs officer	pakid 'meχes	פְּקִיד מֶכֶס (ז)
smuggling	havraχa	הַבְרָחָה (נ)
contraband (smuggled goods)	sχora muv'reχet	סְחוֹרָה מוּבְרַחַת (נ)

109. Finances

share, stock	menaya	מְנָיָה (נ)
bond (certificate)	i'geret χov	אִיגֶּרֶת חוֹב (נ)
promissory note	ʃtar χalifin	שְׁטַר חֲלִיפִין (ז)
stock exchange	'bursa	בּוּרְסָה (נ)
stock price	meχir hamenaya	מְחִיר הַמְנָיָה (ז)
to go down (become cheaper)	la'redet bemeχir	לָרֶדֶת בְּמְחִיר
to go up (become more expensive)	lehityaker	לְהִתְיַיקֵּר
share	menaya	מְנָיָה (נ)
controlling interest	ʃlita	שְׁלִיטָה (נ)
investment	haʃka'ot	הַשְׁקָעוֹת (נ"ר)

to invest (vt)	lehaʃkiʻa	לְהַשְׁקִיעַ
percent	aχuz	אָחוּז (ז)
interest (on investment)	ribit	רִיבִּית (נ)

profit	'revaχ	רֶווַח (ז)
profitable (adj)	rivχi	רִווְחִי
tax	mas	מַס (ז)

currency (foreign ~)	mat'beʻa	מַטְבֵּעַ (ז)
national (adj)	leʻumi	לְאוּמִי
exchange (currency ~)	hamara	הֲמָרָה (נ)

accountant	ro'e χeʃbon	רוֹאֵה חֶשְׁבּוֹן (ז)
accounting	hanhalat χeʃbonot	הַנְהָלַת חֶשְׁבּוֹנוֹת (נ)

bankruptcy	pʃitat 'regel	פְּשִׁיטַת רֶגֶל (נ)
collapse, ruin	krisa	קְרִיסָה (נ)
ruin	pʃitat 'regel	פְּשִׁיטַת רֶגֶל (נ)
to be ruined (financially)	liʃfot 'regel	לִפְשׁוֹט רֶגֶל
inflation	inf'latsya	אִינְפְלַצְיָה (נ)
devaluation	piχut	פִּיחוּת (ז)

capital	hon	הוֹן (ז)
income	haχnasa	הַכְנָסָה (נ)
turnover	maχzor	מַחְזוֹר (ז)
resources	maʃʻabim	מַשְׁאַבִּים (ז"ר)
monetary resources	emtsaʻim kaspiyim	אֶמְצָעִים כַּסְפִּיִים (ז"ר)
overheads	hotsa'ot	הוֹצָאוֹת (נ"ר)
to reduce (expenses)	leʃsamtsem	לְצַמְצֵם

110. Marketing

marketing	ʃivuk	שִׁיווּק (ז)
market	ʃuk	שׁוּק (ז)
market segment	'pelaχ ʃuk	פֶּלַח שׁוּק (ז)
product	mutsar	מוּצָר (ז)
goods (merchandise)	sχora	סְחוֹרָה (נ)

brand	mutag	מוּתָג (ז)
trademark	'semel misχari	סֵמֶל מִסְחָרִי (ז)
logotype	'semel haχevra	סֵמֶל הַחֶבְרָה (ז)
logo	'logo	לוֹגוֹ (ז)
demand	bikuʃ	בִּיקוּשׁ (ז)
supply	he'tseʻa	הֶיצֵעַ (ז)
need	'tsoreχ	צוֹרֶךְ (ז)
consumer	tsarχan	צַרְכָן (ז)

analysis	ni'tuaχ	נִיתוּחַ (ז)
to analyse (vt)	lena'teaχ	לְנַתֵחַ
positioning	mitsuv	מִיצוּב (ז)
to position (vt)	lematsev	לְמַצֵב
price	meχir	מְחִיר (ז)
pricing policy	mediniyut timχur	מְדִינִיוּת תָמְחוּר (נ)
price formation	hamχara	הַמְחָרָה (נ)

111. Advertising

advertising	pirsum	פַּרְסוּם (ז)
to advertise (vt)	lefarsem	לְפַרְסֵם
budget	taktsiv	תַּקְצִיב (ז)
ad, advertisement	pir'somet	פִּרְסוֹמֶת (נ)
TV advertising	pir'somet tele'vizya	פִּרְסוֹמֶת טֶלֶוִוּיזְיָה (נ)
radio advertising	pir'somet 'radyo	פִּרְסוֹמֶת רַדְיוֹ (נ)
outdoor advertising	pirsum xutsot	פַּרְסוּם חוּצוֹת (ז)
mass medias	emtsa'ei tik'sforet hamonim	אֶמְצָעֵי תִקְשוֹרֶת הָמוֹנִים (ז"ר)
periodical (n)	ktav et	כְּתַב עֵת (ז)
image (public appearance)	tadmit	תַּדְמִית (נ)
slogan	sisma	סִיסְמָה (נ)
motto (maxim)	'moto	מוֹטוֹ (ז)
campaign	masa	מַסָע (ז)
advertising campaign	masa pirsum	מַסָע פַּרְסוּם (ז)
target group	oxlusiyat 'ya'ad	אוֹכְלוּסִיַת יַעַד (נ)
business card	kartis bikur	כַּרְטִיס בִּיקוּר (ז)
leaflet (promotional ~)	alon	עָלוֹן (ז)
brochure (e.g. 12 pages ~)	xo'veret	חוֹבֶרֶת (נ)
pamphlet	alon	עָלוֹן (ז)
newsletter	alon meida	עָלוֹן מֵידָע (ז)
signboard (store sign, etc.)	'felet	שֶׁלֶט (ז)
poster	'poster	פּוֹסְטֶר (ז)
hoarding	'luax pirsum	לוּחַ פַּרְסוּם (ז)

112. Banking

bank	bank	בַּנְק (ז)
branch (of bank, etc.)	snif	סְנִיף (ז)
consultant	yo'ets	יוֹעֵץ (ז)
manager (director)	menahel	מְנַהֵל (ז)
bank account	xefbon	חֶשְׁבּוֹן (ז)
account number	mispar xefbon	מִסְפַּר חֶשְׁבּוֹן (ז)
current account	xefbon over vafav	חֶשְׁבּוֹן עוֹבֵר וָשָׁב (ז)
deposit account	xefbon xisaxon	חֶשְׁבּוֹן חִסָכוֹן (ז)
to open an account	lif'toax xefbon	לִפְתוֹחַ חֶשְׁבּוֹן
to close the account	lisgor xefbon	לִסְגוֹר חֶשְׁבּוֹן
to deposit into the account	lehafkid lexefbon	לְהַפְקִיד לְחֶשְׁבּוֹן
to withdraw (vt)	limfox mexefbon	לִמְשׁוֹךְ מֵחֶשְׁבּוֹן
deposit	pikadon	פִּיקָדוֹן (ז)
to make a deposit	lehafkid	לְהַפְקִיד
wire transfer	ha'avara banka'it	הַעֲבָרָה בַּנְקָאִית (נ)

to wire, to transfer	leha'avir 'kesef	לְהַעֲבִיר כָּסֶף
sum	sχum	סכום (ז)
How much?	'kama?	כַּמָה?

| signature | χatima | חֲתִימָה (נ) |
| to sign (vt) | laχtom | לַחתוֹם |

credit card	kartis aʃrai	כַּרטִיס אַשׁרַאי (ז)
code (PIN code)	kod	קוֹד (ז)
credit card number	mispar kartis aʃrai	מִספַּר כַּרטִיס אַשׁרַאי (ז)
cashpoint	kaspomat	כַּספּוֹמָט (ז)

cheque	tʃek	צֶ'ק (ז)
to write a cheque	liχtov tʃek	לִכתוֹב צֶ'ק
chequebook	pinkas 'tʃekim	פִּנקַס צֶ'קִים (ז)

loan (bank ~)	halva'a	הַלוָואָה (נ)
to apply for a loan	levakeʃ halva'a	לְבַקֵשׁ הַלוָואָה
to get a loan	lekabel halva'a	לְקַבֵּל הַלוָואָה
to give a loan	lehalvot	לְהַלווֹת
guarantee	arvut	עַרבוּת (נ)

113. Telephone. Phone conversation

telephone	'telefon	טֶלֶפוֹן (ז)
mobile phone	'telefon nayad	טֶלֶפוֹן נַייָד (ז)
answerphone	meʃivon	מְשִׁיבוֹן (ז)

| to call (by phone) | letsaltsel | לְצַלצֵל |
| call, ring | siχat 'telefon | שִׂיחַת טֶלֶפוֹן (נ) |

to dial a number	leχayeg mispar	לְחַייֵג מִספָּר
Hello!	'halo!	הַלוֹ!
to ask (vt)	liʃol	לִשׁאוֹל
to answer (vi, vt)	la'anot	לַעֲנוֹת
to hear (vt)	liʃmo'a	לִשׁמוֹעַ
well (adv)	tov	טוֹב
not well (adv)	lo tov	לא טוֹב
noises (interference)	hafra'ot	הַפרָעוֹת (נ"ר)

receiver	ʃfo'feret	שׁפוֹפֶרֶת (נ)
to pick up (~ the phone)	leharim ʃfo'feret	לְהָרִים שׁפוֹפֶרֶת
to hang up (~ the phone)	leha'niaχ ʃfo'feret	לְהַנִיחַ שׁפוֹפֶרֶת

busy (engaged)	tafus	תָפוּס
to ring (ab. phone)	letsaltsel	לְצַלצֵל
telephone book	'sefer tele'fonim	סֵפֶר טֶלֶפוֹנִים (ז)

local (adj)	mekomi	מְקוֹמִי
local call	siχa mekomit	שִׂיחָה מְקוֹמִית (נ)
trunk (e.g. ~ call)	bein ironi	בֵּין עִירוֹנִי
trunk call	siχa bein ironit	שִׂיחָה בֵּין עִירוֹנִית (נ)
international (adj)	benle'umi	בֵּינלְאוּמִי
international call	siχa benle'umit	שִׂיחָה בֵּינלְאוּמִית (נ)

114. Mobile telephone

mobile phone	'telefon nayad	טֶלֶפוֹן נַיָּד (ז)
display	masax	מָסָךְ (ז)
button	kaftor	כַּפְתוֹר (ז)
SIM card	kartis sim	כַּרְטִיס סִים (ז)
battery	solela	סוֹלְלָה (נ)
to be flat (battery)	lehitroken	לְהִתְרוֹקֵן
charger	mit'an	מִטְעָן (ז)
menu	tafrit	תַּפְרִיט (ז)
settings	hagdarot	הַגְדָּרוֹת (נ"ר)
tune (melody)	mangina	מַנְגִּינָה (נ)
to select (vt)	livxor	לִבְחוֹר
calculator	maxʃevon	מַחְשְׁבוֹן (ז)
voice mail	ta koli	תָּא קוֹלִי (ז)
alarm clock	ʃa'on me'orer	שָׁעוֹן מְעוֹרֵר (ז)
contacts	anʃei 'keʃer	אַנְשֵׁי קֶשֶׁר (ז"ר)
SMS (text message)	misron	מִסְרוֹן (ז)
subscriber	manui	מָנוּי (ז)

115. Stationery

ballpoint pen	et kaduri	עֵט כַּדּוּרִי (ז)
fountain pen	et no've'a	עֵט נוֹבֵעַ (ז)
pencil	iparon	עִיפָּרוֹן (ז)
highlighter	'marker	מַרְקֵר (ז)
felt-tip pen	tuʃ	טוּשׁ (ז)
notepad	pinkas	פִּנְקָס (ז)
diary	yoman	יוֹמָן (ז)
ruler	sargel	סַרְגֵּל (ז)
calculator	maxʃevon	מַחְשְׁבוֹן (ז)
rubber	'maxak	מַחַק (ז)
drawing pin	'na'ats	נַעַץ (ז)
paper clip	mehadek	מְהַדֵּק (ז)
glue	'devek	דֶּבֶק (ז)
stapler	ʃadxan	שַׁדְכָן (ז)
hole punch	menakev	מְנַקֵּב (ז)
pencil sharpener	maxded	מַחְדֵּד (ז)

116. Various kinds of documents

account (report)	dox	דּוֹחַ (ז)
agreement	heskem	הֶסְכֵּם (ז)

application form	'tofes bakaʃa	טוֹפֶס בַּקָשָׁה (ז)
authentic (adj)	mekori	מְקוֹרִי
badge (identity tag)	tag	תָג (ז)
business card	kartis bikur	פַּרְטִיס בִּיקוּר (ז)

certificate (~ of quality)	te'uda	תְּעוּדָה (נ)
cheque (e.g. draw a ~)	tʃek	צֶ'ק (ז)
bill (in restaurant)	xeʃbon	חֶשְׁבּוֹן (ז)
constitution	xuka	חוּקָה (נ)

contract (agreement)	xoze	חוֹזֶה (ז)
copy	'otek	עוֹתֶק (ז)
copy (of contract, etc.)	'otek	עוֹתֶק (ז)

customs declaration	hatsharat mexes	הַצְהָרַת מֶכֶס (נ)
document	mismax	מִסְמָךְ (ז)
driving licence	riʃyon nehiga	רִשְׁיוֹן נְהִיגָה (ז)
addendum	to'sefet	תּוֹסֶפֶת (נ)
form	'tofes	טוֹפֶס (ז)

ID card (e.g., warrant card)	te'uda mezaha	תְּעוּדָה מְזַהָה (נ)
inquiry (request)	xakira	חֲקִירָה (נ)
invitation card	kartis hazmana	פַּרְטִיס הַזְמָנָה (ז)
invoice	xeʃbonit	חֶשְׁבּוֹנִית (נ)

law	xok	חוֹק (ז)
letter (mail)	mixtav	מִכְתָּב (ז)
letterhead	neyar 'logo	נְיָיר לוֹגוֹ (ז)
list (of names, etc.)	reʃima	רְשִׁימָה (נ)
manuscript	ktav yad	כְּתַב יָד (ז)
newsletter	alon meida	עָלוֹן מֵידָע (ז)
note (short letter)	'petek	פֶּתֶק (ז)

pass (for worker, visitor)	iʃur knisa	אִישׁוּר כְּנִיסָה (ז)
passport	darkon	דַּרְכּוֹן (ז)
permit	riʃayon	רִשָׁיוֹן (ז)
curriculum vitae, CV	korot xayim	קוֹרוֹת חַיִּים (נ״ר)
debt note, IOU	ʃtar xov	שְׁטַר חוֹב (ז)
receipt (for purchase)	kabala	קַבָּלָה (נ)

| till receipt | tʃek | צֶ'ק (ז) |
| report (mil.) | dox | דּוֹח (ז) |

to show (ID, etc.)	lehatsig	לְהַצִּיג
to sign (vt)	laxtom	לַחְתּוֹם
signature	xatima	חֲתִימָה (נ)
seal (stamp)	xo'temet	חוֹתֶמֶת (נ)

| text | tekst | טֶקְסְט (ז) |
| ticket (for entry) | kartis | פַּרְטִיס (ז) |

| to cross out | limxok | לִמְחוֹק |
| to fill in (~ a form) | lemale | לְמַלֵּא |

| waybill (shipping invoice) | ʃtar mit'an | שְׁטַר מִטְעָן (ז) |
| will (testament) | tsava'a | צָוָּאָה (נ) |

117. Kinds of business

accounting services	ʃerutei hanhalat xeʃbonot	שֵׁירוּתֵי הַנְהָלַת חֶשְׁבּוֹנוֹת (ז"ר)
advertising	pirsum	פִּרְסוּם (ז)
advertising agency	soxnut pirsum	סוֹכְנוּת פִּרְסוּם (נ)
air-conditioners	mazganim	מַזְגָנִים (ז"ר)
airline	xevrat te'ufa	חֶבְרַת תְּעוּפָה (נ)
alcoholic beverages	maʃka'ot xarifim	מַשְׁקָאוֹת חֲרִיפִים (נ"ר)
antiques (antique dealers)	atikot	עַתִּיקוֹת (נ"ר)
art gallery (contemporary ~)	ga'lerya le'amanut	גָלֶרְיָה לְאָמָּנוּת (נ)
audit services	ʃerutei bi'koret xeʃbonot	שֵׁירוּתֵי בִּיקוֹרֶת חֶשְׁבּוֹנוֹת (ז"ר)
banking industry	banka'ut	בַּנְקָאוּת (נ)
beauty salon	mexon 'yofi	מְכוֹן יוֹפִי (ז)
bookshop	xanut sfarim	חָנוּת סְפָרִים (נ)
brewery	miv'ʃelet 'bira	מִבְשֶׁלֶת בִּירָה (נ)
business centre	merkaz asakim	מֶרְכַּז עֲסָקִים (ז)
business school	beit 'sefer le'asakim	בֵּית סֵפֶר לַעֲסָקִים (ז)
casino	ka'zino	קָזִינוֹ (ז)
chemist, pharmacy	beit mir'kaxat	בֵּית מִרְקַחַת (ז)
cinema	kol'no‘a	קוֹלְנוֹעַ (ז)
construction	bniya	בְּנִיָה (נ)
consulting	yi'uts	יִיעוּץ (ז)
dental clinic	mirpa'at ʃi'nayim	מִרְפָּאַת שִׁינַיִים (נ)
design	itsuv	עִיצוּב (ז)
dry cleaners	nikui yaveʃ	נִיקוּי יָבֵשׁ (ז)
employment agency	soxnut 'koax adam	סוֹכְנוּת כּוֹחַ אָדָם (נ)
financial services	ʃerutim fi'nansim	שֵׁירוּתִים פִינַנְסִיים (ז"ר)
food products	mutsrei mazon	מוּצְרֵי מָזוֹן (ז"ר)
furniture (e.g. house ~)	rehitim	רָהִיטִים (ז"ר)
clothing, garment	bgadim	בְּגָדִים (ז"ר)
hotel	beit malon	בֵּית מָלוֹן (ז)
ice-cream	'glida	גְלִידָה (נ)
industry (manufacturing)	ta‘asiya	תַּעֲשִׂיָה (נ)
insurance	bi'tuax	בִּיטוּחַ (ז)
Internet	'internet	אִינְטֶרְנֶט (ז)
investments (finance)	haʃka'ot	הַשְׁקָעוֹת (נ"ר)
jeweller	tsoref	צוֹרֵף (ז)
jewellery	taxʃitim	תַּכְשִׁיטִים (ז"ר)
laundry (shop)	mixbasa	מִכְבָּסָה (נ)
legal adviser	yo‘ets miʃpati	יוֹעֵץ מִשְׁפָּטִי (ז)
light industry	ta‘asiya kala	תַּעֲשִׂיָה קַלָּה (נ)
magazine	ʒurnal	ז'וּרְנָל (ז)
mail-order selling	mexira be'do'ar	מְכִירָה בְּדוֹאַר (נ)
medicine	refu'a	רְפוּאָה (נ)
museum	muze'on	מוּזֵיאוֹן (ז)
news agency	soxnut yedi‘ot	סוֹכְנוּת יְדִיעוֹת (נ)
newspaper	iton	עִיתּוֹן (ז)

nightclub	mo'adon 'laila	מוֹעֲדוֹן לַיְלָה (ז)
oil (petroleum)	neft	נֶפְט (ז)
courier services	ʃirut ʃliχim	שֵׁירוּת שְׁלִיחִים (ז)
pharmaceutics	rokχut	רוֹקְחוּת (נ)
printing (industry)	beit dfus	בֵּית דְפוּס (ז)
pub	- bar	בָּר (ז)
publishing house	hotsa'a la'or	הוֹצָאָה לָאוֹר (נ)

radio (~ station)	'radyo	רַדְיוֹ (ז)
real estate	nadlan	נַדְלַ"ן (ז)
restaurant	mis'ada	מִסְעָדָה (נ)

security company	χevrat ʃmira	חֶבְרַת שְׁמִירָה (נ)
shop	χanut	חָנוּת (נ)
sport	sport	סְפּוֹרְט (ז)
stock exchange	'bursa	בּוּרְסָה (נ)
supermarket	super'market	סוּפֶּרְמַרְקֶט (ז)
swimming pool (public ~)	breχat sχiya	בְּרֵיכַת שְׂחִיָה (נ)

tailor shop	mitpara	מִתְפָּרָה (נ)
television	tele'vizya	טֶלֶווִיזְיָה (נ)
theatre	te'atron	תֵיאַטְרוֹן (ז)
trade (commerce)	misχar	מִסְחָר (ז)
transport companies	hovalot	הוֹבָלוֹת (נ"ר)
travel	tayarut	תַיָירוּת (נ)

undertakers	beit levayot	בֵּית לְוָויוֹת (ז)
veterinary surgeon	veterinar	וֶטֶרִינָר (ז)
warehouse	maχsan	מַחְסָן (ז)
waste collection	isuf 'zevel	אִיסוּף זֶבֶל (ז)

Job. Business. Part 2

118. Show. Exhibition

exhibition, show	ta'aruxa	חֲעָרוּכָה (נ)
trade show	ta'aruxa misxarit	חֲעָרוּכָה מִסְחָרִית (נ)
participation	hiʃtatfut	הִשְׁתַּתְּפוּת (נ)
to participate (vi)	lehiʃtatef	לְהִשְׁתַּתֵּף
participant (exhibitor)	miʃtatef	מִשְׁתַּתֵּף (ז)
director	menahel	מְנַהֵל (ז)
organizers' office	misrad hame'argenim	מִשְׂרַד הַמְּאַרְגְּנִים (ז)
organizer	me'argen	מְאַרְגֵּן (ז)
to organize (vt)	le'argen	לְאַרְגֵּן
participation form	'tofes hiʃtatfut	טוֹפֶס הִשְׁתַּתְּפוּת (ז)
to fill in (vt)	lemale	לְמַלֵּא
details	pratim	פְּרָטִים (ז״ר)
information	meida	מֵידָע (ז)
price (cost, rate)	mexir	מְחִיר (ז)
including	kolel	כּוֹלֵל
to include (vt)	lixlol	לִכְלוֹל
to pay (vi, vt)	leʃalem	לְשַׁלֵּם
registration fee	dmei riʃum	דְּמֵי רִישׁוּם (ז״ר)
entrance	knisa	כְּנִיסָה (נ)
pavilion, hall	bitan	בִּיתָן (ז)
to register (vt)	lirʃom	לִרְשׁוֹם
badge (identity tag)	tag	תָּג (ז)
stand	duxan	דּוּכָן (ז)
to reserve, to book	liʃmor	לִשְׁמוֹר
display case	madaf tetsuga	מַדָּף תְּצוּגָה (ז)
spotlight	menorat spot	מְנוֹרַת סְפּוֹט (נ)
design	itsuv	עִיצוּב (ז)
to place (put, set)	la'arox	לַעֲרוֹךְ
to be placed	lehimatse	לְהִימָצֵא
distributor	mefits	מֵפִיץ (ז)
supplier	sapak	סַפָּק (ז)
to supply (vt)	lesapek	לְסַפֵּק
country	medina	מְדִינָה (נ)
foreign (adj)	mexul	מַחוּ״ל
product	mutsar	מוּצָר (ז)
association	amuta	עֲמוּתָה (נ)
conference hall	ulam knasim	אוּלָם כְּנָסִים (ז)

| congress | kongres | קוֹנגרֶס (ז) |
| contest (competition) | taχarut | תַחֲרוּת (נ) |

visitor (attendee)	mevaker	מְבַקֵר (ז)
to visit (attend)	levaker	לְבַקֵר
customer	la'koaχ	לָקוֹחַ (ז)

119. Mass Media

newspaper	iton	עִיתוֹן (ז)
magazine	ʒurnal	ז'וּרנָל (ז)
press (printed media)	itonut	עִיתוֹנוּת (נ)
radio	'radyo	רַדיוֹ (ז)
radio station	taχanat 'radyo	תַחֲנַת רַדיוֹ (נ)
television	tele'vizya	טֶלֶוִוידִיָה (נ)

presenter, host	manχe	מַנחֶה (ז)
newsreader	karyan	קַריָן (ז)
commentator	parʃan	פַרשָן (ז)

journalist	itonai	עִיתוֹנַאי (ז)
correspondent (reporter)	katav	כַּתָב (ז)
press photographer	tsalam itonut	צַלָם עִיתוֹנוּת (ז)
reporter	katav	כַּתָב (ז)

| editor | oreχ | עוֹרֵךְ (ז) |
| editor-in-chief | oreχ raʃi | עוֹרֵךְ רָאשִי (ז) |

to subscribe (to ...)	lehasdir manui	לְהַסדִיר מָנוּי
subscription	minui	מָנוּי (ז)
subscriber	manui	מָנוּי (ז)
to read (vi, vt)	likro	לִקרוֹא
reader	kore	קוֹרֵא (ז)

circulation (of newspaper)	tfutsa	תפוּצָה (נ)
monthly (adj)	χodʃi	חוֹדשִי
weekly (adj)	ʃvu'i	שבוּעִי
issue (edition)	gilayon	גִילָיוֹן (ז)
new (~ issue)	tari	טָרִי

headline	ko'teret	כּוֹתֶרֶת (נ)
short article	katava ktsara	כַּתָבָה קצָרָה (נ)
column (regular article)	tur	טוּר (ז)
article	ma'amar	מַאֲמָר (ז)
page	amud	עַמוּד (ז)

reportage, report	katava	כַּתָבָה (נ)
event (happening)	ei'ru'a	אֵירוּעַ (ז)
sensation (news)	sen'satsya	סֶנסַציָה (נ)
scandal	ʃa'aruriya	שַעֲרוּרִיָיה (נ)
scandalous (adj)	meviʃ	מֵבִיש
great (~ scandal)	gadol	גָדוֹל
programme (e.g. cooking ~)	toχnit	תוֹכנִית (נ)
interview	ra'ayon	רַאֲיוֹן (ז)

| live broadcast | ʃidur χai | שִׁידוּר חַי (ז) |
| channel | aruts | עָרוּץ (ז) |

120. Agriculture

agriculture	χakla'ut	חַקְלָאוּת (נ)
peasant (masc.)	ikar	אִיכָּר (ז)
peasant (fem.)	χakla'ut	חַקְלָאִית (נ)
farmer	χavai	חַוַּאי (ז)

| tractor | 'traktor | טְרַקְטוֹר (ז) |
| combine, harvester | kombain | קוֹמְבַּיין (ז) |

plough	maχreʃa	מַחְרֵשָׁה (נ)
to plough (vi, vt)	laχaroʃ	לַחֲרוֹשׁ
ploughland	sade χaruʃ	שָׂדֶה חָרוּשׁ (ז)
furrow (in field)	'telem	תֶּלֶם (ז)

to sow (vi, vt)	liz'ro'a	לִזְרוֹעַ
seeder	mazre'a	מַזְרֵעָה (נ)
sowing (process)	zri'a	זְרִיעָה (נ)

| scythe | χermeʃ | חֶרְמֵשׁ (ז) |
| to mow, to scythe | liktsor | לִקְצוֹר |

| spade (tool) | et | אֵת (ז) |
| to till (vt) | leta'teaχ | לְתַתֵּחַ |

hoe	ma'ader	מַעְדֵּר (ז)
to hoe, to weed	lenakeʃ	לְנַכֵּשׁ
weed (plant)	'esev ʃote	עֵשֶׂב שׁוֹטֶה (ז)

watering can	maʃpeχ	מַשְׁפֵּךְ (ז)
to water (plants)	lehaʃkot	לְהַשְׁקוֹת
watering (act)	haʃkaya	הַשְׁקָיָה (נ)

| pitchfork | kilʃon | קִלְשׁוֹן (ז) |
| rake | magrefa | מַגְרֵפָה (נ) |

fertiliser	'deʃen	דֶּשֶׁן (ז)
to fertilise (vt)	ledaʃen	לְדַשֵּׁן
manure (fertiliser)	'zevel	זֶבֶל (ז)

field	sade	שָׂדֶה (ז)
meadow	aχu	אָחוּ (ז)
vegetable garden	gan yarak	גַּן יָרָק (ז)
orchard (e.g. apple ~)	bustan	בּוּסְתָּן (ז)

to graze (vt)	lir'ot	לִרְעוֹת
herdsman	ro'e tson	רוֹעֶה צֹאן (ז)
pasture	mir'e	מִרְעֶה (ז)

| cattle breeding | gidul bakar | גִּידּוּל בָּקָר (ז) |
| sheep farming | gidul kvasim | גִּידּוּל כְּבָשִׂים (ז) |

plantation	mata	מַטָּע (ז)
row (garden bed ~s)	aruga	עֲרוּגָה (נ)
hothouse	χamama	חֲמָמָה (נ)

drought (lack of rain)	ba'tsoret	בַּצֹּרֶת (נ)
dry (~ summer)	yaveʃ	יָבֵשׁ

grain	tvu'a	תְבוּאָה (נ)
cereal crops	gidulei dagan	גִּידוּלֵי דָּגָן (ז"ר)
to harvest, to gather	liktof	לִקְטוֹף

miller (person)	toχen	טוֹחֵן (ז)
mill (e.g. gristmill)	taχanat 'kemaχ	טַחֲנַת קֶמַח (נ)
to grind (grain)	litχon	לִטְחוֹן
flour	'kemaχ	קֶמַח (ז)
straw	kaʃ	קַשׁ (ז)

121. Building. Building process

building site	atar bniya	אֲתַר בְּנִיָּה (ז)
to build (vt)	livnot	לִבְנוֹת
building worker	banai	בַּנַאי (ז)

project	proyekt	פְּרוֹיֶקְט (ז)
architect	adriχal	אַדְרִיכָל (ז)
worker	po'el	פּוֹעֵל (ז)

foundations (of a building)	yesodot	יְסוֹדוֹת (ז"ר)
roof	gag	גַּג (ז)
foundation pile	amud yesod	עַמּוּד יְסוֹד (ז)
wall	kir	קִיר (ז)

reinforcing bars	mot χizuk	מוֹט חִיזּוּק (ז)
scaffolding	pigumim	פִּיגּוּמִים (ז"ר)

concrete	beton	בֶּטוֹן (ז)
granite	granit	גְּרָנִיט (ז)
stone	'even	אֶבֶן (נ)
brick	levena	לְבֵנָה (נ)

sand	χol	חוֹל (ז)
cement	'melet	מֶלֶט (ז)
plaster (for walls)	'tiaχ	טִיחַ (ז)
to plaster (vt)	leta'yeaχ	לְטַיֵּחַ
paint	'tseva	צֶבַע (ז)
to paint (~ a wall)	lits'bo'a	לִצְבּוֹעַ
barrel	χavit	חָבִית (נ)

crane	aguran	עֲגוּרָן (ז)
to lift, to hoist (vt)	lehanif	לְהָנִיף
to lower (vt)	lehorid	לְהוֹרִיד

bulldozer	daχpor	דַּחְפּוֹר (ז)
excavator	maχper	מַחְפֵּר (ז)

scoop, bucket	ʃa'ov	שְׁאוֹב (ז)
to dig (excavate)	laχpor	לַחְפּוֹר
hard hat	kasda	קַסְדָּה (נ)

122. Science. Research. Scientists

science	mada	מַדָּע (ז)
scientific (adj)	mada'i	מַדָּעִי
scientist	mad'an	מַדְעָן (ז)
theory	te''orya	תֵּאוֹרְיָה (נ)

axiom	aks'yoma	אַקְסִיוֹמָה (נ)
analysis	ni'tuaχ	נִיתוּחַ (ז)
to analyse (vt)	lena'teaχ	לְנַתֵּחַ
argument (strong ~)	nimuk	נִימוּק (ז)
substance (matter)	'χomer	חוֹמֶר (ז)

hypothesis	hipo'teza	הִיפּוֹתֵזָה (נ)
dilemma	di'lema	דִּילֶמָה (נ)
dissertation	diser'tatsya	דִּיסֶרְטַצְיָה (נ)
dogma	'dogma	דּוֹגְמָה (נ)

doctrine	dok'trina	דּוֹקְטְרִינָה (נ)
research	meχkar	מֶחְקָר (ז)
to research (vt)	laχkor	לַחְקוֹר
tests (laboratory ~)	nuisuyim	נִיסּוּיִים (ז"ר)
laboratory	ma'abada	מַעֲבָּדָה (נ)

method	ʃita	שִׁיטָה (נ)
molecule	mo'lekula	מוֹלֶקוּלָה (נ)
monitoring	nitur	נִיטוּר (ז)
discovery (act, event)	gilui	גִּילוּי (ז)

postulate	aks'yoma	אַקְסִיוֹמָה (נ)
principle	ikaron	עִיקָּרוֹן (ז)
forecast	taχazit	תַּחֲזִית (נ)
to forecast (vt)	laχazot	לַחֲזוֹת

synthesis	sin'teza	סִינְתֶּזָה (נ)
trend (tendency)	megama	מְגַמָּה (נ)
theorem	miʃpat	מִשְׁפָּט (ז)

| teachings | tora | תּוֹרָה (נ) |
| fact | uvda | עוּבְדָה (נ) |

| expedition | miʃ'laχat | מִשְׁלַחַת (נ) |
| experiment | nisui | נִיסּוּי (ז) |

academician	akademai	אָקָדֵמַאי (ז)
bachelor (e.g. ~ of Arts)	'to'ar riʃon	תּוֹאַר רִאשׁוֹן (ז)
doctor (PhD)	'doktor	דּוֹקְטוֹר (ז)
Associate Professor	martse baχir	מַרְצֶה בָּכִיר (ז)
Master (e.g. ~ of Arts)	musmaχ	מוּסְמָךְ (ז)
professor	pro'fesor	פְּרוֹפֶסוֹר (ז)

Professions and occupations

123. Job search. Dismissal

job	avoda	עֲבוֹדָה (נ)
staff (work force)	'segel	סֶגֶל (ז)
personnel	'segel	סֶגֶל (ז)
career	kar'yera	קַרְיֶירָה (נ)
prospects (chances)	efʃaruyot	אֶפְשָׁרוּיוֹת (נ"ר)
skills (mastery)	meyumanut	מְיוּמָנוּת (נ)
selection (screening)	sinun	סִינּוּן (ז)
employment agency	soχnut 'koaχ adam	סוֹכְנוּת כּוֹחַ אָדָם (נ)
curriculum vitae, CV	korot χayim	קוֹרוֹת חַיִּים (נ"ר)
job interview	ra'ayon avoda	רַאֲיוֹן עֲבוֹדָה (ז)
vacancy	misra pnuya	מִשְׂרָה פְּנוּיָה (נ)
salary, pay	mas'koret	מַשְׂכּוֹרֶת (נ)
fixed salary	mas'koret kvu'a	מַשְׂכּוֹרֶת קְבוּעָה (נ)
pay, compensation	taʃlum	תַּשְׁלוּם (ז)
position (job)	tafkid	תַּפְקִיד (ז)
duty (of employee)	χova	חוֹבָה (נ)
range of duties	tχum aχrayut	תְּחוּם אַחְרָיוּת (ז)
busy (I'm ~)	asuk	עָסוּק
to fire (dismiss)	lefater	לְפַטֵּר
dismissal	pitur	פִּיטוּר (ז)
unemployment	avtala	אַבְטָלָה (נ)
unemployed (n)	muvtal	מוּבְטָל (ז)
retirement	'pensya	פֶּנְסִיָה (נ)
to retire (from job)	latset legimla'ot	לָצֵאת לְגִימְלָאוֹת

124. Business people

director	menahel	מְנַהֵל (ז)
manager (director)	menahel	מְנַהֵל (ז)
boss	bos	בּוֹס (ז)
superior	memune	מְמוּנֶה (ז)
superiors	memunim	מְמוּנִים (ז"ר)
president	nasi	נָשִׂיא (ז)
chairman	yoʃev roʃ	יוֹשֵׁב רֹאשׁ (ז)
deputy (substitute)	sgan	סְגָן (ז)
assistant	ozer	עוֹזֵר (ז)

secretary	mazkir	מַזְכִּיר (ז)
personal assistant	mazkir iʃi	מַזְכִּיר אִישִׁי (ז)
businessman	iʃ asakim	אִישׁ עֲסָקִים (ז)
entrepreneur	yazam	יָזָם (ז)
founder	meyased	מְיַיסֵד (ז)
to found (vt)	leyased	לְייַסֵד
founding member	meχonen	מְכוֹנֵן (ז)
partner	ʃutaf	שׁוּתָף (ז)
shareholder	'ba'al menayot	בַּעַל מְנָיוֹת (ז)
millionaire	milyoner	מִילְיוֹנֵר (ז)
billionaire	milyarder	מִילְיַארְדֵר (ז)
owner, proprietor	be'alim	בְּעָלִים (ז)
landowner	'ba'al adamot	בַּעַל אֲדָמוֹת (ז)
client	la'koaχ	לָקוֹחַ (ז)
regular client	la'koaχ ka'vu'a	לָקוֹחַ קָבוּעַ (ז)
buyer (customer)	kone	קוֹנֶה (ז)
visitor	mevaker	מְבַקֵר (ז)
professional (n)	miktso'an	מִקְצוֹעָן (ז)
expert	mumχe	מוּמְחֶה (ז)
specialist	mumχe	מוּמְחֶה (ז)
banker	bankai	בַּנְקַאי (ז)
broker	soχen	סוֹכֵן (ז)
cashier	kupai	קוּפַּאי (ז)
accountant	menahel χeʃbonot	מְנַהֵל חֶשְׁבּוֹנוֹת (ז)
security guard	ʃomer	שׁוֹמֵר (ז)
investor	maʃki'a	מַשְׁקִיעַ (ז)
debtor	'ba'al χov	בַּעַל חוֹב (ז)
creditor	malve	מַלְווֶה (ז)
borrower	love	לוֹוֶה (ז)
importer	yevu'an	יְבוּאָן (ז)
exporter	yetsu'an	יְצוּאָן (ז)
manufacturer	yatsran	יַצְרָן (ז)
distributor	mefits	מֵפִיץ (ז)
middleman	metaveχ	מְתַווֵךְ (ז)
consultant	yo'ets	יוֹעֵץ (ז)
sales representative	natsig meχirot	נָצִיג מְכִירוֹת (ז)
agent	soχen	סוֹכֵן (ז)
insurance agent	soχen bi'tuaχ	סוֹכֵן בִּיטוּחַ (ז)

125. Service professions

cook	tabaχ	טַבָּח (ז)
chef (kitchen chef)	ʃef	שֵׁף (ז)

baker	ofe	אוֹפֶה (ז)
barman	'barmen	בַּרמָן (ז)
waiter	meltsar	מֶלצָר (ז)
waitress	meltsarit	מֶלצָרִית (נ)

lawyer, barrister	orex din	עוֹרֵך דִין (ז)
lawyer (legal expert)	orex din	עוֹרֵך דִין (ז)
notary	notaryon	נוֹטַריוֹן (ז)

electrician	xaʃmalai	חַשמַלַאי (ז)
plumber	ʃravrav	שְרַברַב (ז)
carpenter	nagar	נַגָר (ז)

masseur	ma'ase	מְעַסֶה (ז)
masseuse	masa'ʒistit	מַסָזִ'יסטִית (נ)
doctor	rofe	רוֹפֵא (ז)

taxi driver	nahag monit	נֶהָג מוֹנִית (ז)
driver	nahag	נֶהָג (ז)
delivery man	ʃa'liax	שָלִיחַ (ז)

chambermaid	xadranit	חַדרָנִית (נ)
security guard	ʃomer	שוֹמֵר (ז)
flight attendant (fem.)	da'yelet	דַייֶלֶת (נ)

schoolteacher	more	מוֹרֶה (ז)
librarian	safran	סַפרָן (ז)
translator	metargem	מְתַרגֵם (ז)
interpreter	meturgeman	מְתוּרגְמָן (ז)
guide	madrix tiyulim	מַדרִיך טִיוּלִים (ז)

hairdresser	sapar	סַפָּר (ז)
postman	davar	דַוָור (ז)
salesman (store staff)	moxer	מוֹכֵר (ז)

gardener	ganan	גַנָן (ז)
domestic servant	meʃaret	מְשָרֵת (ז)
maid (female servant)	meʃa'retet	מְשָרֶתֶת (נ)
cleaner (cleaning lady)	menaka	מְנַקָה (נ)

126. Military professions and ranks

private	turai	טוּרַאי (ז)
sergeant	samal	סַמָל (ז)
lieutenant	'segen	סֶגֶן (ז)
captain	'seren	סֶרֶן (ז)

major	rav 'seren	רַב־סֶרֶן (ז)
colonel	aluf miʃne	אַלוּף מִשנֶה (ז)
general	aluf	אַלוּף (ז)
marshal	'marʃal	מַרשָל (ז)
admiral	admiral	אַדמִירָל (ז)
military (n)	iʃ tsava	אִיש צָבָא (ז)
soldier	xayal	חַייָל (ז)

| officer | kaʦin | קָצִין (ז) |
| commander | mefaked | מְפַקֵד (ז) |

border guard	ʃomer gvul	שׁוֹמֵר גְבוּל (ז)
radio operator	alχutai	אַלחוּטַאי (ז)
scout (searcher)	iʃ modi'in kravi	אִישׁ מוֹדִיעִין קְרָבִי (ז)
pioneer (sapper)	χablan	חַבְּלָן (ז)
marksman	ʦalaf	צַלָף (ז)
navigator	navat	נַוָוט (ז)

127. Officials. Priests

| king | 'meleχ | מֶלֶךְ (ז) |
| queen | malka | מַלְכָּה (נ) |

| prince | nasiχ | נָסִיךְ (ז) |
| princess | nesiχa | נְסִיכָה (נ) |

| czar | ʦar | צָאר (ז) |
| czarina | ʦa'rina | צָארִינָה (נ) |

president	nasi	נָשִׂיא (ז)
Secretary (minister)	sar	שַׂר (ז)
prime minister	roʃ memʃala	רֹאשׁ מֶמְשָׁלָה (ז)
senator	se'nator	סֶנָאטוֹר (ז)

diplomat	diplomat	דִיפלוֹמָט (ז)
consul	'konsul	קוֹנסוּל (ז)
ambassador	ʃagrir	שַׁגרִיר (ז)
counsillor (diplomatic officer)	yo'eʦ	יוֹעֵץ (ז)

official, functionary (civil servant)	pakid	פָּקִיד (ז)
prefect	prefekt	פּרֶפֶקט (ז)
mayor	roʃ ha'ir	רֹאשׁ הָעִיר (ז)

| judge | ʃofet | שׁוֹפֵט (ז) |
| prosecutor | to've'a | תוֹבֵעַ (ז) |

missionary	misyoner	מִיסיוֹנֶר (ז)
monk	nazir	נָזִיר (ז)
abbot	roʃ minzar ka'toli	רֹאשׁ מִנזָר קָתוֹלִי (ז)
rabbi	rav	רַב (ז)

vizier	vazir	וָזִיר (ז)
shah	ʃaχ	שָׁאח (ז)
sheikh	ʃeiχ	שֵׁיח (ז)

128. Agricultural professions

| beekeeper | kavran | כַּוָורָן (ז) |
| shepherd | ro'e ʦon | רוֹעֶה צֹאן (ז) |

agronomist	agronom	אַגְרוֹנוֹם (ז)
cattle breeder	megadel bakar	מְגַדֵּל בָּקָר (ז)
veterinary surgeon	veterinar	וֶטֶרִינָר (ז)

farmer	χavai	חַוַּאי (ז)
winemaker	yeinan	יֵינָן (ז)
zoologist	zo'olog	זוֹאוֹלוֹג (ז)
cowboy	'ka'uboi	קָאוּבּוֹי (ז)

129. Art professions

| actor | saχkan | שַׂחְקָן (ז) |
| actress | saχkanit | שַׂחְקָנִית (נ) |

| singer (masc.) | zamar | זַמָּר (ז) |
| singer (fem.) | za'meret | זַמֶּרֶת (נ) |

| dancer (masc.) | rakdan | רַקְדָּן (ז) |
| dancer (fem.) | rakdanit | רַקְדָּנִית (נ) |

| performer (masc.) | saχkan | שַׂחְקָן (ז) |
| performer (fem.) | saχkanit | שַׂחְקָנִית (נ) |

musician	muzikai	מוּזִיקַאי (ז)
pianist	psantran	פְּסַנְתְּרָן (ז)
guitar player	nagan gi'tara	נַגָּן גִּיטָרָה (ז)

conductor (orchestra ~)	mena'tseaχ	מְנַצֵּחַ (ז)
composer	malχin	מַלְחִין (ז)
impresario	amargan	אָמַרְגָּן (ז)

film director	bamai	בַּמַאי (ז)
producer	mefik	מֵפִיק (ז)
scriptwriter	tasritai	תַּסְרִיטַאי (ז)
critic	mevaker	מְבַקֵּר (ז)

writer	sofer	סוֹפֵר (ז)
poet	meʃorer	מְשׁוֹרֵר (ז)
sculptor	pasal	פַּסָּל (ז)
artist (painter)	tsayar	צַיָּיר (ז)

juggler	lahatutan	לַהֲטוּטָן (ז)
clown	leitsan	לֵיצָן (ז)
acrobat	akrobat	אַקְרוֹבָּט (ז)
magician	kosem	קוֹסֵם (ז)

130. Various professions

doctor	rofe	רוֹפֵא (ז)
nurse	aχot	אָחוֹת (נ)
psychiatrist	psiχi''ater	פְּסִיכִיאָטֶר (ז)
dentist	rofe ʃi'nayim	רוֹפֵא שִׁינַיִּים (ז)

surgeon	kirurg	כִּירוּרג (ז)
astronaut	astro'na'ut	אַסְטרוֹנָאוּט (ז)
astronomer	astronom	אַסְטרוֹנוֹם (ז)
pilot	tayas	טַיָּס (ז)
driver (of taxi, etc.)	nahag	נֶהָג (ז)
train driver	nahag ra'kevet	נֶהָג רַכָּבֶת (ז)
mechanic	meχonai	מְכוֹנַאי (ז)
miner	kore	כּוֹרֶה (ז)
worker	po'el	פּוֹעֵל (ז)
locksmith	misgad	מַסְגֵּד (ז)
joiner (carpenter)	nagar	נַגָּר (ז)
turner (lathe machine operator)	χarat	חָרָט (ז)
building worker	banai	בַּנַּאי (ז)
welder	rataχ	רַתָּך (ז)
professor (title)	pro'fesor	פְּרוֹפֶסוֹר (ז)
architect	adriχal	אַדרִיכָל (ז)
historian	historyon	הִיסטוֹרִיוֹן (ז)
scientist	mad'an	מַדְעָן (ז)
physicist	fizikai	פִיזִיקַאי (ז)
chemist (scientist)	χimai	כִימַאי (ז)
archaeologist	arχe'olog	אַרכֵיאוֹלוֹג (ז)
geologist	ge'olog	גֵיאוֹלוֹג (ז)
researcher (scientist)	χoker	חוֹקֵר (ז)
babysitter	ʃmartaf	שׁמַרטַף (ז)
teacher, educator	more, meχaneχ	מוֹרֶה, מְחַנֵּך (ז)
editor	oreχ	עוֹרֵך (ז)
editor-in-chief	oreχ raʃi	עוֹרֵך רָאשִׁי (ז)
correspondent	katav	כַּתָּב (ז)
typist (fem.)	kaldanit	קַלְדָּנִית (נ)
designer	me'atsev	מְעַצֵּב (ז)
computer expert	mumχe maχʃevim	מוּמְחֶה מַחשְׁבִים (ז)
programmer	metaχnet	מְתַכְנֵת (ז)
engineer (designer)	mehandes	מְהַנדֵּס (ז)
sailor	yamai	יַמַאי (ז)
seaman	malaχ	מַלָּח (ז)
rescuer	matsil	מַצִּיל (ז)
firefighter	kabai	כַּבַּאי (ז)
police officer	ʃoter	שׁוֹטֵר (ז)
watchman	ʃomer	שׁוֹמֵר (ז)
detective	balaʃ	בַּלָּשׁ (ז)
customs officer	pakid 'meχes	פָּקִיד מֶכֶס (ז)
bodyguard	ʃomer roʃ	שׁוֹמֵר רֹאשׁ (ז)
prison officer	soher	סוֹהֵר (ז)
inspector	mefa'keaχ	מְפַקֵּחַ (ז)
sportsman	sportai	סְפּוֹרטַאי (ז)

trainer, coach	me'amen	מְאַמֵן (ז)
butcher	katsav	קַצָב (ז)
cobbler (shoe repairer)	sandlar	סַנְדְלָר (ז)
merchant	soχer	סוֹחֵר (ז)
loader (person)	sabal	סַבָּל (ז)

| fashion designer | me'atsev ofna | מְעַצֵב אוֹפְנָה (ז) |
| model (fem.) | dugmanit | דוּגְמָנִית (נ) |

131. Occupations. Social status

| schoolboy | talmid | תַלְמִיד (ז) |
| student (college ~) | student | סְטוּדֶנְט (ז) |

philosopher	filosof	פִילוֹסוֹף (ז)
economist	kalkelan	כַּלְכְּלָן (ז)
inventor	mamtsi	מַמְצִיא (ז)

unemployed (n)	muvtal	מוּבְטָל (ז)
pensioner	pensyoner	פֶּנְסְיוֹנֵר (ז)
spy, secret agent	meragel	מְרַגֵל (ז)

prisoner	asir	אָסִיר (ז)
striker	ʃovet	שוֹבֵת (ז)
bureaucrat	birokrat	בִּירוֹקְרָט (ז)
traveller (globetrotter)	metayel	מְטַיֵיל (ז)

gay, homosexual (n)	'lesbit, 'homo	לֶסְבִּית (נ), הוֹמוֹ (ז)
hacker	'haker	הָאקֵר (ז)
hippie	'hipi	הִיפִּי (ז)

bandit	ʃoded	שוֹדֵד (ז)
hit man, killer	ro'tseaχ saχir	רוֹצֵחַ שָׂכִיר (ז)
drug addict	narkoman	נַרְקוֹמָן (ז)
drug dealer	soχer samim	סוֹחֵר סַמִים (ז)
prostitute (fem.)	zona	זוֹנָה (נ)
pimp	sarsur	סַרְסוּר (ז)

sorcerer	meχaʃef	מְכַשֵף (ז)
sorceress (evil ~)	maχʃefa	מְכַשֵפָה (נ)
pirate	ʃoded yam	שוֹדֵד יָם (ז)
slave	ʃifχa, 'eved	שִפְחָה (נ), עֶבֶד (ז)
samurai	samurai	סָמוּרַאי (ז)
savage (primitive)	'pere adam	פֶּרֶא אָדָם (ז)

116

Sports

132. Kinds of sports. Sportspersons

sportsman	sportai	ספּוֹרְטַאי (ז)
kind of sport	anaf sport	עָנָף סְפּוֹרְט (ז)
basketball	kadursal	כַּדוּרְסַל (ז)
basketball player	kadursalan	כַּדוּרְסַלָן (ז)
baseball	'beisbol	בֵּייסְבּוֹל (ז)
baseball player	saxkan 'beisbol	שַׂחְקָן בֵּייסְבּוֹל (ז)
football	kadu'regel	כַּדוּרֶגֶל (ז)
football player	kaduraglan	כַּדוּרַגְלָן (ז)
goalkeeper	ʃo'er	שׁוֹעֵר (ז)
ice hockey	'hoki	הוֹקִי (ז)
ice hockey player	saxkan 'hoki	שַׂחְקָן הוֹקִי (ז)
volleyball	kadur'af	כַּדוּרְעָף (ז)
volleyball player	saxkan kadur'af	שַׂחְקָן כַּדוּרְעָף (ז)
boxing	igruf	אִיגְרוּף (ז)
boxer	mit'agref	מִתְאַגְרֵף (ז)
wrestling	he'avkut	הֵיאָבְקוּת (נ)
wrestler	mit'abek	מִתְאַבֵּק (ז)
karate	karate	קָרָטֶה (ז)
karate fighter	karatist	קָרָטִיסְט (ז)
judo	'dʒudo	גּ'וּדוֹ (ז)
judo athlete	dʒudai	גּ'וּדָאִי (ז)
tennis	'tenis	טֶנִיס (ז)
tennis player	tenisai	טֶנִיסַאי (ז)
swimming	sxiya	שְׂחִייָה (נ)
swimmer	saxyan	שַׂחְייָן (ז)
fencing	'sayif	סַיִף (ז)
fencer	sayaf	סַייָף (ז)
chess	'ʃaxmat	שַׁחְמָט (ז)
chess player	ʃaxmetai	שַׁחְמְטַאי (ז)
alpinism	tipus harim	טִיפּוּס הָרִים (ז)
alpinist	metapes harim	מְטַפֵּס הָרִים (ז)
running	ritsa	רִיצָה (נ)

runner	atsan	אָצָן (ז)
athletics	at'letika kala	אַתלֵטִיקָה קַלָה (נ)
athlete	atlet	אַתלֵט (ז)

| horse riding | rexiva al sus | רְכִיבָה עַל סוּס (נ) |
| horse rider | paraʃ | פָּרָש (ז) |

figure skating	haxlaka omanutit	הַחלָקָה אוֹמָנוּתִית (נ)
figure skater (masc.)	maxlik amanuti	מַחלִיק אָמָנוּתִי (ז)
figure skater (fem.)	maxlika amanutit	מַחלִיקָה אָמָנוּתִית (נ)

| powerlifting | haramat miʃkolot | הֲרָמַת מִשקוֹלוֹת (נ) |
| powerlifter | miʃkolan | מִשקוֹלָן (ז) |

| car racing | merots mexoniyot | מֵירוֹץ מְכוֹנִיוֹת (ז) |
| racing driver | nahag merotsim | נַהַג מֵרוֹצִים (ז) |

| cycling | rexiva al ofa'nayim | רְכִיבָה עַל אוֹפַנַיִים (נ) |
| cyclist | roxev ofa'nayim | רוֹכֵב אוֹפַנַיִים (ז) |

long jump	kfitsa la'roxav	קפִיצָה לָרוֹחַק (נ)
pole vaulting	kfitsa bemot	קפִיצָה בָּמוֹט (נ)
jumper	kofets	קוֹפֵץ (ז)

133. Kinds of sports. Miscellaneous

American football	'futbol	פוּטבּוֹל (ז)
badminton	notsit	נוֹצִית (ז)
biathlon	bi'atlon	בִּיאַתלוֹן (ז)
billiards	bilyard	בִּילִיַארד (ז)

bobsleigh	miz'xelet	מִזחֶלֶת (נ)
bodybuilding	pi'tuax guf	פִּיתוּחַ גוּף (ז)
water polo	polo 'mayim	פּוֹלוֹ מַיִם (ז)
handball	kadur yad	כַּדוּר-יָד (ז)
golf	golf	גוֹלף (ז)

rowing	xatira	חֲתִירָה (נ)
scuba diving	tslila	צלִילָה (נ)
cross-country skiing	ski bemiʃor	סקִי בַּמִישוֹר (ז)
table tennis (ping-pong)	'tenis ʃulxan	טֶנִיס שוּלחָן (ז)

sailing	'ʃayit	שַיִט (ז)
rally	'rali	רָאלִי (ז)
rugby	'rogbi	רוֹגבִּי (ז)
snowboarding	gliʃat 'ʃeleg	גלִישַת שֶלֶג (נ)
archery	kaʃatut	קַשָתוּת (נ)

134. Gym

| barbell | miʃkolet | מִשקוֹלֶת (נ) |
| dumbbells | miʃkolot | מִשקוֹלוֹת (נ"ר) |

training machine	maχʃir 'koʃer	מַכְשִׁיר כּוֹשֶׁר (ז)
exercise bicycle	ofanei 'koʃer	אוֹפַנֵּי כּוֹשֶׁר (ז״ר)
treadmill	haliχon	הֲלִיכוֹן (ז)
horizontal bar	'metaχ	מָתָח (ז)
parallel bars	makbilim	מַקְבִּילִים (ז״ר)
vault (vaulting horse)	sus	סוּס (ז)
mat (exercise ~)	mizron	מִזְרוֹן (ז)
skipping rope	dalgit	דַּלְגִּית (נ)
aerobics	ei'robika	אֵירוֹבִּיקָה (נ)
yoga	'yoga	יוֹגָה (נ)

135. Ice hockey

ice hockey	'hoki	הוֹקִי (ז)
ice hockey player	saχkan 'hoki	שַׂחְקָן הוֹקִי (ז)
to play ice hockey	lesaχek 'hoki	לְשַׂחֵק הוֹקִי
ice	'keraχ	קֶרַח (ז)
puck	diskit	דִּיסְקִית (נ)
ice hockey stick	makel 'hoki	מַקֵּל הוֹקִי (ז)
ice skates	maχli'kayim	מַחְלִיקַיִם (ז״ר)
board (ice hockey rink ~)	'dofen	דּוֹפֶן (ז)
shot	kli'a	קְלִיעָה (נ)
goaltender	ʃo'er	שׁוֹעֵר (ז)
goal (score)	'ʃa'ar	שַׁעַר (ז)
to score a goal	lehav'ki'a 'ʃa'ar	לְהַבְקִיעַ שַׁעַר
period	ʃliʃ	שְׁלִישׁ (ז)
second period	ʃliʃ ʃeni	שְׁלִישׁ שֵׁנִי (ז)
substitutes bench	safsal maχlifim	סַפְסַל מַחְלִיפִים (ז)

136. Football

football	kadu'regel	כַּדּוּרֶגֶל (ז)
football player	kaduraglan	כַּדּוּרַגְלָן (ז)
to play football	lesaχek kadu'regel	לְשַׂחֵק כַּדּוּרֶגֶל
major league	'liga elyona	לִינָה עֶלְיוֹנָה (נ)
football club	mo'adon kadu'regel	מוֹעֲדוֹן כַּדּוּרֶגֶל (ז)
coach	me'amen	מְאַמֵּן (ז)
owner, proprietor	be'alim	בְּעָלִים (ז)
team	kvutsa, niv'χeret	קְבוּצָה, נִבְחֶרֶת (נ)
team captain	'kepten	קַפְּטָן (ז)
player	saχkan	שַׂחְקָן (ז)
substitute	saχkan maχlif	שַׂחְקָן מַחְלִיף (ז)
forward	χaluts	חָלוּץ (ז)
centre forward	χaluts merkazi	חָלוּץ מֶרְכָּזִי (ז)

scorer	mavki	מַבְקִיעַ (ז)
defender, back	balam, megen	בַּלָם, מָגֵן (ז)
midfielder, halfback	mekaʃer	מְקַשֵׁר (ז)
match	misχak	מִשְׂחָק (ז)
to meet (vi, vt)	lehipageʃ	לְהִיפָּגֵשׁ
final	gmar	גְמָר (ז)
semi-final	χatsi gmar	חֲצִי גְמָר (ז)
championship	alifut	אֲלִיפוּת (נ)
period, half	maχatsit	מַחֲצִית (נ)
first period	maχatsit riʃona	מַחֲצִית רִאשׁוֹנָה (נ)
half-time	hafsaka	הַפְסָקָה (נ)
goal	ʃaʿar	שַׁעַר (ז)
goalkeeper	ʃoʿer	שׁוֹעֵר (ז)
goalpost	amud haʃʃaʿar	עַמוּד הַשַׁעַר (ז)
crossbar	maʃkof	מַשְׁקוֹף (ז)
net	reʃet	רֶשֶׁת (נ)
to concede a goal	lispog ʃaʿar	לִסְפּוֹג שַׁעַר
ball	kadur	כַּדוּר (ז)
pass	mesira	מְסִירָה (נ)
kick	beʿita	בְּעִיטָה (נ)
to kick (~ the ball)	livʿot	לִבְעוֹט
free kick (direct ~)	beʿitat onʃin	בְּעִיטַת עוֹנְשִׁין (נ)
corner kick	beʿitat keren	בְּעִיטַת קֶרֶן (נ)
attack	hatkafa	הַתְקָפָה (נ)
counterattack	hatkafat neged	הַתְקָפַת נֶגֶד (נ)
combination	ʃiluv	שִׁילוּב (ז)
referee	ʃofet	שׁוֹפֵט (ז)
to blow the whistle	liʃrok	לִשְׁרוֹק
whistle (sound)	ʃrika	שְׁרִיקָה (נ)
foul, misconduct	avira	עֲבִירָה (נ)
to commit a foul	levaʿtseʿa avira	לְבַצֵעַ עֲבִירָה
to send off	leharχik	לְהַרְחִיק
yellow card	kartis tsahov	כַּרְטִיס צָהוֹב (ז)
red card	kartis adom	כַּרְטִיס אָדוֹם (ז)
disqualification	psila, ʃlila	פְּסִילָה, שְׁלִילָה (נ)
to disqualify (vt)	lefsol	לִפְסוֹל
penalty kick	pendel	פֶּנְדֶל (ז)
wall	χoma	חוֹמָה (נ)
to score (vi, vt)	lehavʿkiʿa	לְהַבְקִיעַ
goal (score)	ʃaʿar	שַׁעַר (ז)
to score a goal	lehavʿkiʿa ʃaʿar	לְהַבְקִיעַ שַׁעַר
substitution	haχlata	הַחְלָטָה (נ)
to replace (a player)	lehaχlif	לְהַחְלִיף
rules	klalim	כְּלָלִים (ז"ר)
tactics	taktika	טַקְטִיקָה (נ)
stadium	itstadyon	אִצְטַדְיוֹן (ז)
terrace	bama	בָּמָה (נ)

fan, supporter	ohed	אוֹהֵד (ז)
to shout (vi)	lits'ok	לִצְעוֹק
scoreboard	'luax totsa'ot	לוּחַ תּוֹצָאוֹת (ז)
score	totsa'a	תּוֹצָאָה (נ)
defeat	tvusa	תְּבוּסָה (נ)
to lose (not win)	lehafsid	לְהַפְסִיד
draw	'teku	תֵּיקוּ (ז)
to draw (vi)	lesayem be'teku	לְסַיֵּם בְּתֵיקוּ
victory	nitsaxon	נִיצָּחוֹן (ז)
to win (vi, vt)	lena'tseax	לְנַצֵּחַ
champion	aluf	אַלּוּף (ז)
best (adj)	hatov beyoter	הַטּוֹב בְּיוֹתֵר
to congratulate (vt)	levarex	לְבָרֵך
commentator	parʃan	פַּרְשָׁן (ז)
to commentate (vt)	lefarʃen	לְפַרְשֵׁן
broadcast	ʃidur	שִׁידּוּר (ז)

137. Alpine skiing

skis	migla'ʃayim	מִגְלָשַׁיִים (ז"ר)
to ski (vi)	la'asot ski	לַעֲשׂוֹת סְקִי
mountain-ski resort	atar ski	אֲתַר סְקִי (ז)
ski lift	ma'alit ski	מַעֲלִית סְקִי (נ)
ski poles	maklot ski	מַקְלוֹת סְקִי (ז"ר)
slope	midron	מִדְרוֹן (ז)
slalom	merots akalaton	מֵירוֹץ עֲקַלָּתוֹן (ז)

138. Tennis. Golf

golf	golf	גּוֹלְף (ז)
golf club	mo'adon golf	מוֹעֲדוֹן גּוֹלְף (ז)
golfer	saxkan golf	שַׂחְקַן גּוֹלְף (ז)
hole	guma	גּוּמָה (נ)
club	makel golf	מַקֵּל גּוֹלְף (ז)
golf trolley	eglat golf	עֶגְלַת גּוֹלְף (נ)
tennis	'tenis	טֶנִיס (ז)
tennis court	migraʃ 'tenis	מִגְרַשׁ טֶנִיס (ז)
serve	xavatat hagaʃa	חֲבָטַת הַגָּשָׁה (נ)
to serve (vt)	lehagiʃ	לְהַגִּישׁ
racket	maxbet 'tenis	מַחְבֵּט טֶנִיס (ז)
net	'reʃet	רֶשֶׁת (נ)
ball	kadur	כַּדּוּר (ז)

139. Chess

chess	'ʃaχmat	שַׁחְמָט (ז)
chessmen	klei 'ʃaχmat	כְּלֵי שַׁחְמָט (ז"ר)
chess player	ʃaχmetai	שַׁחְמְטַאי (ז)
chessboard	'luaχ 'ʃaχmat	לוּחַ שַׁחְמָט (ז)
chessman	kli	כְּלִי (ז)
White (white pieces)	levanim	לְבָנִים (ז)
Black (black pieces)	ʃχorim	שְׁחוֹרִים (ז)
pawn	χayal	חַיָּל (ז)
bishop	rats	רָץ (ז)
knight	paraʃ	פָּרָשׁ (ז)
rook	'tsriaχ	צְרִיחַ (ז)
queen	malka	מַלְכָּה (נ)
king	'meleχ	מֶלֶךְ (ז)
move	'tsa'ad	צַעַד (ז)
to move (vi, vt)	la'nu'a	לָנוּעַ
to sacrifice (vt)	lehakriv	לְהַקְרִיב
castling	hatsraχa	הַצְרָחָה (נ)
check	ʃaχ	שָׁח (ז)
checkmate	mat	מָט (ז)
chess tournament	taχarut 'ʃaχmat	תַּחֲרוּת שַׁחְמָט (נ)
Grand Master	rav oman	רַב־אוֹמָן (ז)
combination	ʃiluv	שִׁילּוּב (ז)
game (in chess)	misχak	מִשְׂחָק (ז)
draughts	'damka	דָּמְקָה (נ)

140. Boxing

boxing	igruf	אִיגְרוּף (ז)
fight (bout)	krav	קְרָב (ז)
boxing match	du krav	דּוּ־קְרָב (ז)
round (in boxing)	sivuv	סִיבּוּב (ז)
ring	zira	זִירָה (נ)
gong	gong	גּוֹנְג (ז)
punch	mahaluma	מַהֲלוּמָה (נ)
knockdown	nefila lekraʃim	נְפִילָה לְקְרָשִׁים (נ)
knockout	'nok'a'ut	נוֹקְאָאוּט (ז)
to knock out	liʃ'loaχ le'nok'a'ut	לִשְׁלוֹחַ לְנוֹקְאָאוּט
boxing glove	kfafat igruf	כְּפָפַת אִיגְרוּף (נ)
referee	ʃofet	שׁוֹפֵט (ז)
lightweight	miʃkal notsa	מִשְׁקָל נוֹצָה (ז)
middleweight	miʃkal beinoni	מִשְׁקָל בֵּינוֹנִי (ז)
heavyweight	miʃkal kaved	מִשְׁקָל כָּבֵד (ז)

141. Sports. Miscellaneous

Olympic Games	hamisχakim ha'o'limpiyim	הַמְּשֹׁחָקִים הָאוֹלִימְפָּיִים (ז"ר)
winner	mena'tseaχ	מְנַצֵּחַ (ז)
to be winning	lena'tseaχ	לְנַצֵּחַ
to win (vi)	lena'tseaχ	לְנַצֵּחַ
leader	manhig	מַנְהִיג (ז)
to lead (vi)	lehovil	לְהוֹבִיל
first place	makom riʃon	מָקוֹם רָאשׁוֹן (ז)
second place	makom ʃeni	מָקוֹם שֵׁנִי (ז)
third place	makom ʃliʃi	מָקוֹם שְׁלִישִׁי (ז)
medal	me'dalya	מֶדַלְיָה (נ)
trophy	pras	פְּרָס (ז)
prize cup (trophy)	ga'vi'a nitsaχon	גָּבִיעַ נִיצָּחוֹן (ז)
prize (in game)	pras	פְּרָס (ז)
main prize	pras riʃon	פְּרָס רָאשׁוֹן (ז)
record	si	שִׂיא (ז)
to set a record	lik'bo'a si	לִקְבּוֹעַ שִׂיא
final	gmar	גְּמָר (ז)
final (adj)	ʃel hagmar	שֶׁל הַגְּמָר
champion	aluf	אַלוּף (ז)
championship	alifut	אֲלִיפוּת (נ)
stadium	itstadyon	אָצְטַדְיוֹן (ז)
terrace	bama	בָּמָה (נ)
fan, supporter	ohed	אוֹהֵד (ז)
opponent, rival	yariv	יָרִיב (ז)
start (start line)	kav zinuk	קַו זִינוּק (ז)
finish line	kav hagmar	קַו הַגְּמָר (ז)
defeat	tvusa	תְּבוּסָה (נ)
to lose (not win)	lehafsid	לְהַפְסִיד
referee	ʃofet	שׁוֹפֵט (ז)
jury (judges)	χaver ʃoftim	חֶבֶר שׁוֹפְטִים (ז)
score	totsa'a	תּוֹצָאָה (נ)
draw	'teku	תֵּיקוּ (ז)
to draw (vi)	lesayem be'teku	לְסַיֵּם בְּתֵיקוּ
point	nekuda	נְקוּדָה (נ)
result (final score)	totsa'a	תּוֹצָאָה (נ)
period	sivuv	סִיבוּב (ז)
half-time	hafsaka	הַפְסָקָה (נ)
doping	sam	סָם (ז)
to penalise (vt)	leha'aniʃ	לְהַעֲנִישׁ
to disqualify (vt)	lefsol	לִפְסוֹל
apparatus	maχʃir	מַכְשִׁיר (ז)
javelin	kidon	כִּידוֹן (ז)

| shot (metal ball) | kadur barzel | כַּדוּר בַּרְזָל (ז) |
| ball (snooker, etc.) | kadur | כַּדוּר (ז) |

aim (target)	matara	מַטָּרָה (נ)
target	matara	מַטָּרָה (נ)
to shoot (vi)	lirot	לִירוֹת
accurate (~ shot)	meduyak	מְדוּיָק

trainer, coach	me'amen	מְאַמֵּן (ז)
to train (sb)	le'amen	לְאַמֵּן
to train (vi)	lehit'amen	לְהִתְאַמֵּן
training	imun	אִימּוּן (ז)

gym	'xeder 'koʃer	חֶדֶר כּוֹשֶׁר (ז)
exercise (physical)	imun	אִימּוּן (ז)
warm-up (athlete ~)	ximum	חִימּוּם (ז)

Education

142. School

school	beit 'sefer	בֵּית סֵפֶר (ז)
headmaster	menahel beit 'sefer	מְנַהֵל בֵּית סֵפֶר (ז)
pupil (boy)	talmid	תַּלְמִיד (ז)
pupil (girl)	talmida	תַּלְמִידָה (נ)
schoolboy	talmid	תַּלְמִיד (ז)
schoolgirl	talmida	תַּלְמִידָה (נ)
to teach (sb)	lelamed	לְלַמֵּד
to learn (language, etc.)	lilmod	לִלְמוֹד
to learn by heart	lilmod be'al pe	לִלְמוֹד בְּעַל פֶּה
to learn (~ to count, etc.)	lilmod	לִלְמוֹד
to be at school	lilmod	לִלְמוֹד
to go to school	la'leχet le'beit 'sefer	לָלֶכֶת לְבֵית סֵפֶר
alphabet	alefbeit	אָלֶפְבֵּית (ז)
subject (at school)	mik'tso'a	מִקְצוֹעַ (ז)
classroom	kita	כִּיתָה (נ)
lesson	ʃi'ur	שִׁיעוּר (ז)
playtime, break	hafsaka	הַפְסָקָה (נ)
school bell	pa'amon	פַּעֲמוֹן (ז)
school desk	ʃulχan limudim	שׁוּלְחַן לִימוּדִים (ז)
blackboard	'luaχ	לוּחַ (ז)
mark	tsiyun	צִיּוּן (ז)
good mark	tsiyun tov	צִיּוּן טוֹב (ז)
bad mark	tsiyun ga'ru'a	צִיּוּן גָּרוּעַ (ז)
to give a mark	latet tsiyun	לָתֵת צִיּוּן
mistake, error	ta'ut	טָעוּת (נ)
to make mistakes	la'asot ta'uyot	לַעֲשׂוֹת טָעוּיוֹת
to correct (an error)	letaken	לְתַקֵּן
crib	ʃlif	שְׁלִיף (ז)
homework	ʃi'urei 'bayit	שִׁיעוּרֵי בַּיִת (ז״ר)
exercise (in education)	targil	תַּרְגִּיל (ז)
to be present	lihyot no'χeaχ	לִהְיוֹת נוֹכֵחַ
to be absent	lehe'ader	לְהֵיעָדֵר
to miss school	lehaχsir	לְהַחְסִיר
to punish (vt)	leha'aniʃ	לְהַעֲנִישׁ
punishment	'oneʃ	עוֹנֶשׁ (ז)
conduct (behaviour)	hitnahagut	הִתְנַהֲגוּת (נ)

125

school report	yoman beit 'sefer	יוֹמָן בֵּית סֵפֶר (ז)
pencil	iparon	עִיפָּרוֹן (ז)
rubber	'maχak	מַחַק (ז)
chalk	gir	גִּיר (ז)
pencil case	kalmar	קַלְמָר (ז)

schoolbag	yalkut	יַלְקוּט (ז)
pen	et	עֵט (ז)
exercise book	maχ'beret	מַחְבֶּרֶת (נ)
textbook	'sefer limud	סֵפֶר לִימוּד (ז)
compasses	meχuga	מְחוּגָה (נ)

| to make technical drawings | lesartet | לְשַׂרְטֵט |
| technical drawing | sirtut | שִׂרְטוּט (ז) |

poem	ʃir	שִׁיר (ז)
by heart (adv)	be'al pe	בְּעַל פֶּה
to learn by heart	lilmod be'al pe	לִלְמוֹד בְּעַל פֶּה

school holidays	χufʃa	חוּפְשָׁה (נ)
to be on holiday	lihyot beχufʃa	לִהְיוֹת בְּחוּפְשָׁה
to spend holidays	leha'avir 'χofeʃ	לְהַעֲבִיר חוֹפֶשׁ

test (at school)	mivχan	מִבְחָן (ז)
essay (composition)	χibur	חִיבּוּר (ז)
dictation	haχtava	הַכְתָּבָה (נ)
exam (examination)	bχina	בְּחִינָה (נ)
to do an exam	lehibaχen	לְהִיבָּחֵן
experiment (e.g., chemistry ~)	nisui	נִיסוּי (ז)

143. College. University

academy	aka'demya	אָקָדֶמְיָה (נ)
university	uni'versita	אוּנִיבֶרְסִיטָה (נ)
faculty (e.g., ~ of Medicine)	fa'kulta	פָקוּלְטָה (נ)

student (masc.)	student	סְטוּדֶנְט (ז)
student (fem.)	stu'dentit	סְטוּדֶנְטִית (נ)
lecturer (teacher)	martse	מַרְצֶה (ז)

| lecture hall, room | ulam hartsa'ot | אוּלָם הַרְצָאוֹת (ז) |
| graduate | boger | בּוֹגֵר (ז) |

| diploma | di'ploma | דִיפְלוֹמָה (נ) |
| dissertation | diser'tatsya | דִיסֶרְטַצְיָה (נ) |

| study (report) | meχkar | מֶחְקָר (ז) |
| laboratory | ma'abada | מַעֲבָּדָה (נ) |

lecture	hartsa'a	הַרְצָאָה (נ)
coursemate	χaver lelimudim	חָבֵר לְלִימוּדִים (ז)
scholarship, bursary	milga	מִלְגָה (נ)
academic degree	'to'ar aka'demi	תוֹאַר אָקָדֶמִי (ז)

144. Sciences. Disciplines

mathematics	mate'matika	מָתֶמָטִיקָה (נ)
algebra	'algebra	אַלְגֶּבְרָה (נ)
geometry	geʼo'metriya	גֵּיאוֹמֶטְרִיָה (נ)
astronomy	astro'nomya	אַסְטְרוֹנוֹמְיָה (נ)
biology	bio'logya	בִּיוֹלוֹגְיָה (נ)
geography	geʼo'grafya	גֵּיאוֹגְרַפְיָה (נ)
geology	geʼo'logya	גֵּיאוֹלוֹגְיָה (נ)
history	his'torya	הִיסְטוֹרְיָה (נ)
medicine	refu'a	רְפוּאָה (נ)
pedagogy	χinuχ	חִינוּךְ (ז)
law	miʃpatim	מִשְׁפָּטִים (ז"ר)
physics	'fizika	פִיזִיקָה (נ)
chemistry	'χimya	כִימְיָה (נ)
philosophy	filo'sofya	פִילוֹסוֹפְיָה (נ)
psychology	psiχo'logya	פְּסִיכוֹלוֹגְיָה (נ)

145. Writing system. Orthography

grammar	dikduk	דִקְדוּק (ז)
vocabulary	otsar milim	אוֹצַר מִילִים (ז)
phonetics	torat ha'hege	תוֹרַת הַהֶגֶה (נ)
noun	ʃem 'etsem	שֵׁם עֶצֶם (ז)
adjective	ʃem 'to'ar	שֵׁם תּוֹאַר (ז)
verb	po'el	פּוֹעַל (ז)
adverb	'to'ar 'po'al	תּוֹאַר פּוֹעַל (ז)
pronoun	ʃem guf	שֵׁם גּוּף (ז)
interjection	milat kri'a	מִילַת קְרִיאָה (נ)
preposition	milat 'yaχas	מִילַת יַחַס (נ)
root	'ʃoreʃ	שׁוֹרֶשׁ (ז)
ending	si'yomet	סִיוֹמֶת (נ)
prefix	tχilit	תְּחִילִית (נ)
syllable	havara	הֲבָרָה (נ)
suffix	si'yomet	סִיוֹמֶת (נ)
stress mark	'ta'am	טַעַם (ז)
apostrophe	'gereʃ	גֶּרֶשׁ (ז)
full stop	nekuda	נְקוּדָה (נ)
comma	psik	פְּסִיק (ז)
semicolon	nekuda ufsik	נְקוּדָה וּפְסִיק (נ)
colon	nekudo'tayim	נְקוּדוֹתַיִים (נ"ר)
ellipsis	ʃaloʃ nekudot	שָׁלוֹשׁ נְקוּדוֹת (נ"ר)
question mark	siman ʃe'ela	סִימַן שְׁאֵלָה (ז)
exclamation mark	siman kri'a	סִימַן קְרִיאָה (ז)

inverted commas	merχa'ot	מֵרְכָאוֹת (נ״ר)
in inverted commas	bemerχa'ot	בְּמֵרְכָאוֹת
parenthesis	sog'rayim	סוֹגְרַיִם (נ״ר)
in parenthesis	besog'rayim	בְּסוֹגְרַיִם

hyphen	makaf	מַקָּף (ז)
dash	kav mafrid	קַו מַפְרִיד (ז)
space (between words)	'revaχ	רֶוַוח (ז)

| letter | ot | אוֹת (נ) |
| capital letter | ot gdola | אוֹת גְּדוֹלָה (נ) |

| vowel (n) | tnu'a | תְּנוּעָה (נ) |
| consonant (n) | iʦur | עִיצוּר (ז) |

sentence	miʃpat	מִשְׁפָּט (ז)
subject	nose	נוֹשֵׂא (ז)
predicate	nasu	נָשׂוּא (ז)

line	ʃura	שׁוּרָה (נ)
on a new line	beʃura χadaʃa	בְּשׁוּרָה חֲדָשָׁה
paragraph	piska	פִּסְקָה (נ)

word	mila	מִילָה (נ)
group of words	ʦiruf milim	צֵירוּף מִילִים (ז)
expression	bitui	בִּיטוּי (ז)
synonym	mila nir'defet	מִילָה נִרְדֶּפֶת (נ)
antonym	'hefeχ	הֵפֶךְ (ז)

rule	klal	כְּלָל (ז)
exception	yoʦe min haklal	יוֹצֵא מִן הַכְּלָל (ז)
correct (adj)	naχon	נָכוֹן

conjugation	hataya	הַטָּיָיה (נ)
declension	hataya	הַטָּיָיה (נ)
nominal case	yaχasa	יַחֲסָה (נ)
question	ʃe'ela	שְׁאֵלָה (נ)
to underline (vt)	lehadgiʃ	לְהַדְגִּיש
dotted line	kav nakud	קַו נָקוּד (ז)

146. Foreign languages

language	safa	שָׂפָה (נ)
foreign (adj)	zar	זָר
foreign language	safa zara	שָׂפָה זָרָה (נ)
to study (vt)	lilmod	לִלְמוֹד
to learn (language, etc.)	lilmod	לִלְמוֹד

to read (vi, vt)	likro	לִקְרוֹא
to speak (vi, vt)	ledaber	לְדַבֵּר
to understand (vt)	lehavin	לְהָבִין
to write (vt)	liχtov	לִכְתּוֹב
fast (adv)	maher	מַהֵר
slowly (adv)	le'at	לְאַט

fluently (adv)	χofʃi	חוֹפְשִׁי
rules	klalim	כְּלָלִים (ז״ר)
grammar	dikduk	דְּקְדּוּק (ז)
vocabulary	oʦar milim	אוֹצַר מִילִים (ז)
phonetics	torat ha'hege	תּוֹרַת הַהֶגֶה (נ)

textbook	'sefer limud	סֵפֶר לִימוּד (ז)
dictionary	milon	מִילוֹן (ז)
teach-yourself book	'sefer lelimud aʦmi	סֵפֶר לְלִימוּד עַצְמִי (ז)
phrasebook	siχon	שִׂיחוֹן (ז)

cassette, tape	ka'letet	קַלֶטֶת (נ)
videotape	ka'letet 'vide'o	קַלֶטֶת וִידֵיאוֹ (נ)
CD, compact disc	taklitor	תַּקְלִיטוֹר (ז)
DVD	di vi di	דִי. וִי. דִי. (ז)

alphabet	alefbeit	אָלֶפְבֵּית (ז)
to spell (vt)	le'ayet	לְאַיֵית
pronunciation	hagiya	הֲגִיָּיה (נ)

accent	mivta	מִבְטָא (ז)
with an accent	im mivta	עִם מִבְטָא
without an accent	bli mivta	בְּלִי מִבְטָא

| word | mila | מִילָה (נ) |
| meaning | maʃma'ut | מַשְׁמָעוּת (נ) |

course (e.g. a French ~)	kurs	קוּרְס (ז)
to sign up	leheraʃem lekurs	לְהֵירָשֵׁם לְקוּרְס
teacher	more	מוֹרֶה (ז)

translation (process)	tirgum	תַּרְגּוּם (ז)
translation (text, etc.)	tirgum	תַּרְגּוּם (ז)
translator	metargem	מְתַרְגֵּם (ז)
interpreter	meturgeman	מְתוּרְגְּמָן (ז)

| polyglot | poliglot | פּוֹלִיגְלוֹט (ז) |
| memory | zikaron | זִיכָּרוֹן (ז) |

147. Fairy tale characters

Santa Claus	'santa 'kla'us	סַנְטָה קְלָאוּס (ז)
Cinderella	sinde'rela	סִינדֶרֶלָה
mermaid	bat yam, betulat hayam	בַּת יָם, בְּתוּלַת הַיָם (נ)
Neptune	neptun	נֶפְטוּן (ז)

magician, wizard	kosem	קוֹסֵם (ז)
fairy	'feya	פֵיָה (נ)
magic (adj)	kasum	קָסוּם
magic wand	ʃarvit 'kesem	שַׁרְבִיט קֶסֶם (ז)

fairy tale	agada	אַגָדָה (נ)
miracle	nes	נֵס (ז)
dwarf	gamad	גַמָד (ז)

to turn into ...	lahafox le...	...לַהֲפוֹך ל
ghost	'ruax refa"im	רוּחַ רְפָאִים (ז)
phantom	'ruax refa"im	רוּחַ רְפָאִים (ז)
monster	mif'letset	מִפְלֶצֶת (נ)
dragon	drakon	דְרָקוֹן (ז)
giant	anak	עֲנָק (ז)

148. Zodiac Signs

Aries	tale	טָלֶה (ז)
Taurus	ʃor	שׁוֹר (ז)
Gemini	te'omim	תְאוֹמִים (ז"ר)
Cancer	sartan	סַרְטָן (ז)
Leo	arye	אַרְיֵה (ז)
Virgo	betula	בְּתוּלָה (נ)

Libra	moz'nayim	מֹאזְנַיִם (ז"ר)
Scorpio	akrav	עַקְרָב (ז)
Sagittarius	kaʃat	קַשָׁת (ז)
Capricorn	gdi	גְדִי (ז)
Aquarius	dli	דְלִי (ז)
Pisces	dagim	דָגִים (ז"ר)

character	'ofi	אוֹפִי (ז)
character traits	tʃunot 'ofi	תְכוּנוֹת אוֹפִי (נ"ר)
behaviour	hitnahagut	הִתְנַהֲגוּת (נ)
to tell fortunes	lenabe et ha'atid	לְנַבֵּא אֶת הָעָתִיד
fortune-teller	ma'gedet atidot	מַגֶדֶת עֲתִידוֹת (נ)
horoscope	horoskop	הוֹרוֹסְקוֹפ (ז)

Arts

149. Theatre

theatre	te'atron	תֵּיאַטרוֹן (ז)
opera	'opera	אוֹפֶּרָה (נ)
operetta	ope'reta	אוֹפֶּרֶטָּה (נ)
ballet	balet	בָּלֶט (ז)
theatre poster	kraza	כְּרָזָה (נ)
theatre company	lahaka	לַהֲקָה (נ)
tour	masa hofa'ot	מַסַּע הוֹפָעוֹת (ז)
to be on tour	latset lemasa hofa'ot	לָצֵאת לְמַסַּע הוֹפָעוֹת
to rehearse (vi, vt)	la'aroχ χazara	לַעֲרוֹך חֲזָרָה
rehearsal	χazara	חֲזָרָה (נ)
repertoire	repertu'ar	רֶפֶּרְטוּאָר (ז)
performance	hofa'a	הוֹפָעָה (נ)
theatrical show	hatsaga	הַצָּגָה (נ)
play	maχaze	מַחֲזֶה (ז)
ticket	kartis	כַּרְטִיס (ז)
booking office	kupa	קוּפָּה (נ)
lobby, foyer	'lobi	לוֹבִּי (ז)
coat check (cloakroom)	meltaχa	מֶלְתָּחָה (נ)
cloakroom ticket	mispar meltaχa	מִסְפַּר מֶלְתָּחָה (ז)
binoculars	miʃ'kefet	מִשְׁקֶפֶת (נ)
usher	sadran	סַדְרָן (ז)
stalls (orchestra seats)	parter	פַּרְטֶר (ז)
balcony	mir'peset	מִרְפֶּסֶת (נ)
dress circle	ya'tsi'a	יָצִיעַ (ז)
box	ta	תָּא (ז)
row	ʃura	שׁוּרָה (נ)
seat	moʃav	מוֹשָׁב (ז)
audience	'kahal	קָהָל (ז)
spectator	tsofe	צוֹפֶה (ז)
to clap (vi, vt)	limχo ka'payim	לִמְחוֹא כַּפַּיִם
applause	meχi'ot ka'payim	מְחִיאוֹת כַּפַּיִם (נ״ר)
ovation	tʃu'ot	תְּשׁוּאוֹת (נ״ר)
stage	bama	בָּמָה (נ)
curtain	masaχ	מָסָך (ז)
scenery	taf'ura	תַּפְאוּרָה (נ)
backstage	klayim	קְלָעִים
scene (e.g. the last ~)	'stsena	סְצֵינָה (נ)
act	ma'araχa	מַעֲרָכָה (נ)
interval	hafsaka	הַפְסָקָה (נ)

150. Cinema

actor	saχkan	שַׂחְקָן (ז)
actress	saχkanit	שַׂחְקָנִית (נ)
cinema (industry)	kol'noʻa	קוֹלְנוֹעַ (ז)
film	'seret	סֶרֶט (ז)
episode	epi'zoda	אֶפִּיזוֹדָה (נ)
detective film	'seret balaʃi	סֶרֶט בַּלָשִׁי (ז)
action film	ma'arvon	מַעַרְבוֹן (ז)
adventure film	'seret harpatka'ot	סֶרֶט הַרְפַּתְקָאוֹת (ז)
science fiction film	'seret mada bidyoni	סֶרֶט מַדָע בִּדְיוֹנִי (ז)
horror film	'seret eima	סֶרֶט אֵימָה (ז)
comedy film	ko'medya	קוֹמֶדְיָה (נ)
melodrama	melo'drama	מֶלוֹדְרָמָה (נ)
drama	'drama	דְרָמָה (נ)
fictional film	'seret alilati	סֶרֶט עֲלִילָתִי (ז)
documentary	'seret ti'udi	סֶרֶט תִיעוּדִי (ז)
cartoon	'seret ani'matsya	סֶרֶט אָנִימַצְיָה (ז)
silent films	sratim ilmim	סְרָטִים אִילְמִים (ז״ר)
role (part)	tafkid	תַפְקִיד (ז)
leading role	tafkid raʃi	תַפְקִיד רָאשִׁי (ז)
to play (vi, vt)	lesaχek	לְשַׂחֵק
film star	koχav kol'noʻa	כּוֹכַב קוֹלְנוֹעַ (ז)
well-known (adj)	mefursam	מְפוּרְסָם
famous (adj)	mefursam	מְפוּרְסָם
popular (adj)	popu'lari	פּוֹפּוּלָרִי
script (screenplay)	tasrit	תַסְרִיט (ז)
scriptwriter	tasritai	תַסְרִיטַאי (ז)
film director	bamai	בַּמַאי (ז)
producer	mefik	מֵפִיק (ז)
assistant	ozer	עוֹזֵר (ז)
cameraman	tsalam	צַלָם (ז)
stuntman	pa'alulan	פַּעֲלוּלָן (ז)
double (stuntman)	saχkan maχlif	שַׂחְקָן מַחֲלִיף (ז)
to shoot a film	letsalem 'seret	לְצַלֵם סֶרֶט
audition, screen test	mivdak	מִבְדָק (ז)
shooting	hasrata	הַסְרָטָה (נ)
film crew	'tsevet ha'seret	צֶוֶות הַסֶרֶט (ז)
film set	atar hatsilum	אָתַר הַצִילוּם (ז)
camera	matslema	מַצְלֵמָה (נ)
cinema	beit kol'noʻa	בֵּית קוֹלְנוֹעַ (ז)
screen (e.g. big ~)	masaχ	מָסָך (ז)
to show a film	lehar'ot 'seret	לְהַרְאוֹת סֶרֶט
soundtrack	paskol	פַּסְקוֹל (ז)
special effects	e'fektim meyuχadim	אֶפָקְטִים מְיוּחָדִים (ז״ר)

subtitles	ktuviyot	כְּתוּבִיוֹת (נ"ר)
credits	ktuviyot	כְּתוּבִיוֹת (נ"ר)
translation	tirgum	תִּרְגּוּם (ז)

151. Painting

art	amanut	אָמָנוּת (נ)
fine arts	omanuyot yafot	אוֹמָנוּיוֹת יָפוֹת (נ"ר)
art gallery	ga'lerya le'amanut	גָּלֶרְיָה לְאָמָנוּת (נ)
art exhibition	ta'aruxat amanut	תַּעֲרוּכַת אָמָנוּת (נ)
painting (art)	tsiyur	צִיּוּר (ז)
graphic art	'grafika	גְּרָפִיקָה (נ)
abstract art	amanut muf'ʃetet	אָמָנוּת מוּפְשֶׁטֶת (נ)
impressionism	impresyonizm	אִימְפְּרֶסְיוֹנִיזְם (ז)
picture (painting)	tmuna	תְּמוּנָה (נ)
drawing	tsiyur	צִיּוּר (ז)
poster	'poster	פּוֹסְטֶר (ז)
illustration (picture)	iyur	אִיּוּר (ז)
miniature	minya'tura	מִינְיָאטוּרָה (נ)
copy (of painting, etc.)	he'etek	הֶעְתֵּק (ז)
reproduction	ʃi'atuk	שִׁעְתּוּק (ז)
mosaic	psefas	פְּסֵיפָס (ז)
stained glass window	vitraʒ	וִיטְרָאז' (ז)
fresco	fresko	פְרֶסְקוֹ (ז)
engraving	taxrit	תַּחְרִיט (ז)
bust (sculpture)	pro'toma	פְּרוֹטוֹמָה (נ)
sculpture	'pesel	פֶּסֶל (ז)
statue	'pesel	פֶּסֶל (ז)
plaster of Paris	'geves	גֶּבֶס (ז)
plaster (as adj)	mi'geves	מְגֻבָּס
portrait	dyukan	דְּיוֹקָן (ז)
self-portrait	dyukan atsmi	דְּיוֹקָן עַצְמִי (ז)
landscape painting	tsiyur nof	צִיּוּר נוֹף (ז)
still life	'teva domem	טֶבַע דּוֹמֵם (ז)
caricature	karika'tura	קָרִיקָטוּרָה (נ)
sketch	tarʃim	תַּרְשִׁים (ז)
paint	'tseva	צֶבַע (ז)
watercolor paint	'tseva 'mayim	צֶבַע מַיִם (ז)
oil (paint)	'ʃemen	שֶׁמֶן (ז)
pencil	iparon	עִפָּרוֹן (ז)
Indian ink	tuʃ	טוּש (ז)
charcoal	pexam	פֶּחָם (ז)
to draw (vi, vt)	letsayer	לְצַיֵּיר
to paint (vi, vt)	letsayer	לְצַיֵּיר
to pose (vi)	ledagmen	לְדַגְמֵן
artist's model (masc.)	dugman eirom	דּוּגְמָן עֵירוֹם (ז)

artist's model (fem.)	dugmanit erom	דּוּגְמָנִית עֵירוֹם (נ)
artist (painter)	tsayar	צַיָּר (ז)
work of art	yetsirat amanut	יְצִירַת אָמָּנוּת (נ)
masterpiece	yetsirat mofet	יְצִירַת מוֹפֵת (נ)
studio (artist's workroom)	'studyo	סְטוּדְיוֹ (ז)

canvas (cloth)	bad piʃtan	בַּד פִּשְׁתָּן (ז)
easel	kan tsiyur	כַּן צִיּוּר (ז)
palette	'plata	פָּלֶטָה (נ)

frame (picture ~, etc.)	mis'geret	מִסְגֶּרֶת (נ)
restoration	ʃixzur	שִׁחְזוּר (ז)
to restore (vt)	leʃaxzer	לְשַׁחְזֵר

152. Literature & Poetry

literature	sifrut	סִפְרוּת (נ)
author (writer)	sofer	סוֹפֵר (ז)
pseudonym	ʃem badui	שֵׁם בָּדוּי (ז)

book	'sefer	סֵפֶר (ז)
volume	'kerex	כֶּרֶךְ (ז)
table of contents	'toxen inyanim	תּוֹכֶן עִנְיָנִים (ז)
page	amud	עַמּוּד (ז)
main character	hagibor haraʃi	הַגִּבּוֹר הָרָאשִׁי (ז)
autograph	xatima	חֲתִימָה (נ)

short story	sipur katsar	סִיפּוּר קָצָר (ז)
story (novella)	sipur	סִיפּוּר (ז)
novel	roman	רוֹמָן (ז)
work (writing)	xibur	חִיבּוּר (ז)
fable	maʃal	מָשָׁל (ז)
detective novel	roman balaʃi	רוֹמָן בַּלָּשִׁי (ז)

poem (verse)	ʃir	שִׁיר (ז)
poetry	ʃira	שִׁירָה (נ)
poem (epic, ballad)	po''ema	פּוֹאֵמָה (נ)
poet	meʃorer	מְשׁוֹרֵר (ז)

fiction	sifrut yafa	סִפְרוּת יָפָה (נ)
science fiction	mada bidyoni	מַדָּע בִּדְיוֹנִי (ז)
adventures	harpatka'ot	הַרְפַּתְקָאוֹת (נ"ר)
educational literature	sifrut limudit	סִפְרוּת לִימוּדִית (נ)
children's literature	sifrut yeladim	סִפְרוּת יְלָדִים (נ)

153. Circus

circus	kirkas	קִרְקָס (ז)
travelling circus	kirkas nayad	קִרְקָס נַיָּיד (ז)
programme	toxnit	תּוֹכְנִית (נ)
performance	hofa'a	הוֹפָעָה (נ)
act (circus ~)	hofa'a	הוֹפָעָה (נ)

circus ring	zira	זִירָה (נ)
pantomime (act)	panto'mima	פַּנְטוֹמִימָה (נ)
clown	leitsan	לֵיצָן (ז)

acrobat	akrobat	אַקְרוֹבָּט (ז)
acrobatics	akro'batika	אַקְרוֹבָּטִיקָה (נ)
gymnast	mit'amel	מִתְעַמֵל (ז)
gymnastics	hit'amlut	הִתְעַמְלוּת (נ)
somersault	'salta	סַלְטָה (נ)

strongman	atlet	אַתְלֵט (ז)
tamer (e.g., lion ~)	me'alef	מְאַלֵף (ז)
rider (circus horse ~)	roxev	רוֹכֵב (ז)
assistant	ozer	עוֹזֵר (ז)

stunt	pa'alul	פַּעֲלוּל (ז)
magic trick	'kesem	קֶסֶם (ז)
conjurer, magician	kosem	קוֹסֵם (ז)

juggler	lahatutan	לַהֲטוּטָן (ז)
to juggle (vi, vt)	lelahtet	לְלַהְטֵט
animal trainer	me'alef hayot	מְאַלֵף חַיּוֹת (ז)
animal training	iluf xayot	אִילוּף חַיּוֹת (ז)
to train (animals)	le'alef	לְאַלֵף

154. Music. Pop music

music	'muzika	מוּזִיקָה (נ)
musician	muzikai	מוּזִיקַאי (ז)
musical instrument	kli negina	כְּלִי נְגִינָה (ז)
to play ...	lenagen be...	לְנַגֵּן בְּ...

guitar	gi'tara	גִּיטָרָה (נ)
violin	kinor	כִּינוֹר (ז)
cello	'tʃelo	צֶ'לוֹ (ז)
double bass	kontrabas	קוֹנְטְרַבָּס (ז)
harp	'nevel	נֵבֶל (ז)

piano	psanter	פְּסַנְתֵּר (ז)
grand piano	psanter kanaf	פְּסַנְתֵּר כָּנָף (ז)
organ	ugav	עוּגָב (ז)

wind instruments	klei neʃifa	כְּלֵי נְשִיפָה (ז"ר)
oboe	abuv	אַבּוּב (ז)
saxophone	saksofon	סַקְסוֹפוֹן (ז)
clarinet	klarinet	קְלָרִינֵט (ז)
flute	xalil	חָלִיל (ז)
trumpet	xatsotsra	חֲצוֹצְרָה (נ)

| accordion | akordyon | אָקוֹרְדִּיוֹן (ז) |
| drum | tof | תּוֹף (ז) |

| duo | 'du'o | דּוּאוֹ (ז) |
| trio | ʃliʃiya | שְׁלִישִׁיָּה (נ) |

quartet	revi'iya	רְבִיעִיָּה (נ)
choir	makhela	מַקְהֵלָה (נ)
orchestra	tiz'moret	תִזְמוֹרֶת (נ)

pop music	'muzikat pop	מוּזִיקַת פּוֹפ (נ)
rock music	'muzikat rok	מוּזִיקַת רוֹק (נ)
rock group	lehakat rok	לַהֲקַת רוֹק (נ)
jazz	dʒez	גַ'ז (ז)

| idol | koχav | כּוֹכָב (ז) |
| admirer, fan | ohed | אוֹהֵד (ז) |

concert	kontsert	קוֹנְצֶרְט (ז)
symphony	si'fonya	סִימְפוֹנְיָה (נ)
composition	yetsira	יְצִירָה (נ)
to compose (write)	leχaber	לְחַבֵּר

singing (n)	ʃira	שִׁירָה (נ)
song	ʃir	שִׁיר (ז)
tune (melody)	mangina	מַנְגִּינָה (נ)
rhythm	'ketsev	קֶצֶב (ז)
blues	bluz	בְּלוּז (ז)

sheet music	tavim	תָּוִים (ז"ר)
baton	ʃarvit ni'tsuaχ	שַׁרְבִיט נִיצּוּחַ (ז)
bow	'keʃet	קֶשֶׁת (נ)
string	meitar	מֵיתָר (ז)
case (e.g. guitar ~)	nartik	נַרְתִּיק (ז)

Rest. Entertainment. Travel

155. Trip. Travel

tourism, travel	tayarut	תַּיָּירוּת (נ)
tourist	tayar	תַּיָּיר (ז)
trip, voyage	tiyul	טִיּוּל (ז)
adventure	harpatka	הַרְפַּתְקָה (נ)
trip, journey	nesi'a	נְסִיעָה (נ)
holiday	xuffa	חוּפְשָׁה (נ)
to be on holiday	lihyot bexuffa	לִהְיוֹת בָּחוּפְשָׁה
rest	menuxa	מְנוּחָה (נ)
train	ra'kevet	רַכֶּבֶת (נ)
by train	bera'kevet	בְּרַכֶּבֶת
aeroplane	matos	מָטוֹס (ז)
by aeroplane	bematos	בְּמָטוֹס
by car	bemexonit	בִּמְכוֹנִית
by ship	be'oniya	בָּאוֹנִיָּה
luggage	mit'an	מִטְעָן (ז)
suitcase	mizvada	מִזְוָדָה (נ)
luggage trolley	eglat mit'an	עֶגְלַת מִטְעָן (נ)
passport	darkon	דַּרְכּוֹן (ז)
visa	'viza, affra	וִיזָה, אַשְׁרָה (נ)
ticket	kartis	כַּרְטִיס (ז)
air ticket	kartis tisa	כַּרְטִיס טִיסָה (ז)
guidebook	madrix	מַדְרִיךְ (ז)
map (tourist ~)	mapa	מַפָּה (נ)
area (rural ~)	ezor	אֵזוֹר (ז)
place, site	makom	מָקוֹם (ז)
exotica (n)	ek'zotika	אֶקְזוֹטִיקָה (נ)
exotic (adj)	ek'zoti	אֶקְזוֹטִי
amazing (adj)	nifla	נִפְלָא
group	kvutsa	קְבוּצָה (נ)
excursion, sightseeing tour	tiyul	טִיּוּל (ז)
guide (person)	madrix tiyulim	מַדְרִיךְ טִיּוּלִים (ז)

156. Hotel

hotel	malon	מָלוֹן (ז)
motel	motel	מוֹטֶל (ז)
three-star (~ hotel)	ffloffa koxavim	שְׁלוֹשָׁה כּוֹכָבִים

five-star	χamiʃa koχavim	חֲמִישָׁה כּוֹכָבִים
to stay (in a hotel, etc.)	lehit'aχsen	לְהִתְאַכְסֵן
room	'χeder	חֶדֶר (ז)
single room	'χeder yaχid	חֶדֶר יָחִיד (ז)
double room	'χeder zugi	חֶדֶר זוּגִי (ז)
to book a room	lehazmin 'χeder	לְהַזְמִין חֶדֶר
half board	χatsi pensiyon	חֲצִי פֶּנְסִיוֹן (ז)
full board	pensyon male	פֶּנְסִיוֹן מָלֵא (ז)
with bath	im am'batya	עִם אַמְבַּטְיָה
with shower	im mik'laχat	עִם מִקְלַחַת
satellite television	tele'vizya bekvalim	טֶלֶוִויזְיָה בְּכְבָלִים (נ)
air-conditioner	mazgan	מַזְגָּן (ז)
towel	ma'gevet	מַגֶּבֶת (נ)
key	maf'teaχ	מַפְתֵּחַ (ז)
administrator	amarkal	אֲמַרְכָּל (ז)
chambermaid	χadranit	חַדְרָנִית (נ)
porter	sabal	סַבָּל (ז)
doorman	pakid kabala	פְּקִיד קַבָּלָה (ז)
restaurant	mis'ada	מִסְעָדָה (נ)
pub, bar	bar	בָּר (ז)
breakfast	aruχat 'boker	אֲרוּחַת בּוֹקֶר (נ)
dinner	aruχat 'erev	אֲרוּחַת עֶרֶב (נ)
buffet	miznon	מִזְנוֹן (ז)
lobby	'lobi	לוֹבִּי (ז)
lift	ma'alit	מַעֲלִית (נ)
DO NOT DISTURB	lo lehaf'ri'a	לֹא לְהַפְרִיעַ
NO SMOKING	asur le'aʃen!	אָסוּר לְעַשֵׁן!

157. Books. Reading

book	'sefer	סֵפֶר (ז)
author	sofer	סוֹפֵר (ז)
writer	sofer	סוֹפֵר (ז)
to write (~ a book)	liχtov	לִכְתּוֹב
reader	kore	קוֹרֵא (ז)
to read (vi, vt)	likro	לִקְרוֹא
reading (activity)	kri'a	קְרִיאָה (נ)
silently (to oneself)	belev, be'ʃeket	בְּלֵב, בְּשֶׁקֶט
aloud (adv)	bekol ram	בְּקוֹל רָם
to publish (vt)	lehotsi la'or	לְהוֹצִיא לָאוֹר
publishing (process)	hotsa'a la'or	הוֹצָאָה לָאוֹר (נ)
publisher	motsi le'or	מוֹצִיא לָאוֹר (ז)
publishing house	hotsa'a la'or	הוֹצָאָה לָאוֹר (נ)
to come out (be released)	latset le'or	לָצֵאת לָאוֹר

release (of a book)	hafatsa	הֲפָצָה (נ)
print run	tfutsa	תְּפוּצָה (נ)
bookshop	χanut sfarim	חֲנוּת סְפָרִים (נ)
library	sifriya	סְפְרִיָּה (נ)
story (novella)	sipur	סִיפּוּר (ז)
short story	sipur katsar	סִיפּוּר קָצָר (ז)
novel	roman	רוֹמָן (ז)
detective novel	roman balaʃi	רוֹמָן בַּלָשִׁי (ז)
memoirs	ziχronot	זִיכְרוֹנוֹת (ז״ר)
legend	agada	אַגָדָה (נ)
myth	'mitos	מִיתוֹס (ז)
poetry, poems	ʃirim	שִׁירִים (ז״ר)
autobiography	otobio'grafya	אוֹטוֹבְּיוֹגְרַפְיָה (נ)
selected works	mivχar ktavim	מִבְחַר כְּתָבִים (ז)
science fiction	mada bidyoni	מַדָע בִּדְיוֹנִי (ז)
title	kotar	כּוֹתָר (ז)
introduction	mavo	מָבוֹא (ז)
title page	amud ha'ʃa'ar	עַמוּד הַשַּׁעַר (ז)
chapter	'perek	פֶּרֶק (ז)
extract	'keta	קֶטַע (ז)
episode	epi'zoda	אָפִּיזוֹדָה (נ)
plot (storyline)	alila	עֲלִילָה (נ)
contents	'toχen	תּוֹכֶן (ז)
table of contents	'toχen inyanim	תּוֹכֶן עִנְיָינִים (ז)
main character	hagibor haraʃi	הַגִּיבּוֹר הָרָאשִׁי (ז)
volume	'kereχ	כֶּרֶךְ (ז)
cover	kriχa	כְּרִיכָה (נ)
binding	kriχa	כְּרִיכָה (נ)
bookmark	simaniya	סִימָנִיָּה (נ)
page	amud	עַמוּד (ז)
to page through	ledafdef	לְדַפְדֵף
margins	ʃu'layim	שׁוּלַיִם (ז״ר)
annotation (marginal note, etc.)	he'ara	הֶעָרָה (נ)
footnote	he'arat ʃu'layim	הֶעָרַת שׁוּלַיִם (נ)
text	tekst	טֶקְסְט (ז)
type, fount	gufan	גּוּפָן (ז)
misprint, typo	ta'ut dfus	טָעוֹת דְפוּס (נ)
translation	tirgum	תַּרְגוּם (ז)
to translate (vt)	letargem	לְתַרְגֵּם
original (n)	makor	מָקוֹר (ז)
famous (adj)	mefursam	מְפוּרְסָם
unknown (not famous)	lo ya'du'a	לֹא יָדוּעַ
interesting (adj)	me'anyen	מְעַנְיֵין

bestseller	rav 'meχer	רַב־מֶכֶר (ז)
dictionary	milon	מִילוֹן (ז)
textbook	'sefer limud	סֵפֶר לִימוּד (ז)
encyclopedia	entsiklo'pedya	אֶנצִיקלוֹפֶּדיָה (נ)

158. Hunting. Fishing

hunting	'tsayid	צַיִד (ז)
to hunt (vi, vt)	latsud	לָצוּד
hunter	tsayad	צַיָּיד (ז)

to shoot (vi)	lirot	לִירוֹת
rifle	rove	רוֹבֶה (ז)
bullet (shell)	kadur	כַּדּוּר (ז)
shot (lead balls)	kaduriyot	כַּדּוּרִיּוֹת (נ"ר)

steel trap	mal'kodet	מַלכּוֹדֶת (נ)
snare (for birds, etc.)	mal'kodet	מַלכּוֹדֶת (נ)
to fall into the steel trap	lehilaχed bemal'kodet	לְהִילָכֵד בְּמַלכּוֹדֶת
to lay a steel trap	leha'niaχ mal'kodet	לְהָנִיחַ מַלכּוֹדֶת

poacher	tsayad lelo reʃut	צַיָּיד לְלֹא רְשׁוּת (ז)
game (in hunting)	χayot bar	חַיּוֹת בַּר (נ"ר)
hound dog	'kelev 'tsayid	כֶּלֶב צַיִד (ז)
safari	sa'fari	סַפָארִי (ז)
mounted animal	puχlats	פּוּחלָץ (ז)

fisherman	dayag	דַּיָּיג (ז)
fishing (angling)	'dayig	דַּיִג (ז)
to fish (vi)	ladug	לָדוּג

fishing rod	χaka	חַכָּה (נ)
fishing line	χut haχaka	חוּט הַחַכָּה (ז)
hook	'keres	קֶרֶס (ז)
float	matsof	מָצוֹף (ז)
bait	pitayon	פִּיתָיוֹן (ז)

| to cast a line | lizrok et haχaka | לִזרוֹק אֶת הַחַכָּה |
| to bite (ab. fish) | liv'lo'a pitayon | לִבלוֹעַ פִּיתָיוֹן |

| catch (of fish) | ʃlal 'dayig | שׁלַל דַּיִג (ז) |
| ice-hole | mivka 'keraχ | מִבקַע קֶרַח (ז) |

| fishing net | 'reʃet dayagim | רֶשֶׁת דַּיָּיגִים (נ) |
| boat | sira | סִירָה (נ) |

to net (to fish with a net)	ladug be'reʃet	לָדוּג בְּרֶשֶׁת
to cast[throw] the net	lizrok 'reʃet	לִזרוֹק רֶשֶׁת
to haul the net in	ligror 'reʃet	לִגרוֹר רֶשֶׁת
to fall into the net	lehilaχed be'reʃet	לְהִילָכֵד בְּרֶשֶׁת

whaler (person)	tsayad livyatanim	צַיָּיד לְוויָיתָנִים (ז)
whaleboat	sfinat tseid livyetanim	סְפִינַת צֵיד לְוויָיתָנִית (נ)
harpoon	tsiltsal	צִלצָל (ז)

159. Games. Billiards

billiards	bilyard	בִּילְיַארד (ז)
billiard room, hall	'xeder bilyard	חֶדֶר בִּילְיַארד (ז)
ball (snooker, etc.)	kadur bilyard	כַּדוּר בִּילְיַארד (ז)
to pocket a ball	lehaxnis kadur lekis	לְהַכְנִיס כַּדוּר לְכִּיס
cue	makel bilyard	מַקֵל בִּילְיַארד (ז)
pocket	kis	כִּיס (ז)

160. Games. Playing cards

diamonds	yahalom	יַהֲלוֹם (ז)
spades	ale	עָלֶה (ז)
hearts	lev	לֵב (ז)
clubs	tiltan	תִלְתָן (ז)
ace	as	אָס (ז)
king	'melex	מֶלֶך (ז)
queen	malka	מַלְכָּה (נ)
jack, knave	nasix	נָסִיך (ז)
playing card	klaf	קְלָף (ז)
cards	klafim	קְלָפִים (ז"ר)
trump	klaf nitsaxon	קְלָף נִיצָחוֹן (ז)
pack of cards	xafisat klafim	חֲפִיסַת קְלָפִים (נ)
point	nekuda	נְקוּדָה (נ)
to deal (vi, vt)	lexalek klafim	לְחַלֵק קְלָפִים
to shuffle (cards)	litrof	לִטְרוֹף
lead, turn (n)	tor	תוֹר (ז)
cardsharp	noxel klafim	נוֹכֵל קְלָפִים (ז)

161. Casino. Roulette

casino	ka'zino	קָזִינוֹ (ז)
roulette (game)	ru'leta	רוּלֶטָה (נ)
bet	menat misxak	מְנָת מִשְׂחָק (נ)
to place bets	leha'niax menat misxak	לְהָנִיחַ מְנָת מִשְׂחָק
red	adom	אָדוֹם
black	ʃaxor	שָׁחוֹר
to bet on red	lehamer al adom	לְהַמֵר עַל אָדוֹם
to bet on black	lehamer al ʃaxor	לְהַמֵר עַל שָׁחוֹר
croupier (dealer)	'diler	דִילֶר (ז)
to spin the wheel	lesovev et hagalgal	לְסוֹבֵב אֶת הַגַלְגַל
rules (of game)	klalei hamisxak	כְּלָלֵי הַמִשְׂחָק (ז"ר)
chip	asimon	אָסִימוֹן (ז)
to win (vi, vt)	lizkot	לִזְכּוֹת
win (winnings)	zxiya	זְכִיָה (נ)

| to lose (~ 100 dollars) | lehafsid | לְהַפְסִיד |
| loss (losses) | hefsed | הֶפְסֵד (ז) |

player	saχkan	שֹׂחְקָן (ז)
blackjack (card game)	esrim ve'eχad	עֶשְׂרִים וְאֶחָד (ז)
craps (dice game)	misχak kubiyot	מִשְׂחַק קוּבִּיּוֹת (ז)
dice (a pair of ~)	kubiyot	קוּבִּיּוֹת (נ״ר)
fruit machine	meχonat misχak	מְכוֹנַת מִשְׂחָק (נ)

162. Rest. Games. Miscellaneous

to stroll (vi, vt)	letayel ba'regel	לְטַיֵּל בָּרֶגֶל
stroll (leisurely walk)	tiyul ragli	טִיּוּל רַגְלִי (ז)
car ride	nesi'a bameχonit	נְסִיעָה בָּמְכוֹנִית (נ)
adventure	harpatka	הַרְפַּתְקָה (נ)
picnic	'piknik	פִּיקְנִיק (ז)

game (chess, etc.)	misχak	מִשְׂחָק (ז)
player	saχkan	שֹׂחְקָן (ז)
game (one ~ of chess)	misχak	מִשְׂחָק (ז)

collector (e.g. philatelist)	asfan	אַסְפָן (ז)
to collect (stamps, etc.)	le'esof	לֶאֱסוֹף
collection	'osef	אוֹסֶף (ז)

crossword puzzle	taʃbets	תַּשְׁבֵּץ (ז)
racecourse (hippodrome)	hipodrom	הִיפּוֹדְרוֹם (ז)
disco (discotheque)	diskotek	דִיסְקוֹטֶק (ז)

| sauna | 'sa'una | סָאוּנָה (נ) |
| lottery | 'loto | לוֹטוֹ (ז) |

camping trip	tiyul maχana'ut	טִיּוּל מַחֲנָאוּת (ז)
camp	maχane	מַחֲנֶה (ז)
tent (for camping)	'ohel	אוֹהֶל (ז)
compass	matspen	מַצְפֵּן (ז)
camper	maχnai	מַחֲנַאי (ז)

to watch (film, etc.)	lir'ot	לִרְאוֹת
viewer	tsofe	צוֹפֶה (ז)
TV show (TV program)	toχnit tele'vizya	תּוֹכְנִית טֶלֶוִיזְיָה (נ)

163. Photography

| camera (photo) | matslema | מַצְלֵמָה (נ) |
| photo, picture | tmuna | תְמוּנָה (נ) |

photographer	tsalam	צַלָּם (ז)
photo studio	'studyo letsilum	סְטוּדְיוֹ לְצִילוּם (ז)
photo album	albom tmunot	אַלְבּוֹם תְמוּנוֹת (ז)
camera lens	adaʃa	עֲדָשָׁה (נ)
telephoto lens	a'deʃet teleskop	עֲדֶשֶׁת טֶלֶסְקוֹפּ (נ)

filter	masnen	מַסְנֵן (ז)
lens	adaʃa	עֲדָשָׁה (נ)
optics (high-quality ~)	'optika	אוֹפְּטִיקָה (נ)
diaphragm (aperture)	tsamtsam	צַמְצָם (ז)
exposure time (shutter speed)	zman hahe'ara	זְמַן הַהָאָרָה (ז)
viewfinder	einit	עֵינִית (נ)
digital camera	matslema digi'talit	מַצְלֵמָה דִיגִיטָלִית (נ)
tripod	χatsuva	חֲצוּבָה (נ)
flash	mavzek	מַבְזֵק (ז)
to photograph (vt)	letsalem	לְצַלֵם
to take pictures	letsalem	לְצַלֵם
to have one's picture taken	lehitstalem	לְהִצְטַלֵם
focus	moked	מוֹקֵד (ז)
to focus	lemaked	לְמַקֵד
sharp, in focus (adj)	χad, memukad	חַד, מְמוּקָד
sharpness	χadut	חַדוּת (נ)
contrast	nigud	נִיגוּד (ז)
contrast (as adj)	menugad	מְנוּגָד
picture (photo)	tmuna	תְמוּנָה (נ)
negative (n)	taʃlil	תַשְׁלִיל (ז)
film (a roll of ~)	'seret	סֶרֶט (ז)
frame (still)	freim	פְרֵיִים (ז)
to print (photos)	lehadpis	לְהַדְפִּיס

164. Beach. Swimming

beach	χof yam	חוֹף יָם (ז)
sand	χol	חוֹל (ז)
deserted (beach)	ʃomem	שׁוֹמֵם
suntan	ʃizuf	שִׁיזוּף (ז)
to get a tan	lehiʃtazef	לְהִשְׁתַזֵף
tanned (adj)	ʃazuf	שָׁזוּף
sunscreen	krem hagana	קְרֶם הֲגָנָה (ז)
bikini	bi'kini	בִּיקִינִי (ז)
swimsuit, bikini	'beged yam	בֶּגֶד יָם (ז)
swim trunks	'beged yam	בֶּגֶד יָם (ז)
swimming pool	breχa	בְּרֵיכָה (נ)
to swim (vi)	lisχot	לִשְׂחוֹת
shower	mik'laχat	מִקְלַחַת (נ)
to change (one's clothes)	lehaχlif bgadim	לְהַחֲלִיף בְּגָדִים
towel	ma'gevet	מַגֶבֶת (נ)
boat	sira	סִירָה (נ)
motorboat	sirat ma'no'a	סִירַת מָנוֹעַ (נ)

water ski	ski 'mayim	סְקִי מַיִם (ז)
pedalo	sirat pe'dalim	סִירַת פֶּדָלִים (נ)
surfing	gliʃat galim	גְלִישַׁת גַלִים
surfer	goleʃ	גוֹלֵשׁ (ז)
scuba set	'skuba	סְקוּבָּה (נ)
flippers (swim fins)	snapirim	סְנַפִּירִים (ז"ר)
mask (diving ~)	maseχa	מַסֵכָה (נ)
diver	tsolelan	צוֹלְלָן (ז)
to dive (vi)	litslol	לִצְלוֹל
underwater (adv)	mi'taχat lifnei ha'mayim	מִתַחַת לִפְנֵי הַמַיִם
beach umbrella	ʃimʃiya	שִׁמְשִׁיָה (נ)
beach chair (sun lounger)	kise 'noaχ	כִּיסֵא נוֹחַ (ז)
sunglasses	miʃkefei 'ʃemeʃ	מִשְׁקְפֵי שֶׁמֶשׁ (ז"ר)
air mattress	mizron mitna'peaχ	מִזְרוֹן מִתְנַפֵּחַ (ז)
to play (amuse oneself)	lesaχek	לְשַׂחֵק
to go for a swim	lehitraχets	לְהִתְרַחֵץ
beach ball	kadur yam	כַּדוּר יָם (ז)
to inflate (vt)	lena'peaχ	לְנַפֵּחַ
inflatable, air (adj)	menupaχ	מְנוּפָּח
wave	gal	גַל (ז)
buoy (line of ~s)	matsof	מָצוֹף (ז)
to drown (ab. person)	lit'boʻa	לִטְבּוֹעַ
to save, to rescue	lehatsil	לְהַצִיל
life jacket	χagorat hatsala	חֲגוֹרַת הַצָלָה (נ)
to observe, to watch	litspot, lehaʃkif	לִצְפוֹת, לְהַשְׁקִיף
lifeguard	matsil	מַצִיל (ז)

TECHNICAL EQUIPMENT. TRANSPORT

Technical equipment

165. Computer

computer	maxſev	מַחְשֵׁב (ז)
notebook, laptop	maxſev nayad	מַחְשֵׁב נַיָּיד (ז)
to turn on	lehadlik	לְהַדְלִיק
to turn off	lexabot	לְכַבּוֹת
keyboard	mik'ledet	מִקְלֶדֶת (נ)
key	makaſ	מַקָּשׁ (ז)
mouse	axbar	עַכְבָּר (ז)
mouse mat	ſa'tiax le'axbar	שָׁטִיחַ לְעַכְבָּר (ז)
button	kaftor	כַּפְתּוֹר (ז)
cursor	saman	סַמָּן (ז)
monitor	masax	מָסָךְ (ז)
screen	tsag	צַג (ז)
hard disk	disk ka'ſiax	דִּיסְק קָשִׁיחַ (ז)
hard disk capacity	'nefax disk ka'ſiax	נֶפַח דִּיסְק קָשִׁיחַ (ז)
memory	zikaron	זִכָּרוֹן (ז)
random access memory	zikaron giſa akra'it	זִכָּרוֹן גִּישָׁה אַקְרַאִית (ז)
file	'kovets	קוֹבֶץ (ז)
folder	tikiya	תִּיקִיָּיה (נ)
to open (vt)	lif'toax	לִפְתּוֹחַ
to close (vt)	lisgor	לִסְגּוֹר
to save (vt)	liſmor	לִשְׁמוֹר
to delete (vt)	limxok	לִמְחוֹק
to copy (vt)	leha'atik	לְהַעֲתִיק
to sort (vt)	lemayen	לְמַיֵּין
to transfer (copy)	leha'avir	לְהַעֲבִיר
programme	toxna	תּוֹכְנָה (נ)
software	toxna	תּוֹכְנָה (נ)
programmer	metaxnet	מְתַכְנֵת (ז)
to program (vt)	letaxnet	לְתַכְנֵת
hacker	'haker	הָאקֵר (ז)
password	sisma	סִיסְמָה (נ)
virus	'virus	וִירוּס (ז)
to find, to detect	limtso, le'ater	לְמַצוֹא, לְאַתֵּר
byte	bait	בַּייְט (ז)

megabyte	megabait	מֶגָבַּייט (ז)
data	netunim	נְתוּנִים (ז״ר)
database	bsis netunim	בְּסִיס נְתוּנִים (ז)

cable (USB, etc.)	'kevel	כֶּבֶל (ז)
to disconnect (vt)	lenatek	לְנַתֵּק
to connect (sth to sth)	leχaber	לְחַבֵּר

166. Internet. E-mail

Internet	'internet	אִינְטֶרְנֶט (ז)
browser	dafdefan	דַפְדְפָן (ז)
search engine	ma'no'a χipus	מָנוֹעַ חִיפּוּשׂ (ז)
provider	sapak	סַפָּק (ז)

webmaster	menahel ha'atar	מְנַהֵל הָאֲתָר (ז)
website	atar	אֲתָר (ז)
webpage	daf 'internet	דַף אִינְטֶרְנֶט (ז)

| address (e-mail ~) | 'ktovet | כְּתוֹבֶת (נ) |
| address book | 'sefer ktovot | סֵפֶר כְּתוֹבוֹת (ז) |

postbox	teivat 'do'ar	תֵּיבַת דוֹאַר (נ)
post	'do'ar, 'do'al	דוֹאַר (ז), דוֹאַ״ל (ז)
full (adj)	gaduʃ	גָדוּשׁ

message	hoda'a	הוֹדָעָה (נ)
incoming messages	hoda'ot niχnasot	הוֹדָעוֹת נִכְנָסוֹת (נ״ר)
outgoing messages	hoda'ot yots'ot	הוֹדָעוֹת יוֹצְאוֹת (נ״ר)
sender	ʃo'leaχ	שׁוֹלֵחַ (ז)
to send (vt)	liʃ'loaχ	לִשְׁלוֹחַ
sending (of mail)	ʃliχa	שְׁלִיחָה (נ)
receiver	nim'an	נִמְעָן (ז)
to receive (vt)	lekabel	לְקַבֵּל

| correspondence | hitkatvut | הִתְכַּתְבוּת (נ) |
| to correspond (vi) | lehitkatev | לְהִתְכַּתֵּב |

file	'kovets	קוֹבֶץ (ז)
to download (vt)	lehorid	לְהוֹרִיד
to create (vt)	litsor	לִיצוֹר
to delete (vt)	limχok	לִמְחוֹק
deleted (adj)	maχuk	מָחוּק

connection (ADSL, etc.)	χibur	חִיבּוּר (ז)
speed	mehirut	מְהִירוּת (נ)
modem	'modem	מוֹדֶם (ז)
access	giʃa	גִישָׁה (נ)
port (e.g. input ~)	port	פּוֹרְט (ז)

connection (make a ~)	χibur	חִיבּוּר (ז)
to connect to … (vi)	lehitχaber	לְהִתְחַבֵּר
to select (vt)	livχor	לִבְחוֹר
to search (for …)	leχapes	לְחַפֵּשׂ

167. Electricity

electricity	χaʃmal	חַשְׁמַל (ז)
electric, electrical (adj)	χaʃmali	חַשְׁמַלִי
electric power station	taχanat 'koaχ	תַּחֲנַת כּוֹחַ (נ)
energy	e'nergya	אֶנֶרְגְיָה (נ)
electric power	e'nergya χaʃmalit	אֶנֶרְגְיָה חַשְׁמַלִית (נ)

light bulb	nura	נוּרָה (נ)
torch	panas	פָּנָס (ז)
street light	panas reχov	פָּנָס רְחוֹב (ז)

light	or	אוֹר (ז)
to turn on	lehadlik	לְהַדְלִיק
to turn off	leχabot	לְכַבּוֹת
to turn off the light	leχabot	לְכַבּוֹת

to burn out (vi)	lehisaref	לְהִישָׂרֵף
short circuit	'keʦer	קֶצֶר (ז)
broken wire	χut ka'ru'a	חוּט קָרוּעַ (ז)
contact (electrical ~)	maga	מַגָּע (ז)

light switch	'meteg	מֶתֶג (ז)
socket outlet	'ʃeka	שֶׁקַע (ז)
plug	'teka	תֶּקַע (ז)
extension lead	'kabel ma'ariχ	כֶּבֶל מַאֲרִיךְ (ז)

fuse	natiχ	נָתִיךְ (ז)
cable, wire	χut	חוּט (ז)
wiring	χivut	חִיווּט (ז)

ampere	amper	אַמְפֶּר (ז)
amperage	'zerem χaʃmali	זֶרֶם חַשְׁמַלִי (ז)
volt	volt	ווֹלְט (ז)
voltage	'metaχ	מֶתַח (ז)

| electrical device | maχʃir χaʃmali | מַכְשִׁיר חַשְׁמַלִי (ז) |
| indicator | maχvan | מַחְווָן (ז) |

electrician	χaʃmalai	חַשְׁמַלַאי (ז)
to solder (vt)	lehalχim	לְהַלְחִים
soldering iron	malχem	מַלְחֵם (ז)
electric current	'zerem	זֶרֶם (ז)

168. Tools

tool, instrument	kli	כְּלִי (ז)
tools	klei avoda	כְּלֵי עֲבוֹדָה (ז"ר)
equipment (factory ~)	ʦiyud	צִיוּד (ז)

hammer	patiʃ	פַּטִּישׁ (ז)
screwdriver	mavreg	מַבְרֵג (ז)
axe	garzen	גַּרְזֶן (ז)

saw	masor	מָסוֹר (ז)
to saw (vt)	lenaser	לְנַסֵּר
plane (tool)	maktso'a	מַקְצוּעָה (נ)
to plane (vt)	lehak'tsi'a	לְהַקְצִיעַ
soldering iron	malxem	מַלְחֵם (ז)
to solder (vt)	lehalxim	לְהַלְחִים

file (tool)	ptsira	פְּצִירָה (נ)
carpenter pincers	tsvatot	צְבָתוֹת (נ״ר)
combination pliers	mel'kaxat	מֶלְקַחַת (נ)
chisel	izmel	אִזְמֵל (ז)

drill bit	mak'deax	מַקְדֵּחַ (ז)
electric drill	makdexa	מַקְדֵּחָה (נ)
to drill (vi, vt)	lik'doax	לִקְדּוֹחַ

knife	sakin	סַכִּין (ז, נ)
pocket knife	olar	אוֹלָר (ז)
blade	'lahav	לַהַב (ז)

sharp (blade, etc.)	xad	חַד
dull, blunt (adj)	kehe	קֵהֶה
to get blunt (dull)	lehitkahot	לְהִתְקַהוֹת
to sharpen (vt)	lehaʃxiz	לְהַשְׁחִיז

bolt	'boreg	בּוֹרֶג (ז)
nut	om	אוֹם (ז)
thread (of a screw)	tavrig	תַּבְרִיג (ז)
wood screw	'boreg	בּוֹרֶג (ז)

| nail | masmer | מַסְמֵר (ז) |
| nailhead | roʃ hamasmer | רֹאשׁ הַמַּסְמֵר (ז) |

ruler (for measuring)	sargel	סַרְגֵּל (ז)
tape measure	'seret meida	סֶרֶט מִידָה (ז)
spirit level	'peles	פֶּלֶס (ז)
magnifying glass	zxuxit mag'delet	זְכוּכִית מַגְדֶּלֶת (נ)

measuring instrument	maxʃir medida	מַכְשִׁיר מְדִידָה (ז)
to measure (vt)	limdod	לִמְדֹּד
scale (of thermometer, etc.)	'skala	סְקָאלָה (נ)
readings	medida	מְדִידָה (נ)

| compressor | madxes | מַדְחֵס (ז) |
| microscope | mikroskop | מִיקְרוֹסְקוֹפ (ז) |

pump (e.g. water ~)	maʃeva	מַשְׁאֵבָה (נ)
robot	robot	רוֹבּוֹט (ז)
laser	'leizer	לֵייזֶר (ז)

spanner	maf'teax bragim	מַפְתֵּחַ בְּרָגִים (ז)
adhesive tape	neyar 'devek	נְיָיר דֶּבֶק (ז)
glue	'devek	דֶּבֶק (ז)

| sandpaper | neyar zxuxit | נְיָיר זְכוּכִית (ז) |
| spring | kfits | קְפִיץ (ז) |

magnet	magnet	מַגְנֵט (ז)
gloves	kfafot	כְּפָפוֹת (נ״ר)
rope	'xevel	חֶבֶל (ז)
cord	srox	שָׂרוֹךְ (ז)
wire (e.g. telephone ~)	xut	חוּט (ז)
cable	'kevel	כֶּבֶל (ז)
sledgehammer	kurnas	קוּרְנָס (ז)
prybar	lom	לוֹם (ז)
ladder	sulam	סוּלָם (ז)
stepladder	sulam	סוּלָם (ז)
to screw (tighten)	lehavrig	לְהַבְרִיג
to unscrew (lid, filter, etc.)	lif'toax, lehavrig	לִפְתוֹחַ, לְהַבְרִיג
to tighten (e.g. with a clamp)	lehadek	לְהַדֵּק
to glue, to stick	lehadbik	לְהַדְבִּיק
to cut (vt)	laxtox	לַחְתּוֹךְ
malfunction (fault)	takala	תַּקָלָה (נ)
repair (mending)	tikun	תִּיקוּן (ז)
to repair, to fix (vt)	letaken	לְתַקֵּן
to adjust (machine, etc.)	lexavnen	לְכַוְוֵן
to check (to examine)	livdok	לִבְדּוֹק
checking	bdika	בְּדִיקָה (נ)
readings	kri'a	קְרִיאָה (נ)
reliable, solid (machine)	amin	אָמִין
complex (adj)	murkav	מוּרְכָּב
to rust (get rusted)	lehaxlid	לְהַחְלִיד
rusty (adj)	xalud	חָלוּד
rust	xaluda	חֲלוּדָה (נ)

Transport

169. Aeroplane

aeroplane	matos	מָטוֹס (ז)
air ticket	kartis tisa	כַּרְטִיס טִיסָה (ז)
airline	xevrat te'ufa	חֶבְרַת תְּעוּפָה (נ)
airport	nemal te'ufa	נְמַל תְּעוּפָה (ז)
supersonic (adj)	al koli	עַל קוֹלִי
captain	kabarnit	קַבַּרְנִיט (ז)
crew	'tsevet	צֶוֶת (ז)
pilot	tayas	טַיָּס (ז)
stewardess	da'yelet	דַיֶּלֶת (נ)
navigator	navat	נַוָּט (ז)
wings	kna'fayim	כְּנָפַיִם (נ"ר)
tail	zanav	זָנָב (ז)
cockpit	'kokpit	קוֹקְפִּיט (ז)
engine	ma'no'a	מָנוֹעַ (ז)
undercarriage (landing gear)	kan nesi'a	כַּן נְסִיעָה (ז)
turbine	tur'bina	טוּרְבִּינָה (נ)
propeller	madxef	מַדְחֵף (ז)
black box	kufsa ʃxora	קוּפְסָה שְׁחוֹרָה (נ)
yoke (control column)	'hege	הֶגֶה (ז)
fuel	'delek	דֶּלֶק (ז)
safety card	hora'ot betixut	הוֹרָאוֹת בְּטִיחוּת (נ"ר)
oxygen mask	masexat xamtsan	מַסֵּכַת חַמְצָן (נ)
uniform	madim	מַדִּים (ז"ר)
lifejacket	xagorat hatsala	חֲגוֹרַת הַצָּלָה (נ)
parachute	mitsnax	מִצְנָח (ז)
takeoff	hamra'a	הַמְרָאָה (נ)
to take off (vi)	lehamri	לְהַמְרִיא
runway	maslul hamra'a	מַסְלוּל הַמְרָאָה (ז)
visibility	re'ut	רְאוּת (נ)
flight (act of flying)	tisa	טִיסָה (נ)
altitude	'gova	גּוֹבַהּ (ז)
air pocket	kis avir	כִּיס אֲוִיר (ז)
seat	moʃav	מוֹשָׁב (ז)
headphones	ozniyot	אָזְנִיּוֹת (נ"ר)
folding tray (tray table)	magaʃ mitkapel	מַגָּשׁ מִתְקַפֵּל (ז)
airplane window	tsohar	צוֹהַר (ז)
aisle	ma'avar	מַעֲבָר (ז)

170. Train

train	ra'kevet	רַכֶּבֶת (נ)
commuter train	ra'kevet parvarim	רַכֶּבֶת פַּרְבָרִים (נ)
express train	ra'kevet mehira	רַכֶּבֶת מְהִירָה (נ)
diesel locomotive	katar 'dizel	קַטָר דִיזֶל (ז)
steam locomotive	katar	קַטָר (ז)
coach, carriage	karon	קָרוֹן (ז)
buffet car	kron mis'ada	קָרוֹן מִסְעָדָה (ז)
rails	mesilot	מְסִילוֹת (נ״ר)
railway	mesilat barzel	מְסִילַת בַּרְזֶל (נ)
sleeper (track support)	'eden	אֶדֶן (ז)
platform (railway ~)	ratsif	רָצִיף (ז)
platform (~ 1, 2, etc.)	mesila	מְסִילָה (נ)
semaphore	ramzor	רַמְזוֹר (ז)
station	taxana	תַחֲנָה (נ)
train driver	nahag ra'kevet	נָהַג רַכֶּבֶת (ז)
porter (of luggage)	sabal	סַבָּל (ז)
carriage attendant	sadran ra'kevet	סַדְרָן רַכֶּבֶת (ז)
passenger	no'se'a	נוֹסֵעַ (ז)
ticket inspector	bodek	בּוֹדֵק (ז)
corridor (in train)	prozdor	פְּרוֹזְדוֹר (ז)
emergency brake	ma'atsar xirum	מַעֲצָר חִירוּם (ז)
compartment	ta	תָא (ז)
berth	dargaʃ	דַרְגָש (ז)
upper berth	dargaʃ elyon	דַרְגָש עֶלְיוֹן (ז)
lower berth	dargaʃ taxton	דַרְגָש תַחְתוֹן (ז)
bed linen, bedding	matsa'im	מַצָעִים (ז״ר)
ticket	kartis	כַּרְטִיס (ז)
timetable	'luax zmanim	לוּחַ זְמַנִים (ז)
information display	'ʃelet meida	שֶׁלֶט מֵידָע (ז)
to leave, to depart	latset	לָצֵאת
departure (of train)	yetsi'a	יְצִיאָה (נ)
to arrive (ab. train)	leha'gi'a	לְהַגִּיעַ
arrival	haga'a	הַגָעָה (נ)
to arrive by train	leha'gi'a bera'kevet	לְהַגִּיעַ בְּרַכֶּבֶת
to get on the train	la'alot lera'kevet	לַעֲלוֹת לְרַכֶּבֶת
to get off the train	la'redet mehara'kevet	לָרֶדֶת מֵהַרַכֶּבֶת
train crash	hitraskut	הִתְרַסְקוּת (נ)
to derail (vi)	la'redet mipasei ra'kevet	לָרֶדֶת מִפַּסֵי רַכֶּבֶת
steam locomotive	katar	קַטָר (ז)
stoker, fireman	masik	מַסִיק (ז)
firebox	kivʃan	כִּבְשָׁן (ז)
coal	pexam	פֶּחָם (ז)

171. Ship

ship	sfina	סְפִינָה (נ)
vessel	sfina	סְפִינָה (נ)
steamship	oniyat kitor	אוֹנִיַּת קִיטוֹר (נ)
riverboat	sfinat nahar	סְפִינַת נָהָר (נ)
cruise ship	oniyat ta'anugot	אוֹנִיַּת תַּעֲנוּגוֹת (נ)
cruiser	sa'yeret	סַיֶּרֶת (נ)
yacht	'yaχta	יַבְטָה (נ)
tugboat	go'reret	גוֹרֶרֶת (נ)
barge	arba	אַרְבָּה (נ)
ferry	ma'a'boret	מַעֲבּוֹרֶת (נ)
sailing ship	sfinat mifras	סְפִינַת מִפְרָשׂ (נ)
brigantine	briganit	בְּרִיגָנִית (נ)
ice breaker	ʃo'veret 'keraχ	שׁוֹבֶרֶת קֶרַח (נ)
submarine	tso'lelet	צוֹלֶלֶת (נ)
boat (flat-bottomed ~)	sira	סִירָה (נ)
dinghy	sira	סִירָה (נ)
lifeboat	sirat hatsala	סִירַת הַצָּלָה (נ)
motorboat	sirat ma'no'a	סִירַת מָנוֹעַ (נ)
captain	rav χovel	רַב-חוֹבֵל (ז)
seaman	malaχ	מַלָּח (ז)
sailor	yamai	יַמַּאי (ז)
crew	'tsevet	צֶוֶת (ז)
boatswain	rav malaχim	רַב-מַלָּחִים (ז)
ship's boy	'na'ar sipun	נַעַר סִיפּוּן (ז)
cook	tabaχ	טַבָּח (ז)
ship's doctor	rofe ha'oniya	רוֹפֵא הָאוֹנִיָּה (ז)
deck	sipun	סִיפּוּן (ז)
mast	'toren	תּוֹרֶן (ז)
sail	mifras	מִפְרָשׂ (ז)
hold	'beten oniya	בֶּטֶן אוֹנִיָּה (נ)
bow (prow)	χartom	חַרְטוֹם (ז)
stern	yarketei hasfina	יַרְכְּתֵי הַסְּפִינָה (ז"ר)
oar	maʃot	מָשׁוֹט (ז)
screw propeller	madχef	מַדְחֵף (ז)
cabin	ta	תָּא (ז)
wardroom	mo'adon ktsinim	מוֹעֲדוֹן קְצִינִים (ז)
engine room	χadar meχonot	חֲדַר מְכוֹנוֹת (ז)
bridge	'geʃer hapikud	גֶּשֶׁר הַפִּיקּוּד (ז)
radio room	ta alχutan	תָּא אַלְחוּטָן (ז)
wave (radio)	'teder	תֶּדֶר (ז)
logbook	yoman ha'oniya	יוֹמַן הָאוֹנִיָּה (ז)
spyglass	miʃ'kefet	מִשְׁקֶפֶת (נ)
bell	pa'amon	פַּעֲמוֹן (ז)

flag	'degel	דֶּגֶל (ז)
hawser (mooring ~)	avot ha'oniya	עֲבוֹת הָאֳנִיָּה (נ)
knot (bowline, etc.)	'keʃer	קֶשֶׁר (ז)
deckrails	ma'ake hasipun	מַעֲקֵה הַסִּפּוּן (ז)
gangway	'keveʃ	כֶּבֶשׁ (ז)
anchor	'ogen	עֹגֶן (ז)
to weigh anchor	leharim 'ogen	לְהָרִים עֹגֶן
to drop anchor	la'agon	לַעֲגוֹן
anchor chain	ʃar'ʃeret ha'ogen	שַׁרְשֶׁרֶת הָעֹגֶן (נ)
port (harbour)	namal	נָמֵל (ז)
quay, wharf	'mezax	מֵזַח (ז)
to berth (moor)	la'agon	לַעֲגוֹן
to cast off	lehaflig	לְהַפְלִיג
trip, voyage	masa, tiyul	מַסָּע (ז), טִיּוּל (ז)
cruise (sea trip)	'ʃayit	שַׁיִט (ז)
course (route)	kivun	כִּיוּוּן (ז)
route (itinerary)	nativ	נָתִיב (ז)
fairway (safe water channel)	nativ 'ʃayit	נָתִיב שַׁיִט (ז)
shallows	sirton	שִׂרְטוֹן (ז)
to run aground	la'alot al hasirton	לַעֲלוֹת עַל הַשִּׂרְטוֹן
storm	sufa	סוּפָה (נ)
signal	ot	אוֹת (ז)
to sink (vi)	lit'bo'a	לִטְבּוֹעַ
Man overboard!	adam ba'mayim!	אָדָם בַּמַּיִם!
SOS (distress signal)	kri'at hatsala	קְרִיאַת הַצָּלָה
ring buoy	galgal hatsala	גַּלְגַּל הַצָּלָה (ז)

172. Airport

airport	nemal te'ufa	נְמֵל תְּעוּפָה (ז)
aeroplane	matos	מָטוֹס (ז)
airline	xevrat te'ufa	חֶבְרַת תְּעוּפָה (נ)
air traffic controller	bakar tisa	בַּקָּר טִיסָה (ז)
departure	hamra'a	הַמְרָאָה (נ)
arrival	nexita	נְחִיתָה (נ)
to arrive (by plane)	leha'gi'a betisa	לְהַגִּיעַ בְּטִיסָה
departure time	zman hamra'a	זְמַן הַמְרָאָה (ז)
arrival time	zman nexita	זְמַן נְחִיתָה (ז)
to be delayed	lehit'akev	לְהִתְעַכֵּב
flight delay	ikuv hatisa	עִיכּוּב הַטִּיסָה (ז)
information board	'luax meida	לוּחַ מֵידָע (ז)
information	meida	מֵידָע (ז)
to announce (vt)	leho'dia	לְהוֹדִיעַ
flight (e.g. next ~)	tisa	טִיסָה (נ)

| customs | 'meχes | מֶכֶס (ז) |
| customs officer | pakid 'meχes | פָּקִיד מֶכֶס (ז) |

customs declaration	hatsharat meχes	הַצהָרַת מֶכֶס (נ)
to fill in (vt)	lemale	לְמַלֵא
to fill in the declaration	lemale 'tofes hatshara	לְמַלֵא טוֹפֶס הַצהָרָה
passport control	bdikat darkonim	בּדִיקַת דַרכּוֹנִים (נ)

luggage	kvuda	כּבוּדָה (נ)
hand luggage	kvudat yad	כּבוּדַת יָד (נ)
luggage trolley	eglat kvuda	עֶגלַת כּבוּדָה (נ)

landing	neχita	נְחִיתָה (נ)
landing strip	maslul neχita	מַסלוּל נְחִיתָה (ז)
to land (vi)	linχot	לִנחוֹת
airstairs	'keveʃ	כֶּבֶשׁ (ז)

check-in	tʃek in	צֶ'ק אִין (ז)
check-in counter	dalpak tʃek in	דַלפַּק צֶ'ק אִין (ז)
to check-in (vi)	leva'tse'a tʃek in	לְבַצֵע צֶ'ק אִין
boarding card	kartis aliya lematos	כַּרטִיס עֲלִייָה לְמָטוֹס (ז)
departure gate	'ʃa'ar yetsi'a	שַׁעַר יְצִיאָה (ז)

transit	ma'avar	מַעֲבָר (ז)
to wait (vt)	lehamtin	לְהַמתִין
departure lounge	traklin tisa	טרַקלִין טִיסָה (ז)
to see off	lelavot	לְלַווֹת
to say goodbye	lomar lehitra'ot	לוֹמַר לְהִתרָאוֹת

173. Bicycle. Motorcycle

bicycle	ofa'nayim	אוֹפַנַיים (ז״ר)
scooter	kat'no'a	קַטנוֹעַ (ז)
motorbike	of'no'a	אוֹפנוֹעַ (ז)

to go by bicycle	lirkov al ofa'nayim	לִרכּוֹב עַל אוֹפַנַיים
handlebars	kidon	כִּידוֹן (ז)
pedal	davʃa	דַווְשָׁה (נ)
brakes	blamim	בּלָמִים (ז״ר)
bicycle seat (saddle)	ukaf	אוּכָּף (ז)

pump	maʃeva	מַשׁאֵבָה (נ)
luggage rack	sabal	סַבָּל (ז)
front lamp	panas kidmi	פָּנָס קִדמִי (ז)
helmet	kasda	קַסדָה (נ)

wheel	galgal	גַלגַל (ז)
mudguard	kanaf	כָּנָף (נ)
rim	χiʃuk	חִישׁוּק (ז)
spoke	χiʃur	חִישׁוּר (ז)

Cars

174. Types of cars

car	meχonit	מְכוֹנִית (נ)
sports car	meχonit sport	מְכוֹנִית סְפּוֹרְט (נ)
limousine	limu'zina	לִימוּזִינָה (נ)
off-road vehicle	'reχev 'ʃetaχ	רֶכֶב שֶׁטַח (ז)
drophead coupé (convertible)	meχonit gag niftaχ	מְכוֹנִית גַג נִפְתָּח (נ)
minibus	'minibus	מִינִיבּוּס (ז)
ambulance	'ambulans	אַמְבּוּלָנְס (ז)
snowplough	maf'leset 'ʃeleg	מַפְלֶסֶת שֶׁלֶג (נ)
lorry	masa'it	מַשָׂאִית (נ)
road tanker	meχalit 'delek	מֵיכָלִית דֶלֶק (נ)
van (small truck)	masa'it kala	מַשָׂאִית קַלָה (נ)
tractor unit	gorer	גוֹרֵר (ז)
trailer	garur	גָרוּר (ז)
comfortable (adj)	'noaχ	נוֹחַ
used (adj)	meʃumaʃ	מְשׁוּמָשׁ

175. Cars. Bodywork

bonnet	miχse hama'no'a	מִכְסֵה הַמָנוֹעַ (ז)
wing	kanaf	כָּנָף (נ)
roof	gag	גַג (ז)
windscreen	ʃimʃa kidmit	שִׁמְשָׁה קִדְמִית (נ)
rear-view mirror	mar'a aχorit	מַרְאָה אֲחוֹרִית (נ)
windscreen washer	mataz	מַתָז (ז)
windscreen wipers	magev	מַגָב (ז)
side window	ʃimʃat tsad	שִׁמְשַׁת צַד (נ)
electric window	χalon χaʃmali	חַלוֹן חַשְׁמַלִי (ז)
aerial	an'tena	אַנְטֶנָה (נ)
sunroof	χalon gag	חַלוֹן גַג (ז)
bumper	pagoʃ	פָּגוֹשׁ (ז)
boot	ta mit'an	תָא מִטְעָן (ז)
roof luggage rack	gagon	גָגוֹן (ז)
door	'delet	דֶלֶת (נ)
door handle	yadit	יָדִית (נ)
door lock	man'ul	מַנְעוֹל (ז)
number plate	luχit riʃui	לוֹחִית רִישׁוּי (נ)
silencer	am'am	עַמְעָם (ז)

petrol tank	meixal 'delek	מֵיכָל דֶּלֶק (ז)
exhaust pipe	maflet	מַפְלֵט (ז)

accelerator	gaz	גָּז (ז)
pedal	davʃa	דַּוְושָׁה (נ)
accelerator pedal	davʃat gaz	דַּוְושַׁת גָּז (נ)

brake	'belem	בֶּלֶם (ז)
brake pedal	davʃat hablamim	דַּוְושַׁת הַבְּלָמִים (נ)
to brake (use the brake)	livlom	לִבְלוֹם
handbrake	'belem xaniya	בֶּלֶם חֲנִיָּה (ז)

clutch	matsmed	מַצְמֵד (ז)
clutch pedal	davʃat hamatsmed	דַּוְושַׁת הַמַּצְמֵד (נ)
clutch disc	luxit hamatsmed	לוּחִית הַמַּצְמֵד (נ)
shock absorber	bolem za'a'zu'a	בּוֹלֵם זַעֲזוּעִים (ז)

wheel	galgal	גַּלְגַּל (ז)
spare tyre	galgal xilufi	גַּלְגַּל חִלּוּפִי (ז)
tyre	tsmig	צְמִיג (ז)
wheel cover (hubcap)	tsa'laxat galgal	צַלַּחַת גַּלְגַּל (נ)

driving wheels	galgalim meni'im	גַּלְגַּלִּים מֵנִיעִים (ז"ר)
front-wheel drive (as adj)	shel hana'a kidmit	שֶׁל הֲנָעָה קִדְמִית
rear-wheel drive (as adj)	shel hana'a axorit	שֶׁל הֲנָעָה אֲחוֹרִית
all-wheel drive (as adj)	shel hana'a male'a	שֶׁל הֲנָעָה מָלֵאָה

gearbox	teivat hiluxim	תֵּיבַת הִילּוּכִים (נ)
automatic (adj)	oto'mati	אוֹטוֹמָטִי
mechanical (adj)	me'xani	מֵכָנִי
gear lever	yadit hiluxim	יָדִית הִילּוּכִים (נ)

headlamp	panas kidmi	פָּנָס קִדְמִי (ז)
headlights	panasim	פָּנָסִים (ז"ר)

dipped headlights	or namux	אוֹר נָמוּךְ (ז)
full headlights	or ga'voha	אוֹר גָּבוֹהַּ (ז)
brake light	or 'belem	אוֹר בֶּלֶם (ז)

sidelights	orot xanaya	אוֹרוֹת חֲנִיָּה (ז"ר)
hazard lights	orot xerum	אוֹרוֹת חֵירוּם (ז"ר)
fog lights	orot arafel	אוֹרוֹת עֲרָפֶל (ז"ר)
turn indicator	panas itut	פָּנָס אִיתּוּת (ז)
reversing light	orot revers	אוֹרוֹת רֶבֶרְס (ז"ר)

176. Cars. Passenger compartment

car inside (interior)	ta hanos'im	תָּא הַנּוֹסְעִים (ז)
leather (as adj)	asui me'or	עָשׂוּי מֵעוֹר
velour (as adj)	ktifati	קְטִיפָתִי
upholstery	ripud	רִיפּוּד (ז)

instrument (gage)	maxven	מַכְוֵן (ז)
dashboard	'luax maxvenim	לוּחַ מַכְוֵנִים (ז)

| speedometer | mad mehirut | מַד מְהִירוּת (ז) |
| needle (pointer) | 'maxat | מַחַט (נ) |

mileometer	mad merxak	מַד מֶרְחָק (ז)
indicator (sensor)	xaiʃan	חַיְישָׁן (ז)
level	ramat mi'lui	רָמַת מִילּוּי (נ)
warning light	nurat azhara	נוּרַת אַזְהָרָה (נ)

steering wheel	'hege	הֶגֶה (ז)
horn	tsofar	צוֹפָר (ז)
button	kaftor	כַּפְתּוֹר (ז)
switch	'meteg	מֶתֶג (ז)

seat	moʃav	מוֹשָׁב (ז)
backrest	miʃ'enet	מִשְׁעֶנֶת (נ)
headrest	miʃ'enet roʃ	מִשְׁעֶנֶת רֹאשׁ (נ)
seat belt	xagorat betixut	חֲגוֹרַת בְּטִיחוּת (נ)
to fasten the belt	lehadek xagora	לְהַדֵּק חֲגוֹרָה
adjustment (of seats)	kivnun	כִּיווּנוּן (ז)

| airbag | karit avir | כָּרִית אֲווִיר (נ) |
| air-conditioner | mazgan | מַזְגָּן (ז) |

radio	'radyo	רַדְיוֹ (ז)
CD player	'diskmen	דִיסְקְמָן (ז)
to turn on	lehadlik	לְהַדְלִיק
aerial	an'tena	אַנְטֶנָה (נ)
glove box	ta kfafot	תָּא כְּפָפוֹת (ז)
ashtray	ma'afera	מַאֲפֵרָה (נ)

177. Cars. Engine

engine, motor	ma'no‘a	מָנוֹעַ (ז)
diesel (as adj)	shel 'dizel	שֶׁל דִיזָל
petrol (as adj)	'delek	דֶלֶק

engine volume	'nefax ma'no‘a	נֶפַח מָנוֹעַ (ז)
power	otsma	עוֹצְמָה (נ)
horsepower	'koax sus	כּוֹחַ סוּס (ז)
piston	buxna	בּוּכְנָה (נ)
cylinder	tsi'linder	צִילִינְדֶר (ז)
valve	ʃastom	שַׁסְתּוֹם (ז)

injector	mazrek	מַזְרֵק (ז)
generator (alternator)	mexolel	מְחוֹלֵל (ז)
carburettor	me'ayed	מְאַיֵּד (ז)
motor oil	'ʃemen mano'im	שֶׁמֶן מָנוֹעִים (ז)

radiator	matsnen	מַצְנֵן (ז)
coolant	nozel kirur	נוֹזֵל קִירוּר (ז)
cooling fan	me'avrer	מְאַווְרֵר (ז)

| battery (accumulator) | matsber | מַצְבֵּר (ז) |
| starter | mat'ne‘a | מַתְנֵעַ (ז) |

ignition	haʦata	הַצָּתָה (נ)
sparking plug	maʦet	מַצֵּת (ז)

terminal (of battery)	'hedek	הֶדֵק (ז)
positive terminal	'hedek χiyuvi	הֶדֵק חִיּוּבִי (ז)
negative terminal	'hedek ʃlili	הֶדֵק שְׁלִילִי (ז)
fuse	natiχ	נָתִיךְ (ז)

air filter	masnen avir	מַסְנֵן אֲוִיר (ז)
oil filter	masnen 'ʃemen	מַסְנֵן שֶׁמֶן (ז)
fuel filter	masnen 'delek	מַסְנֵן דֶּלֶק (ז)

178. Cars. Crash. Repair

car crash	te'una	תְּאוּנָה (נ)
traffic accident	te'unat draχim	תְּאוּנַת דְּרָכִים (נ)
to crash (into the wall, etc.)	lehitnageʃ	לְהִתְנַגֵּשׁ
to get smashed up	lehima'eχ	לְהִימָּעֵךְ
damage	'nezek	נֶזֶק (ז)
intact (unscathed)	ʃalem	שָׁלֵם

breakdown	takala	תַּקָּלָה (נ)
to break down (vi)	lehitkalkel	לְהִתְקַלְקֵל
towrope	'χevel grar	חֶבֶל גְּרָר (ז)

puncture	'teker	תֶּקֶר (ז)
to have a puncture	lehitpanʦ'er	לְהִתְפַּנְצֵ'ר
to pump up	lena'peaχ	לְנַפֵּחַ
pressure	'laχaʦ	לַחַץ (ז)
to check (to examine)	livdok	לִבְדּוֹק

repair	ʃipuʦ	שִׁיפּוּץ (ז)
auto repair shop	musaχ	מוּסָךְ (ז)
spare part	'χelek χiluf	חֵלֶק חִילוּף (ז)
part	'χelek	חֵלֶק (ז)

bolt (with nut)	'boreg	בּוֹרֶג (ז)
screw (fastener)	'boreg	בּוֹרֶג (ז)
nut	om	אוֹם (ז)
washer	diskit	דִּיסְקִית (נ)
bearing	mesav	מֵסַב (ז)

tube	ʦinorit	צִינוֹרִית (נ)
gasket (head ~)	'etem	אֶטֶם (ז)
cable, wire	χut	חוּט (ז)

jack	dʒek	גַ'ק (ז)
spanner	maf'teaχ bragim	מַפְתֵּחַ בְּרָגִים (ז)
hammer	patiʃ	פַּטִּישׁ (ז)
pump	maʃeva	מַשְׁאֵבָה (נ)
screwdriver	mavreg	מַבְרֵג (ז)

fire extinguisher	mataf	מַטָּף (ז)
warning triangle	meʃulaʃ χirum	מְשׁוּלָשׁ חִירוּם (ז)

to stall (vi)	ledomem	לִדוֹמֵם
stall (n)	hadmama	הַדמָמָה (נ)
to be broken	lihyot ʃavur	לִהיוֹת שָבוּר

to overheat (vi)	lehitχamem yoter midai	לְהִתחַמֵם יוֹתֵר מִדַי
to be clogged up	lehisatem	לְהִיסָתֵם
to freeze up (pipes, etc.)	likpo	לִקפּוֹא
to burst (vi, ab. tube)	lehitpa'ke'a	לְהִתפַּקֵעַ

pressure	'laχats	לַחַץ (ז)
level	ramat mi'lui	רָמַת מִילוּי (נ)
slack (~ belt)	rafe	רָפֶה

dent	dfika	דפִיקָה (נ)
knocking noise (engine)	'ra'aʃ	רַעַש (ז)
crack	'sedek	סֶדֶק (ז)
scratch	srita	שֹרִיטָה (נ)

179. Cars. Road

road	'dereχ	דֶרֶך (ז)
motorway	kviʃ mahir	כּבִיש מָהִיר (ז)
highway	kviʃ mahir	כּבִיש מָהִיר (ז)
direction (way)	kivun	כִּיווּן (ז)
distance	merχak	מֶרחָק (ז)

bridge	'geʃer	גֶשֶר (ז)
car park	χanaya	חֲנָיָה (נ)
square	kikar	כִּיכָּר (נ)
road junction	meχlaf	מֶחלָף (ז)
tunnel	minhara	מִנהָרָה (נ)

petrol station	taχanat 'delek	תַחֲנַת דֶלֶק (נ)
car park	migraʃ χanaya	מִגרַש חֲנָיָה (ז)
petrol pump	maʃevat 'delek	מַשאֵבַת דֶלֶק (נ)
auto repair shop	musaχ	מוּסָך (ז)
to fill up	letadlek	לְתַדלֵק
fuel	'delek	דֶלֶק (ז)
jerrycan	'dʒerikan	גֶ'רִיקָן (ז)

asphalt, tarmac	asfalt	אַספַלט (ז)
road markings	simun	סִימוּן (ז)
kerb	sfat midraχa	שֹפַת מִדרָכָה (נ)
crash barrier	ma'ake betiχut	מַעֲקֶה בְּטִיחוּת (ז)
ditch	te'ala	תְעָלָה (נ)
roadside (shoulder)	ʃulei ha'dereχ	שוּלֵי הַדֶרֶך (ז"ר)
lamppost	amud te'ura	עַמוּד תְאוֹרָה (ז)

to drive (a car)	linhog	לִנהוֹג
to turn (e.g., ~ left)	lifnot	לִפנוֹת
to make a U-turn	leva'tse'a pniyat parsa	לְבַצֵע פּנִיַית פַּרסָה
reverse (~ gear)	hiluχ aχori	הִילוּך אָחוֹרִי (ז)
to honk (vi)	litspor	לִצפּוֹר
honk (sound)	tsfira	צפִירָה (נ)

to get stuck (in the mud, etc.)	lehitaka	לְהֵיתָקַע
to spin the wheels	lesovev et hagalgal al rek	לְסוֹבֵב אֶת הַגַּלְגַּלִים עַל רֵיק
to cut, to turn off (vt)	ledomem	לְדוֹמֵם

speed	mehirut	מְהִירוּת (נ)
to exceed the speed limit	linhog bemehirut muf'rezet	לִנְהוֹג בְּמְהִירוּת מוּפְרֶזֶת
to give a ticket	liknos	לִקְנוֹס
traffic lights	ramzor	רַמְזוֹר (ז)
driving licence	riʃyon nehiga	רִשְׁיוֹן נְהִיגָה (ז)

level crossing	ma'avar pasei ra'kevet	מַעֲבַר פַּסֵּי רַכֶּבֶת (ז)
crossroads	'tsomet	צוֹמֶת (ז)
zebra crossing	ma'avar xatsaya	מַעֲבַר חֲצָיָה (ז)
bend, curve	pniya	פְּנִיָּה (נ)
pedestrian precinct	midrexov	מִדְרְחוֹב (ז)

180. Signs

Highway Code	xukei hatnu'a	חוּקֵי הַתְּנוּעָה (ז"ר)
road sign (traffic sign)	tamrur	תַּמְרוּר (ז)
overtaking	akifa	עֲקִיפָה (נ)
curve	pniya	פְּנִיָּה (נ)
U-turn	sivuv parsa	סִיבוּב פַּרְסָה (ז)
roundabout	ma'agal tnu'a	מַעֲגַל תְּנוּעָה (ז)

No entry	ein knisa	אֵין כְּנִיסָה
All vehicles prohibited	ein knisat rexavim	אֵין כְּנִיסַת רְכָבִים
No overtaking	akifa asura	עֲקִיפָה אֲסוּרָה
No parking	xanaya asura	חֲנָיָה אֲסוּרָה
No stopping	atsira asura	עֲצִירָה אֲסוּרָה

dangerous curve	sivuv xad	סִיבוּב חַד (ז)
steep descent	yerida tlula	יְרִידָה תְּלוּלָה (נ)
one-way traffic	tnu'a xad sitrit	תְּנוּעָה חַד־סִטְרִית (נ)
zebra crossing	ma'avar xatsaya	מַעֲבַר חֲצָיָה (ז)
slippery road	kviʃ xalaklak	כְּבִישׁ חֲלַקְלַק (ז)
GIVE WAY	zxut kdima	זְכוּת קְדִימָה

PEOPLE. LIFE EVENTS

Life events

181. Holidays. Event

celebration, holiday	χagiga	חֲגִיגָה (נ)
national day	χag le'umi	חַג לְאוּמִי (ז)
public holiday	yom χag	יוֹם חַג (ז)
to commemorate (vt)	laχgog	לַחְגֹג
event (happening)	hitraχaʃut	הִתְרַחֲשׁוּת (נ)
event (organized activity)	ei'ru'a	אֵירוּעַ (ז)
banquet (party)	se'uda χagigit	סְעוּדָה חֲגִיגִית (נ)
reception (formal party)	ei'ruaχ	אֵירוּחַ (ז)
feast	miʃte	מִשְׁתֶּה (ז)
anniversary	yom haʃana	יוֹם הַשָּׁנָה (ז)
jubilee	χag hayovel	חַג הַיּוֹבֵל (ז)
to celebrate (vt)	laχgog	לַחְגֹג
New Year	ʃana χadaʃa	שָׁנָה חֲדָשָׁה (נ)
Happy New Year!	ʃana tova!	שָׁנָה טוֹבָה!
Father Christmas	'santa 'kla'us	סַנְטָה קְלָאוּס
Christmas	χag hamolad	חַג הַמּוֹלָד (ז)
Merry Christmas!	χag hamolad sa'meaχ!	חַג הַמּוֹלָד שָׂמֵחַ!
Christmas tree	eʦ χag hamolad	עֵץ חַג הַמּוֹלָד (ז)
fireworks (fireworks show)	zikukim	זִיקּוּקִים (ז״ר)
wedding	χatuna	חֲתוּנָה (נ)
groom	χatan	חָתָן (ז)
bride	kala	כַּלָּה (נ)
to invite (vt)	lehazmin	לְהַזְמִין
invitation card	hazmana	הַזְמָנָה (נ)
guest	o'reaχ	אוֹרֵחַ (ז)
to visit (~ your parents, etc.)	levaker	לְבַקֵּר
to meet the guests	lekabel orχim	לְקַבֵּל אוֹרְחִים
gift, present	matana	מַתָּנָה (נ)
to give (sth as present)	latet matana	לָתֵת מַתָּנָה
to receive gifts	lekabel matanot	לְקַבֵּל מַתָּנוֹת
bouquet (of flowers)	zer	זֵר (ז)
congratulations	braχa	בְּרָכָה (נ)
to congratulate (vt)	levareχ	לְבָרֵךְ
greetings card	kartis braχa	כַּרְטִיס בְּרָכָה (ז)

to send a postcard	liʃloaχ gluya	לִשְׁלוֹחַ גְּלוּיָה
to get a postcard	lekabel gluya	לְקַבֵּל גְּלוּיָה
toast	leharim kosit	לְהָרִים כּוֹסִית
to offer (a drink, etc.)	leχabed	לְכַבֵּד
champagne	ʃam'panya	שַׁמְפַּנְיָה (נ)
to enjoy oneself	lehanot	לֵיהָנוֹת
merriment (gaiety)	alitsut	עֲלִיצוּת (נ)
joy (emotion)	simχa	שִׂמְחָה (נ)
dance	rikud	רִיקוּד (ז)
to dance (vi, vt)	lirkod	לִרְקוֹד
waltz	vals	וַלְס (ז)
tango	'tango	טַנְגּוֹ (ז)

182. Funerals. Burial

cemetery	beit kvarot	בֵּית קְבָרוֹת (ז)
grave, tomb	'kever	קֶבֶר (ז)
cross	tslav	צְלָב (ז)
gravestone	matseva	מַצֵּבָה (נ)
fence	gader	גָּדֵר (נ)
chapel	beit tfila	בֵּית תְּפִילָה (ז)
death	'mavet	מָוֶות (ז)
to die (vi)	lamut	לָמוּת
the deceased	niftar	נִפְטָר (ז)
mourning	'evel	אֵבֶל (ז)
to bury (vt)	likbor	לִקְבּוֹר
undertakers	beit levayot	בֵּית לְוָויוֹת (ז)
funeral	levaya	לְוָויָה (נ)
wreath	zer	זֵר (ז)
coffin	aron metim	אֲרוֹן מֵתִים (ז)
hearse	kron hamet	קְרוֹן הַמֵּת (ז)
shroud	taχriχim	תַּכְרִיכִים (ז"ר)
funeral procession	tahaluχat 'evel	תַּהֲלוּכַת אֵבֶל (נ)
funerary urn	kad 'efer	כַּד אֵפֶר (ז)
crematorium	misrafa	מִשְׂרָפָה (נ)
obituary	moda'at 'evel	מוֹדָעַת אֵבֶל (נ)
to cry (weep)	livkot	לִבְכּוֹת
to sob (vi)	lehitya'peaχ	לְהִתְיַפַּח

183. War. Soldiers

platoon	maχlaka	מַחְלָקָה (נ)
company	pluga	פְּלוּגָה (נ)

regiment	χativa	חֲטִיבָה (נ)
army	tsava	צָבָא (ז)
division	ugda	אוּגְדָּה (נ)
section, squad	kita	כִּיתָה (נ)
host (army)	'χayil	חַיִל (ז)
soldier	χayal	חַיָּל (ז)
officer	katsin	קָצִין (ז)
private	turai	טוּרָאי (ז)
sergeant	samal	סַמָּל (ז)
lieutenant	'segen	סֶגֶן (ז)
captain	'seren	סֶרֶן (ז)
major	rav 'seren	רַב־סֶרֶן (ז)
colonel	aluf miʃne	אַלּוּף מִשְׁנֶה (ז)
general	aluf	אַלּוּף (ז)
sailor	yamai	יַמַּאי (ז)
captain	rav χovel	רַב־חוֹבֵל (ז)
boatswain	rav malaχim	רַב־מַלָּחִים (ז)
artilleryman	totχan	תּוֹתְחָן (ז)
paratrooper	tsanχan	צַנְחָן (ז)
pilot	tayas	טַיָּס (ז)
navigator	navat	נַוָּט (ז)
mechanic	meχonai	מְכוֹנַאי (ז)
pioneer (sapper)	χablan	חַבְּלָן (ז)
parachutist	tsanχan	צַנְחָן (ז)
reconnaissance scout	iʃ modi'in kravi	אִישׁ מוֹדִיעִין קְרָבִי (ז)
sniper	tsalaf	צַלָּף (ז)
patrol (group)	siyur	סִיּוּר (ז)
to patrol (vt)	lefatrel	לְפַטְרֵל
sentry, guard	zakif	זָקִיף (ז)
warrior	loχem	לוֹחֵם (ז)
patriot	patriyot	פַּטְרִיוֹט (ז)
hero	gibor	גִּיבּוֹר (ז)
heroine	gibora	גִּיבּוֹרָה (נ)
traitor	boged	בּוֹגֵד (ז)
to betray (vt)	livgod	לִבְגּוֹד
deserter	arik	עָרִיק (ז)
to desert (vi)	la'arok	לַעֲרוֹק
mercenary	sχir 'χerev	שְׂכִיר חֶרֶב (ז)
recruit	tiron	טִירוֹן (ז)
volunteer	mitnadev	מִתְנַדֵּב (ז)
dead (n)	harug	הָרוּג (ז)
wounded (n)	pa'tsu'a	פָּצוּעַ (ז)
prisoner of war	ʃavui	שָׁבוּי (ז)

184. War. Military actions. Part 1

war	milχama	מִלְחָמָה (נ)
to be at war	lehilaχem	לְהִילָחֵם
civil war	mil'χemet ezraχim	מִלְחֶמֶת אֶזְרָחִים (נ)
treacherously (adv)	bogdani	בּוֹגְדָנִי
declaration of war	haχrazat milχama	הַכְרָזַת מִלְחָמָה (נ)
to declare (~ war)	lehaχriz	לְהַכְרִיז
aggression	tokfanut	תּוֹקְפָנוּת (נ)
to attack (invade)	litkof	לִתְקוֹף
to invade (vt)	liχboʃ	לִכְבּוֹשׁ
invader	koveʃ	כּוֹבֵשׁ (ז)
conqueror	koveʃ	כּוֹבֵשׁ (ז)
defence	hagana	הֲגָנָה (נ)
to defend (a country, etc.)	lehagen al	לְהָגֵן עַל
to defend (against ...)	lehitgonen	לְהִתְגּוֹנֵן
enemy	oyev	אוֹיֵב (ז)
foe, adversary	yariv	יָרִיב (ז)
enemy (as adj)	ʃel oyev	שֶׁל אוֹיֵב
strategy	astra'tegya	אַסְטְרָטֶגְיָה (נ)
tactics	'taktika	טַקְטִיקָה (נ)
order	pkuda	פְּקוּדָה (נ)
command (order)	pkuda	פְּקוּדָה (נ)
to order (vt)	lifkod	לִפְקוֹד
mission	mesima	מְשִׂימָה (נ)
secret (adj)	sodi	סוֹדִי
battle	ma'araχa	מַעֲרָכָה (נ)
combat	krav	קְרָב (ז)
attack	hatkafa	הַתְקָפָה (נ)
charge (assault)	hista'arut	הִסְתָּעֲרוּת (נ)
to storm (vt)	lehista'er	לְהִסְתָּעֵר
siege (to be under ~)	maʦor	מָצוֹר (ז)
offensive (n)	mitkafa	מִתְקָפָה (נ)
to go on the offensive	laʦet lemitkafa	לָצֵאת לְמִתְקָפָה
retreat	nesiga	נְסִיגָה (נ)
to retreat (vi)	la'seget	לָסֶגֶת
encirclement	kitur	כִּיתּוּר (ז)
to encircle (vt)	leχater	לְכַתֵּר
bombing (by aircraft)	haftsatsa	הַפְצָצָה (נ)
to drop a bomb	lehatil ptsatsa	לְהָטִיל פְּצָצָה
to bomb (vt)	lehaftsits	לְהַפְצִיץ
explosion	pitsuts	פִּיצּוּץ (ז)
shot	yeriya	יְרִיָּה (נ)

| to fire (~ a shot) | lirot | לִירוֹת |
| firing (burst of ~) | 'yeri | יְרִי (ז) |

to aim (to point a weapon)	leχaven 'neʃek	לְכַוֵּון נֶשֶׁק
to point (a gun)	leχaven	לְכַוֵּון
to hit (the target)	lik'lo'a	לִקְלוֹעַ

to sink (~ a ship)	lehat'bi'a	לְהַטְבִּיעַ
hole (in a ship)	pirtsa	פִּרְצָה (נ)
to founder, to sink (vi)	lit'bo'a	לִטְבּוֹעַ

front (war ~)	χazit	חָזִית (נ)
evacuation	pinui	פִּינוּי (ז)
to evacuate (vt)	lefanot	לְפַנּוֹת

trench	te'ala	תְּעָלָה (נ)
barbed wire	'tayil dokrani	חַיִל דּוֹקְרָנִי (ז)
barrier (anti tank ~)	maχsom	מַחְסוֹם (ז)
watchtower	migdal ʃmira	מִגְדַּל שְׁמִירָה (ז)

military hospital	beit χolim tsva'i	בֵּית חוֹלִים צְבָאִי (ז)
to wound (vt)	lif'tso'a	לִפְצוֹעַ
wound	'petsa	פֶּצַע (ז)
wounded (n)	pa'tsu'a	פָּצוּעַ (ז)
to be wounded	lehipatsa	לְהִיפָּצַע
serious (wound)	kaʃe	קָשֶׁה

185. War. Military actions. Part 2

captivity	'ʃevi	שְׁבִי (ז)
to take captive	la'kaχat be'ʃevi	לָקַחַת בְּשֶׁבִי
to be held captive	lihyot be'ʃevi	לִהְיוֹת בְּשֶׁבִי
to be taken captive	lipol be'ʃevi	לִיפּוֹל בְּשֶׁבִי

concentration camp	maχane rikuz	מַחֲנֵה רִיכּוּז (ז)
prisoner of war	ʃavui	שָׁבוּי (ז)
to escape (vi)	liv'roaχ	לִבְרוֹחַ

to betray (vt)	livgod	לִבְגּוֹד
betrayer	boged	בּוֹגֵד (ז)
betrayal	bgida	בְּגִידָה (נ)

| to execute (by firing squad) | lehotsi la'horeg | לְהוֹצִיא לַהוֹרֵג |
| execution (by firing squad) | hotsa'a le'horeg | הוֹצָאָה לַהוֹרֵג (נ) |

equipment (military gear)	tsiyud	צִיּוּד (ז)
shoulder board	ko'tefet	כּוֹתֶפֶת (נ)
gas mask	maseχat 'abaχ	מַסֵיכַת אַבָּ"ך (נ)

field radio	maχʃir 'keʃer	מַכְשִׁיר קֶשֶׁר (ז)
cipher, code	'tsofen	צוֹפֶן (ז)
secrecy	χaʃa'iut	חֲשָׁאִיוּת (נ)
password	sisma	סִיסְמָה (נ)
land mine	mokeʃ	מוֹקֵשׁ (ז)

| to mine (road, etc.) | lemakeʃ | לְמַקֵּשׁ |
| minefield | sde mokʃim | שְׂדֵה מוֹקְשִׁים (ז) |

air-raid warning	az'aka	אַזְעָקָה (נ)
alarm (alert signal)	az'aka	אַזְעָקָה (נ)
signal	ot	אוֹת (ז)
signal flare	zikuk az'aka	זִיקוּק אַזְעָקָה (ז)

headquarters	mifkada	מִפְקָדָה (נ)
reconnaissance	isuf modi'in	אִיסוּף מוֹדִיעִין (ז)
situation	matsav	מַצָּב (ז)
report	doχ	דוֹ"ח (ז)
ambush	ma'arav	מַאֲרָב (ז)
reinforcement (of army)	tig'boret	תִּגְבּוֹרֶת (נ)

target	matara	מַטָּרָה (נ)
training area	sde imunim	שְׂדֵה אִימוּנִים (ז)
military exercise	timronim	תִּמְרוֹנִים (ז"ר)

panic	behala	בֶּהָלָה (נ)
devastation	'heres	הֶרֶס (ז)
destruction, ruins	harisot	הֲרִיסוֹת (נ"ר)
to destroy (vt)	laharos	לַהֲרוֹס

to survive (vi, vt)	lisrod	לִשְׂרוֹד
to disarm (vt)	lifrok mi'neʃek	לִפְרוֹק מִנֶּשֶׁק
to handle (~ a gun)	lehiʃtameʃ be...	לְהִשְׁתַּמֵּשׁ בְּ...

| Attention! | amod dom! | עֲמוֹד דּוֹם! |
| At ease! | amod 'noaχ! | עֲמוֹד נוֹחַ! |

act of courage	ma'ase gvura	מַעֲשֵׂה גְּבוּרָה (ז)
oath (vow)	ʃvu'a	שְׁבוּעָה (נ)
to swear (an oath)	lehiʃava	לְהִישָּׁבַע

decoration (medal, etc.)	itur	עִיטּוּר (ז)
to award (give medal to)	leha'anik	לְהַעֲנִיק
medal	me'dalya	מֶדַלְיָה (נ)
order (e.g. ~ of Merit)	ot hitstainut	אוֹת הִצְטַיְּינוּת (ז)

victory	nitsaχon	נִיצָּחוֹן (ז)
defeat	tvusa	תְּבוּסָה (נ)
armistice	hafsakat eʃ	הַפְסָקַת אֵשׁ (נ)

standard (battle flag)	'degel	דֶּגֶל (ז)
glory (honour, fame)	tehila	תְּהִילָה (נ)
parade	mits'ad	מִצְעָד (ז)
to march (on parade)	lits'od	לִצְעוֹד

186. Weapons

weapons	'neʃek	נֶשֶׁק (ז)
firearms	'neʃek χam	נֶשֶׁק חַם (ז)
cold weapons (knives, etc.)	'neʃek kar	נֶשֶׁק קַר (ז)

chemical weapons	'neʃek 'χimi	נֶשֶׁק כִּימִי (ז)
nuclear (adj)	gar'ini	גַרְעִינִי
nuclear weapons	'neʃek gar'ini	נֶשֶׁק גַרְעִינִי (ז)

| bomb | pʦaʦa | פְּצָצָה (נ) |
| atomic bomb | pʦaʦa a'tomit | פְּצָצָה אָטוֹמִית (נ) |

pistol (gun)	ekdaχ	אֶקְדָח (ז)
rifle	rove	רוֹבֶה (ז)
submachine gun	tat mak'le'a	תַת-מַקְלֵעַ (ז)
machine gun	mak'le'a	מַקְלֵעַ (ז)

muzzle	kane	קָנֶה (ז)
barrel	kane	קָנֶה (ז)
calibre	ka'liber	קָלִיבָּר (ז)

trigger	'hedek	הֶדֶק (ז)
sight (aiming device)	ka'venet	כַּוֶנֶת (נ)
magazine	maχsanit	מַחְסָנִית (נ)
butt (shoulder stock)	kat	קַת (נ)

| hand grenade | rimon | רִימוֹן (ז) |
| explosive | 'χomer 'nefeʦ | חוֹמֶר נֶפֶץ (ז) |

bullet	ka'li'a	קְלִיעַ (ז)
cartridge	kadur	כַּדוּר (ז)
charge	te'ina	טְעִינָה (נ)
ammunition	taχ'moʃet	תַחְמוֹשֶׁת (נ)

bomber (aircraft)	mafʦiʦ	מַפְצִיץ (ז)
fighter	metos krav	מְטוֹס קְרָב (ז)
helicopter	masok	מָסוֹק (ז)

anti-aircraft gun	totaχ 'neged metosim	תוֹתָח נֶגֶד מְטוֹסִים (ז)
tank	tank	טַנְק (ז)
tank gun	totaχ	תוֹתָח (ז)

artillery	arti'lerya	אַרְטִילָרְיָה (נ)
gun (cannon, howitzer)	totaχ	תוֹתָח (ז)
to lay (a gun)	leχaven	לְכַוֵון

shell (projectile)	pagaz	פָּגָז (ז)
mortar bomb	pʦaʦat margema	פְּצָצַת מַרְגֵמָה (נ)
mortar	margema	מַרְגֵמָה (נ)
splinter (shell fragment)	resis	רְסִיס (ז)

submarine	ʦo'lelet	צוֹלֶלֶת (נ)
torpedo	tor'pedo	טוֹרְפֶּדוֹ (ז)
missile	til	טִיל (ז)

to load (gun)	lit'on	לִטְעוֹן
to shoot (vi)	lirot	לִירוֹת
to point at (the cannon)	leχaven	לְכַוֵון
bayonet	kidon	כִּידוֹן (ז)
rapier	'χerev	חֶרֶב (נ)
sabre (e.g. cavalry ~)	'χerev paraʃim	חֶרֶב פָּרָשִׁים (ז)

spear (weapon)	χanit	חֲנִית (נ)
bow	'keʃet	קֶשֶׁת (נ)
arrow	χets	חֵץ (ז)
musket	musket	מוּסְקֶט (ז)
crossbow	'keʃet metsu'levet	קֶשֶׁת מְצוּלֶבֶת (נ)

187. Ancient people

primitive (prehistoric)	kadmon	קַדְמוֹן
prehistoric (adj)	prehis'tori	פְּרֶהִיסְטוֹרִי
ancient (~ civilization)	atik	עַתִּיק
Stone Age	idan ha''even	עִידָן הָאֶבֶן (ז)
Bronze Age	idan ha'arad	עִידָן הָאָרָד (ז)
Ice Age	idan ha'keraχ	עִידָן הַקֶּרַח (ז)
tribe	'ʃevet	שֵׁבֶט (ז)
cannibal	oχel adam	אוֹכֵל אָדָם (ז)
hunter	tsayad	צַיָּיד (ז)
to hunt (vi, vt)	latsud	לָצוּד
mammoth	ma'muta	מָמוּטָה (נ)
cave	me'ara	מְעָרָה (נ)
fire	eʃ	אֵשׁ (נ)
campfire	medura	מְדוּרָה (נ)
cave painting	pet'roglif	פֶּטְרוֹגְלִיף (ז)
tool (e.g. stone axe)	kli	כְּלִי (ז)
spear	χanit	חֲנִית (נ)
stone axe	garzen ha'even	גַּרְזֶן הָאֶבֶן (ז)
to be at war	lehilaχem	לְהִילָחֵם
to domesticate (vt)	levayet	לְבַיֵּית
idol	'pesel	פֶּסֶל (ז)
to worship (vt)	la'avod et	לַעֲבוֹד אֶת
superstition	emuna tfela	אֱמוּנָה תְּפֵלָה (נ)
rite	'tekes	טֶקֶס (ז)
evolution	evo'lutsya	אֶבוֹלוּצְיָה (נ)
development	hitpatχut	הִתְפַּתְּחוּת (נ)
disappearance (extinction)	he'almut	הֵיעָלְמוּת (נ)
to adapt oneself	lehistagel	לְהִסְתַּגֵּל
archaeology	arχe'o'logya	אַרְכֵיאוֹלוֹגְיָה (נ)
archaeologist	arχe'olog	אַרְכֵיאוֹלוֹג (ז)
archaeological (adj)	arχe'o'logi	אַרְכֵיאוֹלוֹגִי
excavation site	atar χafirot	אָתַר חֲפִירוֹת (ז)
excavations	χafirot	חֲפִירוֹת (נ"ר)
find (object)	mimtsa	מִמְצָא (ז)
fragment	resis	רְסִיס (ז)

188. Middle Ages

people (ethnic group)	am	עַם (ז)
peoples	amim	עַמִּים (ז״ר)
tribe	'ʃevet	שֵׁבֶט (ז)
tribes	ʃvatim	שְׁבָטִים (ז״ר)
barbarians	bar'barim	בַּרְבָּרִים (ז״ר)
Gauls	'galim	גָּאלִים (ז״ר)
Goths	'gotim	גּוֹתִים (ז״ר)
Slavs	'slavim	סְלָאבִים (ז״ר)
Vikings	'vikingim	וִיקִינְגִים (ז״ר)
Romans	roma'im	רוֹמָאִים (ז״ר)
Roman (adj)	'romi	רוֹמִי
Byzantines	bi'zantim	בִּיזַנְטִים (ז״ר)
Byzantium	bizantion, bizants	בִּיזַנְטִיוֹן, בִּיזַנְץ (נ)
Byzantine (adj)	bi'zanti	בִּיזַנְטִי
emperor	keisar	קֵיסָר (ז)
leader, chief (tribal ~)	manhig	מַנְהִיג (ז)
powerful (~ king)	rav 'koax	רַב־כּוֹחַ
king	'melex	מֶלֶךְ (ז)
ruler (sovereign)	ʃalit	שַׁלִּיט (ז)
knight	abir	אַבִּיר (ז)
feudal lord	fe'odal	פֵיאוֹדָל (ז)
feudal (adj)	fe'o'dali	פֵיאוֹדָלִי
vassal	vasal	וַסָל (ז)
duke	dukas	דוּכָּס (ז)
earl	rozen	רוֹזֵן (ז)
baron	baron	בָּרוֹן (ז)
bishop	'biʃof	בִּישׁוֹף (ז)
armour	ʃiryon	שִׁרְיוֹן (ז)
shield	magen	מָגֵן (ז)
sword	'xerev	חֶרֶב (נ)
visor	magen panim	מָגֵן פָּנִים (ז)
chainmail	ʃiryon kaskasim	שִׁרְיוֹן קַשְׂקַשִּׂים (ז)
Crusade	masa tslav	מַסָע צְלָב (ז)
crusader	tsalban	צַלְבָּן (ז)
territory	'ʃetax	שֶׁטַח (ז)
to attack (invade)	litkof	לִתְקוֹף
to conquer (vt)	lixboʃ	לִכְבּוֹשׁ
to occupy (invade)	lehiʃtalet	לְהִשְׁתַּלֵּט
siege (to be under ~)	matsor	מָצוֹר (ז)
besieged (adj)	natsur	נָצוּר
to besiege (vt)	latsur	לָצוּר
inquisition	inkvi'zitsya	אִינְקְוִוִיזִיצְיָה (נ)
inquisitor	inkvi'zitor	אִינְקְוִוִיזִיטוֹר (ז)

torture	inui	עִנּוּי (ז)
cruel (adj)	aχzari	אַכְזָרִי
heretic	kofer	כּוֹפֵר (ז)
heresy	kfira	כְּפִירָה (נ)

seafaring	haflaga bayam	הַפְלָגָה בַּיָם (נ)
pirate	ʃoded yam	שׁוֹדֵד יָם (ז)
piracy	pi'ratiyut	פִּירָטִיוּת (נ)
boarding (attack)	la'alot al	לַעֲלוֹת עַל
loot, booty	ʃalal	שָׁלָל (ז)
treasures	otsarot	אוֹצָרוֹת (ז"ר)

discovery	taglit	תַּגְלִית (נ)
to discover (new land, etc.)	legalot	לְגַלּוֹת
expedition	miʃlaχat	מִשְׁלַחַת (נ)

musketeer	musketer	מוּסְקֵטֵר (ז)
cardinal	χaʃman	חַשְׁמָן (ז)
heraldry	he'raldika	הֶרַלְדִיקָה (נ)
heraldic (adj)	he'raldi	הֶרַלְדִי

189. Leader. Chief. Authorities

king	'meleχ	מֶלֶךְ (ז)
queen	malka	מַלְכָּה (נ)
royal (adj)	malχuti	מַלְכוּתִי
kingdom	mamlaχa	מַמְלָכָה (נ)

prince	nasiχ	נָסִיךְ (ז)
princess	nesiχa	נְסִיכָה (נ)

president	nasi	נָשִׂיא (ז)
vice-president	sgan nasi	סְגַן נָשִׂיא (ז)
senator	se'nator	סֵנָאטוֹר (ז)

monarch	'meleχ	מֶלֶךְ (ז)
ruler (sovereign)	ʃalit	שַׁלִיט (ז)
dictator	rodan	רוֹדָן (ז)
tyrant	aruts	עָרוּץ (ז)
magnate	eil hon	אֵיל הוֹן (ז)

director	menahel	מְנַהֵל (ז)
chief	menahel, roʃ	מְנַהֵל (ז), רֹאשׁ (ז)
manager (director)	menahel	מְנַהֵל (ז)
boss	bos	בּוֹס (ז)
owner	'ba'al	בַּעַל (ז)

leader	manhig	מַנְהִיג (ז)
head (~ of delegation)	roʃ	רֹאשׁ (ז)
authorities	ʃiltonot	שִׁלְטוֹנוֹת (ז"ר)
superiors	memunim	מְמוּנִים (ז"ר)

governor	moʃel	מוֹשֵׁל (ז)
consul	'konsul	קוֹנְסוּל (ז)

diplomat	diplomat	דִּיפּלוֹמָט (ז)
mayor	roʃ ha'ir	רֹאשׁ הָעִיר (ז)
sheriff	ʃerif	שֶׁרִיף (ז)

emperor	keisar	קֵיסָר (ז)
tsar, czar	tsar	צָאר (ז)
pharaoh	par'o	פַּרְעֹה (ז)
khan	χan	חָאן (ז)

190. Road. Way. Directions

| road | 'dereχ | דֶּרֶךְ (נ) |
| way (direction) | kivun | כִּיווּן (ז) |

highway	kviʃ mahir	כְּבִישׁ מָהִיר (ז)
motorway	kviʃ mahir	כְּבִישׁ מָהִיר (ז)
trunk road	kviʃ le'umi	כְּבִישׁ לְאוּמִי (ז)

| main road | kviʃ raʃi | כְּבִישׁ רָאשִׁי (ז) |
| dirt road | 'dereχ afar | דֶּרֶךְ עָפָר (נ) |

| pathway | ʃvil | שְׁבִיל (ז) |
| footpath (troddenpath) | ʃvil | שְׁבִיל (ז) |

Where?	'eifo?	אֵיפֹה?
Where (to)?	le'an?	לְאָן?
From where?	me''eifo?	מֵאֵיפֹה?

| direction (way) | kivun | כִּיווּן (ז) |
| to point (~ the way) | lenatev | לְנַתֵּב |

to the left	'smola	שְׂמֹאלָה
to the right	ya'mina	יָמִינָה
straight ahead (adv)	yaʃar	יָשָׁר
back (e.g. to turn ~)	a'χora	אֲחוֹרָה

bend, curve	ikul	עִיקּוּל (ז)
to turn (e.g., ~ left)	lifnot	לִפְנוֹת
to make a U-turn	leva'tse'a pniyat parsa	לְבַצֵּעַ פְּנִיַּת פַּרְסָה

| to be visible (mountains, castle, etc.) | lihyot nir'a | לִהְיוֹת נִרְאָה |
| to appear (come into view) | leho'fi'a | לְהוֹפִיעַ |

stop, halt (e.g., during a trip)	taχana	תַּחֲנָה (נ)
to rest, to pause (vi)	la'nuaχ	לָנוּחַ
rest (pause)	menuχa	מְנוּחָה (נ)

to lose one's way	lit'ot	לִתְעוֹת
to lead to ... (ab. road)	lehovil le...	לְהוֹבִיל לְ...
to came out (e.g., on the highway)	latset le...	לָצֵאת לְ...
stretch (of road)	'keta	קֶטַע (ז)
asphalt	asfalt	אַסְפַלְט (ז)

kerb	sfat midraxa	שְׂפַת מִדְרָכָה (נ)
ditch	te'ala	תְּעָלָה (נ)
manhole	bor	בּוֹר (ז)
roadside (shoulder)	ʃulei ha'derex	שׁוּלֵי הַדֶּרֶךְ (ז"ר)
pit, pothole	bor	בּוֹר (ז)

| to go (on foot) | la'lexet | לָלֶכֶת |
| to overtake (vt) | la'akof | לַעֲקוֹף |

| step (footstep) | 'tsa'ad | צַעַד (ז) |
| on foot (adv) | ba'regel | בָּרֶגֶל |

to block (road)	laxsom	לַחְסוֹם
boom gate	maxsom	מַחְסוֹם (ז)
dead end	mavoi satum	מָבוֹי סָתוּם (ז)

191. Breaking the law. Criminals. Part 1

bandit	ʃoded	שׁוֹדֵד (ז)
crime	'peʃa	פֶּשַׁע (ז)
criminal (person)	po'ʃe'a	פּוֹשֵׁעַ (ז)

thief	ganav	גַּנָּב (ז)
to steal (vi, vt)	lignov	לִגְנוֹב
stealing (larceny)	gneva	גְּנֵיבָה (נ)
theft	gneva	גְּנֵיבָה (נ)

to kidnap (vt)	laxatof	לַחֲטוֹף
kidnapping	xatifa	חֲטִיפָה (נ)
kidnapper	xotef	חוֹטֵף (ז)

| ransom | 'kofer | כּוֹפֶר (ז) |
| to demand ransom | lidroʃ 'kofer | לִדְרוֹשׁ כּוֹפֶר |

to rob (vt)	liʃdod	לִשְׁדּוֹד
robbery	ʃod	שׁוֹד (ז)
robber	ʃoded	שׁוֹדֵד (ז)

to extort (vt)	lisxot	לִסְחוֹט
extortionist	saxtan	סַחְטָן (ז)
extortion	saxtanut	סַחְטָנוּת (נ)

to murder, to kill	lir'tsoax	לִרְצוֹחַ
murder	'retsax	רֶצַח (ז)
murderer	ro'tseax	רוֹצֵחַ (ז)

gunshot	yeriya	יְרִיָּה (נ)
to fire (~ a shot)	lirot	לִירוֹת
to shoot to death	lirot la'mavet	לִירוֹת לַמָּוֶת
to shoot (vi)	lirot	לִירוֹת
shooting	'yeri	יֶרִי (ז)

| incident (fight, etc.) | takrit | תַּקְרִית (נ) |
| fight, brawl | ktata | קְטָטָה (נ) |

Help!	ha'tsilu!	הַצִּילוּ!
victim	nifga	נִפְגָּע (ז)
to damage (vt)	lekalkel	לְקַלְקֵל
damage	'nezek	נֶזֶק (ז)
dead body, corpse	gufa	גּוּפָה (נ)
grave (~ crime)	xamur	חָמוּר
to attack (vt)	litkof	לִתְקוֹף
to beat (to hit)	lehakot	לְהַכּוֹת
to beat up	lehakot	לְהַכּוֹת
to take (rob of sth)	la'kaxat be'koax	לָקַחַת בְּכוֹחַ
to stab to death	lidkor le'mavet	לִדְקוֹר לְמָוֶת
to maim (vt)	lehatil mum	לְהָטִיל מוּם
to wound (vt)	lif'tso‘a	לִפְצוֹעַ
blackmail	saxtanut	סַחְטָנוּת (נ)
to blackmail (vt)	lisxot	לִסְחוֹט
blackmailer	saxtan	סַחְטָן (ז)
protection racket	dmei xasut	דְּמֵי חָסוּת (ז"ר)
racketeer	gove xasut	גּוֹבֶה חָסוּת (ז)
gangster	'gangster	גַּנְגְסְטֶר (ז)
mafia	'mafya	מָאפְיָה (נ)
pickpocket	kayas	כַּיָּיס (ז)
burglar	porets	פּוֹרֵץ (ז)
smuggling	havraxa	הַבְרָחָה (נ)
smuggler	mav'riax	מַבְרִיחַ (ז)
forgery	ziyuf	זִיּוּף (ז)
to forge (counterfeit)	lezayef	לְזַיֵּיף
fake (forged)	mezuyaf	מְזוּיָּף

192. Breaking the law. Criminals. Part 2

rape	'ones	אוֹנֶס (ז)
to rape (vt)	le’enos	לֶאֱנוֹס
rapist	anas	אַנָּס (ז)
maniac	'manyak	מַנְיָאק (ז)
prostitute (fem.)	zona	זוֹנָה (נ)
prostitution	znut	זְנוּת (נ)
pimp	sarsur	סַרְסוּר (ז)
drug addict	narkoman	נַרְקוֹמָן (ז)
drug dealer	soxer samim	סוֹחֵר סַמִּים (ז)
to blow up (bomb)	lefotsets	לְפוֹצֵץ
explosion	pitsuts	פִּיצוּץ (ז)
to set fire	lehatsit	לְהַצִּית
arsonist	matsit	מַצִּית (ז)
terrorism	terorizm	טֶרוֹרִיזְם (ז)
terrorist	mexabel	מְחַבֵּל (ז)

hostage	ben aruba	בֶּן עֲרוּבָּה (ז)
to swindle (deceive)	lehonot	לְהוֹנוֹת
swindle, deception	hona'a	הוֹנָאָה (נ)
swindler	ramai	רַמַאי (ז)
to bribe (vt)	leʃaxed	לְשַׁחֵד
bribery	ʃoxad	שׁוֹחַד (ז)
bribe	ʃoxad	שׁוֹחַד (ז)
poison	'ra'al	רַעַל (ז)
to poison (vt)	lehar'il	לְהַרְעִיל
to poison oneself	lehar'il et atsmo	לְהַרְעִיל אֶת עַצְמוֹ
suicide (act)	hit'abdut	הִתְאַבְּדוּת (נ)
suicide (person)	mit'abed	מִתְאַבֵּד (ז)
to threaten (vt)	le'ayem	לְאַיֵּם
threat	iyum	אִיּוּם (ז)
to make an attempt	lehitnakeʃ	לְהִתְנַקֵּשׁ
attempt (attack)	nisayon hitnakʃut	נִיסָיוֹן הִתְנַקְּשׁוּת (ז)
to steal (a car)	lignov	לִגְנוֹב
to hijack (a plane)	laxatof matos	לַחֲטוֹף מָטוֹס
revenge	nekama	נְקָמָה (נ)
to avenge (get revenge)	linkom	לִנְקוֹם
to torture (vt)	la'anot	לְעַנּוֹת
torture	inui	עִינּוּי (ז)
to torment (vt)	leyaser	לְיַיסֵּר
pirate	ʃoded yam	שׁוֹדֵד יָם (ז)
hooligan	xuligan	חוּלִיגָאן (ז)
armed (adj)	mezuyan	מְזוּיָן
violence	alimut	אַלִּימוּת (נ)
illegal (unlawful)	'bilti le'gali	בִּלְתִּי לֶגָלִי
spying (espionage)	rigul	רִיגּוּל (ז)
to spy (vi)	leragel	לְרַגֵּל

193. Police. Law. Part 1

justice	'tsedek	צֶדֶק (ז)
court (see you in ~)	beit miʃpat	בֵּית מִשְׁפָּט (ז)
judge	ʃofet	שׁוֹפֵט (ז)
jurors	muʃba'im	מוּשׁבָּעִים (ז"ר)
jury trial	xaver muʃba'im	חֶבֶר מוּשׁבָּעִים (ז)
to judge (vt)	liʃpot	לִשְׁפּוֹט
lawyer, barrister	orex din	עוֹרֵךְ דִּין (ז)
defendant	omed lemiʃpat	עוֹמֵד לְמִשְׁפָּט (ז)
dock	safsal ne'eʃamim	סַפְסַל נֶאֱשָׁמִים (ז)
charge	ha'aʃama	הַאֲשָׁמָה (נ)

accused	ne'eʃam	נֶאֱשָׁם (ז)
sentence	gzar din	גְּזַר דִּין (ז)
to sentence (vt)	lifsok	לִפְסוֹק

guilty (culprit)	aʃem	אָשֵׁם (ז)
to punish (vt)	leha'aniʃ	לְהַעֲנִיש
punishment	'oneʃ	עוֹנֶש (ז)

fine (penalty)	knas	קְנָס (ז)
life imprisonment	ma'asar olam	מַאֲסַר עוֹלָם (ז)
death penalty	'oneʃ 'mavet	עוֹנֶש מָוֶת (ז)
electric chair	kise χaʃmali	כִּיסֵא חַשְׁמַלִּי (ז)
gallows	gardom	גַרְדוֹם (ז)

| to execute (vt) | lehotsi la'horeg | לְהוֹצִיא לַהוֹרֵג |
| execution | hatsa'a le'horeg | הוֹצָאָה לַהוֹרֵג (נ) |

prison	beit 'sohar	בֵּית סוֹהַר (ז)
cell	ta	תָא (ז)
escort	miʃmar livui	מִשְׁמָר לִיוּוי (ז)
prison officer	soher	סוֹהֵר (ז)
prisoner	asir	אָסִיר (ז)

| handcuffs | azikim | אֲזִיקִים (ז"ר) |
| to handcuff (vt) | liχbol be'azikim | לִכְבּוֹל בָּאֲזִיקִים |

prison break	briχa	בְּרִיחָה (נ)
to break out (vi)	liv'roaχ	לִבְרוֹח
to disappear (vi)	lehe'alem	לְהֵיעָלֵם
to release (from prison)	leʃaχrer	לְשַׁחְרֵר
amnesty	χanina	חֲנִינָה (נ)

police	miʃtara	מִשְׁטָרָה (נ)
police officer	ʃoter	שׁוֹטֵר (ז)
police station	taχanat miʃtara	תַחֲנַת מִשְׁטָרָה (נ)
truncheon	ala	אַלָה (נ)
megaphone (loudhailer)	megafon	מֶגָפוֹן (ז)

patrol car	na'yedet	נַיֶּידֶת (נ)
siren	tsofar	צוֹפָר (ז)
to turn on the siren	lehaf'il tsofar	לְהַפְעִיל צוֹפָר
siren call	tsfira	צְפִירָה (נ)

crime scene	zirat 'peʃa	זִירַת פֶּשַׁע (נ)
witness	ed	עֵד (ז)
freedom	'χofeʃ	חוֹפֶש (ז)
accomplice	ʃutaf	שׁוּתָף (ז)
to flee (vi)	lehiχave	לְהֵיחָבֵא
trace (to leave a ~)	akev	עָקֵב (ז)

194. Police. Law. Part 2

| search (investigation) | χipus | חִיפּוּש (ז) |
| to look for ... | leχapes | לְחַפֵּש |

suspicion	ʃaʃad	חָשָׁד (ז)
suspicious (e.g., ~ vehicle)	ʃaʃud	חָשׁוּד
to stop (cause to halt)	la'atsor	לַעֲצֹר
to detain (keep in custody)	la'atsor	לַעֲצֹר

case (lawsuit)	tik	תִּיק (ז)
investigation	ʃakira	חֲקִירָה (נ)
detective	balaʃ	בַּלָּשׁ (ז)
investigator	ʃoker	חוֹקֵר (ז)
hypothesis	haʃʔara	הַשְׁעָרָה (נ)

motive	me'ni'a	מֵנִיעַ (ז)
interrogation	ʃakira	חֲקִירָה (נ)
to interrogate (vt)	laʃkor	לַחְקֹר
to question (~ neighbors, etc.)	letaʃel	לְתַשְׁאֵל
check (identity ~)	bdika	בְּדִיקָה (נ)

round-up	matsod	מָצוֹד (ז)
search (~ warrant)	ʃipus	חִיפּוּשׂ (ז)
chase (pursuit)	mirdaf	מִרְדָּף (ז)
to pursue, to chase	lirdof aʃarei	לִרְדּוֹף אַחֲרֵי
to track (a criminal)	la'akov aʃarei	לַעֲקוֹב אַחֲרֵי

arrest	ma'asar	מַאֲסָר (ז)
to arrest (sb)	le'esor	לָאֱסוֹר
to catch (thief, etc.)	lilkod	לִלְכּוֹד
capture	leʃida	לְכִידָה (נ)

document	mismaʃ	מִסְמָךְ (ז)
proof (evidence)	hoʃaʃa	הוֹכָחָה (נ)
to prove (vt)	leho'ʃiaʃ	לְהוֹכִיחַ
footprint	akev	עָקֵב (ז)
fingerprints	tvi'ot etsba'ot	טְבִיעוֹת אֶצְבָּעוֹת (נ״ר)
piece of evidence	re'aya	רְאָיָה (נ)

alibi	'alibi	אָלִיבִּי (ז)
innocent (not guilty)	ʃaf mi'peʃa	חַף מִפֶּשַׁע
injustice	i 'tsedek	אִי צֶדֶק (ז)
unjust, unfair (adj)	lo tsodek	לֹא צוֹדֵק

criminal (adj)	plili	פְּלִילִי
to confiscate (vt)	lehaʃrim	לְהַחְרִים
drug (illegal substance)	sam	סַם (ז)
weapon, gun	'neʃek	נֶשֶׁק (ז)
to disarm (vt)	lifrok mi'neʃek	לְפָרֹק מִנֶּשֶׁק

to order (command)	lifkod	לִפְקֹד
to disappear (vi)	lehe'alem	לְהֵיעָלֵם

law	ʃok	חֹק (ז)
legal, lawful (adj)	ʃuki	חוּקִי
illegal, illicit (adj)	'bilti ʃuki	בִּלְתִּי חוּקִי

responsibility (blame)	aʃrayut	אַחְרָיוּת (נ)
responsible (adj)	aʃrai	אַחְרַאי

NATURE

The Earth. Part 1

195. Outer space

space	χalal	חָלָל (ז)
space (as adj)	ʃel χalal	שֶׁל חָלָל
outer space	χalal χitson	חָלָל חִיצוֹן (ז)
world	olam	עוֹלָם (ז)
universe	yekum	יְקוּם (ז)
galaxy	ga'laksya	גָּלַקְסְיָה (נ)
star	koχav	כּוֹכָב (ז)
constellation	tsvir koχavim	צְבִיר כּוֹכָבִים (ז)
planet	koχav 'leχet	כּוֹכָב לֶכֶת (ז)
satellite	lavyan	לַוְיָן (ז)
meteorite	mete'orit	מֶטֵאוֹרִיט (ז)
comet	koχav ʃavit	כּוֹכָב שָׁבִיט (ז)
asteroid	aste'ro'id	אַסְטֵרוֹאִיד (ז)
orbit	maslul	מַסְלוּל (ז)
to revolve	lesovev	לְסוֹבֵב
(~ around the Earth)		
atmosphere	atmos'fera	אַטְמוֹסְפֶרָה (נ)
the Sun	'ʃemeʃ	שֶׁמֶשׁ (נ)
solar system	ma'a'reχet ha'ʃemeʃ	מַעֲרֶכֶת הַשֶׁמֶשׁ (נ)
solar eclipse	likui χama	לִיקוּי חַמָּה (ז)
the Earth	kadur ha''arets	כַּדּוּר הָאָרֶץ (ז)
the Moon	ya'reaχ	יָרֵחַ (ז)
Mars	ma'adim	מַאֲדִים (ז)
Venus	'noga	נוֹגַהּ (ז)
Jupiter	'tsedek	צֶדֶק (ז)
Saturn	ʃabtai	שַׁבְתַאי (ז)
Mercury	koχav χama	כּוֹכָב חַמָּה (ז)
Uranus	u'ranus	אוּרָנוּס (ז)
Neptune	neptun	נֶפְּטוּן (ז)
Pluto	'pluto	פְּלוּטוֹ (ז)
Milky Way	ʃvil haχalav	שְׁבִיל הֶחָלָב (ז)
Great Bear (Ursa Major)	duba gdola	דֻּבָּה גְדוֹלָה (נ)
North Star	koχav hatsafon	כּוֹכָב הַצָּפוֹן (ז)
Martian	toʃav ma'adim	תּוֹשַׁב מַאֲדִים (ז)
extraterrestrial (n)	χutsan	חוּצָן (ז)

| alien | χaizar | חַייזָר (ז) |
| flying saucer | tsa'laχat me'o'fefet | צַלַחַת מְעוֹפֶפֶת (נ) |

spaceship	χalalit	חֲלָלִית (נ)
space station	taχanat χalal	תַחֲנַת חָלָל (נ)
blast-off	hamra'a	הַמרָאָה (נ)

engine	ma'no'a	מָנוֹעַ (ז)
nozzle	neχir	נְחִיר (ז)
fuel	'delek	דֶלֶק (ז)

cockpit, flight deck	'kokpit	קוֹקפִּיט (ז)
aerial	an'tena	אַנטֶנָה (נ)
porthole	eʃnav	אֶשׁנָב (ז)
solar panel	'luaχ so'lari	לוּחַ סוֹלָרִי (ז)
spacesuit	χalifat χalal	חֲלִיפַת חָלָל (נ)

| weightlessness | 'χoser miʃkal | חוֹסֶר מִשׁקָל (ז) |
| oxygen | χamtsan | חַמצָן (ז) |

| docking (in space) | agina | עֲגִינָה (נ) |
| to dock (vi, vt) | la'agon | לַעֲגוֹן |

observatory	mitspe koχavim	מִצפֶּה כּוֹכָבִים (ז)
telescope	teleskop	טֶלֶסקוֹפּ (ז)
to observe (vt)	litspot, lehaʃkif	לִצפּוֹת, לְהַשׁקִיף
to explore (vt)	laχkor	לַחקוֹר

196. The Earth

the Earth	kadur ha''arets	כַּדוּר הָאָרֶץ (ז)
the globe (the Earth)	kadur ha''arets	כַּדוּר הָאָרֶץ (ז)
planet	koχav 'leχet	כּוֹכַב לֶכֶת (ז)

atmosphere	atmos'fera	אַטמוֹספֶרָה (נ)
geography	ge'o'grafya	גֵיאוֹגרַפיָה (נ)
nature	'teva	טֶבַע (ז)

globe (table ~)	'globus	גלוֹבּוּס (ז)
map	mapa	מַפָּה (נ)
atlas	'atlas	אַטלָס (ז)

| Europe | ei'ropa | אֵירוֹפָּה (נ) |
| Asia | 'asya | אַסיָה (נ) |

| Africa | 'afrika | אַפרִיקָה (נ) |
| Australia | ost'ralya | אוֹסטרַליָה (נ) |

America	a'merika	אָמֶרִיקָה (נ)
North America	a'merika hatsfonit	אָמֶרִיקָה הַצפוֹנִית (נ)
South America	a'merika hadromit	אָמֶרִיקָה הַדרוֹמִית (נ)

| Antarctica | ya'beʃet an'tarktika | יַבֶּשֶׁת אַנטאַרקטִיקָה (נ) |
| the Arctic | 'arktika | אַרקטִיקָה (נ) |

197. Cardinal directions

north	tsafon	צָפוֹן (ז)
to the north	tsa'fona	צָפוֹנָה
in the north	batsafon	בַּצָפוֹן
northern (adj)	tsfoni	צְפוֹנִי

south	darom	דָרוֹם (ז)
to the south	da'roma	דָרוֹמָה
in the south	badarom	בַּדָרוֹם
southern (adj)	dromi	דרוֹמִי

west	ma'arav	מַעֲרָב (ז)
to the west	ma'a'rava	מַעֲרָבָה
in the west	bama'arav	בַּמַעֲרָב
western (adj)	ma'aravi	מַעֲרָבִי

east	mizraχ	מִזרָח (ז)
to the east	miz'raχa	מִזרָחָה
in the east	bamizraχ	בַּמִזרָח
eastern (adj)	mizraχi	מִזרָחִי

198. Sea. Ocean

sea	yam	יָם (ז)
ocean	ok'yanos	אוֹקיָאנוֹס (ז)
gulf (bay)	mifrats	מִפרָץ (ז)
straits	meitsar	מֵיצָר (ז)

land (solid ground)	yabaʃa	יַבָּשָׁה (נ)
continent (mainland)	ya'beʃet	יַבָּשֶׁת (נ)
island	i	אִי (ז)
peninsula	χatsi i	חֲצִי אִי (ז)
archipelago	arχipelag	אַרכִיפֶּלָג (ז)

bay, cove	mifrats	מִפרָץ (ז)
harbour	namal	נָמָל (ז)
lagoon	la'guna	לָגוּנָה (נ)
cape	kef	כֵּף (ז)

atoll	atol	אָטוֹל (ז)
reef	ʃunit	שׁוּנִית (נ)
coral	almog	אַלמוֹג (ז)
coral reef	ʃunit almogim	שׁוּנִית אַלמוֹגִים (נ)

deep (adj)	amok	עָמוֹק
depth (deep water)	'omek	עוֹמֶק (ז)
abyss	tehom	תְהוֹם (נ)
trench (e.g. Mariana ~)	maχteʃ	מִכתָשׁ (ז)

current (Ocean ~)	'zerem	זֶרֶם (ז)
to surround (bathe)	lehakif	לְהַקִיף
shore	χof	חוֹף (ז)

coast	χof yam	חוֹף יָם (ז)
flow (flood tide)	ge'ut	גֵּאוּת (נ)
ebb (ebb tide)	'ʃefel	שֵׁפֶל (ז)
shoal	sirton	שִׂרטוֹן (ז)
bottom (~ of the sea)	karka'it	קַרקָעִית (נ)

wave	gal	גַּל (ז)
crest (~ of a wave)	pisgat hagal	פִּסגַת הַגַּל (נ)
spume (sea foam)	'ketsef	קֶצֶף (ז)

storm (sea storm)	sufa	סוּפָה (נ)
hurricane	hurikan	הוֹרִיקָן (ז)
tsunami	tsu'nami	צוּנָאמִי (ז)
calm (dead ~)	'roga	רוֹגַע (ז)
quiet, calm (adj)	ʃalev	שָׁלֵו

| pole | 'kotev | קוֹטֶב (ז) |
| polar (adj) | kotbi | קוֹטבִּי |

latitude	kav 'roχav	קַו רוֹחַב (ז)
longitude	kav 'oreχ	קַו אוֹרֶך (ז)
parallel	kav 'roχav	קַו רוֹחַב (ז)
equator	kav hamaʃve	קַו הַמַשׁווֶה (ז)

sky	ʃa'mayim	שָׁמַיִים (ז"ר)
horizon	'ofek	אוֹפֶק (ז)
air	avir	אֲווִיר (ז)

lighthouse	migdalor	מִגדָלוֹר (ז)
to dive (vi)	litslol	לִצלוֹל
to sink (ab. boat)	lit'bo'a	לִטבּוֹעַ
treasures	otsarot	אוֹצָרוֹת (ז"ר)

199. Seas & Oceans names

Atlantic Ocean	ha'ok'yanus ha'at'lanti	הָאוֹקיָינוֹס הָאַטלַנטִי (ז)
Indian Ocean	ha'ok'yanus ha'hodi	הָאוֹקיָינוֹס הַהוֹדִי (ז)
Pacific Ocean	ha'ok'yanus haʃaket	הָאוֹקיָינוֹס הַשָׁקֵט (ז)
Arctic Ocean	ok'yanos ha'keraχ hatsfoni	אוֹקיָינוֹס הַקֶרַח הַצפוֹנִי (ז)

Black Sea	hayam haʃaχor	הַיָם הַשָׁחוֹר (ז)
Red Sea	yam suf	יַם סוּף (ז)
Yellow Sea	hayam hatsahov	הַיָם הַצָהוֹב (ז)
White Sea	hayam halavan	הַיָם הַלָבָן (ז)

Caspian Sea	hayam ha'kaspi	הַיָם הַכַּספִי (ז)
Dead Sea	yam ha'melaχ	יַם הַמֶלַח (ז)
Mediterranean Sea	hayam hatiχon	הַיָם הַתִיכוֹן (ז)

| Aegean Sea | hayam ha'e'ge'i | הַיָם הָאֶגֵאִי (ז) |
| Adriatic Sea | hayam ha'adri'yati | הַיָם הָאַדרִיָאתִי (ז) |

| Arabian Sea | hayam ha'aravi | הַיָם הָעֲרָבִי (ז) |
| Sea of Japan | hayam haya'pani | הַיָם הַיָפָנִי (ז) |

Bering Sea	yam 'bering	יַם בֶּרִינג (ז)
South China Sea	yam sin hadromi	יַם סִין הַדְרוֹמִי (ז)
Coral Sea	yam ha'almogim	יַם הָאַלְמוֹגִים (ז)
Tasman Sea	yam tasman	יַם טַסְמַן (ז)
Caribbean Sea	hayam haka'ribi	הַיָם הַקָרִיבִּי (ז)
Barents Sea	yam 'barents	יַם בָּרֶנְץ (ז)
Kara Sea	yam 'kara	יַם קָאַרָה (ז)
North Sea	hayam hatsfoni	הַיָם הַצְפוֹנִי (ז)
Baltic Sea	hayam ha'balti	הַיָם הַבַּלְטִי (ז)
Norwegian Sea	hayam hanor'vegi	הַיָם הַנוֹרְבֶגִי (ז)

200. Mountains

mountain	har	הַר (ז)
mountain range	'rexes harim	רֶכֶס הָרִים (ז)
mountain ridge	'rexes har	רֶכֶס הַר (ז)
summit, top	pisga	פִּסְגָה (נ)
peak	pisga	פִּסְגָה (נ)
foot (~ of the mountain)	margelot	מַרְגְלוֹת (נ"ר)
slope (mountainside)	midron	מִדְרוֹן (ז)
volcano	har 'ga'aʃ	הַר גַעַשׁ (ז)
active volcano	har 'ga'aʃ pa'il	הַר גַעַשׁ פָּעִיל (ז)
dormant volcano	har 'ga'aʃ radum	הַר גַעַשׁ רָדוּם (ז)
eruption	hitpartsut	הִתְפָּרְצוּת (נ)
crater	lo'a	לוֹעַ (ז)
magma	megama	מֶגְמָה (נ)
lava	'lava	לָאבָה (נ)
molten (~ lava)	lohet	לוֹהֵט
canyon	kanyon	קַנְיוֹן (ז)
gorge	gai	גַיְא (ז)
crevice	'beka	בֶּקַע (ז)
abyss (chasm)	tehom	תְהוֹם (נ)
pass, col	ma'avar harim	מַעֲבַר הָרִים (ז)
plateau	rama	רָמָה (נ)
cliff	tsuk	צוּק (ז)
hill	giv'a	גִבְעָה (נ)
glacier	karxon	קַרְחוֹן (ז)
waterfall	mapal 'mayim	מַפַּל מַיִם (ז)
geyser	'geizer	גֵייְזֶר (ז)
lake	agam	אֲגַם (ז)
plain	miʃor	מִישׁוֹר (ז)
landscape	nof	נוֹף (ז)
echo	hed	הֵד (ז)
alpinist	metapes harim	מְטַפֵּס הָרִים (ז)

rock climber	metapes sla'im	מְטַפֵּס סְלָעִים (ז)
to conquer (in climbing)	liχbo∫	לִכְבּוֹשׁ
climb (an easy ~)	tipus	טִיפּוּס (ז)

201. Mountains names

The Alps	harei ha''alpim	הָרֵי הָאָלְפִּים (ז"ר)
Mont Blanc	mon blan	מוֹן בְּלָאן (ז)
The Pyrenees	pire'ne'im	פִּירֶנֶאִים (ז"ר)
The Carpathians	kar'patim	קַרְפָּטִים (ז"ר)
The Ural Mountains	harei ural	הָרֵי אוּרָל (ז"ר)
The Caucasus Mountains	harei hakavkaz	הָרֵי הַקַּווֹקָז (ז"ר)
Mount Elbrus	elbrus	אֶלְבְּרוּס (ז)
The Altai Mountains	harei altai	הָרֵי אַלְטַאי (ז"ר)
The Tian Shan	tyan ∫an	טִיאָן שָׁאן (ז)
The Pamir Mountains	harei pamir	הָרֵי פָּאמִיר (ז"ר)
The Himalayas	harei hehima'laya	הָרֵי הֶהִימָלַאיָה (ז"ר)
Mount Everest	everest	אֶוֶרֶסְט (ז)
The Andes	harei ha''andim	הָרֵי הָאַנְדִּים (ז"ר)
Mount Kilimanjaro	kiliman'dʒaro	קִילִימַנְגִ'רוֹ (ז)

202. Rivers

river	nahar	נָהָר (ז)
spring (natural source)	ma'ayan	מַעְיָן (ז)
riverbed (river channel)	afik	אָפִיק (ז)
basin (river valley)	agan nahar	אֲגַן נָהָר (ז)
to flow into ...	lehi∫apeχ	לְהִישָׁפֵךְ
tributary	yuval	יוּבַל (ז)
bank (of river)	χof	חוֹף (ז)
current (stream)	'zerem	זֶרֶם (ז)
downstream (adv)	bemorad hanahar	בְּמוֹרַד הַנָּהָר
upstream (adv)	bema'ale hanahar	בְּמַעֲלֶה הַנָּהָר
inundation	hatsafa	הֲצָפָה (נ)
flooding	∫itafon	שִׁיטָפוֹן (ז)
to overflow (vi)	la'alot al gdotav	לַעֲלוֹת עַל גְּדוֹתָיו
to flood (vt)	lehatsif	לְהָצִיף
shallow (shoal)	sirton	שִׂרְטוֹן (ז)
rapids	'e∫ed	אֶשֶׁד (ז)
dam	'seχer	סֶכֶר (ז)
canal	te'ala	תְּעָלָה (נ)
reservoir (artificial lake)	ma'agar 'mayim	מַאֲגַר מַיִם (ז)
sluice, lock	ta '∫ayit	תָּא שַׁיִט (ז)
water body (pond, etc.)	ma'agar 'mayim	מַאֲגַר מַיִם (ז)

swamp (marshland)	biƚsa	בִּיצָה (נ)
bog, marsh	biƚsa	בִּיצָה (נ)
whirlpool	me'ar'bolet	מְעַרְבּוֹלֶת (נ)

stream (brook)	'naχal	נַחַל (ז)
drinking (ab. water)	ʃel ʃtiya	שֶׁל שְׁתִיָּה
fresh (~ water)	metukim	מְתוּקִים

ice	'keraχ	קֶרַח (ז)
to freeze over (ab. river, etc.)	likpo	לִקְפוֹא

203. Rivers names

Seine	hasen	הַסֵן (ז)
Loire	lu'ar	לוּאָר (ז)

Thames	'temza	תֶּמְזָה (נ)
Rhine	hrain	הָרַיִן (ז)
Danube	da'nuba	דָּנוּבָּה (נ)

Volga	'volga	וֹוֹלְגָה (נ)
Don	nahar don	נְהַר דּוֹן (ז)
Lena	'lena	לֶנָה (נ)

Yellow River	hvang ho	הוֹוַנג הוֹ (ז)
Yangtze	yangƚse	יַאנגצֶה (ז)
Mekong	mekong	מֶקוֹנג (ז)
Ganges	'ganges	גַנְגֶס (ז)

Nile River	'nilus	נִילוּס (ז)
Congo River	'kongo	קוֹנגוֹ (ז)
Okavango River	ok'vango	אוֹקָבַנגוֹ (ז)
Zambezi River	zam'bezi	זַמְבֶּזִי (ז)
Limpopo River	limpopo	לִימְפּוֹפוֹ (ז)
Mississippi River	misi'sipi	מִיסִיסִיפִּי (ז)

204. Forest

forest, wood	'ya'ar	יַעַר (ז)
forest (as adj)	ʃel 'ya'ar	שֶׁל יַעַר

thick forest	avi ha'ya'ar	עֲבִי הַיַּעַר (ז)
grove	χurʃa	חוֹרְשָׁה (נ)
forest clearing	ka'raχat 'ya'ar	קָרַחַת יַעַר (נ)

thicket	svaχ	סְבַךְ (ז)
scrubland	'siaχ	שִׂיחַ (ז)

footpath (troddenpath)	ʃvil	שְׁבִיל (ז)
gully	'emek ƚsar	עֵמֶק צַר (ז)
tree	eƚs	עֵץ (ז)
leaf	ale	עָלֶה (ז)

183

leaves (foliage)	alva	עָלֶוָה (נ)
fall of leaves	ʃa'leχet	שַׁלֶּכֶת (נ)
to fall (ab. leaves)	linʃor	לִנְשׁוֹר
top (of the tree)	tsa'meret	צַמֶּרֶת (נ)

branch	anaf	עָנָף (ז)
bough	anaf ave	עָנָף עָבֶה (ז)
bud (on shrub, tree)	nitsan	נִיצָן (ז)
needle (of pine tree)	'maχat	מַחַט (נ)
fir cone	itstrubal	אָצְטְרוּבָּל (ז)

hollow (in a tree)	χor ba'ets	חוֹר בָּעֵץ (ז)
nest	ken	קֵן (ז)
burrow (animal hole)	meχila	מְחִילָה (נ)

trunk	'geza	גֶּזַע (ז)
root	'ʃoreʃ	שׁוֹרֶשׁ (ז)
bark	klipa	קְלִיפָּה (נ)
moss	taχav	טַחַב (ז)

to uproot (remove trees or tree stumps)	la'akor	לַעֲקוֹר
to chop down	liχrot	לִכְרוֹת
to deforest (vt)	levare	לְבָרֵא
tree stump	'gedem	גֶּדֶם (ז)

campfire	medura	מְדוּרָה (נ)
forest fire	srefa	שְׂרֵיפָה (נ)
to extinguish (vt)	leχabot	לְכַבּוֹת

forest ranger	ʃomer 'ya'ar	שׁוֹמֵר יַעַר (ז)
protection	ʃmira	שְׁמִירָה (נ)
to protect (~ nature)	liʃmor	לִשְׁמוֹר
poacher	tsayad lelo reʃut	צַיָּיד לְלֹא רְשׁוּת (ז)
steel trap	mal'kodet	מַלְכּוֹדֶת (נ)

| to gather, to pick (vt) | lelaket | לְלַקֵּט |
| to lose one's way | lit'ot | לִתְעוֹת |

205. Natural resources

natural resources	otsarot 'teva	אוֹצְרוֹת טֶבַע (ז"ר)
minerals	mine'ralim	מִינֶרָלִים (ז"ר)
deposits	mirbats	מִרְבָּץ (ז)
field (e.g. oilfield)	mirbats	מִרְבָּץ (ז)

to mine (extract)	liχrot	לִכְרוֹת
mining (extraction)	kriya	כְּרִיָּה (נ)
ore	afra	עַפְרָה (נ)
mine (e.g. for coal)	miχre	מִכְרֶה (ז)
shaft (mine ~)	pir	פִּיר (ז)
miner	kore	כּוֹרֶה (ז)
gas (natural ~)	gaz	גָּז (ז)
gas pipeline	tsinor gaz	צִינוֹר גָּז (ז)

oil (petroleum)	neft	נֵפְט (ז)
oil pipeline	tsinor neft	צִינוֹר נֵפְט (ז)
oil well	be'er neft	בְּאֵר נֵפְט (נ)
derrick (tower)	migdal ki'duax	מִגְדָל קִידוּחַ (ז)
tanker	mexalit	מֵיכָלִית (נ)
sand	xol	חוֹל (ז)
limestone	'even gir	אֶבֶן גִיר (נ)
gravel	xatsats	חָצָץ (ז)
peat	kavul	כָּבוּל (ז)
clay	tit	טִיט (ז)
coal	pexam	פֶּחָם (ז)
iron (ore)	barzel	בַּרְזֶל (ז)
gold	zahav	זָהָב (ז)
silver	'kesef	כֶּסֶף (ז)
nickel	'nikel	נִיקֶל (ז)
copper	ne'xoʃet	נְחוֹשֶת (נ)
zinc	avats	אָבָץ (ז)
manganese	mangan	מַנְגָן (ז)
mercury	kaspit	כַּסְפִּית (נ)
lead	o'feret	עוֹפֶרֶת (נ)
mineral	mineral	מִינְרָל (ז)
crystal	gaviʃ	גָבִיש (ז)
marble	'ʃayiʃ	שַיִש (ז)
uranium	u'ranyum	אוּרָנְיוּם (ז)

The Earth. Part 2

206. Weather

weather	'mezeg avir	מֶזֶג אֲוִיר (ז)
weather forecast	taxazit 'mezeg ha'avir	תַּחֲזִית מֶזֶג הָאֲוִיר (נ)
temperature	tempera'tura	טֶמְפֶּרָטוּרָה (נ)
thermometer	madxom	מַדחוֹם (ז)
barometer	ba'rometer	בָּרוֹמֶטֶר (ז)

humid (adj)	lax	לַח
humidity	laxut	לַחוּת (נ)
heat (extreme ~)	xom	חוֹם (ז)
hot (torrid)	xam	חַם
it's hot	xam	חַם

| it's warm | xamim | חָמִים |
| warm (moderately hot) | xamim | חָמִים |

| it's cold | kar | קַר |
| cold (adj) | kar | קַר |

sun	'ʃemeʃ	שֶׁמֶשׁ (נ)
to shine (vi)	lizhor	לִזהוֹר
sunny (day)	ʃimʃi	שִׁמשִׁי
to come up (vi)	liz'roax	לִזרוֹחַ
to set (vi)	liʃ'koʻa	לִשׁקוֹעַ

cloud	anan	עָנָן (ז)
cloudy (adj)	meʻunan	מְעוּנָן
rain cloud	av	עָב (ז)
somber (gloomy)	sagriri	סַגרִירִי

| rain | 'geʃem | גֶּשֶׁם (ז) |
| it's raining | yored 'geʃem | יוֹרֵד גֶּשֶׁם |

| rainy (~ day, weather) | gaʃum | גָּשׁוּם |
| to drizzle (vi) | letaftef | לְטַפטֵף |

pouring rain	matar	מָטָר (ז)
downpour	mabul	מַבּוּל (ז)
heavy (e.g. ~ rain)	xazak	חָזָק

| puddle | ʃlulit | שְׁלוּלִית (נ) |
| to get wet (in rain) | lehitratev | לְהִתרַטֵב |

fog (mist)	arapel	עֲרָפֶל (ז)
foggy	meʻurpal	מְעוּרפָּל
snow	'ʃeleg	שֶׁלֶג (ז)
it's snowing	yored 'ʃeleg	יוֹרֵד שֶׁלֶג

207. Severe weather. Natural disasters

thunderstorm	sufat re'amim	סוּפַת רְעָמִים (נ)
lightning (~ strike)	barak	בָּרָק (ז)
to flash (vi)	livhok	לִבְהוֹק
thunder	'ra'am	רַעַם (ז)
to thunder (vi)	lir'om	לִרְעוֹם
it's thundering	lir'om	לִרְעוֹם
hail	barad	בָּרָד (ז)
it's hailing	yored barad	יוֹרֵד בָּרָד
to flood (vt)	lehatsif	לְהָצִיף
flood, inundation	ʃitafon	שִׁיטָפוֹן (ז)
earthquake	re'idat adama	רְעִידַת אֲדָמָה (נ)
tremor, quake	re'ida	רְעִידָה (נ)
epicentre	moked	מוֹקֵד (ז)
eruption	hitpartsut	הִתְפָּרְצוּת (נ)
lava	'lava	לָאבָה (נ)
twister	hurikan	הוֹרִיקָן (ז)
tornado	tor'nado	טוֹרְנָדוֹ (ז)
typhoon	taifun	טַייפוּן (ז)
hurricane	hurikan	הוֹרִיקָן (ז)
storm	sufa	סוּפָה (נ)
tsunami	tsu'nami	צוּנָאמִי (ז)
cyclone	tsiklon	צִיקְלוֹן (ז)
bad weather	sagrir	סַגְרִיר (ז)
fire (accident)	srefa	שְׂרֵיפָה (נ)
disaster	ason	אָסוֹן (ז)
meteorite	mete'orit	מֶטְאוֹרִיט (ז)
avalanche	ma'polet ʃlagim	מַפּוֹלֶת שְׁלָגִים (נ)
snowslide	ma'polet ʃlagim	מַפּוֹלֶת שְׁלָגִים (נ)
blizzard	sufat ʃlagim	סוּפַת שְׁלָגִים (נ)
snowstorm	sufat ʃlagim	סוּפַת שְׁלָגִים (נ)

208. Noises. Sounds

silence (quiet)	'ʃeket	שֶׁקֶט (ז)
sound	tslil	צְלִיל (ז)
noise	'ra'aʃ	רַעַשׁ (ז)
to make noise	lir'oʃ	לִרְעוֹשׁ
noisy (adj)	ro'eʃ	רוֹעֵשׁ
loudly (to speak, etc.)	bekol	בְּקוֹל
loud (voice, etc.)	ram	רָם
constant (e.g., ~ noise)	ka'vu'a	קָבוּעַ

cry, shout (n)	tse'aka	צְעָקָה (נ)
to cry, to shout (vi)	lits'ok	לִצְעוֹק
whisper	lexiʃa	לְחִישָׁה (נ)
to whisper (vi, vt)	lilxoʃ	לִלְחוֹשׁ
barking (dog's ~)	nevixa	נְבִיחָה (נ)
to bark (vi)	lin'boax	לִנְבּוֹחַ
groan (of pain, etc.)	anaka	אֲנָקָה (נ)
to groan (vi)	lehe'anek	לְהֵיאָנֵק
cough	ʃi'ul	שִׁיעוּל (ז)
to cough (vi)	lehiʃta'el	לְהִשְׁתַּעֵל
whistle	ʃrika	שְׁרִיקָה (נ)
to whistle (vi)	liʃrok	לִשְׁרוֹק
knock (at the door)	hakaʃa	הַקָּשָׁה (נ)
to knock (at the door)	lidfok	לִדְפוֹק
to crack (vi)	lehitba'ke'a	לְהִתְבַּקֵּעַ
crack (cracking sound)	naftsuts	נַפְצוּץ (ז)
siren	tsofar	צוֹפָר (ז)
whistle (factory ~, etc.)	tsfira	צְפִירָה (נ)
to whistle (ab. train)	litspor	לְצַפּוֹר
honk (car horn sound)	tsfira	צְפִירָה (נ)
to honk (vi)	litspor	לְצַפּוֹר

209. Winter

winter (n)	'xoref	חוֹרֶף (ז)
winter (as adj)	xorpi	חוֹרְפִּי
in winter	ba'xoref	בַּחוֹרֶף
snow	'ʃeleg	שֶׁלֶג (ז)
it's snowing	yored 'ʃeleg	יוֹרֵד שֶׁלֶג
snowfall	yeridat 'ʃeleg	יְרִידַת שֶׁלֶג (נ)
snowdrift	aremat 'ʃeleg	עֲרֵימַת שֶׁלֶג (נ)
snowflake	ptit 'ʃeleg	פְּתִית שֶׁלֶג (ז)
snowball	kadur 'ʃeleg	כַּדּוּר שֶׁלֶג (ז)
snowman	iʃ 'ʃeleg	אִישׁ שֶׁלֶג (ז)
icicle	netif 'kerax	נְטִיף קֶרַח (ז)
December	de'tsember	דֵצֶמְבָּר (ז)
January	'yanu'ar	יָנוּאָר (ז)
February	'febru'ar	פֶבְּרוּאָר (ז)
frost (severe ~, freezing cold)	kfor	כְּפוֹר (ז)
frosty (weather, air)	kfori	כְּפוֹרִי
below zero (adv)	mi'taxat la''efes	מִתַּחַת לָאֶפֶס
first frost	kara	קָרָה (נ)
hoarfrost	kfor	כְּפוֹר (ז)
cold (cold weather)	kor	קוֹר (ז)

it's cold	kar	קַר
fur coat	me'il parva	מְעִיל פַּרְוָה (ז)
mittens	kfafot	כְּפָפוֹת (נ"ר)
to fall ill	laχalot	לַחֲלוֹת
cold (illness)	hitstanenut	הִצְטַנְנוּת (נ)
to catch a cold	lehitstanen	לְהִצְטַנֵן
ice	'keraχ	קֶרַח (ז)
black ice	ʃiχvat 'keraχ	שִׁכְבַת קֶרַח (נ)
to freeze over (ab. river, etc.)	likpo	לִקְפּוֹא
ice floe	karχon	קַרְחוֹן (ז)
skis	ski	סְקִי (ז)
skier	goleʃ	גּוֹלֵשׁ (ז)
to ski (vi)	la'asot ski	לַעֲשׂוֹת סְקִי
to skate (vi)	lehaχlik	לְהַחְלִיק

Fauna

210. Mammals. Predators

predator	χayat 'teref	חַיַּת טֶרֶף (נ)
tiger	'tigris	טִיגְרִיס (ז)
lion	arye	אַרְיֵה (ז)
wolf	ze'ev	זְאֵב (ז)
fox	ʃu'al	שׁוּעָל (ז)
jaguar	yagu'ar	יָגוּאָר (ז)
leopard	namer	נָמֵר (ז)
cheetah	bardelas	בַּרְדְּלָס (ז)
black panther	panter	פַּנְתֵּר (ז)
puma	'puma	פּוּמָה (נ)
snow leopard	namer 'ʃeleg	נָמֵר שֶׁלֶג (ז)
lynx	ʃunar	שׁוּנָר (ז)
coyote	ze'ev ha'aravot	זְאֵב הָעֲרָבוֹת (ז)
jackal	tan	תַּן (ז)
hyena	tsa'vo'a	צָבוֹעַ (ז)

211. Wild animals

animal	'ba'al χaylm	בַּעַל חַיִּים (ז)
beast (animal)	χaya	חַיָּה (נ)
squirrel	sna'i	סְנָאִי (ז)
hedgehog	kipod	קִיפּוֹד (ז)
hare	arnav	אַרְנָב (ז)
rabbit	ʃafan	שָׁפָן (ז)
badger	girit	גִּירִית (נ)
raccoon	dvivon	דְּבִיבוֹן (ז)
hamster	oger	אוֹגֵר (ז)
marmot	mar'mita	מַרְמִיטָה (נ)
mole	χafar'peret	חֲפַרְפֶּרֶת (נ)
mouse	aχbar	עַכְבָּר (ז)
rat	χulda	חוּלְדָּה (נ)
bat	atalef	עֲטַלֵּף (ז)
ermine	hermin	הֶרְמִין (ז)
sable	tsobel	צוֹבֶּל (ז)
marten	dalak	דְּלָק (ז)
weasel	χamus	חָמוּס (ז)
mink	χorfan	חוֹרְפָּן (ז)

| beaver | bone | בּוֹנֶה (ז) |
| otter | lutra | לוּטְרָה (נ) |

horse	sus	סוּס (ז)
moose	ayal hakore	אַיָּל הַקּוֹרֵא (ז)
deer	ayal	אַיָּל (ז)
camel	gamal	גָּמָל (ז)

bison	bizon	בִּיזוֹן (ז)
aurochs	bizon ei'ropi	בִּיזוֹן אֵירוֹפִּי (ז)
buffalo	te'o	תְּאוֹ (ז)

zebra	'zebra	זֶבְּרָה (נ)
antelope	anti'lopa	אַנְטִילוֹפָּה (נ)
roe deer	ayal hakarmel	אַיָּל הַכַּרְמֶל (ז)
fallow deer	yaχmur	יַחְמוּר (ז)
chamois	ya'el	יָעֵל (ז)
wild boar	χazir bar	חֲזִיר בָּר (ז)

whale	livyatan	לִוְיָתָן (ז)
seal	'kelev yam	כֶּלֶב יָם (ז)
walrus	sus yam	סוּס יָם (ז)
fur seal	dov yam	דֹּב יָם (ז)
dolphin	dolfin	דּוֹלְפִין (ז)

bear	dov	דֹּב (ז)
polar bear	dov 'kotev	דֹּב קוֹטֶב (ז)
panda	'panda	פַּנְדָּה (נ)

monkey	kof	קוֹף (ז)
chimpanzee	ʃimpanze	שִׁימְפַּנְזָה (נ)
orangutan	orang utan	אוֹרַנְג-אוּטָן (ז)
gorilla	go'rila	גּוֹרִילָה (נ)
macaque	makak	מָקָק (ז)
gibbon	gibon	גִּיבּוֹן (ז)

elephant	pil	פִּיל (ז)
rhinoceros	karnaf	קַרְנַף (ז)
giraffe	ʤi'rafa	גִ׳ירָפָה (נ)
hippopotamus	hipopotam	הִיפּוֹפּוֹטָם (ז)

| kangaroo | 'kenguru | קֶנְגּוּרוּ (ז) |
| koala (bear) | ko''ala | קוֹאָלָה (ז) |

mongoose	nemiya	נְמִיָּה (נ)
chinchilla	tʃin'tʃila	צִ׳ינְצִ׳ילָה (נ)
skunk	bo'eʃ	בּוֹאֵשׁ (ז)
porcupine	darban	דַּרְבָּן (ז)

212. Domestic animals

cat	χatula	חֲתוּלָה (נ)
tomcat	χatul	חָתוּל (ז)
dog	'kelev	כֶּלֶב (ז)

horse	sus	סוּס (ז)
stallion (male horse)	sus harba'a	סוּס הַרְבָּעָה (ז)
mare	susa	סוּסָה (נ)

cow	para	פָּרָה (נ)
bull	ʃor	שׁוֹר (ז)
ox	ʃor	שׁוֹר (ז)

sheep (ewe)	kivsa	כִּבְשָׂה (נ)
ram	'ayil	אַיִל (ז)
goat	ez	עֵז (נ)
billy goat, he-goat	'tayiʃ	תַּיִשׁ (ז)

| donkey | χamor | חֲמוֹר (ז) |
| mule | 'pered | פֶּרֶד (ז) |

pig	χazir	חֲזִיר (ז)
piglet	χazarzir	חֲזַרְזִיר (ז)
rabbit	arnav	אַרְנָב (ז)

| hen (chicken) | tarne'golet | תַּרְנְגוֹלֶת (נ) |
| cock | tarnegol | תַּרְנְגוֹל (ז) |

duck	barvaz	בַּרְוָז (ז)
drake	barvaz	בַּרְוָז (ז)
goose	avaz	אֲוָז (ז)

| tom turkey, gobbler | tarnegol 'hodu | תַּרְנְגוֹל הוֹדוּ (ז) |
| turkey (hen) | tarne'golet 'hodu | תַּרְנְגוֹלֶת הוֹדוּ (נ) |

domestic animals	χayot 'bayit	חַיּוֹת בַּיִת (נ״ר)
tame (e.g. ~ hamster)	mevuyat	מְבוּיָת
to tame (vt)	levayet	לְבַיֵּת
to breed (vt)	lehar'bi‘a	לְהַרְבִּיעַ

farm	χava	חַוָּה (נ)
poultry	ofot 'bayit	עוֹפוֹת בַּיִת (נ״ר)
cattle	bakar	בָּקָר (ז)
herd (cattle)	'eder	עֵדֶר (ז)

stable	urva	אוּרְוָה (נ)
pigsty	dir χazirim	דִּיר חֲזִירִים (ז)
cowshed	'refet	רֶפֶת (נ)
rabbit hutch	arnaviya	אַרְנָבִיָּה (נ)
hen house	lul	לוּל (ז)

213. Dogs. Dog breeds

dog	'kelev	כֶּלֶב (ז)
sheepdog	'kelev ro'e	כֶּלֶב רוֹעֶה (ז)
German shepherd	ro'e germani	רוֹעֶה גֶּרְמָנִי (ז)
poodle	'pudel	פּוּדֶל (ז)
dachshund	'taχaʃ	תַּחַשׁ (ז)
bulldog	buldog	בּוּלְדּוֹג (ז)

boxer	'bokser	בּוֹקְסֶר (ז)
mastiff	mastif	מַסְטִיף (ז)
Rottweiler	rot'vailer	רוֹטְוַויילֶר (ז)
Doberman	'doberman	דּוֹבֶּרְמָן (ז)

basset	'baset 'ha'und	בָּאסֶט־הָאוּנד (ז)
bobtail	bobteil	בּוֹבְּטֵייל (ז)
Dalmatian	dal'mati	דָלְמָטִי (ז)
cocker spaniel	'koker 'spani'el	קוֹקֶר סְפָּנִיאֶל (ז)

| Newfoundland | nyu'fa'undlend | נְיוּפָאוּנדלֶנד (ז) |
| Saint Bernard | sen bernard | סֶן בֶּרְנָרד (ז) |

husky	'haski	הָאסְקִי (ז)
Chow Chow	'ʧa'u 'ʧa'u	צָ'אוּ צָ'אוּ (ז)
spitz	ʃpits	שְׁפִּיץ (ז)
pug	pag	פָּאג (ז)

214. Sounds made by animals

barking (n)	neviχa	נְבִיחָה (נ)
to bark (vi)	lin'boaχ	לִנְבּוֹחַ
to miaow (vi)	leyalel	לְיַיֵל
to purr (vi)	legarger	לְגַרְגֵּר

to moo (vi)	lig'ot	לִגְעוֹת
to bellow (bull)	lig'ot	לִגְעוֹת
to growl (vi)	linhom	לִנְהוֹם

howl (n)	yelala	יְלָלָה (נ)
to howl (vi)	leyalel	לְיַיֵל
to whine (vi)	leyabev	לְיַבֵּב

to bleat (sheep)	lif'ot	לִפְעוֹת
to oink, to grunt (pig)	leχarχer	לְחַרְחֵר
to squeal (vi)	lits'voaχ	לִצְוֹוֹחַ

to croak (vi)	lekarker	לְקַרְקֵר
to buzz (insect)	lezamzem	לְזַמְזֵם
to chirp (crickets, grasshopper)	letsartser	לְצַרְצֵר

215. Young animals

cub	gur	גּוּר (ז)
kitten	χataltul	חֲתַלְתוּל (ז)
baby mouse	aχbaron	עַכְבָּרוֹן (ז)
puppy	klavlav	כְּלַבְלַב (ז)

leveret	arnavon	אַרְנָבוֹן (ז)
baby rabbit	ʃfanfan	שְׁפַנְפַּן (ז)
wolf cub	gur ze'evim	גּוּר זְאֵבִים (ז)

fox cub	ʃu'alon	שׁוּעָלוֹן (ז)
bear cub	dubon	דּוּבוֹן (ז)

lion cub	gur arye	גּוּר אַרְיֵה (ז)
tiger cub	gur namerim	גּוּר נְמֵרִים (ז)
elephant calf	pilon	פִּילוֹן (ז)

piglet	χazarzir	חֲזַרְזִיר (ז)
calf (young cow, bull)	'egel	עֵגֶל (ז)
kid (young goat)	gdi	גְּדִי (ז)
lamb	tale	טָלֶה (ז)
fawn (young deer)	'ofer	עוֹפֶר (ז)
young camel	'beχer	בֶּכֶר (ז)

snakelet (baby snake)	gur naχaʃim	גּוּר נְחָשִׁים (ז)
froglet (baby frog)	tsfarde'on	צְפַרְדְעוֹן (ז)

baby bird	gozal	גּוֹזָל (ז)
chick (of chicken)	ef'roaχ	אֶפְרוֹחַ (ז)
duckling	barvazon	בַּרְוָזוֹן (ז)

216. Birds

bird	tsipor	צִיפּוֹר (נ)
pigeon	yona	יוֹנָה (נ)
sparrow	dror	דְּרוֹר (ז)
tit (great tit)	yargazi	יַרְגָּזִי (ז)
magpie	orev neχalim	עוֹרֵב נְחָלִים (ז)

raven	orev ʃaχor	עוֹרֵב שָׁחוֹר (ז)
crow	orev afor	עוֹרֵב אָפוֹר (ז)
jackdaw	ka'ak	קָאָק (ז)
rook	orev hamizra	עוֹרֵב הַמִּזְרָע (ז)

duck	barvaz	בַּרְוָז (ז)
goose	avaz	אַוָּז (ז)
pheasant	pasyon	פַּסְיוֹן (ז)

eagle	'ayit	עַיִט (ז)
hawk	nets	נֵץ (ז)
falcon	baz	בַּז (ז)
vulture	ozniya	עוֹזְנִיָה (ז)
condor (Andean ~)	kondor	קוֹנְדּוֹר (ז)

swan	barbur	בַּרְבּוּר (ז)
crane	agur	עָגוּר (ז)
stork	χasida	חֲסִידָה (נ)

parrot	'tuki	תּוּכִּי (ז)
hummingbird	ko'libri	קוֹלִיבְרִי (ז)
peacock	tavas	טַוָּס (ז)

ostrich	bat ya'ana	בַּת יַעֲנָה (נ)
heron	anafa	אֲנָפָה (נ)

| flamingo | fla'mingo | פְלָמִינגוֹ (ז) |
| pelican | saknai | שַׂקְנַאי (ז) |

| nightingale | zamir | זָמִיר (ז) |
| swallow | snunit | סְנוּנִית (נ) |

thrush	kiχli	קִיכְלִי (ז)
song thrush	kiχli mezamer	קִיכְלִי מְזַמֵּר (ז)
blackbird	kiχli ʃaχor	קִיכְלִי שָׁחוֹר (ז)

swift	sis	סִיס (ז)
lark	efroni	עֶפְרוֹנִי (ז)
quail	slav	שְׂלָיו (ז)

woodpecker	'neker	נַקָּר (ז)
cuckoo	kukiya	קוּקִיָּה (נ)
owl	yanʃuf	יַנְשׁוּף (ז)
eagle owl	'oaχ	אוֹחַ (ז)
wood grouse	seχvi 'ya'ar	שְׂכְוִוי יַעַר (ז)
black grouse	seχvi	שְׂכְוִוי (ז)
partridge	χogla	חוֹגְלָה (נ)

starling	zarzir	זַרְזִיר (ז)
canary	ka'narit	קָנָרִית (נ)
hazel grouse	seχvi haya'arot	שְׂכְוִוי הַיְעָרוֹת (ז)
chaffinch	paroʃ	פָּרוּשׁ (ז)
bullfinch	admonit	אַדְמוֹנִית (נ)

seagull	'ʃaχaf	שַׁחַף (ז)
albatross	albatros	אַלְבַּטְרוֹס (ז)
penguin	pingvin	פִּינגְוִוין (ז)

217. Birds. Singing and sounds

to sing (vi)	laʃir	לָשִׁיר
to call (animal, bird)	lits'ok	לִצְעוֹק
to crow (cock)	lekarker	לְקַרְקֵר
cock-a-doodle-doo	kuku'riku	קוּקוּרִיקוּ

to cluck (hen)	lekarker	לְקַרְקֵר
to caw (vi)	lits'roaχ	לִצְרוֹחַ
to quack (duck)	lega'a'ge'a	לְגַעְגֵּעַ
to cheep (vi)	letsayets	לְצַיֵּץ
to chirp, to twitter	letsaftsef, letsayets	לְצַפְצֵף, לְצַיֵּץ

218. Fish. Marine animals

bream	avroma	אַבְרוֹמָה (נ)
carp	karpiyon	קַרְפְּיוֹן (ז)
perch	'okunus	אוֹקוּנוּס (ז)
catfish	sfamnun	שְׂפַמְנוּן (ז)
pike	ze'ev 'mayim	זְאֵב מַיִם (ז)

| salmon | 'salmon | סַלְמוֹן (ז) |
| sturgeon | χidkan | חִדְקָן (ז) |

herring	ma'liaχ	מָלִיחַ (ז)
Atlantic salmon	iltit	אִילְתִּית (נ)
mackerel	makarel	מָקָרֵל (ז)
flatfish	dag moʃe ra'benu	דַּג מֹשֶׁה רַבֵּנוּ (ז)

zander, pike perch	amnun	אַמְנוּן (ז)
cod	ʃibut	שִׁיבּוּט (ז)
tuna	'tuna	טוּנָה (נ)
trout	forel	פּוֹרֶל (ז)

eel	tslofaχ	צְלוֹפַח (ז)
electric ray	trisanit	תְּרִיסָנִית (נ)
moray eel	mo'rena	מוֹרֶנָה (נ)
piranha	pi'ranya	פִּירַנְיָה (נ)

shark	kariʃ	כָּרִישׁ (ז)
dolphin	dolfin	דּוֹלְפִין (ז)
whale	livyatan	לִוְיָתָן (ז)

crab	sartan	סַרְטָן (ז)
jellyfish	me'duza	מֶדוּזָה (נ)
octopus	tamnun	תַּמְנוּן (ז)

starfish	koχav yam	כּוֹכַב יָם (ז)
sea urchin	kipod yam	קִיפּוֹד יָם (ז)
seahorse	suson yam	סוּסוֹן יָם (ז)

oyster	tsidpa	צִדְפָּה (נ)
prawn	χasilon	חֲסִילוֹן (ז)
lobster	'lobster	לוֹבְּסְטֶר (ז)
spiny lobster	'lobster kotsani	לוֹבְּסְטֶר קוֹצָנִי (ז)

219. Amphibians. Reptiles

| snake | naχaʃ | נָחָשׁ (ז) |
| venomous (snake) | arsi | אַרְסִי |

viper	'tsefa	צֶפַע (ז)
cobra	'peten	פֶּתֶן (ז)
python	piton	פִּיתוֹן (ז)
boa	χanak	חָנָק (ז)

grass snake	naχaʃ 'mayim	נָחָשׁ מַיִם (ז)
rattle snake	ʃfifon	שְׁפִיפוֹן (ז)
anaconda	ana'konda	אָנָקוֹנְדָה (נ)

lizard	leta'a	לְטָאָה (נ)
iguana	igu''ana	אִיגוּאָנָה (נ)
monitor lizard	'koaχ	כֹּחַ (ז)
salamander	sala'mandra	סָלָמַנְדְּרָה (נ)
chameleon	zikit	זִיקִית (נ)

scorpion	akrav	עַקְרָב (ז)
turtle	tsav	צָב (ז)
frog	tsfar'de'a	צְפַרְדֵּעַ (נ)
toad	karpada	קַרְפָּדָה (נ)
crocodile	tanin	תַּנִּין (ז)

220. Insects

insect	χarak	חָרָק (ז)
butterfly	parpar	פַּרְפַּר (ז)
ant	nemala	נְמָלָה (נ)
fly	zvuv	זְבוּב (ז)
mosquito	yatuʃ	יַתּוּשׁ (ז)
beetle	χipuʃit	חִיפּוּשִׁית (נ)

wasp	tsir'a	צִרְעָה (נ)
bee	dvora	דְּבוֹרָה (נ)
bumblebee	dabur	דַּבּוּר (ז)
gadfly (botfly)	zvuv hasus	זְבוּב הַסּוּס (ז)

| spider | akaviʃ | עַכָּבִישׁ (ז) |
| spider's web | kurei akaviʃ | קוּרֵי עַכָּבִישׁ (ז"ר) |

dragonfly	ʃapirit	שְׁפִירִית (נ)
grasshopper	χagav	חָגָב (ז)
moth (night butterfly)	aʃ	עָשׁ (ז)

cockroach	makak	מַקָּק (ז)
tick	kartsiya	קַרְצִייָה (נ)
flea	par'oʃ	פַּרְעוֹשׁ (ז)
midge	yavχuʃ	יַבְחוּשׁ (ז)

locust	arbe	אַרְבֶּה (ז)
snail	χilazon	חִילָזוֹן (ז)
cricket	tsartsar	צְרָצַר (ז)
firefly	gaχlilit	גַּחְלִילִית (נ)
ladybird	parat moʃe ra'benu	פָּרַת מֹשֶׁה רַבֵּנוּ (נ)
cockchafer	χipuʃit aviv	חִיפּוּשִׁית אָבִיב (נ)

leech	aluka	עֲלוּקָה (נ)
caterpillar	zaχal	זַחַל (ז)
earthworm	to'la'at	תּוֹלַעַת (נ)
larva	'deren	דֶּרֶן (ז)

221. Animals. Body parts

beak	makor	מָקוֹר (ז)
wings	kna'fayim	כְּנָפַיִם (ז"ר)
foot (of bird)	'regel	רֶגֶל (נ)
feathers (plumage)	pluma	פְּלוּמָה (נ)
feather	notsa	נוֹצָה (נ)
crest	tsitsa	צִיצָה (נ)

gills	zimim	זִימִים (ז״ר)
spawn	beitsei dagim	בֵּיצֵי דָגִים (נ״ר)
larva	'deren	דֶּרֶן (ז)
fin	snapir	סְנַפִּיר (ז)
scales (of fish, reptile)	kaskasim	קַשְׂקַשִׂים (ז״ר)

fang (canine)	niv	נִיב (ז)
paw (e.g. cat's ~)	'regel	רֶגֶל (נ)
muzzle (snout)	partsuf	פַּרְצוּף (ז)
mouth (of cat, dog)	lo'a	לוֹעַ (ז)
tail	zanav	זָנָב (ז)
whiskers	safam	שָׂפָם (ז)

| hoof | parsa | פַּרְסָה (נ) |
| horn | 'keren | קֶרֶן (נ) |

carapace	ʃiryon	שִׁרְיוֹן (ז)
shell (of mollusc)	konχiya	קוֹנְכִּיָה (נ)
eggshell	klipa	קְלִיפָּה (נ)

| animal's hair (pelage) | parva | פַּרְוָה (נ) |
| pelt (hide) | or | עוֹר (ז) |

222. Actions of animals

to fly (vi)	la'uf	לָעוּף
to fly in circles	laχug	לָחוּג
to fly away	la'uf	לָעוּף
to flap (~ the wings)	lenafnef	לְנַפְנֵף

to peck (vi)	lenaker	לְנַקֵר
to sit on eggs	lidgor	לִדְגוֹר
to hatch out (vi)	liv'ko'a	לִבְקוֹעַ
to build a nest	lekanen	לְקַנֵן

to slither, to crawl	lizχol	לִזְחוֹל
to sting, to bite (insect)	la'akots	לַעֲקוֹץ
to bite (ab. animal)	linʃoχ	לִנְשׁוֹך

to sniff (vt)	leraχ'reaχ	לְכַחְרֵחַ
to bark (vi)	lin'boaχ	לִנְבּוֹחַ
to hiss (snake)	lirʃof	לִרְשׁוֹף

| to scare (vt) | lehafχid | לְהַפְחִיד |
| to attack (vt) | litkof | לִתְקוֹף |

to gnaw (bone, etc.)	leχarsem	לְכַרְסֵם
to scratch (with claws)	lisrot	לִשְׂרוֹט
to hide (vi)	lehistater	לְהִסְתַּתֵר

to play (kittens, etc.)	lesaχek	לְשַׂחֵק
to hunt (vi, vt)	latsud	לָצוּד
to hibernate (vi)	laχrof	לַחֲרוֹף
to go extinct	lehikaχed	לְהִיכָּחֵד

223. Animals. Habitats

habitat	beit gidul	בֵּית גִּידוּל (ז)
migration	hagira	הֲגִירָה (נ)
mountain	har	הַר (ז)
reef	ʃunit	שׁוּנִית (נ)
cliff	'sela	סֶלַע (ז)
forest	'yaʿar	יַעַר (ז)
jungle	'dʒungel	גִ'וּנְגֶל (ז)
savanna	sa'vana	סָוָנָה (נ)
tundra	'tundra	טוּנְדְרָה (נ)
steppe	arava	עֲרָבָה (נ)
desert	midbar	מִדְבָּר (ז)
oasis	neve midbar	נְוֵה מִדְבָּר (ז)
sea	yam	יָם (ז)
lake	agam	אֲגַם (ז)
ocean	ok'yanos	אוֹקְיָאנוֹס (ז)
swamp (marshland)	bitsa	בִּיצָה (נ)
freshwater (adj)	ʃel 'mayim metukim	שֶׁל מַיִם מְתוּקִים
pond	breχa	בְּרֵיכָה (נ)
river	nahar	נָהָר (ז)
den (bear's ~)	me'ura	מְאוּרָה (נ)
nest	ken	קֵן (ז)
hollow (in a tree)	χor ba'ets	חוֹר בָּעֵץ (ז)
burrow (animal hole)	meχila	מְחִילָה (נ)
anthill	kan nemalim	קַן נְמָלִים (ז)

224. Animal care

zoo	gan hayot	גַּן חַיּוֹת (ז)
nature reserve	ʃmurat 'teva	שְׁמוּרַת טֶבַע (נ)
breeder (cattery, kennel, etc.)	beit gidul	בֵּית גִּידוּל (ז)
open-air cage	kluv	כְּלוּב (ז)
cage	kluv	כְּלוּב (ז)
kennel	meluna	מְלוּנָה (נ)
dovecot	ʃovaχ	שׁוֹבָךְ (ז)
aquarium (fish tank)	ak'varyum	אָקְוָורְיוּם (ז)
dolphinarium	dolfi'naryum	דוֹלְפִינָרְיוּם (ז)
to breed (animals)	legadel	לְגַדֵּל
brood, litter	tse'etsa'im	צֶאֱצָאִים (ז"ר)
to tame (vt)	levayet	לְבַיֵּת
to train (animals)	le'alef	לְאַלֵּף
feed (fodder, etc.)	mazon, mispo	מָזוֹן (ז), מִסְפּוֹא (ז)
to feed (vt)	leha'axil	לְהַאֲכִיל

pet shop	χanut χayot	חֲנוּת חַיּוֹת (נ)
muzzle (for dog)	maχsom	מַחְסוֹם (ז)
collar (e.g., dog ~)	kolar	קוֹלָר (ז)
name (of animal)	kinui	כִּינוּי (ז)
pedigree (of dog)	ʃal'ʃelet yuχsin	שַׁלְשֶׁלֶת יוֹחֲסִין (נ)

225. Animals. Miscellaneous

pack (wolves)	lahaka	לַהֲקָה (נ)
flock (birds)	lahaka	לַהֲקָה (נ)
shoal, school (fish)	lahaka	לַהֲקָה (נ)
herd (horses)	'eder	עֵדֶר (ז)
male (n)	zaχar	זָכָר (ז)
female (n)	nekeva	נְקֵבָה (נ)
hungry (adj)	ra'ev	רָעֵב
wild (adj)	pra'i	פִּרְאִי
dangerous (adj)	mesukan	מְסוּכָּן

226. Horses

horse	sus	סוּס (ז)
breed (race)	'geza	גֶּזַע (ז)
foal	syaχ	סְיָח (ז)
mare	susa	סוּסָה (נ)
mustang	mustang	מוּסְטַנְג (ז)
pony	'poni	פּוֹנִי (ז)
draught horse	sus avoda	סוּס עֲבוֹדָה (ז)
mane	ra'ama	רַעֲמָה (נ)
tail	zanav	זָנָב (ז)
hoof	parsa	פַּרְסָה (נ)
horseshoe	parsa	פַּרְסָה (נ)
to shoe (vt)	lefarzel	לְפַרְזֵל
blacksmith	'nefaχ	נַפָּח (ז)
saddle	ukaf	אוּכָּף (ז)
stirrup	arkuba	אַרְכּוּבָּה (נ)
bridle	'resen	רֶסֶן (ז)
reins	moʃχot	מוֹשְׁכוֹת (נ"ר)
whip (for riding)	ʃot	שׁוֹט (ז)
rider	roχev	רוֹכֵב (ז)
to saddle up (vt)	le'akef	לְאַכֵּף
to mount a horse	la'alot al sus	לַעֲלוֹת עַל סוּס
gallop	dehira	דְּהִירָה (נ)
to gallop (vi)	lidhor	לִדְהוֹר

trot (n)	tfifa	טְפִיפָה (נ)
at a trot (adv)	bidhira	בִּדְהִירָה
to go at a trot	litpof	לִטְפּוֹף

| racehorse | sus merots | סוּס מֵירוֹץ (ז) |
| horse racing | merots susim | מֵירוֹץ סוּסִים (ז) |

stable	urva	אוּרְוָה (נ)
to feed (vt)	leha'axil	לְהַאֲכִיל
hay	xatsil	חָצִיל (ז)
to water (animals)	lehaʃkot	לְהַשְׁקוֹת
to wash (horse)	lirxots	לִרְחוֹץ

horse-drawn cart	agala	עֲגָלָה (נ)
to graze (vi)	lir'ot	לִרְעוֹת
to neigh (vi)	litshol	לִצְהוֹל
to kick (about horse)	liv'ot	לִבְעוֹט

Flora

227. Trees

tree	ets	עֵץ (ז)
deciduous (adj)	naʃir	נָשִׁיר
coniferous (adj)	maχtani	מַחטָנִי
evergreen (adj)	yarok ad	יָרוֹק עַד
apple tree	ta'puaχ	תַּפּוּחַ (ז)
pear tree	agas	אַגָס (ז)
sweet cherry tree	gudgedan	גּוּדגְדָן (ז)
sour cherry tree	duvdevan	דּוּבדְבָן (ז)
plum tree	ʃezif	שְׁזִיף (ז)
birch	ʃadar	שְׁדָר (ז)
oak	alon	אַלּוֹן (ז)
linden tree	'tilya	טִילִיָה (נ)
aspen	aspa	אַספָּה (נ)
maple	'eder	אֶדֶר (ז)
spruce	a'ʃuaχ	אַשּׁוּחַ (ז)
pine	'oren	אוֹרֶן (ז)
larch	arzit	אַרזִית (נ)
fir tree	a'ʃuaχ	אַשּׁוּחַ (ז)
cedar	'erez	אֶרֶז (ז)
poplar	tsaftsefa	צַפצָפָה (נ)
rowan	ben χuzrar	בֶּן-חוּזרָר (ז)
willow	arava	עֲרָבָה (נ)
alder	alnus	אַלנוּס (ז)
beech	aʃur	אָשׁוּר (ז)
elm	bu'kitsa	בּוּקִיצָה (נ)
ash (tree)	mela	מֵילָה (נ)
chestnut	armon	עַרמוֹן (ז)
magnolia	mag'nolya	מַגנוֹלִיָה (נ)
palm tree	'dekel	דֶּקֶל (ז)
cypress	broʃ	בְּרוֹשׁ (ז)
mangrove	mangrov	מַנגרוֹב (ז)
baobab	ba'obab	בָּאוֹבַּב (ז)
eucalyptus	eika'liptus	אֵיקָלִיפּטוּס (ז)
sequoia	sek'voya	סְקוֹוִיָה (נ)

228. Shrubs

bush	'siaχ	שִׂיחַ (ז)
shrub	'siaχ	שִׂיחַ (ז)

| grapevine | 'gefen | גֶּפֶן (ז) |
| vineyard | 'kerem | כֶּרֶם (ז) |

raspberry bush	'petel	פֶּטֶל (ז)
blackcurrant bush	'siaχ dumdemaniyot ʃχorot	שִׂיחַ דּוּמְדְּמָנִיּוֹת שְׁחוֹרוֹת (ז)
redcurrant bush	'siaχ dumdemaniyot adumot	שִׂיחַ דּוּמְדְּמָנִיּוֹת אֲדוּמוֹת (ז)
gooseberry bush	χazarzar	חֲזַרְזַר (ז)

acacia	ʃita	שִׁיטָה (נ)
barberry	berberis	בֶּרְבֶּרִיס (ז)
jasmine	yasmin	יַסְמִין (ז)

juniper	ar'ar	עַרְעָר (ז)
rosebush	'siaχ vradim	שִׂיחַ וְרָדִים (ז)
dog rose	'vered bar	וֶרֶד בָּר (ז)

229. Mushrooms

mushroom	pitriya	פִּטְרִיָּה (נ)
edible mushroom	pitriya ra'uya lema'aχal	פִּטְרִיָּה רְאוּיָה לְמַאֲכָל
poisonous mushroom	pitriya ra'ila	פִּטְרִיָּה רְעִילָה (נ)
cap (of mushroom)	kipat pitriya	כִּיפַת פִּטְרִיָּה (נ)
stipe (of mushroom)	'regel	רֶגֶל (נ)

cep, penny bun	por'ʧini	פּוֹרְצִ'ינִי (ז)
orange-cap boletus	pitriyat 'kova aduma	פִּטְרִיַּת כּוֹבַע אֲדוּמָה (נ)
birch bolete	pitriyat 'ya'ar	פִּטְרִיַּת יַעַר (נ)
chanterelle	gvi'onit ne'e'χelet	גְּבִיעוֹנִית נֶאֱכֶלֶת (נ)
russula	χarifit	חֲרִיפִית (נ)

morel	gamʦuʦ	גַּמְצוּץ (ז)
fly agaric	zvuvanit	זְבוּבָנִית (נ)
death cap	pitriya ra'ila	פִּטְרִיָּה רְעִילָה (נ)

230. Fruits. Berries

fruit	pri	פְּרִי (ז)
fruits	perot	פֵּירוֹת (ז״ר)
apple	ta'puaχ	תַּפּוּחַ (ז)
pear	agas	אַגָּס (ז)
plum	ʃezif	שְׁזִיף (ז)

strawberry (garden ~)	tut sade	תּוּת שָׂדֶה (ז)
sour cherry	duvdevan	דּוּבְדְּבָן (ז)
sweet cherry	gudgedan	גּוּדְגְּדָן (ז)
grape	anavim	עֲנָבִים (ז״ר)

raspberry	'petel	פֶּטֶל (ז)
blackcurrant	dumdemanit ʃχora	דּוּמְדְּמָנִית שְׁחוֹרָה (נ)
redcurrant	dumdemanit aduma	דּוּמְדְּמָנִית אֲדוּמָה (נ)
gooseberry	χazarzar	חֲזַרְזַר (ז)
cranberry	χamuʦit	חֲמוּצִית (נ)

orange	tapuz	תַּפּוּז (ז)
tangerine	klemen'tina	קְלֶמֶנְטִינָה (נ)
pineapple	'ananas	אֲנָנָס (ז)
banana	ba'nana	בָּנָנָה (נ)
date	tamar	תָּמָר (ז)

lemon	limon	לִימוֹן (ז)
apricot	'miʃmeʃ	מִשְׁמֵשׁ (ז)
peach	afarsek	אֲפַרְסֵק (ז)
kiwi	'kivi	קִיוִי (ז)
grapefruit	eʃkolit	אֶשְׁכּוֹלִית (נ)

berry	garger	גַּרְגֵּר (ז)
berries	gargerim	גַּרְגְּרִים (ז"ר)
cowberry	uχmanit aduma	אוּכְמָנִית אֲדֻמָּה (נ)
wild strawberry	tut 'ya'ar	תּוּת יַעַר (ז)
bilberry	uχmanit	אוּכְמָנִית (נ)

231. Flowers. Plants

| flower | 'peraχ | פֶּרַח (ז) |
| bouquet (of flowers) | zer | זֵר (ז) |

rose (flower)	'vered	וֶרֶד (ז)
tulip	tsiv'oni	צִבְעוֹנִי (ז)
carnation	tsi'poren	צִיפּוֹרֶן (ז)
gladiolus	glad'yola	גְּלָדְיוֹלָה (נ)

cornflower	dganit	דְּגָנִית (נ)
harebell	pa'amonit	פַּעֲמוֹנִית (נ)
dandelion	ʃinan	שִׁינָן (ז)
camomile	kamomil	קָמוֹמִיל (ז)

aloe	alvai	אַלְוַוי (ז)
cactus	'kaktus	קַקְטוּס (ז)
rubber plant, ficus	'fikus	פִיקוּס (ז)

lily	ʃoʃana	שׁוֹשַׁנָּה (נ)
geranium	ge'ranyum	גֵּרַנְיוּם (ז)
hyacinth	yakinton	יָקִינְטוֹן (ז)

mimosa	mi'moza	מִימוֹזָה (נ)
narcissus	narkis	נַרְקִיס (ז)
nasturtium	'kova hanazir	כּוֹבַע הַנָּזִיר (ז)

orchid	saχlav	סַחְלָב (ז)
peony	admonit	אַדְמוֹנִית (נ)
violet	sigalit	סִיגָלִית (נ)

pansy	amnon vetamar	אַמְנוֹן וְתָמָר (ז)
forget-me-not	ziχ'rini	זִכְרִינִי (ז)
daisy	marganit	מַרְגָּנִית (נ)
poppy	'pereg	פֶּרֶג (ז)
hemp	ka'nabis	קָנַאבִּיס (ז)

mint	'menta	מֶנְתָה (נ)
lily of the valley	zivanit	זִיווָנִית (נ)
snowdrop	ga'lantus	גָלַנְטוּס (ז)
nettle	sirpad	סִרְפָּד (ז)
sorrel	χum'a	חוֹמְעָה (נ)
water lily	nufar	נוּפָר (ז)
fern	ʃaraχ	שְׁרָךְ (ז)
lichen	χazazit	חֲזָזִית (נ)
greenhouse (tropical ~)	χamama	חֲמָמָה (נ)
lawn	midʃa'a	מִדְשָׁאָה (נ)
flowerbed	arugat praχim	עֲרוּגַת פְּרָחִים (נ)
plant	'tsemaχ	צֶמַח (ז)
grass	'deʃe	דֶשֶׁא (ז)
blade of grass	giv'ol 'esev	גִבְעוֹל עֵשֶׂב (ז)
leaf	ale	עָלֶה (ז)
petal	ale ko'teret	עָלֶה כּוֹתֶרֶת (ז)
stem	giv'ol	גִבְעוֹל (ז)
tuber	'pka'at	פְּקַעַת (נ)
young plant (shoot)	'nevet	נֶבֶט (ז)
thorn	kots	קוֹץ (ז)
to blossom (vi)	lif'roaχ	לִפְרוֹח
to fade, to wither	linbol	לִנְבּוֹל
smell (odour)	'reaχ	רֵיח (ז)
to cut (flowers)	ligzom	לִגְזוֹם
to pick (a flower)	liktof	לִקְטוֹף

232. Cereals, grains

grain	tvu'a	תְבוּאָה (נ)
cereal crops	dganim	דְגָנִים (ז"ר)
ear (of barley, etc.)	ʃi'bolet	שִׁיבּוֹלֶת (נ)
wheat	χita	חִיטָה (נ)
rye	ʃifon	שִׁיפוֹן (ז)
oats	ʃi'bolet ʃu'al	שִׁיבּוֹלֶת שׁוּעָל (נ)
millet	'doχan	דוֹחַן (ז)
barley	se'ora	שְׂעוֹרָה (נ)
maize	'tiras	תִירָס (ז)
rice	'orez	אוֹרֶז (ז)
buckwheat	ku'semet	כּוּסֶמֶת (נ)
pea plant	afuna	אֲפוּנָה (נ)
kidney bean	ʃu'it	שְׁעוּעִית (נ)
soya	'soya	סוֹיָה (נ)
lentil	adaʃim	עֲדָשִׁים (נ"ר)
beans (pulse crops)	pol	פּוֹל (ז)

233. Vegetables. Greens

vegetables	yerakot	יְרָקוֹת (ז״ר)
greens	'yerek	יָרָק (ז)
tomato	agvaniya	עַגְבָנִיָּה (נ)
cucumber	melafefon	מְלָפְפוֹן (ז)
carrot	'gezer	גֶּזֶר (ז)
potato	ta'puaχ adama	תַּפּוּחַ אֲדָמָה (ז)
onion	batsal	בָּצָל (ז)
garlic	ʃum	שׁוּם (ז)
cabbage	kruv	כְּרוּב (ז)
cauliflower	kruvit	כְּרוּבִית (נ)
Brussels sprouts	kruv nitsanim	כְּרוּב נִצָּנִים (ז)
broccoli	'brokoli	בְּרוֹקוֹלִי (ז)
beetroot	'selek	סֶלֶק (ז)
aubergine	χatsil	חָצִיל (ז)
marrow	kiʃu	קִישׁוּא (ז)
pumpkin	'dla'at	דְּלַעַת (נ)
turnip	'lefet	לֶפֶת (נ)
parsley	petro'zilya	פֶּטְרוֹזִילְיָה (נ)
dill	ʃamir	שָׁמִיר (ז)
lettuce	'χasa	חַסָּה (נ)
celery	'seleri	סֶלֶרִי (ז)
asparagus	aspa'ragos	אַסְפָּרָגוֹס (ז)
spinach	'tered	תֶּרֶד (ז)
pea	afuna	אֲפוּנָה (נ)
beans	pol	פּוֹל (ז)
maize	'tiras	תִּירָס (ז)
kidney bean	ʃu'it	שְׁעוּעִית (נ)
pepper	'pilpel	פִּלְפֵּל (ז)
radish	tsnonit	צְנוֹנִית (נ)
artichoke	artiʃok	אַרְטִישׁוֹק (ז)

REGIONAL GEOGRAPHY

Countries. Nationalities

234. Western Europe

Europe	ei'ropa	אֵירוֹפָּה (נ)
European Union	ha'iχud ha'eiro'pe'i	הָאִיחוּד הָאֵירוֹפִּי (ז)
European (n)	eiro'pe'i	אֵירוֹפָּאִי (ז)
European (adj)	eiro'pe'i	אֵירוֹפָּאִי

Austria	'ostriya	אוֹסְטְרִיָה (נ)
Austrian (masc.)	'ostri	אוֹסְטְרִי (ז)
Austrian (fem.)	'ostrit	אוֹסְטְרִית (נ)
Austrian (adj)	'ostri	אוֹסְטְרִי

Great Britain	bri'tanya hagdola	בְּרִיטַנְיָה הַגְדוֹלָה (נ)
England	'angliya	אַנְגְלִיָה (נ)
British (masc.)	'briti	בְּרִיטִי (ז)
British (fem.)	'btitit	בְּרִיטִית (נ)
English, British (adj)	angli	אַנְגְלִי

Belgium	'belgya	בֶּלְגִיָה (נ)
Belgian (masc.)	'belgi	בֶּלְגִי (ז)
Belgian (fem.)	'belgit	בֶּלְגִית (נ)
Belgian (adj)	'belgi	בֶּלְגִי

Germany	ger'manya	גֶרְמַנְיָה (נ)
German (masc.)	germani	גֶרְמָנִי (ז)
German (fem.)	germaniya	גֶרְמָנִיָה (נ)
German (adj)	germani	גֶרְמָנִי

Netherlands	'holand	הוֹלַנְד (נ)
Holland	'holand	הוֹלַנְד (נ)
Dutch (masc.)	ho'landi	הוֹלַנְדִי (ז)
Dutch (fem.)	ho'landit	הוֹלַנְדִית (נ)
Dutch (adj)	ho'landi	הוֹלַנְדִי

Greece	yavan	יָוָן (נ)
Greek (masc.)	yevani	יְוָנִי (ז)
Greek (fem.)	yevaniya	יְוָנִיָה (נ)
Greek (adj)	yevani	יְוָנִי

Denmark	'denemark	דֶנֶמַרק (נ)
Dane (masc.)	'deni	דֶנִי (ז)
Dane (fem.)	'denit	דֶנִית (נ)
Danish (adj)	'deni	דֶנִי
Ireland	'irland	אִירְלַנְד (נ)
Irish (masc.)	'iri	אִירִי (ז)

Irish (fem.)	ir'landit	אִירְלַנְדִּית (נ)
Irish (adj)	'iri	אִירִי
Iceland	'island	אִיסְלַנְד (נ)
Icelander (masc.)	is'landi	אִיסְלַנְדִּי (ז)
Icelander (fem.)	is'landit	אִיסְלַנְדִּית (נ)
Icelandic (adj)	is'landi	אִיסְלַנְדִּי
Spain	sfarad	סְפָרַד (נ)
Spaniard (masc.)	sfaradi	סְפָרַדִּי (ז)
Spaniard (fem.)	sfaradiya	סְפָרַדִּיָּה (נ)
Spanish (adj)	sfaradi	סְפָרַדִּי
Italy	i'talya	אִיטַלְיָה (נ)
Italian (masc.)	italki	אִיטַלְקִי (ז)
Italian (fem.)	italkiya	אִיטַלְקִיָּה (נ)
Italian (adj)	italki	אִיטַלְקִי
Cyprus	kafrisin	קַפְרִיסִין (נ)
Cypriot (masc.)	kafri'sa'i	קַפְרִיסָאִי (ז)
Cypriot (fem.)	kafri'sa'it	קַפְרִיסָאִית (נ)
Cypriot (adj)	kafri'sa'i	קַפְרִיסָאִי
Malta	'malta	מַלְטָה (נ)
Maltese (masc.)	'malti	מַלְטִי (ז)
Maltese (fem.)	'maltit	מַלְטִית (נ)
Maltese (adj)	'malti	מַלְטִי
Norway	nor'vegya	נוֹרְבֶגְיָה (נ)
Norwegian (masc.)	nor'vegi	נוֹרְבֶגִי (ז)
Norwegian (fem.)	nor'vegit	נוֹרְבֶגִית (נ)
Norwegian (adj)	nor'vegi	נוֹרְבֶגִי
Portugal	portugal	פּוֹרְטוּגָל (נ)
Portuguese (masc.)	portu'gali	פּוֹרְטוּגָלִי (ז)
Portuguese (fem.)	portu'galit	פּוֹרְטוּגָלִית (נ)
Portuguese (adj)	portu'gezi	פּוֹרְטוּגְזִי
Finland	'finland	פִינְלַנְד (נ)
Finn (masc.)	'fini	פִינִי (ז)
Finn (fem.)	'finit	פִינִית (נ)
Finnish (adj)	'fini	פִינִי
France	tsarfat	צָרְפַת (נ)
French (masc.)	tsarfati	צָרְפָתִי (ז)
French (fem.)	tsarfatiya	צָרְפָתִיָּה (נ)
French (adj)	tsarfati	צָרְפָתִי
Sweden	'ʃvedya	שְׁבֶדְיָה (נ)
Swede (masc.)	'ʃvedi	שְׁבֵדִי (ז)
Swede (fem.)	'ʃvedit	שְׁבֵדִית (נ)
Swedish (adj)	'ʃvedi	שְׁבֵדִי
Switzerland	'ʃvaits	שְׁוֵוייץ (נ)
Swiss (masc.)	ʃvei'tsari	שְׁוֵוייצָרִי (ז)
Swiss (fem.)	ʃvei'tsarit	שְׁוֵוייצָרִית (נ)

Swiss (adj)	ʃveˈtsari	שׁוֹויצָרִי
Scotland	ˈskotland	סְקוֹטְלַנְד (ז)
Scottish (masc.)	ˈskoti	סְקוֹטִי (ז)
Scottish (fem.)	ˈskotit	סְקוֹטִית (נ)
Scottish (adj)	ˈskoti	סְקוֹטִי

Vatican	vatikan	וָתִיקָן (ז)
Liechtenstein	liχtenʃtain	לִיכְטֶנְשְׁטַיין (ז)
Luxembourg	luksemburg	לוּקְסֶמְבּוּרְג (ז)
Monaco	moˈnako	מוֹנָקוֹ (ז)

235. Central and Eastern Europe

Albania	alˈbanya	אַלְבַּנְיָה (נ)
Albanian (masc.)	alˈbani	אַלְבָּנִי (ז)
Albanian (fem.)	alˈbanit	אַלְבָּנִית (נ)
Albanian (adj)	alˈbani	אַלְבָּנִי

Bulgaria	bulˈgarya	בּוּלְגַּרְיָה (נ)
Bulgarian (masc.)	bulˈgari	בּוּלְגָּרִי (ז)
Bulgarian (fem.)	bulgariya	בּוּלְגָּרְיָה (נ)
Bulgarian (adj)	bulˈgari	בּוּלְגָּרִי

Hungary	hunˈgarya	הוּנְגַּרְיָה (נ)
Hungarian (masc.)	hungari	הוּנְגָּרִי (ז)
Hungarian (fem.)	hungariya	הוּנְגָּרְיָה (נ)
Hungarian (adj)	hunˈgari	הוּנְגָּרִי

Latvia	ˈlatviya	לַטְבִיָה (נ)
Latvian (masc.)	ˈlatvi	לַטְבִי (ז)
Latvian (fem.)	ˈlatvit	לַטְבִית (נ)
Latvian (adj)	ˈlatvi	לַטְבִי

Lithuania	ˈlita	לִיטָא (נ)
Lithuanian (masc.)	litaˈi	לִיטָאִי (ז)
Lithuanian (fem.)	litaˈit	לִיטָאִית (נ)
Lithuanian (adj)	litaˈi	לִיטָאִי

Poland	polin	פּוֹלִין (נ)
Pole (masc.)	polani	פּוֹלָנִי (ז)
Pole (fem.)	polaniya	פּוֹלָנְיָה (נ)
Polish (adj)	polani	פּוֹלָנִי

Romania	roˈmanya	רוֹמַנְיָה (נ)
Romanian (masc.)	romani	רוֹמָנִי (ז)
Romanian (fem.)	romaniya	רוֹמָנְיָה (נ)
Romanian (adj)	roˈmani	רוֹמָנִי

Serbia	ˈserbya	סֶרְבִּיָה (נ)
Serbian (masc.)	ˈserbi	סֶרְבִּי (ז)
Serbian (fem.)	ˈserbit	סֶרְבִּית (נ)
Serbian (adj)	ˈserbi	סֶרְבִּי
Slovakia	sloˈvakya	סְלוֹבָקְיָה (נ)
Slovak (masc.)	sloˈvaki	סְלוֹבָקִי (ז)

| Slovak (fem.) | slo'vakit | (נ) סְלוֹבָּקִית |
| Slovak (adj) | slo'vaki | סְלוֹבָּקִי |

Croatia	kro''atya	(נ) קְרוֹאָטְיָה
Croatian (masc.)	kro''ati	(ז) קְרוֹאָטִי
Croatian (fem.)	kro''atit	(נ) קְרוֹאָטִית
Croatian (adj)	kro''ati	קְרוֹאָטִי

Czech Republic	'tʃexya	(נ) צֶ'כְיָה
Czech (masc.)	'tʃexi	(ז) צֶ'כִי
Czech (fem.)	'tʃexit	(נ) צֶ'כִית
Czech (adj)	'tʃexi	צֶ'כִי

Estonia	es'tonya	(נ) אֶסְטוֹנְיָה
Estonian (masc.)	es'toni	(ז) אֶסְטוֹנִי
Estonian (fem.)	es'tonit	(נ) אֶסְטוֹנִית
Estonian (adj)	es'toni	אֶסְטוֹנִי

Bosnia and Herzegovina	'bosniya	(נ) בּוֹסְנְיָה
Macedonia (Republic of ~)	make'donya	(נ) מָקֶדוֹנְיָה
Slovenia	slo'venya	(נ) סְלוֹבֶנְיָה
Montenegro	monte'negro	(נ) מוֹנְטֶנֶגְרוֹ

236. Former USSR countries

Azerbaijan	azerbaidʒan	(נ) אֲזֶרְבַּייגָ'ן
Azerbaijani (masc.)	azerbai'dʒani	(ז) אֲזֶרְבַּייגָ'נִי
Azerbaijani (fem.)	azerbai'dʒanit	(נ) אֲזֶרְבַּייגָ'נִית
Azerbaijani, Azeri (adj)	azerbai'dʒani	אֲזֶרְבַּייגָ'נִי

Armenia	ar'menya	(נ) אַרְמֶנְיָה
Armenian (masc.)	ar'meni	(ז) אַרְמֶנִי
Armenian (fem.)	ar'menit	(נ) אַרְמֶנִית
Armenian (adj)	ar'meni	אַרְמֶנִי

Belarus	'belarus	(נ) בֶּלָרוּס
Belarusian (masc.)	bela'rusi	(ז) בֶּלָרוּסִי
Belarusian (fem.)	bela'rusit	(נ) בֶּלָרוּסִית
Belarusian (adj)	byelo'rusi	בְּיֶלוֹרוּסִי

Georgia	'gruzya	(נ) גְרוּזְיָה
Georgian (masc.)	gru'zini	(ז) גְרוּזִינִי
Georgian (fem.)	gru'zinit	(נ) גְרוּזִינִית
Georgian (adj)	gru'zini	גְרוּזִינִי

Kazakhstan	kazaxstan	(נ) קָזַחְסְטָן
Kazakh (masc.)	ka'zaxi	(ז) קָזַחִי
Kazakh (fem.)	ka'zaxit	(נ) קָזַחִית
Kazakh (adj)	ka'zaxi	קָזַחִי

Kirghizia	kirgizstan	(נ) קִירְגִיזְסְטָן
Kirghiz (masc.)	kir'gizi	(ז) קִירְגִיזִי
Kirghiz (fem.)	kir'gizit	(נ) קִירְגִיזִית
Kirghiz (adj)	kir'gizi	קִירְגִיזִי

Moldova, Moldavia	mol'davya	מוֹלדַבְיָה (נ)
Moldavian (masc.)	mol'davi	מוֹלדַבִי (ז)
Moldavian (fem.)	mol'davit	מוֹלדַבִית (נ)
Moldavian (adj)	mol'davi	מוֹלדַבִי

Russia	'rusya	רוּסִיָה (נ)
Russian (masc.)	rusi	רוּסִי (ז)
Russian (fem.)	rusiya	רוּסִיָיה (נ)
Russian (adj)	rusi	רוּסִי

Tajikistan	tadʒikistan	טַגִ'יקִיסטָן (נ)
Tajik (masc.)	ta'dʒiki	טַגִ'יקִי (ז)
Tajik (fem.)	ta'dʒikit	טַגִ'יקִית (נ)
Tajik (adj)	ta'dʒiki	טַגִ'יקִי

Turkmenistan	turkmenistan	טוּרקמֶנִיסטָן (נ)
Turkmen (masc.)	turk'meni	טוּרקמֶנִי (ז)
Turkmen (fem.)	turk'menit	טוּרקמֶנִית (נ)
Turkmenian (adj)	turk'meni	טוּרקמֶנִי

Uzbekistan	uzbekistan	אוּזבָּקִיסטָן (נ)
Uzbek (masc.)	uz'beki	אוּזבָּקִי (ז)
Uzbek (fem.)	uz'bekit	אוּזבָּקִית (נ)
Uzbek (adj)	uz'beki	אוּזבָּקִי

Ukraine	uk'rayna	אוּקרָאִינָה (נ)
Ukrainian (masc.)	ukra''ini	אוּקרָאִינִי (ז)
Ukrainian (fem.)	ukra''init	אוּקרָאִינִית (נ)
Ukrainian (adj)	ukra''ini	אוּקרָאִינִי

237. Asia

| Asia | 'asya | אַסיָה (נ) |
| Asian (adj) | as'yati | אַסיָיתִי |

Vietnam	vyetnam	וְיֶיטנָאם (נ)
Vietnamese (masc.)	vyet'nami	וְיֶיטנָאמִי (ז)
Vietnamese (fem.)	vyet'namit	וְיֶיטנָאמִית (נ)
Vietnamese (adj)	vyet'nami	וְיֶיטנָאמִי

India	'hodu	הוֹדוּ (נ)
Indian (masc.)	'hodi	הוֹדִי (ז)
Indian (fem.)	'hodit	הוֹדִית (נ)
Indian (adj)	'hodi	הוֹדִי

Israel	yisra'el	יִשׂרָאֵל (נ)
Israeli (masc.)	yisra'eli	יִשׂרְאֵלִי (ז)
Israeli (fem.)	yisra'elit	יִשׂרְאֵלִית (נ)
Israeli (adj)	yisra'eli	יִשׂרְאֵלִי

Jew (n)	yehudi	יְהוּדִי (ז)
Jewess (n)	yehudiya	יְהוּדִיָה (נ)
Jewish (adj)	yehudi	יְהוּדִי
China	sin	סִין (נ)

211

Chinese (masc.)	'sini	סִינִי (ז)
Chinese (fem.)	'sinit	סִינִית (נ)
Chinese (adj)	'sini	סִינִי

Korean (masc.)	korei''ani	קוֹרֵיאָנִי (ז)
Korean (fem.)	korei''anit	קוֹרֵיאָנִית (נ)
Korean (adj)	korei''ani	קוֹרֵיאָנִי

Lebanon	levanon	לְבָנוֹן (נ)
Lebanese (masc.)	leva'noni	לְבָנוֹנִי (ז)
Lebanese (fem.)	leva'nonit	לְבָנוֹנִית (נ)
Lebanese (adj)	leva'noni	לְבָנוֹנִי

Mongolia	mon'golya	מוֹנגוֹלְיָה (נ)
Mongolian (masc.)	mon'goli	מוֹנגוֹלִי (ז)
Mongolian (fem.)	mon'golit	מוֹנגוֹלִית (נ)
Mongolian (adj)	mon'goli	מוֹנגוֹלִי

Malaysia	ma'lezya	מָלֶזיָה (נ)
Malaysian (masc.)	ma'la'i	מָלָאִי (ז)
Malaysian (fem.)	ma'la'it	מָלָאִית (נ)
Malaysian (adj)	ma'la'i	מָלָאִי

Pakistan	pakistan	פָּקִיסטָן (נ)
Pakistani (masc.)	pakis'tani	פָּקִיסטָנִי (ז)
Pakistani (fem.)	pakis'tanit	פָּקִיסטָנִית (נ)
Pakistani (adj)	pakis'tani	פָּקִיסטָנִי

Saudi Arabia	arav hasa'udit	עֲרָב הַסָעוּדִית (נ)
Arab (masc.)	aravi	עֲרָבִי (ז)
Arab (fem.)	araviya	עֲרָבִיָה (נ)
Arab, Arabic (adj)	aravi	עֲרָבִי

Thailand	'tailand	תָאִילַנד (נ)
Thai (masc.)	tai'landi	תָאִילַנדִי (ז)
Thai (fem.)	tai'landit	תָאִילַנדִית (נ)
Thai (adj)	tai'landi	תָאִילַנדִי

Taiwan	taivan	טַייוָון (נ)
Taiwanese (masc.)	tai'vani	טַייוָונִי (ז)
Taiwanese (fem.)	tai'vanit	טַייוָונִית (נ)
Taiwanese (adj)	tai'vani	טַייוָונִי

Turkey	'turkiya	טוּרקִיָה (נ)
Turk (masc.)	turki	טוּרקִי (ז)
Turk (fem.)	turkiya	טוּרקִיָה (נ)
Turkish (adj)	turki	טוּרקִי

Japan	yapan	יַפָן (נ)
Japanese (masc.)	ya'pani	יַפָנִי (ז)
Japanese (fem.)	ya'panit	יַפָנִית (נ)
Japanese (adj)	ya'pani	יַפָנִי

Afghanistan	afganistan	אַפגָנִיסטָן (נ)
Bangladesh	bangladeʃ	בַּנגלָדֶש (נ)
Indonesia	indo'nezya	אִינדוֹנֶזיָה (נ)

Jordan	yarden	יַרְדֵן (ג)
Iraq	irak	עִירָאק (ג)
Iran	iran	אִירָן (ג)
Cambodia	kam'bodya	קַמְבּוֹדְיָה (ג)
Kuwait	kuveit	כּוּוֵית (ג)

Laos	la'os	לָאוֹס (ג)
Myanmar	miyanmar	מְיַאנְמָר (ג)
Nepal	nepal	נֵפָּאל (ג)
United Arab Emirates	iχud ha'emi'royot ha'araviyot	אִיחוּד הָאֱמִירוּיוֹת הָעֲרָבִיוֹת (ז)

Syria	'surya	סוּרְיָה (ג)
Palestine	falastin	פָּלֶסְטִין (ג)
South Korea	ko'rei'a hadromit	קוֹרֵיאָה הַדְרוֹמִית (ג)
North Korea	ko'rei'a hatsfonit	קוֹרֵיאָה הַצְפוֹנִית (ג)

238. North America

United States of America	artsot habrit	אַרְצוֹת הַבְּרִית (נ"ר)
American (masc.)	ameri'ka'i	אָמֶרִיקָאי (ז)
American (fem.)	ameri'ka'it	אָמֶרִיקָאית (ג)
American (adj)	ameri'ka'i	אָמֶרִיקָאי

Canada	'kanada	קָנָדָה (ג)
Canadian (masc.)	ka'nadi	קָנָדִי (ז)
Canadian (fem.)	ka'nadit	קָנָדִית (ג)
Canadian (adj)	ka'nadi	קָנָדִי

Mexico	'meksiko	מֶקְסִיקוֹ (ג)
Mexican (masc.)	meksi'kani	מֶקְסִיקָנִי (ז)
Mexican (fem.)	meksi'kanit	מֶקְסִיקָנִית (ג)
Mexican (adj)	meksi'kani	מֶקְסִיקָנִי

239. Central and South America

Argentina	argen'tina	אַרְגֶנְטִינָה (ג)
Argentinian (masc.)	argentinai	אַרְגֶנְטִינָאי (ז)
Argentinian (fem.)	argenti'na'it	אַרְגֶנְטִינָאית (ג)
Argentinian (adj)	argenti'na'it	אַרְגֶנְטִינָאי

Brazil	brazil	בְּרָזִיל (ג)
Brazilian (masc.)	brazil'a'i	בְּרָזִילָאי (ז)
Brazilian (fem.)	brazi'la'it	בְּרָזִילָאית (ג)
Brazilian (adj)	brazi'la'i	בְּרָזִילָאי

Colombia	ko'lombya	קוֹלוֹמְבִּיָה (ג)
Colombian (masc.)	kolom'byani	קוֹלוֹמְבִּיָאנִי (ז)
Colombian (fem.)	kolomb'yanit	קוֹלוֹמְבִּיָאנִית (ג)
Colombian (adj)	kolom'byani	קוֹלוֹמְבִּיָאנִי

| Cuba | 'kuba | קוּבָּה (ג) |
| Cuban (masc.) | ku'bani | קוּבָּנִי (ז) |

| Cuban (fem.) | ku'banit | קוּבָּנִית (נ) |
| Cuban (adj) | ku'bani | קוּבָּנִי |

Chile	'tʃile	צִ׳ילֶה (נ)
Chilean (masc.)	tʃili"ani	צִ׳ילְיָאנִי (ז)
Chilean (fem.)	tʃili"anit	צִ׳ילְיָאנִית (נ)
Chilean (adj)	tʃili"ani	צִ׳ילְיָאנִי

Bolivia	bo'livya	בּוֹלִיבְיָה (נ)
Venezuela	venetsu"ela	וֶנֶצוּאֶלָה (נ)
Paraguay	paragvai	פָּרָגְווָאי (נ)
Peru	peru	פֶּרוּ (נ)

Suriname	surinam	סוּרִינָאם (נ)
Uruguay	urugvai	אוּרוּגְווָאי (נ)
Ecuador	ekvador	אֶקְווָדוֹר (נ)

The Bahamas	iyey ba'hama	אִיֵי בָּהָאמָה (נ״ר)
Haiti	ha"iti	הָאִיטִי (נ)
Dominican Republic	hare'publika hadomeni'kanit	הָרֶפּוּבְּלִיקָה הַדוֹמִינִיקָנִית (נ)
Panama	pa'nama	פָּנָמָה (נ)
Jamaica	dʒa'maika	גָ׳מַייקָה (נ)

240. Africa

Egypt	mits'rayim	מִצְרַיִם (נ)
Egyptian (masc.)	mitsri	מִצְרִי (ז)
Egyptian (fem.)	mitsriya	מִצְרִייָה (נ)
Egyptian (adj)	mitsri	מִצְרִי

Morocco	ma'roko	מָרוֹקוֹ (נ)
Moroccan (masc.)	maro'ka'i	מָרוֹקָאִי (ז)
Moroccan (fem.)	maro'ka'it	מָרוֹקָאִית (נ)
Moroccan (adj)	maro'ka'i	מָרוֹקָאִי

Tunisia	tu'nisya	טוּנִיסְיָה (נ)
Tunisian (masc.)	tuniˈsa'i	טוּנִיסָאִי (ז)
Tunisian (fem.)	tuni'sa'it	טוּנִיסָאִית (נ)
Tunisian (adj)	tuniˈsa'i	טוּנִיסָאִי

Ghana	'gana	גָאנָה (נ)
Zanzibar	zanzibar	זַנְזִיבָּר (נ)
Kenya	'kenya	קֶנְיָה (נ)
Libya	luv	לוּב (נ)
Madagascar	madagaskar	מָדָגַסְקָר (ז)

Namibia	na'mibya	נָמִיבְּיָה (נ)
Senegal	senegal	סֶנֶגָל (נ)
Tanzania	tan'zanya	טַנְזַנְיָה (נ)
South Africa	drom 'afrika	דרוֹם אַפְרִיקָה (נ)

African (masc.)	afri'ka'i	אַפְרִיקָאִי (ז)
African (fem.)	afri'ka'it	אַפְרִיקָאִית (נ)
African (adj)	afri'ka'i	אַפְרִיקָאִי

241. Australia. Oceania

Australia	ost'ralya	אוֹסְטְרַלְיָה (נ)
Australian (masc.)	ost'rali	אוֹסְטְרָלִי (ז)
Australian (fem.)	ost'ralit	אוֹסְטְרָלִית (נ)
Australian (adj)	ost'rali	אוֹסְטְרָלִי

New Zealand	nyu 'ziland	נְיוּ זִילַנְד (נ)
New Zealander (masc.)	nyu zi'landi	נְיוּ זִילַנְדִי (ז)
New Zealander (fem.)	nyu zi'landit	נְיוּ זִילַנְדִית (נ)
New Zealand (as adj)	nyu zi'landi	נְיוּ זִילַנְדִי

| Tasmania | tas'manya | טַסְמַנְיָה (נ) |
| French Polynesia | poli'nezya hatsarfatit | פּוֹלִינֶזְיָה הַצָּרְפָתִית (נ) |

242. Cities

Amsterdam	'amsterdam	אַמְסְטֶרְדָם (נ)
Ankara	ankara	אַנְקָרָה (נ)
Athens	a'tuna	אָתּוּנָה (נ)
Baghdad	bagdad	בַּגְדָד (נ)
Bangkok	bangkok	בַּנְגְקוֹק (נ)
Barcelona	bartse'lona	בַּרְצֶלוֹנָה (נ)

Beijing	beidʒing	בֵּייגִ'ינג (נ)
Beirut	beirut	בֵּירוּת (נ)
Berlin	berlin	בֶּרְלִין (נ)
Mumbai (Bombay)	bombei	בּוֹמְבֵּי (נ)
Bonn	bon	בּוֹן (נ)

Bordeaux	bordo	בּוֹרְדוֹ (נ)
Bratislava	bratis'lava	בְּרָטִיסְלָאבָה (נ)
Brussels	brisel	בְּרִיסֶל (נ)
Bucharest	'bukareʃt	בּוּקָרֶשְט (נ)
Budapest	'budapeʃt	בּוּדַפֶּשְט (נ)

Cairo	kahir	קָהִיר (נ)
Kolkata (Calcutta)	kol'kata	קוֹלְקָטָה (נ)
Chicago	ʃi'kago	שִׁיקָאגוֹ (נ)
Copenhagen	kopen'hagen	קוֹפֶּנְהָגֶן (נ)

Dar-es-Salaam	dar e salam	דָאר אֶ־סַלָאם (נ)
Delhi	'delhi	דֶלְהִי (נ)
Dubai	dubai	דוּבַּאי (נ)
Dublin	'dablin	דַבְּלִין (נ)
Düsseldorf	'diseldorf	דִיסֶלְדּוֹרְף (נ)

Florence	fi'rentse	פִירֶנְצֶה (נ)
Frankfurt	'frankfurt	פְרַנְקְפוֹרְט (נ)
Geneva	dʒe'neva	גֶ'נֶבָה (נ)
The Hague	hag	הָאג (נ)
Hamburg	'hamburg	הַמְבּוּרְג (נ)
Hanoi	hanoi	הָאנוֹי (נ)

Havana	ha'vana	הַוָואנָה (נ)
Helsinki	'helsinki	הֶלְסִינְקִי (נ)
Hiroshima	hiro'ʃima	הִירוֹשִׁימָה (נ)
Hong Kong	hong kong	הוֹנג קוֹנג (נ)

Istanbul	istanbul	אִיסְטַנבּוּל (נ)
Jerusalem	yeruʃa'layim	יְרוּשָׁלַיִם (נ)
Kyiv	'kiyev	קִייֵב (נ)
Kuala Lumpur	ku''ala lumpur	קוּאָלָה לוּמפּוּר (נ)
Lisbon	lisbon	לִיסבּוֹן (נ)
London	'london	לוֹנדוֹן (נ)
Los Angeles	los 'andʒeles	לוֹס אַנגֶ׳לֶס (נ)
Lyons	li'on	לִיאוֹן (נ)

Madrid	madrid	מַדרִיד (נ)
Marseille	marsei	מַרסֵי (נ)
Mexico City	'meksiko 'siti	מֶקסִיקוֹ סִיטִי (נ)
Miami	ma'yami	מָיאָמִי (נ)
Montreal	montri'ol	מוֹנטרִיאוֹל (נ)
Moscow	'moskva	מוֹסקבָה (נ)
Munich	'minχen	מִינכֶן (נ)

Nairobi	nai'robi	נַיירוֹבִּי (נ)
Naples	'napoli	נָפוֹלִי (נ)
New York	nyu york	נִיוּ יוֹרק (נ)
Nice	nis	נִיס (נ)
Oslo	'oslo	אוֹסלוֹ (נ)
Ottawa	'otava	אוֹטָוָוה (נ)

Paris	pariz	פָּרִיז (נ)
Prague	prag	פּרָאג (נ)
Rio de Janeiro	'riyo de ʒa'nero	רִיוֹ דָה זָ׳נֶרוֹ (נ)
Rome	'roma	רוֹמָא (נ)

Saint Petersburg	sant 'petersburg	סַנט פֶּטרסבּוּרג (נ)
Seoul	se'ul	סָאוּל (נ)
Shanghai	ʃanχai	שַׁנחַאי (נ)
Singapore	singapur	סִינגָפּוּר (נ)
Stockholm	'stokholm	סטוֹקהוֹלם (נ)
Sydney	'sidni	סִידנִי (נ)

Taipei	taipe	טַייפֶּה (נ)
Tokyo	'tokyo	טוֹקִיוֹ (נ)
Toronto	to'ronto	טוֹרוֹנטוֹ (נ)

Venice	ve'netsya	וֶנֶציָה (נ)
Vienna	'vina	וִינָה (נ)
Warsaw	'varʃa	וַרשָׁה (נ)
Washington	'voʃington	ווֹשִׁינגטוֹן (נ)

243. Politics. Government. Part 1

| politics | po'litika | פּוֹלִיטִיקָה (נ) |
| political (adj) | po'liti | פּוֹלִיטִי |

politician	politikai	פּוֹלִיטִיקַאי (ז)
state (country)	medina	מְדִינָה (נ)
citizen	ezraχ	אֶזְרָח (ז)
citizenship	ezraχut	אֶזְרָחוּת (נ)

national emblem	'semel le'umi	סֶמֶל לְאוֹמִי (ז)
national anthem	himnon le'umi	הַמְנוֹן לְאוֹמִי (ז)

government	memʃala	מֶמְשָׁלָה (נ)
head of state	roʃ medina	רֹאש מְדִינָה (ז)
parliament	parlament	פַּרְלָמֶנְט (ז)
party	miflaga	מִפְלָגָה (נ)

capitalism	kapitalizm	קָפִּיטָלִיזְם (ז)
capitalist (adj)	kapita'listi	קָפִּיטָלִיסְטִי

socialism	sotsyalizm	סוֹצְיָאלִיזְם (ז)
socialist (adj)	sotsya'listi	סוֹצְיָאלִיסְטִי

communism	komunizm	קוֹמוּנִיזְם (ז)
communist (adj)	komu'nisti	קוֹמוּנִיסְטִי
communist (n)	komunist	קוֹמוּנִיסְט (ז)

democracy	demo'kratya	דֶמוֹקְרַטְיָה (נ)
democrat	demokrat	דֶמוֹקְרָט (ז)
democratic (adj)	demo'krati	דֶמוֹקְרָטִי
Democratic party	miflaga demo'kratit	מִפְלָגָה דֶמוֹקְרָטִית (נ)

liberal (n)	libe'rali	לִיבֶּרָלִי (ז)
Liberal (adj)	libe'rali	לִיבֶּרָלִי
conservative (n)	ʃamran	שַׁמְרָן (ז)
conservative (adj)	ʃamrani	שַׁמְרָנִי

republic (n)	re'publika	רֶפּוּבְּלִיקָה (נ)
republican (n)	republi'kani	רֶפּוּבְּלִיקָנִי (ז)
Republican party	miflaga republi'kanit	מִפְלָגָה רֶפּוּבְּלִיקָנִית (נ)

elections	bχirot	בְּחִירוֹת (נ"ר)
to elect (vt)	livχor	לִבְחוֹר
elector, voter	mats'bi‘a	מַצְבִּיעַ (ז)
election campaign	masa bχirot	מַסַע בְּחִירוֹת (ז)

voting (n)	hatsba‘a	הַצְבָּעָה (נ)
to vote (vi)	lehats'bi‘a	לְהַצְבִּיעַ
suffrage, right to vote	zχut hatsba‘a	זכות הַצְבָּעָה (נ)

candidate	mu‘amad	מוּעֲמָד (ז)
to be a candidate	lehatsig mu‘amadut	לְהַצִּיג מוּעֲמָדוּת
campaign	masa	מַסַע (ז)

opposition (as adj)	opozitsyoni	אוֹפּוֹזִיצְיוֹנִי
opposition (n)	opo'zitsya	אוֹפּוֹזִיצְיָה (נ)

visit	bikur	בִּיקוּר (ז)
official visit	bikur riʃmi	בִּיקוּר רְשְׁמִי (ז)
international (adj)	benle'umi	בֵּינְלְאוֹמִי

negotiations	masa umatan	מַשָׂא וּמַתָן (ז)
to negotiate (vi)	laset velatet	לָשֵׂאת וְלָתֵת

244. Politics. Government. Part 2

society	xevra	חֶבְרָה (נ)
constitution	xuka	חוּקָה (נ)
power (political control)	ʃilton	שִׁלְטוֹן (ז)
corruption	ʃxitut	שְׁחִיתוּת (נ)
law (justice)	xok	חוֹק (ז)
legal (legitimate)	xuki	חוּקִי
justice (fairness)	'tsedek	צֶדֶק (ז)
just (fair)	tsodek	צוֹדֵק
committee	'va'ad	וַעַד (ז)
bill (draft law)	hatsa'at xok	הַצָעַת חוֹק (נ)
budget	taktsiv	תַקְצִיב (ז)
policy	mediniyut	מְדִינִיוּת (נ)
reform	re'forma	רֶפוֹרְמָה (נ)
radical (adj)	radi'kali	רָדִיקָלִי
power (strength, force)	otsma	עוֹצְמָה (נ)
powerful (adj)	rav 'koax	רַב-כּוֹחַ
supporter	tomex	תוֹמֵךְ (ז)
influence	haʃpa'a	הַשְׁפָּעָה (נ)
regime (e.g. military ~)	miʃtar	מִשְׁטָר (ז)
conflict	sixsux	סִכְסוּךְ (ז)
conspiracy (plot)	'keʃer	קֶשֶׁר (ז)
provocation	provo'katsya, hitgarut	פְּרוֹבוֹקַצְיָה, הִתְגָרוּת (נ)
to overthrow (regime, etc.)	leha'diax	לְהַדִיחַ
overthrow (of government)	hadaxa mikes malxut	הַדָחָה מִכֵּס מַלְכוּת (נ)
revolution	mahapexa	מַהְפֵּכָה (נ)
coup d'état	hafixa	הֲפִיכָה (ז)
military coup	mahapax tsva'i	מַהֲפָּךְ צְבָאִי (ז)
crisis	maʃber	מַשְׁבֵּר (ז)
economic recession	mitun kalkali	מִיתוּן כַּלְכָּלִי (ז)
demonstrator (protester)	mafgin	מַפְגִין (ז)
demonstration	hafgana	הַפְגָנָה (נ)
martial law	miʃtar tsva'i	מִשְׁטָר צְבָאִי (ז)
military base	basis tsva'i	בָּסִיס צְבָאִי (ז)
stability	yatsivut	יַצִיבוּת (נ)
stable (adj)	yatsiv	יַצִיב
exploitation	nitsul	נִיצוּל (ז)
to exploit (workers)	lenatsel	לְנַצֵל
racism	giz'anut	גִזְעָנוּת (נ)
racist	giz'ani	גִזְעָנִי (ז)

| fascism | faʃizm | פָּשִׁיזֹם (ז) |
| fascist | faʃist | פָּשִׁיסט (ז) |

245. Countries. Miscellaneous

foreigner	zar	זָר (ז)
foreign (adj)	zar	זָר
abroad (in a foreign country)	beχul	בְּחוּ"ל

emigrant	mehager	מְהַגֵּר (ז)
emigration	hagira	הֲגִירָה (נ)
to emigrate (vi)	lehager	לְהַגֵּר

the West	ma'arav	מַעֲרָב (ז)
the East	mizraχ	מִזרָח (ז)
the Far East	hamizraχ haraχok	הַמִזֹרָח הָרָחוֹק (ז)

civilization	tsivili'zatsya	צִיבִילִיזַצְיָה (נ)
humanity (mankind)	enoʃut	אֱנוֹשׁוּת (נ)
the world (earth)	olam	עוֹלָם (ז)
peace	ʃalom	שָׁלוֹם (ז)
worldwide (adj)	olami	עוֹלָמִי

homeland	mo'ledet	מוֹלֶדֶת (נ)
people (population)	am	עַם (ז)
population	oχlusiya	אוּכְלוּסִיָה (נ)
people (a lot of ~)	anaʃim	אֲנָשִׁים (ז"ר)
nation (people)	uma	אוּמָה (נ)
generation	dor	דוֹר (ז)
territory (area)	'ʃetaχ	שֶׁטַח (ז)
region	ezor	אֵזוֹר (ז)
state (part of a country)	medina	מְדִינָה (נ)

tradition	ma'soret	מָסוֹרֶת (נ)
custom (tradition)	minhag	מִנהָג (ז)
ecology	eko'logya	אֶקוֹלוֹגְיָה (נ)

Indian (Native American)	ind'yani	אִינֹדיָאנִי (ז)
Gypsy (masc.)	tso'ani	צוֹעֲנִי (ז)
Gypsy (fem.)	tso'aniya	צוֹעֲנִיָה (נ)
Gypsy (adj)	tso'ani	צוֹעֲנִי

empire	im'perya	אִימפֶּרִיָה (נ)
colony	ko'lonya	קוֹלוֹנִיָה (נ)
slavery	avdut	עַבֹדוּת (נ)
invasion	pliʃa	פְּלִישָׁה (נ)
famine	'ra'av	רָעָב (ז)

246. Major religious groups. Confessions

| religion | dat | דָת (נ) |
| religious (adj) | dati | דָתִי |

219

faith, belief	emuna	אֱמוּנָה (נ)
to believe (in God)	leha'amin	לְהַאֲמִין
believer	ma'amin	מַאֲמִין
atheism	ate'izm	אָתֵאִיזם (ז)
atheist	ate'ist	אָתֵאִיסט (ז)
Christianity	natsrut	נַצרוּת (נ)
Christian (n)	notsri	נוֹצרִי (ז)
Christian (adj)	notsri	נוֹצרִי
Catholicism	ka'toliyut	קָתוֹליוּת (נ)
Catholic (n)	ka'toli	קָתוֹלִי (ז)
Catholic (adj)	ka'toli	קָתוֹלִי
Protestantism	protes'tantiyut	פרוֹטֶסטַנטִיוּת (נ)
Protestant Church	knesiya protes'tantit	כּנֵסִייָה פרוֹטֶסטַנטִית (נ)
Protestant (n)	protestant	פרוֹטֶסטַנט (ז)
Orthodoxy	natsrut orto'doksit	נַצרוּת אוֹרתוֹדוֹקסִית (נ)
Orthodox Church	knesiya orto'doksit	כּנֵסִייָה אוֹרתוֹדוֹקסִית (נ)
Orthodox (n)	orto'doksi	אוֹרתוֹדוֹקסִי
Presbyterianism	presbiteryanizm	פּרֶסבִּיטֶרְיָאנִיזם (ז)
Presbyterian Church	knesiya presviteri''anit	כּנֵסִייָה פּרֶסבִּיטֶרְיָאנִית (נ)
Presbyterian (n)	presbiter'yani	פּרֶסבִּיטֶרְיָאנִי (ז)
Lutheranism	knesiya lute'ranit	כּנֵסִייָה לוּתֶרָנִית (נ)
Lutheran (n)	lute'rani	לוּתֶרָנִי (ז)
Baptist Church	knesiya bap'tistit	כּנֵסִייָה בַּפּטִיסטִית (נ)
Baptist (n)	baptist	בַּפּטִיסט (ז)
Anglican Church	knesiya angli'kanit	כּנֵסִייָה אַנגלִיקָנִית (נ)
Anglican (n)	angli'kani	אַנגלִיקָנִי (ז)
Mormonism	mor'monim	מוֹרמוֹנִים (ז)
Mormon (n)	mormon	מוֹרמוֹן (ז)
Judaism	yahadut	יַהֲדוּת (נ)
Jew (n)	yehudi, yehudiya	יְהוּדִי (ז), יְהוּדִייָה (נ)
Buddhism	budhizm	בּוּדהִיזם (ז)
Buddhist (n)	budhist	בּוּדהִיסט (ז)
Hinduism	hindu'izm	הִינדוּאִיזם (ז)
Hindu (n)	'hindi	הִינדִי (ז)
Islam	islam	אִיסלָאם (ז)
Muslim (n)	'muslemi	מוּסלְמִי (ז)
Muslim (adj)	'muslemi	מוּסלְמִי
Shiah Islam	islam 'ʃi'i	אִסלָאם שִיעִי (ז)
Shiite (n)	'ʃi'i	שִיעִי (ז)
Sunni Islam	islam 'suni	אִסלָאם סוּנִי (ז)
Sunnite (n)	'suni	סוּנִי (ז)

247. Religions. Priests

priest	'komer	כֹּמֶר (ז)
the Pope	apifyor	אַפִּיפִיוֹר (ז)
monk, friar	nazir	נָזִיר (ז)
nun	nazira	נְזִירָה (נ)
pastor	'komer	כֹּמֶר (ז)
abbot	roʃ minzar	רֹאש מִנזָר (ז)
vicar (parish priest)	'komer hakehila	כֹּמֶר הַקְּהִילָה (ז)
bishop	'biʃof	בִּישוֹף (ז)
cardinal	χaʃman	חַשמָן (ז)
preacher	matif	מַטִיף (ז)
preaching	hatafa, draʃa	הַטָּפָה, דְּרָשָה (נ)
parishioners	χaver kehila	חֲבַר קְהִילָה (ז)
believer	ma'amin	מַאֲמִין (ז)
atheist	ate'ist	אָתֵאִיסט (ז)

248. Faith. Christianity. Islam

Adam	adam	אָדָם
Eve	χava	חַוָּה
God	elohim	אֱלֹוהִים
the Lord	adonai	אֲדוֹנָי
the Almighty	kol yaχol	כָּל יָכוֹל
sin	χet	חֵטא (ז)
to sin (vi)	laχato	לַחֲטוֹא
sinner (masc.)	χote	חוֹטֵא (ז)
sinner (fem.)	χo'ta'at	חוֹטֵאת (נ)
hell	gehinom	גֵּיהִינוֹם (ז)
paradise	gan 'eden	גַּן עֵדֶן (ז)
Jesus	'yeʃu	יֵשו
Jesus Christ	'yeʃu hanotsri	יֵשו הַנוֹצרִי
the Holy Spirit	'ruaχ ha'kodeʃ	רוּחַ הַקוֹדֶש (נ)
the Saviour	mo'ʃi'a	מוֹשִיעַ (ז)
the Virgin Mary	'miryam hakdoʃa	מִריָם הַקְדוֹשָה
the Devil	satan	שָׂטָן (ז)
devil's (adj)	stani	שֹׂטָנִי
Satan	satan	שָׂטָן (ז)
satanic (adj)	stani	שֹׂטָנִי
angel	mal'aχ	מַלאָך (ז)
guardian angel	mal'aχ ʃomer	מַלאָך שוֹמֵר (ז)
angelic (adj)	mal'aχi	מַלאָכִי

221

apostle	ʃa'liaχ	שָׁלִיחַ (ז)
archangel	arχimalaχ	אַרְכִימַלְאָךְ (ז)
the Antichrist	an'tikrist	אַנְטִיכְּרִיסְט (ז)

Church	knesiya	כְּנֵסִיָּה (נ)
Bible	tanaχ	תַּנַ"ךְ (ז)
biblical (adj)	tanaχi	תַּנַ"כִי

Old Testament	habrit hayeʃana	הַבְּרִית הַיְשָׁנָה (נ)
New Testament	habrit haχadaʃa	הַבְּרִית הַחֲדָשָׁה (נ)
Gospel	evangelyon	אֶוַונְגֶלְיוֹן (ז)
Holy Scripture	kitvei ha'kodeʃ	כִּתְבֵי הַקּוֹדֶשׁ (ז"ר)
Heaven	malχut ʃa'mayim, gan 'eden	מַלְכוּת שָׁמַיִם (נ), גַן עֵדֶן (ז)

Commandment	mitsva	מִצְוָה (נ)
prophet	navi	נָבִיא (ז)
prophecy	nevu'a	נְבוּאָה (נ)

Allah	'alla	אַלְלָה
Mohammed	mu'χamad	מוּחַמַד
the Koran	kur'an	קוּרְאָן (ז)

mosque	misgad	מִסְגָד (ז)
mullah	'mula	מוּלָא (ז)
prayer	tfila	תְּפִילָה (נ)
to pray (vi, vt)	lehitpalel	לְהִתְפַּלֵל

pilgrimage	aliya le'regel	עֲלִיָה לְרֶגֶל (נ)
pilgrim	tsalyan	צַלְיָן (ז)
Mecca	'meka	מֶכָּה (נ)

church	knesiya	כְּנֵסִיָּה (נ)
temple	mikdaʃ	מִקְדָשׁ (ז)
cathedral	kated'rala	קָתֶדְרָלָה (נ)
Gothic (adj)	'goti	גוֹתִי
synagogue	beit 'kneset	בֵּית כְּנֶסֶת (ז)
mosque	misgad	מִסְגָד (ז)

chapel	beit tfila	בֵּית תְּפִילָה (ז)
abbey	minzar	מִנְזָר (ז)
convent	minzar	מִנְזָר (ז)
monastery	minzar	מִנְזָר (ז)

bell (church ~s)	pa'amon	פַּעֲמוֹן (ז)
bell tower	migdal pa'amonim	מִגְדַל פַּעֲמוֹנִים (ז)
to ring (ab. bells)	letsaltsel	לְצַלְצֵל

cross	tslav	צְלָב (ז)
cupola (roof)	kipa	כִּיפָּה (נ)
icon	ikonin	אִיקוֹנִין (ז)

soul	neʃama	נְשָׁמָה (נ)
fate (destiny)	goral	גוֹרָל (ז)
evil (n)	'ro'a	רוֹעַ (ז)
good (n)	tuv	טוּב (ז)
vampire	arpad	עַרְפָּד (ז)

witch (evil ~)	maxʃefa	מְכַשֵּׁפָה (נ)
demon	ʃed	שֵׁד (ז)
spirit	'ruax	רוּחַ (נ)

redemption (giving us ~)	kapara	כַּפָּרָה (נ)
to redeem (vt)	lexaper al	לְכַפֵּר עַל

church service, mass	'misa	מִיסָה (נ)
to say mass	la'arox 'misa	לַעֲרוֹךְ מִיסָה
confession	vidui	וִידוּי (ז)
to confess (vi)	lehitvadot	לְהִתְוַדּוֹת

saint (n)	kadoʃ	קָדוֹשׁ (ז)
sacred (holy)	mekudaʃ	מְקוּדָּשׁ
holy water	'mayim kdoʃim	מַיִם קְדוֹשִׁים (ז"ר)

ritual (n)	'tekes	טֶקֶס (ז)
ritual (adj)	ʃel 'tekes	שֶׁל טֶקֶס
sacrifice	korban	קוֹרְבָּן (ז)

superstition	emuna tfela	אֱמוּנָה תְּפֵלָה (נ)
superstitious (adj)	ma'amin emunot tfelot	מַאֲמִין אֱמוּנוֹת תְּפֵלוֹת
afterlife	ha'olam haba	הָעוֹלָם הַבָּא (ז)
eternal life	xayei olam, xayei 'netsax	חַיֵּי עוֹלָם (ז"ר), חַיֵּי נֶצַח (ז"ר)

MISCELLANEOUS

249. Various useful words

background (green ~)	'reka	רֶקַע (ז)
balance (of situation)	izun	אִיזוּן (ז)
barrier (obstacle)	mixʃol	מִכְשׁוֹל (ז)
base (basis)	basis	בָּסִיס (ז)
beginning	hatxala	הַתְחָלָה (נ)
category	kate'gorya	קָטֶגוֹרְיָה (נ)
cause (reason)	siba	סִיבָּה (נ)
choice	bxina	בְּחִינָה (נ)
coincidence	hat'ama	הַתְאָמָה (נ)
comfortable (~ chair)	'noax	נוֹחַ
comparison	haʃva'a	הַשְׁוָאָה (נ)
compensation	pitsui	פִּיצוּי (ז)
degree (extent, amount)	darga	דַרְגָה (נ)
development	hitpatxut	הִתְפַּתְחוּת (נ)
difference	'ʃoni	שׁוֹנִי (ז)
effect (e.g. of drugs)	efekt	אֶפֶקְט (ז)
effort (exertion)	ma'amats	מַאֲמָץ (ז)
element	element	אֶלֶמֶנְט (ז)
end (finish)	sof	סוֹף (ז)
example (illustration)	dugma	דוּגְמָה (נ)
fact	uvda	עוּבְדָה (נ)
frequent (adj)	tadir	תָדִיר
growth (development)	gidul	גִידוּל (ז)
help	ezra	עֶזְרָה (נ)
ideal	ide'al	אִידֵיאָל (ז)
kind (sort, type)	sug	סוּג (ז)
labyrinth	mavox	מָבוֹך (ז)
mistake, error	ta'ut	טָעוּת (נ)
moment	'rega	רֶגַע (ז)
object (thing)	'etsem	עֶצֶם (ז)
obstacle	maxsom	מַחְסוֹם (ז)
original (original copy)	makor	מָקוֹר (ז)
part (~ of sth)	'xelek	חֵלֶק (ז)
particle, small part	xelkik	חֶלְקִיק (ז)
pause (break)	hafuga	הֲפוּגָה (נ)
position	emda	עֶמְדָה (נ)
principle	ikaron	עִיקָרוֹן (ז)
problem	be'aya	בְּעָיָה (נ)
process	tahalix	תַהֲלִיך (ז)

progress	kidma	קִדמָה (נ)
property (quality)	tχuna, sgula	תְבוּנָה, סְגוּלָה (נ)
reaction	tguva	תְגוּבָה (נ)
risk	sikun	סִיכּוּן (ז)

secret	sod	סוֹד (ז)
series	sidra	סִדרָה (נ)
shape (outer form)	tsura	צוּרָה (נ)
situation	matsav	מַצָב (ז)
solution	pitaron	פִּיתָרוֹן (ז)

standard (adj)	tikni	תִקנִי
standard (level of quality)	'teken	תֶקֶן (ז)
stop (pause)	hafsaka	הַפּסָקָה (נ)
style	signon	סִגנוֹן (ז)

system	ʃita	שִיטָה (נ)
table (chart)	tavla	טַבלָה (נ)
tempo, rate	'ketsev	קֶצֶב (ז)
term (word, expression)	musag	מוּשָג (ז)
thing (object, item)	'χefets	חֵפֶץ (ז)

truth (e.g. moment of ~)	emet	אֱמֶת (נ)
turn (please wait your ~)	tor	תוֹר (ז)
type (sort, kind)	min	מִין (ז)
urgent (adj)	daχuf	דָחוּף
urgently	bidχifut	בִּדחִיפוּת

utility (usefulness)	to''elet	תוֹעֶלֶת (נ)
variant (alternative)	girsa	גִירסָה (נ)
way (means, method)	'ofen	אוֹפֶן (ז)
zone	ezor	אֵזוֹר (ז)

250. Modifiers. Adjectives. Part 1

additional (adj)	nosaf	נוֹסָף
ancient (~ civilization)	atik	עָתִיק
artificial (adj)	melaχuti	מְלָאכוּתִי
back, rear (adj)	aχorani	אָחוֹרָנִי
bad (adj)	ra	רַע

beautiful (~ palace)	mefo'ar	מְפוֹאָר
beautiful (person)	yafe	יָפֶה
big (in size)	gadol	גָדוֹל
bitter (taste)	marir	מָרִיר
blind (sightless)	iver	עִיוֵור

calm, quiet (adj)	ʃaket	שָקֵט
careless (negligent)	meruʃal	מְרוּשָל
caring (~ father)	do'eg	דוֹאֵג
central (adj)	merkazi	מֶרכָּזִי

| cheap (low-priced) | zol | זוֹל |
| cheerful (adj) | sa'meaχ | שָמֵחַ |

children's (adj)	yaldi	יַלְדִי
civil (~ law)	ezraχi	אֶזְרָחִי
clandestine (secret)	maχtarti	מַחְתַּרְתִּי

clean (free from dirt)	naki	נָקִי
clear (explanation, etc.)	barur	בָּרוּר
clever (intelligent)	pi'keaχ	פִּיקֵחַ
close (near in space)	karov	קָרוֹב
closed (adj)	sagur	סָגוּר

cloudless (sky)	lelo ananim	לְלֹא עֲנָנִים
cold (drink, weather)	kar	קַר
compatible (adj)	to'em	תּוֹאֵם
contented (satisfied)	merutse	מְרוּצֶה
continuous (uninterrupted)	mitmaʃeχ	מִתְמַשֵּׁךְ

cool (weather)	karir	קָרִיר
dangerous (adj)	mesukan	מְסֻכָּן
dark (room)	χaʃuχ	חָשׁוּךְ
dead (not alive)	met	מֵת
dense (fog, smoke)	tsafuf	צָפוּף

destitute (extremely poor)	ani	עָנִי
different (not the same)	ʃone	שׁוֹנֶה
difficult (decision)	kaʃe	קָשֶׁה
difficult (problem, task)	mesubaχ	מְסֻבָּךְ
dim, faint (light)	amum	עָמוּם

dirty (not clean)	meluχlaχ	מְלֻכְלָךְ
distant (in space)	raχok	רָחוֹק
dry (clothes, etc.)	yaveʃ	יָבֵשׁ
easy (not difficult)	kal	קַל

empty (glass, room)	rek	רֵיק
even (e.g. ~ surface)	χalak	חָלָק
exact (amount)	meduyak	מְדֻיָּק
excellent (adj)	metsuyan	מְצֻיָּן
excessive (adj)	meyutar	מְיוּתָר

expensive (adj)	yakar	יָקָר
exterior (adj)	χitsoni	חִיצוֹנִי
far (the ~ East)	raχok	רָחוֹק
fast (quick)	mahir	מָהִיר
fatty (food)	ʃamen	שָׁמֵן

fertile (land, soil)	pore	פּוֹרֶה
flat (~ panel display)	ʃa'tuaχ	שָׁטוּחַ
foreign (adj)	zar	זָר
fragile (china, glass)	ʃavir	שָׁבִיר

free (at no cost)	χinam	חִינָם
free (unrestricted)	χofʃi	חוֹפְשִׁי
fresh (~ water)	metukim	מְתוּקִים
fresh (e.g. ~ bread)	tari	טָרִי
frozen (food)	kafu	קָפוּא
full (completely filled)	male	מָלֵא

gloomy (house, forecast)	koder	קוֹדֵר
good (book, etc.)	tov	טוֹב
good, kind (kindhearted)	tov	טוֹב
grateful (adj)	asir toda	אָסִיר תּוֹדָה

happy (adj)	me'uʃar	מְאוּשָׁר
hard (not soft)	kaʃe	קָשֶׁה
heavy (in weight)	kaved	כָּבֵד
hostile (adj)	oyen	עוֹיֵן
hot (adj)	χam	חַם

huge (adj)	anaki	עֲנָקִי
humid (adj)	laχ	לַח
hungry (adj)	ra'ev	רָעֵב
ill (sick, unwell)	χole	חוֹלֶה
immobile (adj)	χasar tnu'a	חֲסַר תְּנוּעָה

important (adj)	χaʃuv	חָשׁוּב
impossible (adj)	'bilti efʃari	בִּלְתִּי אֶפְשָׁרִי
incomprehensible	'bilti muvan	בִּלְתִּי מוּבָן
indispensable (adj)	naχuts	נָחוּץ
inexperienced (adj)	χasar nisayon	חֲסַר נִיסָיוֹן

insignificant (adj)	χasar χaʃivut	חֲסַר חֲשִׁיבוּת
interior (adj)	pnimi	פְּנִימִי
joint (~ decision)	meʃutaf	מְשׁוּתָף
last (e.g. ~ week)	ʃe'avar	שֶׁעָבַר

last (final)	aχaron	אַחֲרוֹן
left (e.g. ~ side)	smali	שְׂמָאלִי
legal (legitimate)	χuki	חוּקִי
light (in weight)	kal	קַל
light (pale color)	bahir	בָּהִיר

limited (adj)	mugbal	מוּגבָּל
liquid (fluid)	nozli	נוֹזְלִי
long (e.g. ~ hair)	aroχ	אָרוֹךְ
loud (voice, etc.)	ram	רָם
low (voice)	ʃaket	שָׁקֵט

251. Modifiers. Adjectives. Part 2

main (principal)	raʃi	רָאשִׁי
matt, matte	mat	מַט
meticulous (job)	kapdani	קַפְּדָנִי
mysterious (adj)	mistori	מִסתּוֹרִי
narrow (street, etc.)	tsar	צַר

native (~ country)	ʃel mo'ledet	שֶׁל מוֹלֶדֶת
nearby (adj)	karov	קָרוֹב
needed (necessary)	daruʃ	דָרוּשׁ
negative (~ response)	ʃlili	שְׁלִילִי
neighbouring (adj)	samuχ	סָמוּךְ
nervous (adj)	atsbani	עַצבָּנִי

new (adj)	xadaʃ	חָדָשׁ
next (e.g. ~ week)	haba	הַבָּא
nice (kind)	nexmad	נֶחְמָד
nice (voice)	na'im	נָעִים
normal (adj)	nor'mali	נוֹרְמָלִי
not big (adj)	lo gadol	לֹא גָדוֹל
not difficult (adj)	lo kaʃe	לֹא קָשֶׁה
obligatory (adj)	hexrexi	הֶכְרֵחִי
old (house)	yaʃan	יָשָׁן
open (adj)	pa'tuax	פָּתוּחַ
opposite (adj)	negdi	נֶגְדִי
ordinary (usual)	ragil	רָגִיל
original (unusual)	mekori	מְקוֹרִי
past (recent)	ʃe'avar	שֶׁעָבָר
permanent (adj)	ka'vu'a	קָבוּעַ
personal (adj)	prati	פְּרָטִי
polite (adj)	menumas	מְנוּמָס
poor (not rich)	ani	עָנִי
possible (adj)	efʃari	אֶפְשָׁרִי
present (current)	noxexi	נוֹכְחִי
previous (adj)	kodem	קוֹדֵם
principal (main)	ikari	עִיקָרִי
private (~ jet)	iʃi	אִישִׁי
probable (adj)	efʃari	אֶפְשָׁרִי
prolonged (e.g. ~ applause)	memuʃax	מְמוּשָׁךְ
public (open to all)	tsiburi	צִיבּוּרִי
punctual (person)	daikan	דַייְקָן
quiet (tranquil)	ʃalev	שָׁלֵו
rare (adj)	nadir	נָדִיר
raw (uncooked)	xai	חַי
right (not left)	yemani	יְמָנִי
right, correct (adj)	naxon	נָכוֹן
ripe (fruit)	baʃel	בָּשֵׁל
risky (adj)	mesukan	מְסוּכָּן
sad (~ look)	atsuv	עָצוּב
sad (depressing)	atsuv	עָצוּב
safe (not dangerous)	ba'tuax	בָּטוּחַ
salty (food)	ma'luax	מָלוּחַ
satisfied (customer)	mesupak	מְסוּפָּק
second hand (adj)	meʃumaʃ	מְשׁוּמָשׁ
shallow (water)	radud	רָדוּד
sharp (blade, etc.)	xad	חַד
short (in length)	katsar	קָצָר
short, short-lived (adj)	katsar	קָצָר
short-sighted (adj)	ktsar re'iya	קְצָר רְאִייָה
significant (notable)	xaʃuv	חָשׁוּב

similar (adj)	dome	דּוֹמֶה
simple (easy)	paʃut	פָּשׁוּט
skinny	raze	רָזֶה
small (in size)	katan	קָטָן
smooth (surface)	χalak	חָלָק
soft (~ toys)	raχ	רַך
solid (~ wall)	mutsak	מוּצָק
sour (flavour, taste)	χamuts	חָמוּץ
spacious (house, etc.)	meruvaχ	מְרוּוָח
special (adj)	meyuχad	מְיוּחָד
straight (line, road)	yaʃar	יָשָׁר
strong (person)	χazak	חָזָק
stupid (foolish)	tipeʃ	טִיפֵּשׁ
suitable (e.g. ~ for drinking)	mat'im	מַתְאִים
sunny (day)	ʃimʃi	שִׁמְשִׁי
superb, perfect (adj)	metsuyan	מְצוּיָן
swarthy (adj)	ʃaχum	שָׁחוּם
sweet (sugary)	matok	מָתוֹק
tanned (adj)	ʃazuf	שָׁזוּף
tasty (delicious)	ta'im	טָעִים
tender (affectionate)	raχ	רַך
the highest (adj)	haga'voha beyoter	הַגָּבוֹהַ בְּיוֹתֵר
the most important	haχaʃuv beyoter	הֶחָשׁוּב בְּיוֹתֵר
the nearest	hakarov beyoter	הַקָּרוֹב בְּיוֹתֵר
the same, equal (adj)	zehe	זֶהֶה
thick (e.g. ~ fog)	samuχ	סָמוּך
thick (wall, slice)	ave	עָבֶה
thin (person)	raze	רָזֶה
tight (~ shoes)	tsar	צַר
tired (exhausted)	ayef	עָיֵיף
tiring (adj)	me'ayef	מְעָיֵיף
transparent (adj)	ʃakuf	שָׁקוּף
unclear (adj)	lo barur	לֹא בָּרוּר
unique (exceptional)	meyuχad bemino	מְיוּחָד בְּמִינוֹ
various (adj)	kol minei	כָּל מִינֵי
warm (moderately hot)	χamim	חָמִים
wet (e.g. ~ clothes)	ratuv	רָטוֹב
whole (entire, complete)	ʃalem	שָׁלֵם
wide (e.g. ~ road)	raχav	רָחָב
young (adj)	tsa'ir	צָעִיר

MAIN 500 VERBS

252. Verbs A-C

to accompany (vt)	lelavot	לְלַוּוֹת
to accuse (vt)	leha'aʃim	לְהַאֲשִׁים
to acknowledge (admit)	lehakir be...	לְהַכִּיר בְּ...
to act (take action)	lif'ol	לִפְעוֹל
to add (supplement)	lehosif	לְהוֹסִיף
to address (speak to)	lifnot el	לִפְנוֹת אֶל
to admire (vi)	lehitpa'el	לְהִתְפַּעֵל
to advertise (vt)	lefarsem	לְפַרְסֵם
to advise (vt)	leya'ets	לְיַיעֵץ
to affirm (assert)	lit'on	לִטְעוֹן
to agree (say yes)	lehaskim	לְהַסְכִּים
to aim (to point a weapon)	leχaven	לְכַוון
to allow (sb to do sth)	leharʃot	לְהַרְשׁוֹת
to amputate (vt)	lik'to'a	לִקְטוֹעַ
to answer (vi, vt)	la'anot	לַעֲנוֹת
to apologize (vi)	lehitnatsel	לְהִתְנַצֵּל
to appear (come into view)	leho'fi'a	לְהוֹפִיעַ
to applaud (vi, vt)	limχo ka'payim	לִמְחוֹא כַּפַּיִים
to appoint (assign)	lemanot	לְמַנוֹת
to approach (come closer)	lehitkarev	לְהִתְקָרֵב
to arrive (ab. train)	leha'gi'a	לְהַגִּיעַ
to ask (~ sb to do sth)	levakeʃ	לְבַקֵּשׁ
to aspire to ...	liʃof	לִשְׁאוֹף
to assist (help)	la'azor	לַעֲזוֹר
to attack (mil.)	litkof	לִתְקוֹף
to attain (objectives)	lehasig	לְהַשִּׂיג
to avenge (get revenge)	linkom	לִנְקוֹם
to avoid (danger, task)	lehimana	לְהִימָנַע
to award (give medal to)	leha'anik	לְהַעֲנִיק
to battle (vi)	lehilaχem	לְהִילָחֵם
to be (vi)	lihyot	לִהְיוֹת
to be a cause of ...	ligrom le...	לִגְרוֹם לְ...
to be afraid	lefaχed	לְפַחֵד
to be angry (with ...)	lehitragez	לְהִתְרַגֵּז
to be at war	lehilaχem	לְהִילָחֵם
to be based (on ...)	lehitbases	לְהִתְבַּסֵּס
to be bored	lehiʃta'amem	לְהִשְׁתַּעֲמֵם

to be convinced	lehiʃtax'ne'a	לְהִשְׁתַּכְנֵעַ
to be enough	lehasmik	לְהַסְמִיק
to be envious	lekane	לְקַנֵּא
to be indignant	lehitra'em	לְהִתְרַעֵם
to be interested in …	lehit'anyen	לְהִתְעַנְיֵן
to be lost in thought	liʃko'a bemaxʃavot	לִשְׁקוֹעַ בְּמַחְשָׁבוֹת
to be lying (~ on the table)	lihyot munax	לִהְיוֹת מוּנָח
to be needed	lehidareʃ	לְהִידָרֵשׁ
to be perplexed (puzzled)	lit'moha	לִתְמוֹהַּ
to be preserved	lehiʃtamer	לְהִשְׁתַּמֵּר
to be required	lehidareʃ	לְהִידָרֵשׁ
to be surprised	lehitpale	לְהִתְפַּלֵּא
to be worried	lid'og	לִדְאוֹג
to beat (to hit)	lehakot	לְהַכּוֹת
to become (e.g. ~ old)	lahafox le…	לַהֲפוֹךְ לְ…
to behave (vi)	lehitnaheg	לְהִתְנַהֵג
to believe (think)	leha'amin	לְהַאֲמִין
to belong to …	lehiʃtayex	לְהִשְׁתַּיֵּךְ
to berth (moor)	la'agon	לַעֲגוֹן
to blind (other drivers)	lisanver	לְסַנְוֵר
to blow (wind)	linʃov	לִנְשׁוֹב
to blush (vi)	lehasmik	לְהַסְמִיק
to boast (vi)	lehitravrev	לְהִתְרַבְרֵב
to borrow (money)	lilvot	לִלְווֹת
to break (branch, toy, etc.)	liʃbor	לִשְׁבּוֹר
to breathe (vi)	linʃom	לִנְשׁוֹם
to bring (sth)	lehavi	לְהָבִיא
to burn (paper, logs)	lisrof	לִשְׂרוֹף
to buy (purchase)	liknot	לִקְנוֹת
to call (~ for help)	likro	לִקְרוֹא
to call (yell for sb)	likro le…	לִקְרוֹא לְ…
to calm down (vt)	lehar'gi'a	לְהַרְגִּיעַ
can (v aux)	yaxol	יָכוֹל
to cancel (call off)	levatel	לְבַטֵּל
to cast off (of a boat or ship)	lehaflig	לְהַפְלִיג
to catch (e.g. ~ a ball)	litfos	לִתְפּוֹס
to change (~ one's opinion)	leʃanot	לְשַׁנּוֹת
to change (exchange)	lehaxlif	לְהַחְלִיף
to charm (vt)	lehaksim	לְהַקְסִים
to choose (select)	livxor	לִבְחוֹר
to chop off (with an axe)	lixrot	לִכְרוֹת
to clean (e.g. kettle from scale)	lenakot	לְנַקּוֹת
to clean (shoes, etc.)	lenakot	לְנַקּוֹת
to clean up (tidy)	lesader	לְסַדֵּר
to close (vt)	lisgor	לִסְגּוֹר

to comb one's hair	lehistarek	לְהִסְתָּרֵק
to come down (the stairs)	la'redet	לָרֶדֶת
to come out (book)	latset le'or	לָצֵאת לְאוֹר
to compare (vt)	lehaʃvot	לְהַשְווֹת
to compensate (vt)	lefatsot	לְפַצוֹת
to compete (vi)	lehitχarot	לְהִתְחָרוֹת
to compile (~ a list)	lena'seaχ, la'aroχ	לְנַסֵחַ, לַעֲרוֹך
to complain (vi, vt)	lehitlonen	לְהִתְלוֹנֵן
to complicate (vt)	lesabeχ	לְסַבֵּך
to compose (music, etc.)	lehalχin	לְהַלְחִין
to compromise (reputation)	lehav'iʃ et reχo	לְהַבְאִיש אֶת רֵיחוֹ
to concentrate (vi)	lehitrakez	לְהִתְרַכֵּז
to confess (criminal)	lehodot be...	...לְהוֹדוֹת בְּ
to confuse (mix up)	lehitbalbel	לְהִתְבַּלְבֵּל
to congratulate (vt)	levareχ	לְבָרֵך
to consult (doctor, expert)	lehitya'ets im	לְהִתְייַעֵץ עִם
to continue (~ to do sth)	lehamʃiχ	לְהַמְשִיך
to control (vt)	liʃlot	לִשְלוֹט
to convince (vt)	leʃaχ'ne'a	לְשַכְנֵעַ
to cooperate (vi)	leʃatef pe'ula	לְשַתֵף פְּעוּלָה
to coordinate (vt)	leta'em	לְתָאֵם
to correct (an error)	letaken	לְתַקֵן
to cost (vt)	la'alot	לַעֲלוֹת
to count (money, etc.)	lispor	לִסְפוֹר
to count on ...	lismoχ al	לִסְמוֹך עַל
to crack (ceiling, wall)	lehisadek	לְהִיסָדֵק
to create (vt)	litsor	לִיצוֹר
to crush, to squash (~ a bug)	lirmos	לִרְמוֹס
to cry (weep)	livkot	לִבְכּוֹת
to cut off (with a knife)	laχtoχ	לַחְתוֹך

253. Verbs D-G

to dare (~ to do sth)	leha'ez	לְהָעֵז
to date from ...	leta'areχ	לְתַאֲרֵך
to deceive (vi, vt)	leramot	לְרַמוֹת
to decide (~ to do sth)	lehaχlit	לְהַחְלִיט
to decorate (tree, street)	lekaʃet	לְקַשֵט
to dedicate (book, etc.)	lehakdiʃ	לְהַקְדִיש
to defend (a country, etc.)	lehagen	לְהָגֵן
to defend oneself	lehitgonen	לְהִתְגוֹנֵן
to demand (request firmly)	lidroʃ	לִדְרוֹש
to denounce (vt)	lehalʃim	לְהַלְשִין
to deny (vt)	liʃlol	לִשְלוֹל
to depend on ...	lihyot talui be...	...לִהְיוֹת תָלוּי בְּ
to deprive (vt)	liʃlol	לִשְלוֹל

to deserve (vt)	lihyot ra'ui	לִהְיוֹת רָאוּי
to design (machine, etc.)	letaxnen	לְתַכְנֵן
to desire (want, wish)	lirtsot	לִרְצוֹת
to despise (vt)	lezalzel be…	לְזַלְזֵל בְּ…
to destroy (documents, etc.)	lexasel	לְחַסֵל
to differ (from sth)	lehibadel	לְהִיבָּדֵל
to dig (tunnel, etc.)	laxpor	לַחְפּוֹר
to direct (point the way)	lexaven	לְכַוֵּון
to disappear (vi)	lehe'alem	לְהֵיעָלֵם
to discover (new land, etc.)	legalot	לְגַלּוֹת
to discuss (vt)	ladun	לָדוּן
to distribute (leaflets, etc.)	lehafits	לְהָפִיץ
to disturb (vt)	lehatrid	לְהַטְרִיד
to dive (vi)	litslol	לִצְלוֹל
to divide (math)	lexalek	לְחַלֵּק
to do (vt)	la'asot	לַעֲשׂוֹת
to do the laundry	lexabes	לְכַבֵּס
to double (increase)	lehaxpil	לְהַכְפִּיל
to doubt (have doubts)	lefakpek	לְפַקְפֵּק
to draw a conclusion	lehasik	לְהַסִּיק
to dream (daydream)	laxalom	לַחֲלוֹם
to dream (in sleep)	laxalom	לַחֲלוֹם
to drink (vi, vt)	liʃtot	לִשְׁתּוֹת
to drive a car	linhog	לִנְהוֹג
to drive away (scare away)	legareʃ	לְגָרֵשׁ
to drop (let fall)	lehapil	לְהַפִּיל
to drown (ab. person)	lit'bo'a	לִטְבּוֹעַ
to dry (clothes, hair)	leyabeʃ	לְיַבֵּשׁ
to eat (vi, vt)	le'exol	לֶאֱכוֹל
to eavesdrop (vi)	leha'azin be'seter	לְהַאֲזִין בְּסֵתֶר
to emit (diffuse - odor, etc.)	lehafits	לְהָפִיץ
to enjoy oneself	lehanot	לֵיהָנוֹת
to enter (on the list)	lehosif	לְהוֹסִיף
to enter (room, house, etc.)	lehikanes	לְהִיכָּנֵס
to entertain (amuse)	levader	לְבַדֵּר
to equip (fit out)	letsayed	לְצַיֵּיד
to examine (proposal)	livxon	לִבְחוֹן
to exchange (sth)	lehitxalef	לְהִתְחַלֵּף
to excuse (forgive)	lis'loax	לִסְלוֹחַ
to exist (vi)	lehitkayem	לְהִתְקַיֵּים
to expect (anticipate)	letsapot	לְצַפּוֹת
to expect (foresee)	laxazot	לַחֲזוֹת
to expel (from school, etc.)	lesalek	לְסַלֵּק
to explain (vt)	lehasbir	לְהַסְבִּיר
to express (vt)	levate	לְבַטֵּא
to extinguish (a fire)	lexabot	לְכַבּוֹת

to fall in love (with ...)	lehit'ahev	לְהִתְאַהֵב
to fancy (vt)	limtso χen be'ei'nayim	לִמְצוֹא חֵן בְּעֵינַיִים
to feed (provide food)	leha'aχil	לְהַאֲכִיל

to fight (against the enemy)	lehilaχem	לְהִילָחֵם
to fight (vi)	lehitkotet	לְהִתְקוֹטֵט
to fill (glass, bottle)	lemale	לְמַלֵּא
to find (~ lost items)	limtso	לִמְצוֹא

to finish (vt)	lesayem	לְסַיֵּם
to fish (angle)	ladug	לָדוּג
to fit (ab. dress, etc.)	lehat'im	לְהַתְאִים
to flatter (vt)	lehaχnif	לְהַחְנִיף

to fly (bird, plane)	la'uf	לָעוּף
to follow ... (come after)	la'akov aχarei	לַעֲקוֹב אַחֲרֵי
to forbid (vt)	le'esor	לֶאֱסוֹר
to force (compel)	lehaχ'riaχ	לְהַכְרִים

to forget (vi, vt)	lif'koaχ	לִשְׁכּוֹחַ
to forgive (pardon)	lis'loaχ	לִסְלוֹחַ
to form (constitute)	le'atsev	לְעַצֵּב
to get dirty (vi)	lehitlaχleχ	לְהִתְלַכְלֵךְ

to get infected (with ...)	lehibadek	לְהִידָבֵק
to get irritated	lehitragez	לְהִתְרַגֵּז
to get married	lehitχaten	לְהִתְחַתֵּן
to get rid of ...	lehipater mi...	לְהִיפָּטֵר מ...

to get tired	lehit'ayef	לְהִתְעַיֵּיף
to get up (arise from bed)	lakum	לָקוּם
to give (vt)	latet	לָתֵת
to give a bath (to bath)	lirχots	לִרְחוֹץ

to give a hug, to hug (vt)	leχabek	לְחַבֵּק
to give in (yield to)	levater	לְוַותֵּר
to glimpse (vt)	lir'ot	לִרְאוֹת
to go (by car, etc.)	lin'so'a	לִנְסוֹעַ

to go (on foot)	la'leχet	לָלֶכֶת
to go for a swim	lehitraχets	לְהִתְרַחֵץ
to go out (for dinner, etc.)	latset	לָצֵאת
to go to bed (go to sleep)	liʃkav liʃon	לִשְׁכַּב לִישׁוֹן

to greet (vt)	lomar ʃalom	לוֹמַר שָׁלוֹם
to grow (plants)	legadel	לְגַדֵּל
to guarantee (vt)	lehav'tiaχ	לְהַבְטִיחַ
to guess (the answer)	lenaχeʃ	לְנַחֵשׁ

254. Verbs H-M

to hand out (distribute)	leχalek	לְחַלֵּק
to hang (curtains, etc.)	litlot	לִתְלוֹת
to have (vt)	lehaχzik	לְהַחֲזִיק

| to have a bath | lehitraχets | לְהִתְרַחֵץ |
| to have a try | lenasot | לְנַסּוֹת |

to have breakfast	le'eχol aruχat 'boker	לֶאֱכוֹל אֲרוּחַת בּוֹקֶר
to have dinner	le'eχol aruχat 'erev	לֶאֱכוֹל אֲרוּחַת עֶרֶב
to have lunch	le'eχol aruχat tsaha'rayim	לֶאֱכוֹל אֲרוּחַת צָהֳרַיִם
to head (group, etc.)	la'amod beroʃ	לַעֲמוֹד בְּרֹאש
to hear (vt)	liʃmo'a	לִשְׁמוֹעַ

to heat (vt)	leχamem	לְחַמֵּם
to help (vt)	la'azor	לַעֲזוֹר
to hide (vt)	lehastir	לְהַסְתִּיר
to hire (e.g. ~ a boat)	liskor	לִשְׂכּוֹר
to hire (staff)	leha'asik	לְהַעֲסִיק

to hope (vi, vt)	lekavot	לְקַווֹת
to hunt (for food, sport)	latsud	לָצוּד
to hurry (vi)	lemaher	לְמַהֵר
to imagine (to picture)	ledamyen	לְדַמְיֵן
to imitate (vt)	leχakot	לְחַקּוֹת

to implore (vt)	lehitχanen	לְהִתְחַנֵּן
to import (vt)	leyabe	לְיַיבֵּא
to increase (vi)	ligdol	לִגְדּוֹל
to increase (vt)	lehagdil	לְהַגְדִּיל
to infect (vt)	lehadbik	לְהַדְבִּיק

to influence (vt)	lehaʃpi'a	לְהַשְׁפִּיעַ
to inform (e.g. ~ the police about …)	leya'de'a	לְייַדֵּעַ
to inform (vt)	leho'dia	לְהוֹדִיעַ
to inherit (vt)	la'reʃet	לָרֶשֶׁת
to inquire (about …)	levarer	לְבָרֵר

to insert (put in)	lehaχnis	לְהַכְנִיס
to insinuate (imply)	lirmoz	לִרְמוֹז
to insist (vi, vt)	lehit'akeʃ	לְהִתְעַקֵּשׁ
to inspire (vt)	lehalhiv	לְהַלְהִיב
to instruct (teach)	lehadriχ	לְהַדְרִיךְ

to insult (offend)	leha'aliv	לְהַעֲלִיב
to interest (vt)	le'anyen	לְעַניֵן
to intervene (vi)	lehit'arev	לְהִתְעָרֵב
to introduce (sb to sb)	lehatsig	לְהַצִּיג

to invent (machine, etc.)	lehamtsi	לְהַמְצִיא
to invite (vt)	lehazmin	לְהַזְמִין
to iron (clothes)	legahets	לְגַהֵץ
to irritate (annoy)	le'atsben	לְעַצְבֵּן
to isolate (vt)	levoded	לְבוֹדֵד

to join (political party, etc.)	lehitstaref	לְהִצְטָרֵף
to joke (be kidding)	lehitba'deaχ	לְהִתְבַּדֵּחַ
to keep (old letters, etc.)	liʃmor	לִשְׁמוֹר
to keep silent	liʃtok	לִשְׁתוֹק
to kill (vt)	laharog	לַהֲרוֹג

to knock (at the door)	lidfok	לִדְפוֹק
to know (sb)	lehakir et	לְהַכִּיר אֶת
to know (sth)	la'da'at	לָדַעַת
to laugh (vi)	litsχok	לִצְחוֹק
to launch (start up)	lehaf'il	לְהַפְעִיל
to leave (~ for Mexico)	la'azov	לַעֲזוֹב
to leave (forget sth)	lehaʃ'ir	לְהַשְׁאִיר
to leave (spouse)	la'azov	לַעֲזוֹב
to liberate (city, etc.)	leʃaχrer	לְשַׁחְרֵר
to lie (~ on the floor)	liʃkav	לִשְׁכַּב
to lie (tell untruth)	leʃaker	לְשַׁקֵּר
to light (campfire, etc.)	lehadlik	לְהַדְלִיק
to light up (illuminate)	leha'ir	לְהָאִיר
to limit (vt)	lehagbil	לְהַגְבִּיל
to listen (vi)	lehakʃiv	לְהַקְשִׁיב
to live (~ in France)	lagur	לָגוּר
to live (exist)	liχyot	לִחְיוֹת
to load (gun)	lit'on	לִטְעוֹן
to load (vehicle, etc.)	leha'amis	לְהַעֲמִיס
to look (I'm just ~ing)	lehistakel	לְהִסְתַּכֵּל
to look for ... (search)	leχapes	לְחַפֵּשׂ
to look like (resemble)	lihyot dome	לִהְיוֹת דּוֹמֶה
to lose (umbrella, etc.)	le'abed	לְאַבֵּד
to love (e.g. ~ dancing)	le'ehov	לֶאֱהוֹב
to love (sb)	le'ehov	לֶאֱהוֹב
to lower (blind, head)	lehorid	לְהוֹרִיד
to make (~ dinner)	levaʃel	לְבַשֵּׁל
to make a mistake	lit'ot	לִטְעוֹת
to make angry	lehargiz	לְהַרְגִּיז
to make easier	lehakel al	לְהָקֵל עַל
to make multiple copies	leʃaχpel	לְשַׁכְפֵּל
to make the acquaintance	lehakir	לְהַכִּיר
to make use (of ...)	lehiʃtameʃ be...	לְהִשְׁתַּמֵּשׁ בְּ...
to manage, to run	lenahel	לְנַהֵל
to mark (make a mark)	lesamen	לְסַמֵּן
to mean (signify)	lomar	לוֹמַר
to memorize (vt)	lizkor	לִזְכּוֹר
to mention (talk about)	lehazkir	לְהַזְכִּיר
to miss (school, etc.)	lehaχsir	לְהַחְסִיר
to mix (combine, blend)	le'arbev	לְעַרְבֵּב
to mock (make fun of)	lil'og	לִלְעוֹג
to move (to shift)	lehaziz	לְהָזִיז
to multiply (math)	lehaχpil	לְהַכְפִּיל
must (v aux)	lihyot χayav	לִהְיוֹת חַיָּב

255. Verbs N-R

to name, to call (vt)	likro	לִקְרוֹא
to negotiate (vi)	laset velatet	לָשֵׂאת וְלָתֵת
to note (write down)	lesamen	לְסַמֵן
to notice (see)	lasim lev	לָשִׂים לֵב
to obey (vi, vt)	letsayet	לְצַיֵת
to object (vi, vt)	lehitnaged	לְהִתְנַגֵד
to observe (see)	litspot, lehaʃkif	לִצְפּוֹת, לְהַשְׁקִיף
to offend (vt)	lif'go'a	לִפְגּוֹעַ
to omit (word, phrase)	lehaʃmit	לְהַשְׁמִיט
to open (vt)	lif'toaχ	לִפְתּוֹחַ
to order (in restaurant)	lehazmin	לְהַזְמִין
to order (mil.)	lifkod	לִפְקוֹד
to organize (concert, party)	le'argen	לְאַרְגֵן
to overestimate (vt)	leha'ariχ 'yeter al hamida	לְהַעֲרִיךְ יָתֵר עַל הַמִידָה
to own (possess)	lihyot 'ba'al ʃel	לִהְיוֹת בַּעַל שֶׁל
to participate (vi)	lehiʃtatef	לְהִשְׁתַתֵף
to pass through (by car, etc.)	la'avor	לַעֲבוֹר
to pay (vi, vt)	leʃalem	לְשַׁלֵם
to peep, to spy on	lehatsits	לְהָצִיץ
to penetrate (vt)	laχdor	לַחְדוֹר
to permit (vt)	leharʃot	לְהַרְשׁוֹת
to pick (flowers)	liktof	לִקְטוֹף
to place (put, set)	la'aroχ	לַעֲרוֹךְ
to plan (~ to do sth)	letaχnen	לְתַכְנֵן
to play (actor)	lesaχek	לְשַׂחֵק
to play (children)	lesaχek	לְשַׂחֵק
to point (~ the way)	lenatev	לְנַתֵב
to pour (liquid)	limzog	לִמְזוֹג
to pray (vi, vt)	lehitpalel	לְהִתְפַּלֵל
to prefer (vt)	leha'adif	לְהַעֲדִיף
to prepare (~ a plan)	lehaχin	לְהָכִין
to present (sb to sb)	lehatsig	לְהַצִיג
to preserve (peace, life)	leʃamer	לְשַׁמֵר
to prevail (vt)	ligbor	לִגְבּוֹר
to progress (move forward)	lehitkadem	לְהִתְקַדֵם
to promise (vt)	lehav'tiaχ	לְהַבְטִיחַ
to pronounce (vt)	levate	לְבַטֵא
to propose (vt)	leha'tsi'a	לְהַצִיעַ
to protect (e.g. ~ nature)	liʃmor	לִשְׁמוֹר
to protest (vi)	limχot	לִמְחוֹת
to prove (vt)	leho'χiaχ	לְהוֹכִיחַ
to provoke (vt)	lehitgarot	לְהִתְגָרוֹת
to pull (~ the rope)	limʃoχ	לִמְשׁוֹךְ
to punish (vt)	leha'aniʃ	לְהַעֲנִישׁ

to push (~ the door)	lidχof	לִדְחוֹף
to put away (vt)	lefanot	לְפַנוֹת
to put in order	lesader	לְסַדֵר
to put, to place	lasim	לָשִׂים
to quote (cite)	letsatet	לְצַטֵט
to reach (arrive at)	lehasig	לְהַשִׂיג
to read (vi, vt)	likro	לִקְרוֹא
to realize (a dream)	lehagʃim	לְהַגְשִׁים
to recognize (identify sb)	lezahot	לְזַהוֹת
to recommend (vt)	lehamlits	לְהַמְלִיץ
to recover (~ from flu)	lehaχlim	לְהַחְלִים
to redo (do again)	la'asot meχadaʃ	לַעֲשׂוֹת מֵחָדָשׁ
to reduce (speed, etc.)	lehaktin	לְהַקְטִין
to refuse (~ sb)	lesarev	לְסָרֵב
to regret (be sorry)	lehitsta'er	לְהִצְטַעֵר
to reinforce (vt)	leχazek	לְחַזֵק
to remember (Do you ~ me?)	lizkor	לִזְכּוֹר
to remember (I can't ~ her name)	lehizaχer	לְהִיזָכֵר
to remind of …	lehazkir	לְהַזְכִּיר
to remove (~ a stain)	lehasir	לְהָסִיר
to remove (~ an obstacle)	lehasir	לְהָסִיר
to rent (sth from sb)	liskor	לִשְׂכּוֹר
to repair (mend)	letaken	לְתַקֵן
to repeat (say again)	laχazor al	לַחֲזוֹר עַל
to report (make a report)	leda'veaχ	לְדַוֵוחַ
to reproach (vt)	linzof	לִנְזוֹף
to reserve, to book	leʃaryen	לְשַׁרְיֵן
to restrain (hold back)	lerasen	לְרַסֵן
to return (come back)	laʃuv	לָשׁוּב
to risk, to take a risk	la'kaχat sikun	לָקַחַת סִיכּוּן
to rub out (erase)	limχok	לִמְחוֹק
to run (move fast)	laruts	לָרוּץ
to rush (hurry sb)	lezarez	לְזָרֵז

256. Verbs S-W

to satisfy (please)	lesapek	לְסַפֵּק
to save (rescue)	lehatsil	לְהַצִיל
to say (~ thank you)	lomar	לוֹמַר
to scold (vt)	linzof	לִנְזוֹף
to scratch (with claws)	lisrot	לִשְׂרוֹט
to select (to pick)	livχor	לִבְחוֹר
to sell (goods)	limkor	לִמְכּוֹר
to send (a letter)	liʃloaχ	לִשְׁלוֹחַ
to send back (vt)	liʃloaχ baχazara	לִשְׁלוֹחַ בַּחֲזָרָה

to sense (~ danger)	laχuʃ	לָחוּשׁ
to sentence (vt)	ligzor din	לִגְזוֹר דִין
to serve (in restaurant)	leʃaret	לְשָׁרֵת
to settle (a conflict)	lesader	לְסַדֵר
to shake (vt)	lena'er	לְנַעֵר
to shave (vi)	lehitga'leaχ	לְהִתְגַלֵחַ
to shine (gleam)	lizhor	לִזְהוֹר
to shiver (with cold)	lir'od	לִרְעוֹד
to shoot (vi)	lirot	לִירוֹת
to shout (vi)	lits'ok	לִצְעוֹק
to show (to display)	lehar'ot	לְהַרְאוֹת
to shudder (vi)	lir'od	לִרְעוֹד
to sigh (vi)	lehe'anaχ	לְהֵיאָנַח
to sign (document)	laχtom	לַחְתוֹם
to signify (mean)	lomar	לוֹמַר
to simplify (vt)	lefaʃet	לְפַשֵׁט
to sin (vi)	laχato	לַחֲטוֹא
to sit (be sitting)	la'ʃevet	לָשֶׁבֶת
to sit down (vi)	lehityaʃev	לְהִתְיַישֵׁב
to smell (emit an odor)	leha'riaχ	לְהָרִיחַ
to smell (inhale the odor)	leha'riaχ	לְהָרִיחַ
to smile (vi)	leχayeχ	לְחַיֵיךְ
to snap (vi, ab. rope)	lehikara	לְהִיקָרַע
to solve (problem)	liftor	לִפְתוֹר
to sow (seed, crop)	liz'ro'a	לִזְרוֹעַ
to spill (liquid)	liʃpoχ	לִשְׁפּוֹךְ
to spill out, scatter (flour, etc.)	lehiʃapeχ	לְהִישָׁפֵּךְ
to spit (vi)	lirok	לִירוֹק
to stand (toothache, cold)	lisbol	לִסְבּוֹל
to start (begin)	lehatχil	לְהַתְחִיל
to steal (money, etc.)	lignov	לִגְנוֹב
to stop (for pause, etc.)	la'atsor	לָעֲצוֹר
to stop (please ~ calling me)	lehafsik	לְהַפְסִיק
to stop talking	lehiʃtatek	לְהִשְׁתַתֵק
to stroke (caress)	lelatef	לְלַטֵף
to study (vt)	lilmod	לִלְמוֹד
to suffer (feel pain)	lisbol	לִסְבּוֹל
to support (cause, idea)	litmoχ be...	לִתְמוֹךְ בְּ...
to suppose (assume)	leʃa'er	לְשַׁעֵר
to surface (ab. submarine)	latsuf	לָצוּף
to surprise (amaze)	lehaf'ti'a	לְהַפְתִיעַ
to suspect (vt)	laχʃod	לַחְשׁוֹד
to swim (vi)	lisχot	לִשְׂחוֹת
to take (get hold of)	la'kaχat	לָקַחַת
to take a rest	la'nuaχ	לָנוּחַ

to take away (e.g. about waiter)	lehotsi	לְהוֹצִיא
to take off (aeroplane)	lehamri	לְהַמרִיא
to take off (painting, curtains, etc.)	lehorid	לְהוֹרִיד
to take pictures	letsalem	לְצֶלֶם
to talk to ...	ledaber	לְדַבֵּר
to teach (give lessons)	lelamed	לְלַמֵד
to tear off, to rip off (vt)	litlof	לִתלוֹשׁ
to tell (story, joke)	lesaper	לְסַפֵּר
to thank (vt)	lehodot	לְהוֹדוֹת
to think (believe)	lisbor	לִסבּוֹר
to think (vi, vt)	laxfov	לַחשׁוֹב
to threaten (vt)	le'ayem	לְאַיֵם
to throw (stone, etc.)	lizrok	לִזרוֹק
to tie to ...	likfor	לִקשׁוֹר
to tie up (prisoner)	likfor	לִקשׁוֹר
to tire (make tired)	le'ayef	לְעַיֵף
to touch (one's arm, etc.)	lin'go'a	לִנגּוֹעַ
to tower (over ...)	lehitromem	לְהִתרוֹמֵם
to train (animals)	le'alef	לְאַלֵף
to train (sb)	le'amen	לְאַמֵן
to train (vi)	lehit'amen	לְהִתאַמֵן
to transform (vt)	lefanot tsura	לְשַנוֹת צוּרָה
to translate (vt)	letargem	לְתַרגֵם
to treat (illness)	letapel be...	לְטַפֵּל בְּ...
to trust (vt)	liv'toax	לִבטוֹחַ
to try (attempt)	lenasot	לְנַסוֹת
to turn (e.g., ~ left)	lifnot	לִפנוֹת
to turn away (vi)	lehafnot 'oref le...	לְהַפנוֹת עוֹרֶף לְ...
to turn off (the light)	lexabot	לְכַבּוֹת
to turn on (computer, etc.)	lehadlik	לְהַדלִיק
to turn over (stone, etc.)	lahafox	לַהַפוֹך
to underestimate (vt)	leham'it be''erex	לְהַמעִיט בְּעֵרֶך
to underline (vt)	lehadgif	לְהַדגִישׁ
to understand (vt)	lehavin	לְהָבִין
to undertake (vt)	linkot	לִנקוֹט
to unite (vt)	le'axed	לְאַחֵד
to untie (vt)	lehatir 'kefer	לְהַתִיר קֶשֶׁר
to use (phrase, word)	lehiftamef be...	לְהִשׁתַמֵשׁ בְּ...
to vaccinate (vt)	lexasen	לְחַסֵן
to vote (vi)	lehats'bi'a	לְהַצבִּיעַ
to wait (vt)	lehamtin	לְהַמתִין
to wake (sb)	leha'ir	לְהָעִיר
to want (wish, desire)	lirtsot	לִרצוֹת
to warn (of the danger)	lehazhir	לְהַזהִיר

to wash (clean)	liʃtof	לִשְׁטוֹף
to water (plants)	lehaʃkot	לְהַשְׁקוֹת
to wave (the hand)	lenafnef	לְנַפְנֵף

to weigh (have weight)	liʃkol	לִשְׁקוֹל
to work (vi)	la'avod	לַעֲבוֹד
to worry (make anxious)	lehad'ig	לְהַדְאִיג
to worry (vi)	lid'og	לִדְאוֹג

to wrap (parcel, etc.)	le'eroz	לֶאֱרוֹז
to wrestle (sport)	lehe'avek	לְהֵיאָבֵק
to write (vt)	lixtov	לִכְתּוֹב
to write down	lirʃom	לִרְשׁוֹם